'An important and well-focused contribution to a pressing academic and policy debate.'
Professor Peter Edge, Oxford Brookes University, UK

'The author tackles one of the hardest and most controversial problems in Human rights and Equality Law. By way of calm, careful, and thorough analysis, enhanced by comparative material, she shows that the rigorous application of proportionality's justificatory structure produces balanced solutions which can hope to command a high degree of legitimacy.'
Professor Julian Rivers, University of Bristol Law School, UK

'The legal conflict between freedom of religion and other human rights is one of the most vexed questions of our age. All too often, participants in these debates take entrenched positions and talk past each other. Megan Pearson's scholarly and insightful book is not only a timely and comprehensive guide but also points to the nuanced and practical ways in which seemingly irreconcilable arguments can be treated with full respect.'
Professor Ian Leigh, University of Durham, UK

Proportionality, Equality Laws, and Religion

This book considers how the law should manage conflicts between the right of religious freedom and that of non-discrimination on the grounds of sexual orientation. These disputes are often high-profile and frequently receive a lot of media attention and public debate. Starting from the basis that both these rights are valuable and worthy of protection, but that such disputes are often characterised by animosity, it contends that a proportionality analysis provides the best method for resolving these conflicts. The work takes a comparative approach, examining the law in England and Wales, Canada, and the USA, and examines four main areas of law, considering how a proportionality approach could be used in each. The book will be an invaluable resource for students and researchers in the areas of Public Law, Human Rights Law, Law and Religion, Discrimination Law, and Comparative Law.

Megan Pearson is a Teaching Fellow in Employment and Public Law at the University of Southampton, UK.

ICLARS Series on Law and Religion

Series Editors

Silvio Ferrari, University of Milan, Italy, Russell Sandberg, Cardiff University, UK, Pieter Coertzen, University of Stellenbosch, South Africa, W. Cole Durham, Jr., Brigham Young University, USA, and Tahir Mahmood, Amity International University, India

The *ICLARS Series on Law and Religion* is a new series designed to provide a forum for the rapidly expanding field of research in law and religion. The series is published in association with the International Consortium for Law and Religion Studies, an international network of scholars and experts of law and religion founded in 2007 with the aim of providing a place where information, data and opinions can easily be exchanged among members and made available to the broader scientific community. The series aims to become a primary source for students and scholars while presenting authors with a valuable means to reach a wide and growing readership.

Other titles in this series:

Islam and Women's Income
Farah Deeba Chowdhury, Queen's University, Canada

Blasphemy, Islam and the State
Stewart Fenwick, University of Melbourne, Australia

Religions and Constitutional Transitions in the Muslim Mediterranean
Edited by Alessandro Ferrari, University of Insubria, Italy and James Toronto, Brigham Young University, USA

Religion, Pluralism, and Reconciling Difference
W. Cole Durham, Jr. and Donlu Thayer, both at Brigham Young University, USA

Religion and Equality
Edited by W. Cole Durham, Jr. and Donlu Thayer, both at Brigham Young University, USA

Church and State in Scotland
Francis Lyall, University of Aberdeen, UK

Religion as Empowerment
Edited by Kyriaki Topidi and Lauren Fielder, both at University of Lucerne, Switzerland

Proportionality, Equality Laws, and Religion

Conflicts in England, Canada, and the USA

Megan Pearson

Routledge
Taylor & Francis Group
LONDON AND NEW YORK

First published 2017
by Routledge

2 Park Square, Milton Park, Abingdon, Oxfordshire OX14 4RN
52 Vanderbilt Avenue, New York, NY 10017

Routledge is an imprint of the Taylor & Francis Group, an informa business

First issued in paperback 2018

British Library Cataloguing-in-Publication Data
A catalogue record for this book is available from the British Library

Library of Congress Cataloging-in-Publication Data
Names: Pearson, Megan, author.
Title: Proportionality, equality laws, and religion : conflicts in England, Canada, and the USA / Megan Pearson.
Description: New York : Routledge, 2017. | Series: Iclars series on law and religion | Includes bibliographical references and index.
Identifiers: LCCN 2016038016 | ISBN 9781472456502 (hardback) | ISBN 9781315602592 (e-book)
Subjects: LCSH: Homosexuality--Religious aspects. | Gays--Legal status, laws, etc.--Great Britain. | Gays--Legal status, laws, etc.--Canada. | Gays--Legal status, laws, etc.--United States. | Gay rights--Great Britain. | Gay rights--Canada. | Gay rights--United States. | Equality. | Freedom of religion. | Religion and law.
Classification: LCC K3242.3 .P43 2017 | DDC 342.08/5215664--dc23
LC record available at https://lccn.loc.gov/2016038016

ISBN: 978-1-4724-5650-2 (hbk)
ISBN: 978-0-367-18991-4 (pbk)

Typeset in Galliard
by Taylor & Francis Books

Contents

Preface ix
List of abbreviations x

1 Introduction 1
Culture wars 2
The importance of the rights 3
Conflict of rights 11
Overview 12

2 Legal frameworks 14
England 14
Canada 17
USA 19
Conclusion 24

3 Resolving conflicts between religious and other claims 25
Conduct/belief 25
Public/private 31
Core/periphery 37
Neutral laws of general applicability 39
Hybrid rights? 42
Conclusion 43

4 Interference and justification 44
Defining rights broadly 44
What should be included in the right to religious freedom? 48
What should the right to non-discrimination include? 54
Conclusion 55

5 Proportionality 57
Proportionality: an analysis 57

Proportionality and conflicts between freedom of religion and non-discrimination 68
Potential objections 76
Proportionality in the USA, England, and Canada 79
Conclusion 82

6 Religious claims in secular employment 83
Disputes around same-sex marriage 83
Other 'conscientious objection' case 97
Discriminatory religious expression and the workplace 104
Proportionality and belief 107
Conclusion 109

7 Discrimination and religious employment 110
Collective religious freedom 111
Types of religious activities 113
Religious ministers 113
Teachers 123
Social service organisations 132
Secular function employees 137
Islands of exclusivity? 138
Conclusion 140

8 Religious organisations and services 141
Religious activities 141
University societies 144
Educational contexts 147
Non-members and services 154
Conclusion 167

9 The secular marketplace and religious claims 168
Interference 169
The provision of services and proportionality 179
One-off commercial services 182
Housing 186
Bed and breakfast accommodation 189
Conclusion 191

10 Conclusion 192
Concluding thoughts 195

Bibliography 197
Index 210

Preface

I began thinking about the ideas that led to this book in 2010. I was interested in the number of legal disputes which kept appearing in the UK and elsewhere which seemed to pitch religious freedom against non-discrimination rights in employment and other contexts. The tone of the media and other debates tended to see these disputes as fundamental, not simply in the sense that they were important, but as a conflict between two entirely opposed world views that were not subject to compromise. I was also critical of the way the English courts were dealing with the then fairly new right of religious freedom introduced into domestic law by the Human Rights Act 1998. I therefore began thinking about what legal principles should be used to decide these cases which could help to lessen tensions and decide these cases fairly. Given that similar issues had arisen in different jurisdictions, I decided to take a comparative approach which examined the legal principles behind legislation and court decisions in England and Wales, Canada, and the USA. This led me to argue that proportionality is the best way to resolve these disputes because of its fact-sensitive and nuanced nature and its requirement for justification.

Since I began researching this area there have been many further cases which the courts have had to address and new disputes are still arising. Some of the cases I discuss, such as the Canadian litigation surrounding the proposed law school at Trinity Western University, are still making their way through the courts. The referendum vote in June 2016 to leave the EU may also have important consequences in the future for English discrimination law as much of it is EU law based. Given the constantly changing law in this area, there was no clear end point to the research but a stop had to be made somewhere and I have aimed to provide a framework for deciding future disputes.

There are many people to thank for all their help over the last few years. My thanks in particular are due to Conor Gearty and Kai Möller for their endless support and suggestions and to Russell Sandberg for showing faith in my work and for the very helpful comments as the work was progressing. Thank you too to Julian Rivers and Colm O'Cinneide. I am also grateful to the AHRC for funding. I am very grateful to everyone at Routledge, particularly to Alison Kirk and Jade Lovitt, and appreciate their tolerance for delays. Finally, thank you to my family for putting up with me, especially to my mother for willingly proofreading, and to Graham for making it all possible. And finally, thank you to Theo, born during the writing of this book, for bringing me joy every day, despite the fact that your presence did not speed up the process.

Abbreviations

ACLU	American Civil Liberties Union
ECHR	European Convention on Human Rights
ECtHR	European Court of Human Rights
ENDA	Employment Non-Discrimination Act
EHRC	Equality and Human Rights Commission
EEOC	Equal Employment Opportunity Commission
OGCMA	Ocean Grove Camp Meeting Association
RFRA	Religious Freedom Restoration Act

1 Introduction

A florist refuses to serve a customer because it contradicts her Southern Baptist beliefs to use her 'professional skill to make an arrangement of flowers for use at a same-sex wedding'.[1] A man is refused employment as a Diocesan Youth Officer because the bishop appointing him is concerned that he will not comply with the Church of England's teachings on sexuality as he is gay, although he confirms he will remain celibate.[2] A counsellor refuses to provide counselling to a client on the basis that her religion 'prohibits her from encouraging or supporting same-sex relationships'.[3] Such situations, involving conflicts between claims of religious freedom to act in discriminatory ways and the right not to be subjected to sexual orientation discrimination, have arisen in numerous contexts. These include the refusal of some religious organisations to hire out their premises for same-sex weddings, the refusal of some registrars or town clerks to perform marriages or give marriage licences to gay couples and the refusal of some faith-based social welfare organisations to employ gay people, among many others.

This book considers how such conflicts should be addressed in law. In doing so, it uses cases and situations that have arisen in three jurisdictions: the US, Canada, and England and Wales. These disputes raise important but difficult issues. They can cause a great deal of controversy, characterised in some contexts by bitterness and animosity, often accompanied by much public and media interest. The purpose of this text is not to provide a comprehensive description of the law in each jurisdiction. Instead, cases are selected to give examples of situations that have arisen to demonstrate the general approach of each jurisdiction or to contrast different approaches for the resolution of these issues. The legal problem in a basic sense, that of whether and how to reconcile the conflicting rights, has arisen in all three places. In each, the problem has been litigated, leading to a significant amount of case law, in addition to often detailed legislation. Indeed, some of the same situations have arisen in the different jurisdictions, such as the claim of some Catholic adoption agencies not to place children with gay couples or the demand of some owners of bed-and-breakfast accommodation to be permitted not to allow gay couples to stay. Of course though, the broader social and legal context in which these disputes have arisen is not identical.

My argument will be that an approach based on the concept of proportionality is the best way to resolve these conflicts between non-discrimination and freedom of religion. Proportionality in this sense requires the courts to apply a specific test made up of a number of

1 *State of Washington v Arlene's Flowers Inc* (WA Super. Ct. Feb 28 2015) 6.
2 *Reaney v Hereford Diocesan Board of Finance* ET Case No. 1602844/2006.
3 *Walden v Centers for Disease Control and Prevention* No. 10–11733 (11th Cir., Feb 7 2012).

parts. It requires that any interference with the right under examination must have a legitimate aim and a rational connection between the aim and the action taken. The policy selected must be the least restrictive means of achieving the aim and, finally, it must be proportionate overall. Under proportionality, rights do not operate in an all-or-nothing way: rights are not trumps as they are under a Dworkinian model.[4] Rather, rights are balanced against legitimate public interests or against other rights, with the purpose being to optimise the right to the greatest extent possible. All these aspects will be considered in more detail later, but first it is necessary to consider why this conflict between sexual orientation discrimination and religious freedom matters.

Culture wars

American scholarship was the first to refer to the clash of world views that these conflicts illustrate as amounting to a 'culture war' and such a description has become relevant to the other jurisdictions as well, although to a lesser extent.[5] A culture war involves deep and stark divisions between social groups, whereby 'moral' issues become flashpoints for cultural and political disagreements.[6] In such a culture war, 'the goal is not to go on living with [the other side] but under a new arrangement. It is somehow to root them out, or subjugate them, so that one does not have to deal with what they stand for anymore.'[7] The question of gay rights, including non-discrimination laws, same-sex marriage, and broader claims for social recognition, has become part of this culture war and indeed perhaps one of its most contested issues.[8] An interesting aspect of this situation is that an issue may become highly contested, not necessarily because of its practical importance but because it is symbolically

4 R. Dworkin, *Taking Rights Seriously* (Cambridge, Mass: Harvard UP, 1977).

5 J. Hunter, *Culture Wars: The Struggle to Define America* (New York: Basic Books, 1991); *Before the Shooting Begins: Searching for Democracy in America's Culture War* (New York: Free Press, 1994); D. Rayside and C. Wilcox, 'The Difference that a Border Makes: The Political Intersection of Sexuality and Religion in Canada and the United States' in D. Rayside and C. Wilcox (eds), *Faith, Politics and Sexual Diversity in Canada and the United States* (Vancouver: UBC Press, 2011). The differences between the jurisdictions may be partly due to the lack of the 'religious right' as a powerful social and political force in Canada and England, see: J. Malloy, 'Bush/Harper? Canadian and American Evangelical Politics Compared' (2009) 39 *American Review of Canadian Studies* 352; A. Walton et al., *Is there a 'Religious Right' Emerging in Britain?* (London: Theos, 2013).

6 It should be noted that not all scholars have agreed that a culture war exists. Literature on this topic includes: A. Abramowitz and K. Saunders, 'Is Polarization a Myth?' (2008) 70 *Journal of Politics* 542; J.D. Hunter and A. Wolfe (eds), *Is there a Culture War? A Dialogue on Values and American Public Life* (Washington D.C.: Brookings Institution Press, 2006); W.G. Jacoby, 'Is There a Culture War? Conflicting Value Structures in American Public Opinion' (2014) 108 *American Political Science Review* 754; G. Layman, *The Great Divide: Religious and Cultural Conflict in American Party Politics* (New York: Columbia UP, 2001); J. Nolan (ed.), *The American Culture Wars: Current Contests and Future Prospects* (Charlottesville: University Press of Virginia, 1996); J. Uecker and G. Lucke, 'Protestant Clergy and the Culture Wars: An Empirical Test of Hunter's Thesis' (2011) 50 *J Sci Study Relig* 692.

7 C. Taylor, 'Living with Difference' in A. Allen and M. Regan (eds), *Debating Democracy's Discontent: Essays on American Politics, Law and Public Philosophy* (Oxford: Oxford UP, 1998) 222.

8 A. Wolfe, 'The Culture War that Never Came' in Hunter and Wolfe supra n.5 (arguing that while the existence of a culture war is exaggerated on other issues, gay rights, and particularly same-sex marriage, remain very controversial). See also K. Hull, *Same-Sex Marriage: The Cultural Politics of Love and Law* (Cambridge: Cambridge UP, 2006).

significant or because of fears that it signals the beginning of a slippery slope. Even though the culture war may only involve a small number of participants, even in the US,[9] the analysis is still pertinent. In all three jurisdictions at issue, disputes over gay rights or religious exemptions have on occasion become 'high stakes' issues and a matter of identity politics, where cases and issues can be used 'not simply, or even primarily, to settle ordinary individual disputes, but rather to pursue social and political causes'.[10]

Of course, we should be careful not to overly simplify or misinterpret this controversy. It is very important to remember that there is no straightforward religious/secular divide. There is no intrinsic reason why religious belief should necessarily be discriminatory towards gay people. There are many devoutly religious people who see no conflict between their religious beliefs and a belief that same-sex relationships are as morally worthy as heterosexual ones.[11] Some organised religions' teachings do not argue there is any moral difference between the two, and indeed there are some religious institutions particularly aimed at gay people, such as the Metropolitan Community Churches, as well as groups which campaign for greater inclusiveness in religious organisations, such as Dignity, in the USA, and the Lesbian and Gay Christian Movement, in the UK.[12] Additionally, many religious individuals and organisations would not wish to discriminate in providing services to gay people, for example, regardless of their beliefs or teaching on sexual morality, and therefore do not seek exemptions from equality laws. The number of those who do wish to discriminate in these jurisdictions, by which I mean treat differently those with a non-heterosexual sexual orientation from those with a heterosexual one outside the sphere of intimate relationships, may therefore be small. The number of those with discriminatory views also appears to be decreasing.[13] Even so, numerous conflicts have arisen and continue to arise and can arouse strong feelings.

The importance of the rights

From a political and social perspective this conflict of rights is therefore a controversial and difficult issue. It also poses problems from a legal and philosophical perspective since it gives rise to a weighty dilemma. Both freedom of religion, which may include the freedom to express and act on discriminatory beliefs, and freedom from discrimination, including on the grounds of sexual orientation, are important rights in a liberal society and represent important underlying values.

9 M. Fiorina, *Culture War? The Myth of a Polarized America*, 3rd ed. (Boston: Longman, 2010); C. Muste, 'Reframing Polarization: Social Groups and "Culture Wars"' (2014) 47 *Political Science & Politics* 432.

10 D. Hoover and K. Den Dulk, 'Christian Conservatives Go to Court: Religion and Legal Mobilization in the United States and Canada' (2004) 25 *Int Polit Sci Rev* 9, 11.

11 For example, one British study found 79 per cent of religious people were in favour of extending civil marriage to same-sex couples: Stonewall, *Living Together: British Attitudes to Lesbian, Gay and Bisexual People in 2012* (London: Stonewall, 2012). See also P. Dickey Young, H. Shipley and T. Trothen (eds), *Religion and Sexuality: Diversity and the Limits of Tolerance* (Vancouver: UBC Press, 2014).

12 See Metropolitan Community Churches' 'Who We Are', available at: http://mccchurch.org/overview/; DignityUSA: https://www.dignityusa.org/; and Lesbian and Gay Christian Movement: http://www.lgcm.org.uk/ <last accessed 18 July 2016>.

13 Hoover and Den Dulk supra n.10.

Freedom of religion

Numerous reasons have been put forward for the protection of freedom of religion.[14] Whilst many commentators have argued that there is little that is unique about freedom of religion that could not be covered by other rights such as freedom of association, conscience or expression,[15] it is almost universally included in lists of rights both domestically and internationally.[16]

Arguments for religious toleration and freedom of religion have a long historical background. Many of the early arguments for religious freedom were based on instrumental considerations. Locke, for example, argued that failure to tolerate religious practices would lead to dissatisfaction and societal disorder.[17] However, while there may be some truth to this at various historical moments, it is not evidently true at present in the jurisdictions discussed here in this context. While there have, of course, been violent conflicts over religious matters, this seems far from likely in relation to the conflict between freedom of religion and non-discrimination rights. In general, too, as Rivers points out, those who are subject to religious oppression tend to be minorities who would not have sufficient power to challenge the state.[18] This merely pragmatic argument is contingent on particular circumstances and does not provide justification when these are not present.

A still instrumental, but less contingent, potential justification is Mill's argument that religious liberty is more likely than authoritarianism to lead to the discovery of truth because it permits the pursuit of many competing lifestyles, and therefore allows others to assess the success of such ideas.[19] While there may be some value in this idea, it fails to grasp the importance of freedom of religion for individuals and groups who share particular beliefs, since it only focuses on the utilitarian benefits for society as a whole.

A more important and persuasive reason is that religion may be of great importance to people's lives. Martha Nussbaum argues that it has an important role 'in people's search for the ultimate meaning of life; in consoling people for the deaths of loved ones and in helping them face their own mortality; in transmitting moral values; in giving people a sense of community and civic dignity [and] in giving them imaginative and emotional fulfilment'.[20] Perhaps because of these benefits, religion can have an 'identity-generative'[21] nature: that is, it may be central to a person's identity and 'form a core aspect of the individual's sense of

14 See e.g. R. Ahdar and I. Leigh, *Religious Freedom in the Liberal State*, 2nd ed. (Oxford: Oxford UP, 2013).

15 See e.g. C. Eisgruber and L. Sager, *Religious Freedom and the Constitution* (Cambridge, Mass: Harvard UP, 2010); W.P. Marshall, 'Solving the Free Exercise Dilemma: Free Exercise as Expression' (1983) 67 *Minn L Rev* 545.

16 See e.g. Universal Declaration of Human Rights Art. 18; American Convention on Human Rights Art. 12; African Charter on Human and Peoples' Rights Art. 8.

17 Locke put forward this argument in *A Letter Concerning Toleration,* reproduced in J. Horton and S. Mendus (eds), *John Locke: A Letter Concerning Toleration – In Focus* (Abingdon: Routledge, 1991).

18 J. Rivers, 'Justifying Freedom of Religion: Does Dignity Help?' in C. McCrudden (ed.), *Understanding Human Dignity* (Oxford: Oxford UP, 2013).

19 J.S. Mill, *On Liberty*. Reproduced at http://www.bartleby.com/130/ <last accessed 25 July 2016>.

20 M. Nussbaum, 'A Plea for Difficulty' in S. Okin (ed.), *Is Multiculturalism Bad for Women?* (Princeton: Princeton UP, 1999) 106.

21 D. Salmons, 'Toward a Fuller Understanding of Religious Exercise: Recognizing the Identity-Generative and Expressive Nature of Religious Devotion' (1995) 62 *U Chi L Rev* 1243.

self and purpose in the world.'[22] For some, religion is a nomos: 'a normative universe' providing its own source of 'law', which because of its mixture of a 'divinely ordained normative corpus, common ritual and strong interpersonal obligations' may present a 'potent' combination.[23] Interferences with religious practices may therefore be experienced as intensely burdensome and disorientating.

Freedom of religion is also part of a broader value of autonomy. In a liberal democracy, there is an important ideal that all should be free to seek their own ultimate convictions without state interference and that they should be able to live in accordance with these convictions, where this is possible and compatible with others' rights.[24] Numerous scholars have argued that seeking such convictions is an intrinsic part of what it means to live a flourishing human life. For example, Maclure and Taylor argue that 'it is in choosing values, hierarchizing or reconciling them, and in clarifying the projects based on them that human beings manage to structure their existence, to exercise their judgment, and to conduct their life'.[25] Nussbaum similarly argues, basing her arguments to some extent on the writings of the seventeenth century writer and theologian Roger Williams, that there should be a 'special respect for the faculty in human beings with which they search for life's ultimate meaning'.[26] Along the same lines, Plant uses Bernard Williams' idea of 'ground projects' to point to the importance of such a capacity, arguing that people have 'beliefs that give a sense of meaning and significance to their lives and that may indeed give them the best reasons they have for wanting to live at all.'[27] This last set of arguments have at their core a sense that the opportunity to develop and maintain beliefs is valuable, and indeed part of what it is to be human.

Preserving autonomy does not merely require that people should be free to develop their beliefs, but also requires some scope to live in accordance with them. Religions typically lay down not only patterns of belief, but also an obligation to act in accordance with these beliefs. Given this, an interference with religious practices may affect the conscientious choices people have made. Acting on the basis of beliefs is intrinsically part of being religious and is 'an essential way of bringing meaning to such beliefs'.[28] Therefore, to ban religious practices 'causes serious human suffering: the emotional (psychological) suffering ... that attends one's being legally forbidden to live a life of integrity.'[29] As Childress argues, the infringement of conscience that results from being required to act contrary to one's core ideals 'result[s] not only in such unpleasant feelings as guilt and/or shame but also in a fundamental loss of integrity, wholeness, and harmony in the self.'[30]

Perry argues that the state is under an obligation to try and prevent this harm where this is possible. His argument is based on the idea that each person has inherent dignity and should be treated in accordance with this. Given this, he argues, causing unnecessary severe

22 C. Feldblum, 'Moral Conflict and Liberty: Gay Rights and Religion' (2006) 72 *Brook L Rev* 61.
23 R. Cover, 'The Supreme Court 1982 Term Foreword: Nomos and Narrative' (1983) 97 *Harv L Rev* 4, 14.
24 See the discussion of different concepts of autonomy in K. Möller, *The Global Model of Constitutional Rights* (Oxford: Oxford UP, 2012) Ch. 3.
25 J. Maclure and C. Taylor, *Secularism and Freedom of Conscience* (Cambridge, Mass: Harvard University Press, 2011) 11–12. See also *Planned Parenthood v Casey* 505 US 833, 851 (1992) ('At the heart of liberty is the right to define one's own concept of existence, of meaning, of the universe, and of the mystery of human life.').
26 M. Nussbaum, *Liberty of Conscience* (New York: Basic Books, 2008) 19.
27 R. Plant, 'Religion, Identity and Freedom of Expression' (2011) 17 *Res Publica* 7.
28 Feldblum supra n.22 at 104.
29 M. Perry, *The Political Morality of Liberal Democracy* (Cambridge: Cambridge UP, 2010) 70–1.
30 J.F. Childress, 'Appeals to Conscience' (1979) 89 *Ethics* 319.

emotional suffering infringes a person's dignity and therefore 'we have conclusive reason to do what we can, all things considered, to prevent human beings from doing things that … cause [others] *unwarranted* suffering.'[31] Since preventing a person from acting in accordance with their religious belief would, he maintains, cause them suffering, there is a prima facie reason to seek to avoid this.

Given the complexity of the issues, arguments for freedom of religion can only be outlined here. In summary though, it protects autonomy, a sense of identity and important relationships, as well as being part of freedom of conscience.[32] Chapter 3 will discuss in more detail whether it is sufficient to protect only religious belief itself, or whether conduct based on this belief must also be protected. It will be argued that, given the importance of this interest, while it would of course be impossible and highly undesirable to protect every religious practice no matter what its effects, there should be consideration of whether it is possible to protect people's conscientious actions and, further, that these should be permitted unless the state has 'good reason' to intervene.[33]

Discriminatory beliefs, by which I mean any belief that same-sex relationships are not as morally worthy as those between opposite sexes, may form part of a matrix of beliefs and practices that constitute a person's 'ground project'.[34] They are therefore prima facie worthy of protection. It should be clear from the preceding discussion that approving of the ability to seek and live in accordance with such beliefs does not necessarily rest on a positive approval of the beliefs themselves. As Waldron argues, rights exist at a certain level of generality,[35] which means that 'the right is not justified by the value of the particular choice I make, but rather by the value of being able to choose for myself in this particular aspect of life'.[36] Thus, to return the discussion to the specific context in question, the issue is not whether we agree with, for example, a conservative Evangelical Christian's views on homosexuality, or for that matter with the sexual activities of a gay man who rejects traditional, monogamous, long-term relationship patterns, but on appreciating the value of each having their opportunity to develop, and to live in accordance with, their own view of sexual ethics.

However, because justification for freedom of religion or conscience is based on the idea of a person's ultimate convictions, in making a claim for protection there is a minimum obligation to demonstrate how such discriminatory views are part of broader conscientious beliefs, although this should not be taken to impose too great a burden. While it is possible that a non-religious justification could amount to a conscientious claim, in the vast majority of cases which have reached the courts in the relevant jurisdictions, a clear religious motivation is present, or at least there has been a mixture of religious and non-religious motivations.[37] For this reason, only religious objections to equality claims will be considered. There is also, of

31 Perry supra n.29, 19 (emphasis added).

32 Reasons for the protection of collective religious freedom are considered in more detail in Chapter 7.

33 Perry supra n.29, 71.

34 See Plant supra n.27.

35 J. Waldron, 'A Right to do Wrong' (1981) 92 *Ethics* 21.

36 J. Quong, 'The Rights of Unreasonable Citizens' (2004) 12 *J Polit Philos* 314, 330 referring to Waldron ibid.

37 E.g. *McClintock v Department of Constitutional Affairs* [2008] IRLR 29 (EAT); [2008] EWCA Civ 167 (CA). McClintock was a magistrate on the family panel who did not want to place children with gay adoptive couples. Although he was a Christian, the reasons he gave were rationally based, in that he did not believe that this was in the best interests of the child. This was not accepted as a 'belief'. This conclusion is criticised in A. Hambler, 'A No-Win Situation for Public Officials with Faith Convictions' (2010) 12 *Ecc LJ* 3.

course, considerable disagreement over what counts as a 'religion' or a 'religious belief'.[38] Unsurprisingly, courts have found this a hard question whenever it has arisen.[39] Again though, because the claims I will discuss are clearly accepted as religious by the legal systems at issue, this issue does not have to be decided here.

Freedom of religion is therefore an important right. However, quite clearly, it may conflict with other rights and with the state's interests. This difficulty, and the attitude which the state should take to these dilemmas, was well expressed by Sachs J in the South African Constitutional Court, and has since been quoted by other jurisdictions elsewhere.[40] He stated that:

> The underlying problem in any open and democratic society based on human dignity, equality and freedom in which conscientious and religious freedom has to be regarded with appropriate seriousness, is how far such democracy can and must go in allowing members of religious communities to define for themselves which laws they will obey and which not ... Believers cannot claim an automatic right to be exempted by their beliefs from the laws of the land. At the same time, the state should, wherever reasonably possible, seek to avoid putting believers to extremely painful and intensely burdensome choices of either being true to their faith or else respectful of the law.[41]

Non-discrimination

Non-discrimination, by which I mean any differential treatment on the grounds of sexual orientation outside the sphere of intimate relationships, too is an important right.[42] Most obviously, discrimination can result in tangible deprivation such as loss of particular employment, thus leading to economic disadvantage, and through that social disadvantage.[43] This though is only a partial explanation of the need for a right of non-discrimination and cannot explain why this right may be violated where there is no tangible loss caused apart from mild inconvenience, as occurs, for example, when a person has been denied goods or services but has acquired this elsewhere. There is evidently a moral difference between being told 'we don't make wedding cakes' and 'we won't make a wedding cake for *you*', even if the practical result is the same.

38 See Ahdar and Leigh supra n.14, 139–55; L. Beaman, 'Defining Religion: The Promise and the Peril of Legal Interpretation' in R. Moon (ed.), *Law and Religious Pluralism in Canada* (Vancouver: UBC Press, 2008); G. Freeman, 'The Misguided Search for the Constitutional Definition of Religion' (1983) 71 *Geo LJ* 1519; T.J. Gunn, 'The Complexity of Religion and the Definition of "Religion" in International Law' (2003) 16 *Harv Hum Rts J* 189; C. Kenny, 'Law and the Art of Defining Religion' (2014) 16 *Ecc LJ* 18; W. Sadurski, 'On Legal Definitions of "Religion"' (1989) 63 *Aust LJ* 834.

39 *Church of the New Faith v Commissioner of Pay-Roll Tax (Victoria)* (1983) 154 CLR 136 (Australia); *Malnak v Yogi* 592 F.2d 197 (1979) (USA); *United States v Seeger* 380 U.S 163 (1965). The related question of whether a Scientologist church was a 'place of meeting for religious worship' was at issue in *R v Registrar General ex p Segerdal* [1970] 2 QB 697 and more recently in *R(Hodkin) v Registrar General of Births, Deaths and Marriages* [2013] UKSC 77.

40 E.g. *Islington BC v Ladele* [2010] 1 WLR 955; *R(Williamson) v Secretary of State for Education* [2005] 2 AC 246.

41 *Christian Education South Africa v Minister of Education* [2000] ZACC 11, para 35.

42 For criticism though that this concept is fundamentally empty and does not provide guidance on what should be done see P. Westen, 'The Empty Idea of Equality' (1982) 95 *Harv L Rev* 537.

43 I leave aside here more complex questions about when positive discrimination is permissible as a method of compensating for historical disadvantage.

The full importance of the non-discrimination right is not necessarily recognised by all writers on the conflict between sexual orientation discrimination and freedom of religion. For example, in his discussion of whether there should be exemptions for those who refuse on religious grounds to provide services relating to same-sex marriage, Laycock considers discrimination to involve a practical loss and 'the insult of being refused service.'[44] Since he argues that insult is not a recognised interest under US law, he sees it as an easy decision to protect discriminatory refusals of service related to same-sex marriage because there is little to weigh against the infringement of freedom of religion. This though is not an adequate explanation of what is at stake. A person may of course *feel* insulted in such a situation but this suggests that there is only hurt pride at stake.

Rather, such discrimination undermines a person's sense of self-worth and inclusion and denies them equal respect. This is partly because of its cumulative nature. Discriminatory beliefs are often widely shared. Repeated discrimination causes harm which 'occasional idiosyncratic prejudice'[45] does not, even if this is entirely arbitrary and unjustified. If a person is denied a job because the owner of the company dislikes people with large ear-lobes[46] they of course suffer harm, but this is likely to be an isolated occurrence. However, repeated discrimination leads to a sense of exclusion:[47] a person cannot feel that they are an 'equal citizen'[48] where they fear constant discrimination in performing everyday tasks, in seeking access to benefits or services provided by the state, or in access to social activities.

Widespread discrimination may also have a stigmatic effect: if a person is discriminated against, it may lead others to believe that this is acceptable and to assume that there is a reason why a certain group is stigmatised.[49] Discrimination is thus mutually reinforcing: the more pervasive it is, the more 'natural' it may seem and thus the more likely it is to continue to occur. The stigma of discrimination may also be internalised, leading to low self-esteem and higher rates of mental illness.[50] Sexual orientation discrimination may also lead to other pressures because, in an effort to avoid discrimination or social ostracism, a non-heterosexual orientation may be hidden in contexts such as work. Maintaining this may lead to 'significant stress and disengagement'.[51] The non-discrimination principle therefore 'presumptively insists that the organized society treat each individual as a person, one who is worthy of respect, one who "belongs"'.[52] It is part of a broader principle that the state has an obligation to treat all its citizens with 'equal concern and respect'.[53]

44 D. Laycock, 'Afterword', in D. Laycock et al. (eds), *Same-Sex Marriage and Religious Liberty*: Emerging Conflicts (Lanham, Maryland: Rowman & Littlefield, 2008) 197. See also for a similar argument, I. Leigh and A. Hambler, 'Religious Symbols, Conscience and the Rights of Others' (2014) 3 *OJLR* 2.
45 A. Koppelman, 'Justice for Large Earlobes! A Comment on Richard Arneson's "*What is Wrongful Discrimination?*"' (2006) 43 *San Diego L Rev* 809.
46 Ibid.
47 The exclusion may also be literal e.g. from some organisations or places.
48 K. Karst, 'Equal Citizenship Under the Fourteenth Amendment' (1977) 91 *Harv L Rev* 1.
49 K. Karst, 'Private Discrimination and Public Responsibility: *Patterson* in Context' [1989] *Sup Court Rev* 1.
50 See e.g. M. Hatzenbuehler, 'How Does Sexual Minority Stigma "Get Under the Skin"? A Psychological Mediation Framework' [2009] *Psychol Bull* 135.
51 N. Buddel, 'Queering the Workplace' (2011) 23 *Journal of Gay & Lesbian Social Services* 131, 136.
52 Karst supra n.48, 6.
53 Dworkin supra n.4. This principle also partly explains why freedom of religion must be protected.

As private actors control much of the economic and social opportunities in society and make up a great deal of public life,[54] this obligation means that the state must not only refrain from acting in discriminatory ways itself but also prevent private actors from acting in discriminatory ways in many contexts too. As Dworkin puts it, 'a political and economic system that allows prejudice to destroy some people's lives does not treat all members of the community with equal concern'.[55] To permit private discrimination in public and social life where there is pervasive discrimination demonstrates either an impermissible lack of interest in the welfare of citizens or, probably more likely, that the discriminatory views are tacitly, or perhaps even explicitly, agreed with. After all, it is through the state's choice not to prohibit it that such discrimination may legally continue.[56]

Epstein, though, argues from a libertarian perspective that, while the state should not discriminate, anti-discrimination law should not apply to non-state actors.[57] He contends that there is a right of self-ownership which should mean that people are free to contract their labour with whoever they choose and at whatever price. He also argues that market forces will ameliorate invidious discrimination, although leaving some rationally based discrimination,[58] if it is allowed to function unhindered by, for example, minimum wage laws. However, in this argument, he does not account for the effects of stigma and stereotyping, which lead to the continuation of discrimination even where this is not economically rational.[59] Discrimination laws also have a cultural effect, meaning that they help to change attitudes.[60] Legally prohibiting employment discrimination does reduce discrimination against gay people.[61] For these reasons, although it is far from a perfect mechanism, the law has an important role to play in ending discrimination. Indeed, all three jurisdictions recognise that prohibiting private discrimination is necessary in order to combat discrimination and that the state is required to act to prevent it.[62]

54 Karst argues that 'respected participation in the community's life implies access to all those activities and places, whether managed directly by government or not, that are normally open to the public at large.' supra n.48, 35.

55 R. Dworkin, 'What is Equality? Part 3: The Place of Liberty' (1987) 73 *Iowa L Rev* 1, 36–7.

56 S. Gardbaum, 'The "Horizontal Effect" of Constitutional Rights' (2003) 102 *Mich L Rev* 387.

57 R. Epstein, *Forbidden Grounds: The Case Against Employment Discrimination Laws* (Cambridge, Mass: Harvard UP, 1992).

58 Ibid., 269–74, arguing that there are biological and other factors which mean women and men will choose to specialise in different jobs.

59 See S. Deakin, 'Equality, Non-discrimination and the Labour Market: A Commentary on Richard Epstein's Critique of Anti-discrimination Laws' in R. Epstein, *Equal Opportunity or More Opportunity? The Good Thing About Discrimination* (London: Civitas, 2002).

60 Indeed, Epstein recognises this, but argues that it makes the government intervention inherent in non-discrimination laws even more problematic.

61 L.G. Barron et al., 'The Force of Law: The Effects of Sexual Orientation Antidiscrimination Legislation on Interpersonal Discrimination in Employment' (2013) 19 *Psychology, Public Policy, and Law* 191.

62 Cases prohibiting discrimination between private parties include *Ghaidan v Godin-Mendoza* [2004] 2 AC 557 in the UK and *Shelley v Kraemer* 334 US 1 (1948) in the US. In Canada, it was held that the Charter could not be asserted against a private party in *Retail Wholesale and Department Store Union Local 580 v Dolphin Delivery Ltd* (1985) 33 DLR (4th) 174, although the common law will be developed consistently with 'Charter values', as in *Ontario (Human Rights Commission) v Brockie* (2002) 22 DLR (4th) 174. An individual can also claim that the *state* has breached the Charter by not prohibiting discrimination: *Vriend v Alberta*. See Ahdar and Leigh, supra n.14, 185–92.

In the three jurisdictions under discussion here, Canada, the USA, and England, equality concerns are usually addressed by the prohibition of discrimination on specific grounds, where discrimination is particularly prevalent.[63] It can easily be demonstrated that sexual orientation should be one of these grounds. Gay people have certainly been subject to appalling historical disadvantage in the three jurisdictions.[64] This history is important because it can continue to have psychological effects, leading to fear of discrimination or ill treatment, which can in turn affect behaviour.[65] Furthermore, although there has clearly been an overall trend towards greater protection against sexual orientation discrimination, some of this history is very recent, as will be outlined in the next chapter.

Moreover, in fairly recent studies, high levels of discrimination have still been reported in all three jurisdictions. In the US, a large meta-analysis found that 55 per cent of gay people reported suffering verbal harassment and 41 per cent discrimination.[66] One study by Stonewall, the UK campaigning organisation on gay issues, found that 19 per cent of employees reported that they had experienced verbal bullying from colleagues, customers or service users because of their sexual orientation between 2008–2013 and almost a third of this bullying was from their managers. Only 38 per cent were open about their sexuality to their colleagues.[67] According to another study in England and Wales, 51 per cent of gay men, 61 per cent of lesbians and 25 per cent of bisexual people felt that they had experienced disadvantage as a result of their sexual orientation.[68] In Canada in one study, 44 per cent of gay men and lesbians and 41 per cent of bisexuals reported some form of workplace discrimination in the previous five years.[69] Even more serious is the existence of violent hate crime against gay people.[70] Given this evidence, there is still a demonstrable need for the prohibition of discrimination.

Prohibiting such discrimination in law alone, though, is not sufficient to challenge ingrained attitudes. Moon, for example, has argued that, 'to be meaningful, the acceptance or affirmation of same-sex relationships must involve a public statement or indication that

63 The Equality Act 2010 has a list of 'protected characteristics' (s.4). The US uses concepts of suspect and quasi-suspect grounds to distinguish between different kinds of discrimination and Canada lists various grounds as part of its equality right in the Canadian Charter of Rights and Freedoms s.15, although these are not comprehensive.

64 D.G. Casswell, *Lesbians, Gay Men and Canadian Law* (Toronto: Montgomery, 1996); W. Eskridge, *Gaylaw: Challenging the Apartheid of the Closet* (Cambridge, Mass: Harvard UP, 1999); M. Nussbaum, *Law, Religion and Homosexuality: From Disgust to Humanity: Sexual Orientation and Constitutional Law* (New York: Oxford UP, 2010).

65 G. Ellison and B. Gunstone, *Sexual Orientation Explored: A Study of Identity, Attraction, Behaviour and Attitudes in 2009* (Manchester: Equality and Human Rights Commission, 2009) (Finding that fear of discrimination affects choice of career).

66 S. Katz-Wise and J. Hyde, 'Victimization Experiences of Lesbian, Gay, and Bisexual Individuals: A Meta Analysis' (2012) 49 *J Sex Res* 142.

67 Stonewall, *Gay in Britain: Lesbian, Gay and Bisexual People's Experiences and Expectations of Discrimination* (London: Stonewall, 2013). It is important to note that people's experiences of discrimination may vary considerably. See A.K.T. Kip, 'Homophobia and Ethnic Minority Communities in the United Kingdom' in L. Trappolin, A. Gasparini and R. Wintemute, *Confronting Homophobia in Europe: Social and Legal Perspectives* (Oxford: Hart Publishing, 2011).

68 Equality and Human Rights Commission, *Beyond Tolerance: Making Sexual Orientation a Public Matter* (Manchester: Equality and Human Rights Commission, 2009).

69 Buddel supra n.51.

70 See e.g. M. Smyth and V. Jenness, 'Violence Against Sexual and Gender Minorities' in R. Gartner and B. McCarthy (eds), *The Oxford Handbook of Gender, Sex and Crime* (Oxford: Oxford UP, 2014). The report by Ellison and Gunstone (supra n.64) found that 19 per cent of gay men in the study reported being physically assaulted on the grounds of their sexual orientation.

such relationships are normal and valuable'.[71] There may therefore be a claim for more: to challenge the 'cultural heterosexism' in society, the process whereby heterosexuality is the norm and other sexualities are marginalised[72] by 'a heterosexual assumption'[73] that leads to the invisibility of gay people. Such policies do not fall strictly under the right to non-discrimination but are part of a broader public policy. They may include efforts to challenge the 'heterosexual norm' in education and in other training, and for workplaces to promote inclusivity.

These types of policies may pose greater conflicts for those who have discriminatory views than the mere obligation not to discriminate because they may suggest that positive approval of gay people and relationships is required. Thus when a school board in British Columbia decided not to approve three books which portrayed same-sex parenting positively, this led to serious disputes, with claims on the one side about the use of schools to 'indoctrinate children' against parents' wishes, and on the other, the need of state schools 'to mirror the diversity of the community and teach tolerance and understanding of difference'.[74] Eventually, the Canadian Supreme Court quashed the decision to refuse to approve the books.[75] These types of disputes mirrored arguments in England about the repeal of the law often referred to as 'Section 28'.[76] This law forbade local authorities to promote homosexuality or to 'promote the acceptability of homosexuality as a pretended family relationship' in schools.[77] There were numerous campaigns to abolish it and it was finally repealed in 2003, following an earlier attempt which was defeated in the House of Lords in 2001.

This section has established that non-discrimination, and in particular non-discrimination on the grounds of sexual orientation, is a vital right. However, just as there are limits to the value of freedom of religion, there are limits to how far non-discrimination can be applied. As Koppelman puts it:

> The antidiscrimination project represents a claim of enormous moral power … Yet as soon as we begin to try to carry it out, we find ourselves in collision with other moral considerations, equally powerful, that demand that the project be a limited one.[78]

Conflict of rights

So far it has been demonstrated that conflicts between religious freedom and the prohibition of sexual orientation discrimination are not merely likely but also potentially serious because

71 R. Moon, *Freedom of Conscience and Religion* (Toronto: Irwin Law, 2014) 60. Indeed, he has gone further arguing that 'the commitment to sexual orientation equality involves a public repudiation of the view held by some religious adherents that same-sex relationships are immoral' (ibid., 61). See also for a similar argument A. Galeotti, *Toleration as Recognition* (Cambridge: Cambridge UP, 2002).

72 J. Schacter, '*Romer v Evans*: Democracy's Domain' (1997) 50 *Vanderbilt Law Rev* 411.

73 G. Herek, 'Confronting Sexual Stigma and Prejudice: Theory and Practice' (2007) 4 *J Soc Issues* 905.

74 *Chamberlain v Surrey School District No. 36* (2002) 221 DLR (4th) 156, para 3. See D. Collins, 'Culture, Religion and Curriculum: Lessons from the "Three Books" Controversy in Surrey, BC' (2006) 50 *Can Geogr-Geogr Can* 342.

75 Ibid.

76 The Local Government Act 1988 s.28 added Section 2A to the Local Government Act 1986.

77 See J. Moran, 'Childhood Sexuality and Education: The Case of Section 28' (2001) 4 *Sexualities* 73. As Moran points out, since the law only applied to local authorities rather than schools themselves it had little practical effect but it had significant symbolic significance, not least because of the description of homosexuality as a 'pretended family relationship'.

78 A. Koppelman, *Antidiscrimination Law and Social Equality* (New Haven: Yale UP, 1996) 10.

both rights are important and worthy of protection. As Stychin puts it, 'liberal democracies are faced with what appears to be an irreconcilable clash of two conflicting rights'.[79] A choice must therefore be made about which right to protect, at the cost of infringing another important right. It is this difficulty which is at the heart of this book. In such a dispute, as Minow points out, 'always granting exemptions subverts the civil rights norms. Never granting them disparages religious beliefs and coerces religious believers.'[80] The choice is made paradoxically both harder, in the sense that a straightforward binary answer is unlikely to be sufficient, and easier, in the sense that there is some way to avoid stalemate situations, by the fact that the claims may not be of identical strength in particular situations. Any method of resolving this conflict must be sufficiently nuanced to appreciate these points and should also accept that, given that both these rights are valuable, it should seek to protect both as far as possible, rather than protecting one entirely at the expense of the other.

Because these rights are both important, and because co-existence in society between people who have very different views on this matter is required, it will be argued that the method used to resolve this conflict should promote respect, although of a very limited kind. To be clear, this is not an argument that gay people should respect, in the sense of approve of, those who they may see as seeking to undo hard-fought and precarious rights, or alternatively that religious people must approve of those who they think are behaving in fundamentally immoral ways. A useful distinction between two different kinds of respect is made by Darwall, which he calls moral recognition respect and appraisal respect. It is the former which is appropriate here. Having moral recognition respect for something means that the 'inappropriate consideration or weighing of that fact or feature would result in behaviour that is morally wrong'.[81] Thus when considering whether discrimination should be prohibited, whether and how this affects religious freedom should be taken into account. Similarly, if a religious organisation wishes to discriminate in providing a service, there must be consideration of how this affects those discriminated against. Appraisal respect, or a 'positive appraisal of a person or his character-related features',[82] is not needed.

Overview

This book considers various legal cases and situations that have occurred in the three jurisdictions, the legal principles used to decide these cases and how a proportionality test could be applied to them. I have referred to these jurisdictions as England, Canada, and the USA. By England, I mean the jurisdiction of England and Wales, although much law, such as the Equality Act 2010, applies to Scotland as well. The particular situation relating to Northern Ireland will not be discussed, although sometimes, such as when discussing case law on the ECHR, the law will be applicable throughout the UK. I will therefore refer to Britain or to the UK rather than to England where this is appropriate. Second, both Canada and the US are federal systems and therefore the relevant law is somewhat complex, although state law of course is subject to federal law. As the purpose of the book is to examine situations where there is a clash of rights, it will only rarely address the situation in those US states that do not prohibit sexual orientation discrimination.

79 C.F. Stychin, 'Faith in the Future: Sexuality, Religion and the Public Sphere' (2009) 29 *OJLS* 729.
80 M. Minow, 'Should Religious Groups be Exempt from Civil Rights Laws?' (2007) 48 *BCL Rev* 781, 827.
81 S. Darwall, 'Two Kinds of Respect' (1977) 88 *Ethics* 36, 41.
82 Ibid., 46.

Although the situations and legal problems that have arisen in each jurisdiction are similar, the jurisdictions' legal tests and methods of analysis, and in particular their use of proportionality, varies. This will be explained in greater detail in Chapter 5 but in summary, proportionality is becoming a widely used test in English law, although this is a fairly recent introduction. In Canada, proportionality is an established and major concept in its human rights and discrimination law. In contrast, the US tends to use either categorical tests or tiered standards of review (in decreasing order of scrutiny: strict scrutiny, intermediate scrutiny, rational basis), based on the type of interest at stake. Importantly though, since the US Supreme Court's judgment in 1990 in *Employment Division v Smith*,[83] strict scrutiny, which requires the state to show that there is a compelling government interest and that the law is narrowly tailored to achieve that interest, only applies to religious freedom claims where a law or action deliberately targets a religious practice. It does not apply where there is 'a neutral rule of general applicability'. The current constitutional protection of freedom of religion is therefore narrow. Greater legislative protection is given though through the very important Religious Freedom Restoration Act of 1993, which restored the strict scrutiny test in some contexts. While the US does not explicitly use proportionality in any of these contexts, I will consider whether its use is in fact implicit.

Full agreement over conflicts between sexual orientation discrimination and freedom of religion is extremely unlikely and there is no widely accepted moral answer to this question. Since neither side is likely to completely withdraw its demands, and therefore disputes and cases are likely to continue to arise, these conflicts have to be resolved by the law. Both freedom of religion, which can include the right to express and act on discriminatory beliefs, and non-discrimination are vitally important rights. The aim is therefore to find a way for the law to protect both sides' rights as fully as possible, bearing in mind the impact on the other, ideally in a way which does not exacerbate existing tensions. The argument will be that reliance on the principle of proportionality is a suitable way of adjudicating the balance between freedom of religion and non-discrimination given these considerations.

The structure of the book is as follows. Chapter 2 outlines the legal protection given to both rights in the three jurisdictions. Chapter 3 discusses various tests that have been suggested or used for deciding when religious freedom should be protected, since it evidently cannot be an absolute right, but will conclude that none of these is appropriate. Chapter 4 argues that the law should make a distinction between interference and violation of a right and considers what the right to freedom of religion and to non-discrimination should include. Chapter 5 explains the nature of the proportionality test and its advantages in this context, and proposes it as a method of resolving these issues. Chapters 6–9 provide a detailed analysis of how a proportionality test would work in various situations. Chapter 6 looks at the situation of employees in secular organisations who claim that they face conflicts between their religious beliefs and part of their work, or claim a right to express discriminatory views in a work-related context. Chapter 7 discusses whether religious organisations, including faith-based social service organisations, can require that their employees are not gay or in same-sex relationships. Chapter 8 considers whether religious organisations, including social service organisations and providers of rented premises, can refuse to provide services to gay people. Chapter 9 discusses the same issue with regard to religious individuals, particularly relating to services relating to same-sex marriage and the provision of housing and other accommodation.

83 494 US 872 (1990).

2 Legal frameworks

This chapter provides an outline of the specific provisions protecting freedom of religion and non-discrimination rights in each jurisdiction. Since each jurisdiction protects both rights, although in differing ways, the conflict between them raises not only moral and philosophical issues as described in the previous chapter, but also legal problems, as will become evident.

England

Freedom of religion

Before the Human Rights Act 1998, there was no general right to freedom of religion in English law. Of course, this does not mean that religious freedom itself was non-existent, and there were many pieces of legislation granting particular rights.[1] Race discrimination law also gave protection to members of some religions in certain contexts. The House of Lords held in *Mandla v Dowell Lee*[2] that Sikhs were a group defined by 'ethnic origins' and therefore a racial group for the purposes of the Race Relations Act 1976, giving protection in employment and the provision of goods and services. It was therefore indirect discrimination, a concept explained further below, for a school to prohibit a Sikh boy from wearing a turban. In the earlier case of *Seide v Gillette Industries Ltd*[3] the Employment Appeal Tribunal had accepted that Jews too were a racial group. However, the protection given by race discrimination law was limited as it excluded numerous religious groups, including Christians and Muslims.[4]

In addition to this legislation, as a signatory to the ECHR, the UK was under an obligation to protect the right to freedom of religion under Article 9 of the ECHR and applicants could take their case to Strasbourg if they believed there had been a violation of this right. Article 9 gives an absolute right to 'freedom of thought, conscience and religion' and a right to 'manifest one's religion or beliefs' which is 'subject only to such limitations as are prescribed by law and necessary in a democratic society in the interests of public safety, for the protection of public order, health or morals, or for the protection of the rights and freedoms of others.' There have been relatively few cases brought under Art. 9 though, partly because,

1 See R. Sandberg, *Law and Religion* (Cambridge: Cambridge UP, 2011) Ch. 2.
2 [1983] 2 AC 548.
3 [1980] IRLR 427.
4 *Nyazi v Rymans Ltd* [1988] EAT/6/88.

as will be discussed in Chapter 4, both Strasbourg and the UK courts interpreted this right restrictively until fairly recently.

The Human Rights Act 1998 incorporated the Convention into English law. Claimants can now bring cases claiming violation of their Convention rights to the English courts. Courts have the power to issue a Declaration of Incompatibility if primary legislation is incompatible with a Convention right, although this does not affect its validity.[5] Secondary legislation must be compatible with the Convention and the courts have the power to strike it down if it is not. Furthermore, under the Human Rights Act s.3, 'so far as it is possible to do so', legislation must be interpreted in a way which is compatible with Convention rights. In addition, public authorities may not act contrary to Convention rights, unless they are required to do so by primary legislation.[6]

The Convention only grants rights against the state, as opposed to private persons. However, since the state has a positive obligation to protect these rights it may be of relevance in disputes between private individuals. A party may argue, for example, that the law which the other party is relying on violates its rights and the state is therefore at fault in permitting this. The Human Rights Act too only applies to public bodies. However, since courts and tribunals are included in the definition of public bodies and therefore have an obligation to protect rights, it will be relevant even if a case concerns private parties.

Religious discrimination *per se* was not prohibited until the Employment Equality (Religion or Belief) Regulations 2003 were introduced as a result of an EU Directive.[7] The Equality Act 2006 extended protection against religious discrimination to cover goods and services. These are now both incorporated into the Equality Act 2010. This domestic law is unaffected by the recent vote to leave the EU, although it is of course open to Parliament to issue further legislation. The Equality Act forbids direct and indirect discrimination by the state and private actors on many grounds including religion. Direct discrimination concerns the situation where a person is treated less favourably because of a protected characteristic (such as their religion). Indirect discrimination is where a 'provision, criterion or practice' places people who share a protected characteristic at a disadvantage compared to others, and this is not a proportionate means of achieving a legitimate aim. For example, if an employer forbids employees from wearing head coverings this rule will disadvantage Muslim women more heavily than those who are not Muslim and therefore the employer has the burden of demonstrating that this requirement is proportionate. In addition, the Racial and Religious Hatred Act 2006 prohibits religious hate speech.

There has only been limited success for claimants under both religious discrimination law and the Human Rights Act 1998. One of the first cases, *R (Williamson) v Secretary of State for Education*,[8] which went to the House of Lords, concerned a claim that the ban on corporal punishment in schools was contrary to Article 9 ECHR, since it violated the claimants' Christian beliefs that such punishment was necessary on occasion. The House of Lords held that the interference with the claimants' rights was justified.[9] In *R (Begum) v Denbigh High School*[10] a pupil lost her claim that she should be allowed to wear a niqab at school. This case will be discussed in greater detail in Chapter 4. Furthermore, claims brought to employment

5 Human Rights Act 1998 s.4.
6 Human Rights Act 1998 s.6.
7 Council Directive 2000/78/EC of 27 November establishing a General Framework for Equal Treatment in Employment and Occupation.
8 [2005] 2 AC 246.
9 At earlier stages the ban had been held not to infringe the claimants' rights at all.
10 [2007] 1 AC 100.

tribunals challenging employee dress codes have largely been unsuccessful.[11] Nevertheless, the law remains important.

Sexual orientation discrimination

The legal prohibition of sexual orientation discrimination has been a long and slow process, and has received consistent opposition at every stage, much of it religiously based.[12] The first major legal reforms began with challenges to laws prohibiting same-sex sexual activity. Decriminalisation of sexual activity between men (sexual activity between women was never illegal in the UK) took place in 1967 in England and Wales, although only if there were no more than two men present and only if both participants were aged over 21 (this was in comparison to an age of consent of 16 for heterosexual sex).[13] It is interesting to note that most of the arguments for decriminalisation did not depend on arguments that such sexual activity was not morally reprehensible, but on the narrower basis that this was not a suitable matter for criminal regulation.[14] After a fairly long period, the age of consent was reduced to 18 in 1993 by the Criminal Justice and Public Order Act and was equalised to 16 in 2000, despite the objections of the House of Lords.[15]

Sexual orientation discrimination in employment was prohibited by the Employment Equality (Sexual Orientation) Regulations 2003 as a result of an EU directive.[16] The Equality Act (Sexual Orientation) Regulations 2007 later forbade discrimination in the provision of services. Both these Regulations were later consolidated into the Equality Act 2010. In addition, hate speech against gay people was prohibited by the Criminal Justice and Immigration Act 2008. This prohibits threatening words or behaviour or the display of written material if the person thereby intends to stir up hatred on the grounds of sexual orientation.[17] Most recently, non-discrimination claims have involved claims for equal relationship recognition. The Civil Partnerships Act 2004 introduced civil partnerships, which give the same rights as marriage, across the UK. These can only be entered into by same-sex couples.[18] A challenge to the prohibition on same-sex marriage was unsuccessful[19] but it was legalised by the Marriage (Same Sex Couples) Act 2013 in England and Wales, and in

11 In *Eweida v British Airways* [2010] EWCA Civ 80 and *Chaplin v Royal Devon & Exeter Hospital NHS Foundation Trust* [2010] ET 1702886/2009 it was held that employers could prevent employees from wearing crosses at work. In *Azmi v Kirklees Metropolitan Borough Council* [2007] ICR 1154 a teaching assistant could be prohibited from wearing a niqab while in the classroom. In the school context a pupil was prohibited from wearing a 'purity ring': *Playfoot v Millais School Governing Body* [2007] EWHC 1698 (Admin). However, in a claim brought under race discrimination law it was held that a school had acted unlawfully in refusing to allow a pupil to wear the Sikh kara: *R (Watkins-Singh) v Governing Body of Aberdare Girls' High School* [2008] EWHC 1865 (Admin).

12 P. Johnson and R.M. Vanderbeck, *Law, Religion and Homosexuality* (Abingdon: Routledge, 2014).

13 Decriminalisation took place in Scotland in 1980, and in 1982 in Northern Ireland.

14 Johnson and Vanderbeck supra n.12 at 40–52.

15 Unusually, passing this legislation required use of the Parliament Acts.

16 Council Directive 2000/78/EC of 27 November establishing a General Framework for Equal Treatment in Employment and Occupation.

17 See Johnson and Vanderbeck supra n.12 Ch. 5.

18 The prohibition on *opposite*-sex couples entering into civil partnerships was unsuccessfully challenged in *Steinfeld v Secretary of State for Education* [2016] 4 WLR 41.

19 *Wilkinson v Kitzinger* [2006] 2 FLR 397.

Scotland by the Marriage and Civil Partnership (Scotland) Act 2014. It still does not exist in Northern Ireland.

As with freedom of religion, statutory protection against discrimination lies alongside that given by the ECHR. Early ECtHR case law focused on Art. 8 ECHR, which grants the right to respect for private and family life. It was held in *Dudgeon v UK*[20] that the prohibition on same-sex sexual activity, still in force in Northern Ireland at the time, violated Art. 8. This right is also important outside this narrow context. In *Smith and Grady v UK*[21] and *Lustig-Prean v UK*,[22] for example, it was held that this right was violated when members of the armed forces were discharged because of their homosexuality.

Further protection is given by Article 14 ECHR. Article 14 provides that 'the enjoyment of the rights and freedoms set forth in this Convention shall be secured without discrimination on any ground' and then goes on to provide examples of such grounds. Whilst sexual orientation is not one of these, the list is not exhaustive and in a number of cases the ECtHR has held that 'particularly weighty reasons' are required to justify sexual orientation discrimination.[23] However, it held in *Schalk and Kopf v Austria*[24] that it is not a violation of the Convention to limit marriage to opposite-sex couples, given there was no European consensus on this issue. At the time the case was brought, only six Council of European jurisdictions permitted same-sex marriage. The ruling in *Schalk* was confirmed in 2014 in *Hämäläinen v Finland*.[25] Case law is likely to evolve further on this issue.[26]

Canada

Protection of both freedom of religion and non-discrimination is primarily given by the Canadian Charter of Rights and Freedoms and the federal Canadian Human Rights Act and Human Rights Codes of each province. The Charter entrenches various rights into the Canadian Constitution. Individuals can bring cases claiming that the state has violated their rights under the Charter and if the court finds that a law violates the Charter it can strike down the law.[27] The Charter only applies to the state rather than private individuals, and the state's positive obligations have been interpreted more narrowly than under the ECtHR and the UK Human Rights Act.[28] However, the Canadian Human Rights Act[29] prohibits discrimination by non-state actors in matters under the jurisdiction of the federal government and each province also has its own Human Rights Code covering non-federal matters.

20 (1982) 4 EHRR 149.
21 (1999) 29 EHRR 493.
22 (2000) 29 EHRR 548.
23 This phrase was first used in *SL v Austria* (2003) 37 EHRR 39, a case about whether it was permissible to have a higher age of consent for sexual activity between men. See also *EB v France* (2008) 1 FLR 850 and *Karner v Austria* (2004) 38 EHRR 24.
24 (2011) 53 EHRR 20.
25 (2014) 37 BHRC 55.
26 In *Hämäläinen* the number of states granting same-sex marriage had by this time increased to 10 but this was still not viewed as a consensus. This case was more complex than that of *Schalk* since the case involved a transgender woman who was unable to receive full legal recognition of her gender unless she converted her marriage into a registered partnership. However, see *Oliari v Italy* (App No. 18766/11 and 36030/11, 21 July 2015) (holding that within the Italian context it was a violation of Art. 8 not to provide some legal relationship recognition for same-sex couples).
27 s.52 Constitution Act 1982 c.11.
28 *Retail, Wholesale and Department Store Union v Dolphin Delivery Ltd* [1986] 2 SCR 573.
29 R.S.C., 1985, c H-6.

Freedom of religion

There are two provisions in the Charter concerning freedom of religion. S.2 states that everyone has the right to freedom of conscience and religion. S.15 provides that everyone has the 'equal protection and benefit' of the law without discrimination based on, *inter alia*, religion. Neither of these rights is absolute but rather, under s.1 of the Charter, subject 'to such reasonable limits prescribed by law as can be demonstrably justified in a free and democratic society'.

There have been many important cases under s.2. The first case, *R v Big M Drug Mart Ltd*,[30] involved a challenge to the Lord's Day Act which prevented shops from opening on Sundays. It was held that the legislation was enacted for an invalid purpose of ensuring religious observance and was therefore contrary to the Charter. Later cases, such as *Multani v Commission Scolaire Marguerite-Bourgeoys*,[31] have included claims for exemptions on religious grounds. Multani was a Sikh pupil who believed he was religiously obligated to wear a kirpan (a small ceremonial dagger) at all times but was prohibited from wearing it at school, even though he agreed that it would be sewn up inside his clothing. The Supreme Court held that this was a violation of s.2 since, although there was a pressing and substantial aim in ensuring safety in schools, an absolute prohibition on wearing a kirpan was not the least restrictive means of achieving this. However, other claims for religious exemptions have been unsuccessful. In *Alberta v Hutterian Brethren of Wilson Colony*,[32] Hutterites, who refused for religious reasons to have photographs taken of them, claimed that a new policy requiring them to have driving licences containing photographs was a violation of their Charter rights. However, the Supreme Court held by 4 votes to 3 that the state's actions were justified and so this did not contravene their rights under the Charter.[33]

In addition to the Charter, human rights legislation is also extremely important. As stated, these laws prohibit religious discrimination in employment and other contexts, although there is usually an exception where being of a particular religion is a bona fide occupational requirement (BFOR). Importantly, these rights have been interpreted as including a right of reasonable accommodation: that is religious practices must be accommodated, unless this would cause undue hardship.[34] One of the first cases to consider this issue was *Ontario Human Rights Division v Simpson-Sears*.[35] An employee of Simpson-Sears, O'Malley, was required to work on Friday evenings and Saturdays contrary to her Seventh-Day Adventist beliefs. She claimed this was a violation of the Ontario Human Rights Code. The Supreme Court held that the employer had an obligation to reasonably accommodate her religious beliefs, which it had failed to do since it could have rearranged her work schedule.[36]

Sexual orientation discrimination

While historically Canada's treatment of gay people has, like the UK's, been characterised by discrimination and repression, there have been many legal reforms and its courts in particular

30 [1985] 1 SCR 295.
31 [2006] 1 SCR 256.
32 [2009] 2 SCR 567.
33 See also *R v N.S.* [2012] 3 SCR 726.
34 *British Columbia (Public Service Employee Relations Commission) v BCGSEU* [1999] 3 SCR 3.
35 [1985] 2 SCR 536.
36 See B. Ryder, 'The Canadian Conception of Equal Religious Citizenship' in R. Moon (ed.), *Law and Religious Pluralism in Canada* (Vancouver: UBC Press, 2008) 89–91.

have been activist in this area. Parliament decriminalised 'buggery' and gross indecency (which had criminalised other sexual activity between men and also sexual activity between women) by the Criminal Law Amendment Act 1969.[37] Since then it has been one of the first jurisdictions to prohibit discrimination in numerous contexts.

The Supreme Court held in *Egan v Canada*[38] in 1995 that sexual orientation discrimination was a prohibited ground of discrimination under s.15 of the Charter. Egan was in a homosexual relationship. If he had been in a heterosexual relationship, he would have been entitled to claim a spousal allowance once his partner reached the age of 65 and began receiving old age security payments. He therefore claimed this difference in treatment was a violation of the Charter. Although the majority found that this was not a violation, the importance of the case lies in the fact that it was accepted that discrimination on the grounds of sexual orientation was 'analogous' to the grounds listed in s.16 and therefore such discrimination would have to be justified, leaving open the possibility of a violation being found in future cases.

Subsequently, in *Vriend v Alberta*[39] it was held that each province's Human Rights Code must prohibit sexual orientation discrimination by private actors. Vriend was dismissed from a private religious college due to his sexual orientation. It was held that there was a violation of the Charter as there was no way of challenging such discrimination. The Court did not, however, decide that the particular situation must in itself necessarily be a violation of the Human Rights Code. This is of importance given that the discrimination may be justified because of the college's right to freedom of religion in ensuring its employees followed religious rules.

The introduction of same-sex marriage similarly resulted from court decisions. Numerous cases, including *Halpern v Canada*[40] and *Hendricks and Leboeuf v Quebec*[41] in provincial courts had held the state was required to allow same-sex couples to marry. As a result, the federal government brought forward legislation to permit it across the jurisdiction. It also made a reference to the Supreme Court asking it to consider whether the bill was consistent with the Charter, in particular the provisions on freedom of religion.[42] The Supreme Court held that it was and the Civil Marriage Act came into force in 2005, making Canada only the fourth country in the world to introduce same-sex marriage.

Finally, Canada's criminal code prohibits 'hate propaganda' against gay people.[43] In addition there are provisions in each province or territory's Human Rights Codes prohibiting hate speech on the ground of sexual orientation in matters under provincial control. The Supreme Court has upheld such laws as constitutional.[44]

USA

As is well known, the US protects freedom of religion in its constitution, although the interpretation of this provision has been subject to considerable debate and change. In contrast, the extent to which the constitution protects against sexual orientation

37 S.C. 1968–69, c. 38.
38 [1995] 2 SCR 513.
39 [1998] 1 SCR 493.
40 65 OR (3d) 161.
41 [2002] JQ no 3816.
42 *Re Same-Sex Marriage* [2004] 3 SCR 698.
43 Criminal Code, R.S.C. 1985, c.46 s.319.
44 *Saskatchewan (Human Rights Commission) v Whatcott* [2013] 1 SCR 467.

discrimination has not yet been definitively decided. Both rights are also protected by legislation, although largely only at the state rather than federal level as far as sexual orientation discrimination is concerned.

Freedom of religion

Out of the jurisdictions discussed in this book, the USA has the longest legal guarantee of freedom of religion. The First Amendment states that 'Congress shall make no law respecting an establishment of religion, or prohibiting the free exercise thereof'. As will be explored in the following chapters, while some aspects of this right are very broad, others are narrow. Its interpretation also has changed over time.

The right was initially defined extremely restrictively to include only protection of belief rather than actions based on these beliefs. However, in *Sherbert v Verner*[45] it was held that a test of strict scrutiny should be applied to this context. Under this test, the state must be able to demonstrate that the law furthers a 'compelling government interest', is narrowly tailored and is the least restrictive means to achieve this interest. As its name implies, this is a searching test, although it was interpreted much less stringently than in other areas such as free speech.[46] *Sherbert v Verner* involved a woman who was dismissed from her employment because she refused to work on Saturdays due to her Seventh-Day Adventist beliefs. She could not find alternative employment because other similar employers also required Saturday work. She was then refused unemployment benefit on the grounds she had not accepted suitable work. She challenged this decision. It was held that the state had imposed a substantial burden on her religious belief and there was no compelling state interest in doing so.

The 'high watermark'[47] of the Free Exercise Clause came in *Yoder v Wisconsin.*[48] Yoder was prosecuted under a law which required all children to attend school up to the age of 16. He claimed this was contrary to his Amish beliefs that children should not receive formal education after the eighth grade (about age 14). Again, the Court applied strict scrutiny and held there was no compelling state interest in ensuring such compulsory education. This case is not wholly representative though, and there were numerous cases rejecting religious claims.[49]

Quite unexpectedly, the constitutional structure changed in *Employment Division v Smith.*[50] Smith took part in a Native American religious ceremony which involved the use of peyote, a banned substance under Oregon law. He was dismissed from his employment as a drug and alcohol counsellor as a result and was then denied unemployment benefit because he was considered to have been dismissed because of work-related misconduct. He claimed this decision was a violation of his free exercise rights. Since the Supreme Court considered that

45 [2004] 3 SCR. 698. Earlier cases had foreshadowed this: see *Cantwell v Connecticut* 310 US 296 (1940).

46 Sager and Eisgruber described it as 'strict in theory, feeble in fact', a play on Gerald Gunther's description of strict scrutiny as it related to free speech and race discrimination as 'strict in theory, fatal in fact': C.L. Eisgruber and L.G. Sager, 'The Vulnerability of Conscience: The Constitutional Basis for Protecting Religious Conduct' (1994) 61 *U Chi L Rev* 1245, 1247; G. Gunther, 'In Search of Evolving Doctrine on a Changing Court: A Model for a Newer Equal Protection' (1972) 86 *Harv L Rev* 1, 8.

47 R.S. Myers, 'The Right to Conscience and the First Amendment' (2011) 9 *Ave Maria L Rev* 123, 127.

48 406 US. 205 (1972).

49 See I. Lupu, 'The Trouble with Accommodation' (1991) 60 *Geo Wash L Rev* 743, 756; M. McConnell, 'Religious Freedom at a Crossroads' (1992) 59 *U Chi L Rev* 115.

50 494 US 872 (1990).

it was impossible to separate the question of whether he should be denied unemployment benefit from Oregon's prohibition of peyote for religious activities, the issue became whether Smith could demand an exemption from the law prohibiting its use because of his religious beliefs. Although *Sherbert v Verner* was not formally overruled, the majority of the Court held that a law would only be subject to strict scrutiny if it was not 'neutral' or 'generally applicable'. That is, rather than requiring strict scrutiny for all government acts which substantially burden the free exercise of religion, as long as a religion is not targeted in some way, the act will pose no constitutional problem under the Free Exercise Clause.[51]

This decision was highly controversial. The political opposition to it was such that it led to the Religious Freedom Restoration Act (RFRA),[52] passed with overwhelming bipartisan support.[53] This sought to reinstate the compelling state interest test. It states that the 'government shall not substantially burden a person's exercise of religion even if the burden results from a rule of general applicability', unless 'it demonstrates that the burden is in furtherance of a compelling governmental interest and is the least restrictive means of furthering that compelling governmental interest.' As is evident from its terms, this Act is very wide ranging. As a result, in *City of Boerne v Flores,*[54] it was held to be unconstitutional as far as it related to the states, since Congress had exceeded its authority under the Fourteenth Amendment to control state law. However, it still applies to federal action.[55] Additionally, 21 states have state RFRAs, providing similar protection to the federal RFRA to state laws, and some state constitutions provide similar protection. Whilst these states' RFRAs are the subject of increasing popular controversy, perhaps oddly, they have not so far been widely used in litigation, although this may be changing.[56]

In addition to this constitutional law, federal legislation, Title VII of the Civil Rights Act 1964,[57] also prohibits discrimination on the grounds of religion in the context of employment or public accommodations. The term 'Public accommodations' has been interpreted very broadly and includes places such as hotels, restaurants and shops.[58] The right to non-discrimination includes a right to reasonable accommodation, although this has been interpreted restrictively. Anything that imposes more than a *de minimis* burden will not be considered reasonable.[59]

Sexual orientation discrimination

The US law relating to sexual orientation discrimination is fairly complex. In contrast to the other two jurisdictions, the protection given against sexual orientation discrimination at the

51 Although other rights such as freedom of speech or association may be relevant.

52 42 U.S.C. § 2000bb.

53 It was passed unanimously by the House of Representatives and only three dissenting votes in the Senate.

54 521 US 507 (1997).

55 *Gonzales v O Centro Espirita Beneficente Uniao do Vegetal* 546 US 418 (2006).

56 See C. Lund, 'Religious Liberty After *Gonzales*: A Look at State RFRAs' (2010) 55 *SD L Rev* 466.

57 42 U.S.C. § 2000e. It does not apply to religious organisations or to employers with fewer than 15 employees.

58 E.g. the Boy Scouts were held to be a public accommodation in *Boy Scouts of America v Dale* 530 US 640 (2000). See also *Hurley v Irish-American Gay, Lesbian and Bisexual Group of Boston, Inc* 515 US 557 (1995) (public accommodations law applied to parade, but held to be unconstitutional).

59 *TWA v Hardison* 432 US 63 (1977).

federal level is currently limited, although, depending on the state, there may be considerable protection at state level.

Prohibitions on 'sodomy' existed until much later than the other jurisdictions discussed. Although many US states overturned such laws much earlier, and such bans were in any case rarely enforced, it was not until 2003 in *Lawrence v Texas*[60] that the US Supreme Court ruled that prohibiting 'sodomy' violated the Due Process Clause of the Fourteenth Amendment, and even then there were three dissents. One of the dissenters, Scalia J, argued that:

> Many Americans do not want persons who openly engage in homosexual conduct as partners in their business, as scoutmasters for their children, as teachers in their children's schools, or as boarders in their home. They view this as protecting themselves and their families from a lifestyle that they believe to be immoral and destructive.[61]

In an earlier case, *Bowers v Hardwick*,[62] decided as recently as 1986, the Supreme Court had upheld the prohibition. In doing so, Burger CJ stated that 'condemnation of those practices is firmly rooted in Judeo-Christian moral and ethical standards' and quoted Blackstone, who described 'sodomy' as 'the infamous crime against nature', as an offense of 'deeper malignity' than rape, a heinous act 'the very mention of which is a disgrace to human nature', and 'a crime not fit to be named'.[63] This was a prominent example of a legal failure to recognise even basic interests in privacy and non-discrimination. Although such laws were rarely enforced, *Bowers v Hardwick* served as justification for discriminatory treatment, for example, to deny custody of children to gay parents.[64]

Unlike Canada and the UK, there is no protection across the jurisdiction from discrimination in employment or in the provision of services. A bill known as the Employment Non-Discrimination Act (ENDA), which would give protection in private employment, although with blanket exemptions for religious organisations and small businesses,[65] has not yet gained the necessary support to be passed, despite being introduced in every Congress apart from one since 1994. However, since the District of Columbia prohibited discrimination in employment and public accommodations in 1973, a growing number of states have prohibited such discrimination. Currently 22 states, plus the District of Columbia, and many local laws, applying to cities and counties, prohibit such discrimination in employment and public accommodations.[66] In addition, rather unexpectedly, the Equal

60 539 US 558 (2003).
61 Ibid., 604.
62 478 US 186 (1986).
63 Ibid., 197.
64 W. Eskridge, *Gaylaw: Challenging the Apartheid of the Closet* (Cambridge, Mass: Harvard UP, 1999).
65 Although some have now withdrawn support claiming that the religious exemptions are too broad. See I. Lupu, 'Moving Targets: Obergefell, *Hobby Lobby*, and the Future of LGBT Rights' (2015) 7 *Ala CR & CL L Rev* 1, 26–9.
66 Recently some states have introduced legislation *prohibiting* anti-discrimination legislation e.g. the Protecting Freedom of Conscience from Government Discrimination Act 2016 Mississippi HB1523; but see *Barber v Bryant* Case no. 3:16-CV-417-CWR-LRA.

Employment Opportunity Commission (EEOC) held in *Baldwin v Foxx*[67] that sexual orientation is inherently sex discrimination and therefore forbidden by existing legislation because 'discrimination on the basis of sexual orientation is premised on sex-based preferences, assumptions, expectations, stereotypes, or norms.' The courts have thus far, though, not accepted this argument, and the EEOC only has direct jurisdiction over employees of the federal government, so while this decision is significant it has not fully decided the issue.[68]

In a very significant decision, a federal right to same-sex marriage was introduced by the Supreme Court's decision in *Obergefell v Hodges.*[69] By 5–4, the Supreme Court held that the lack of same-sex marriage was contrary to the due process of the Fifth Amendment[70] and equal protection clauses of the Fourteenth Amendment.[71] Justice Kennedy held that the due process clause protected 'certain personal choices central to individual dignity and autonomy, including intimate choices that define personal identity and beliefs', and the reasons for protecting marriage applied just as strongly to same-sex as different-sex couples. Even before this decision there had been a rapid increase in the number of states which permitted it, going from eight states plus the District of Columbia in 2012, the first being Massachusetts in 2004 as a result of a state court decision,[72] to 36 states in 2015.

Many states had decided to legalise same-sex marriage following the Supreme Court's earlier decisions in *United States v Windsor* and *Hollingsworth v Perry.*[73] *United States v Windsor* concerned the Defense of Marriage Act (DOMA),[74] which prohibited the recognition of same-sex marriages by the federal government for any purpose. A majority held that this law violated the due process and equal protection clauses of the Constitution. Although this decision is extremely important, much of the reasoning depends on the fact that marriage is a matter for regulation by the states. Nevertheless, the Court certainly moved towards a finding that such discrimination in itself is a violation of the Constitution. The majority held that the 'purpose and practical effect of the law ... are to impose a disadvantage, a separate status and so a stigma upon all who enter into same-sex marriage' and described its effect on couples in same-sex marriages as telling the world 'that their otherwise valid marriages are unworthy of federal recognition.'

Finally, and unusually, in contrast to the other two jurisdictions discussed, laws restricting hate speech on any ground are constitutionally prohibited as an impermissible viewpoint

67 App No 0120133080, 2015 WL 4397641 (EEOC July 16, 2015).

68 See R. Nelson, 'Sexual Orientation Discrimination Under Title VII after *Baldwin v Foxx*' (2015) 72 *Wash & Lee L Rev Online* 255.

69 576 US ____ (2015).

70 This states: 'No person ... shall be deprived of life, liberty or property without due process of law.' The courts have developed a concept of 'substantive due process', meaning that intrusions into rights must be reasonable and have a legitimate government purpose. See E. Chemerinsky, 'Substantive Due Process' (1998) 15 *Touro L Rev* 1501.

71 This states: 'No state shall deny to any person within its jurisdiction the equal protection of the laws.'

72 *Goodridge v Department of Public Health* 798 N.E. 2d 941 (Mass. 2003). Hawaii lower courts did initially find the refusal to grant same-sex marriage discriminatory in 1993 (*Baehr v Lewin* 74 Haw. 530, 852 P.2d 44 (1993)), but the Hawaii constitution was changed in response.

73 570 U.S. 12 (2013).

74 1 U.S.C. § 7 and 28 U.S.C. § 1738C.

restriction,[75] and so speech which promotes hatred against gay people cannot be prohibited on this basis.[76]

Conclusion

As can be seen, there are considerable variations in the law in each jurisdiction. However, in all, freedom of religion is a constitutionally or quasi-constitutionally protected right. Religious discrimination is also prohibited in employment and the provision of goods and services. There is variation, though, in how extensive this protection is. Sexual orientation anti-discrimination rights are newer and there remain gaps in their protection, particularly in the USA. There also remain significant problems in the interpretation of both rights. What kind of test should we use in deciding whether each right has been violated? What does each right include? What happens when these rights conflict? It is to these questions that the discussion now turns.

75 *RAV v St Pauls* 505 U.S. 377 (1992).

76 There is a large amount of literature on American exceptionalism in this context. See e.g. M. Rosenfeld, 'Hate Speech in Constitutional Jurisprudence: A Comparative Analysis' (2003) 24 *Cardozo L Rev* 1523.

3 Resolving conflicts between religious and other claims

As the previous chapter may have suggested, the problem of determining how to decide conflicts between freedom of religion and other rights or the public interest is not a new one, although the specific context relating to conflicts between religious freedom and sexual orientation discrimination is. Clearly there can be no absolute right to follow the dictates of one's religious conscience. Even leaving aside the chaos that would inevitably result, to do so would strongly conflict with the rights of others. Various 'limiting strategies'[1] have therefore been suggested or used as ways of restricting freedom of religion and thereby ensuring that it does not encroach too heavily on other rights.

This chapter therefore takes a step back from the specific issues under discussion, and considers more generally what criteria should be used to decide when religious claims should be protected. Since the US has the longest constitutional protection of freedom of religion in the three jurisdictions discussed, and a concomitant history of disputes over what this constitutional protection requires, much of the discussion will use case law drawn from this jurisdiction. While this chapter will draw on cases from Canada, England and Wales, and the USA, the purpose is not to describe the legal situation in any particular jurisdiction but rather to examine the mechanisms underlying these decisions.

Four approaches will be outlined in this chapter, three of which rest on a dichotomy between different forms of religious activity. It will consider tests based on distinctions between conduct and belief, public and private, core and non-core religious activities, as well as the current test in US constitutional law that requires justification for infringing religious practices only where a law is not neutral or generally applicable. All draw categorical distinctions, rather than balance the various interests. It will be demonstrated that while they may highlight factors that should be taken into account, none of these approaches is sufficient by itself, and that a more nuanced account is needed.

Conduct/belief

The first possible test distinguishes between conduct and belief and provides that while freedom of belief is protected, no special protection should be given to conduct motivated by that belief. Such an analysis would therefore permit people to hold discriminatory views but would not protect conduct based on this.

This understanding of religious freedom, as leaving religious belief free from coercion but not affecting the government's power to regulate behaviour, has deep historical roots. It is,

1 R. Ahdar and I. Leigh, *Religious Freedom in the Liberal State,* 2nd ed. (Oxford: Oxford UP, 2013).

for example, crucial to Thomas Jefferson's understanding of the First Amendment and has proved to be extremely influential in its interpretation. Jefferson argued that:

> Religion is a matter which lies solely between man and his God; that he owes account to none other for his faith or his worship: that the legislative powers of the government reach actions only, and not opinions.[2]

A clear distinction between belief and action can also be seen in the approach taken in Art. 9 ECHR. This gives absolute protection to thought, conscience and religion[3] and only limited protection to the manifestation of religion or belief, thereby implying that these concepts are separate and distinguishable. This distinction is often referred to as the distinction between the *forum internum* and *forum externum*.

Hamilton outlines how the distinction between belief and action was central to the US Supreme Court's understanding of religious freedom in the nineteenth and first half of the twentieth centuries.[4] The distinction is particularly noticeable in the first case on the Free Exercise Clause[5] decided by the US Supreme Court, *Reynolds v US*.[6] The Church of Latter Day Saints (Mormons) claimed there was a religious obligation for male members of the church to practise polygamy. Following his prosecution for bigamy, Reynolds, an eminent member of the church, claimed the law was a violation of his free exercise of religion. His argument failed. In its decision, the Supreme Court made a distinction between 'legislative power over mere opinion' and 'actions which were in violation of social duties or subversive of good order'.[7] It held that 'laws are made for the government of actions, and while they cannot interfere with mere religious belief and opinions, they may with practices.'[8] Since the case involved religious conduct and did not in theory affect the right to religious belief, it received no protection.

The result itself is unsurprising. Polygamy was an extremely shocking practice by the standards of the time, considered to be particularly barbaric and, through its challenge to monogamy and to established Christian morality, perceived as capable of undermining the very basis of society.[9] Even now, with a far greater acceptance of different forms of relationships beyond heterosexual monogamous marriage, protecting the interests of women (since polygamy seems almost invariably to mean polygyny) appears to be sufficient justification for its prohibition.[10] The major importance of *Reynolds*, though, in terms of

2 T. Jefferson, 'Letter to the Danbury Baptists', available at: http://www.loc.gov/loc/lcib/9806/danpre.html <last accessed 20 July 2016>. This distinction between belief and action is also evident in Locke's *Letter Concerning Toleration*.

3 Article 9(1) refers to 'freedom of thought, conscience and religion'. Art. 9(2) states, 'Freedom to manifest religion or belief shall be subject only to such limits as are prescribed by law and necessary in a democratic society in the interests of public safety, for the protection of public order, health or morals, or for the protection of the rights and freedoms of others.'

4 M. Hamilton, 'The Belief/Conduct Paradigm in the Supreme Court's Free Exercise Jurisprudence' (1993) 54 *Ohio St LJ* 713.

5 The First Amendment states, 'Congress shall make no law respecting an establishment of religion, or prohibiting the free exercise thereof'.

6 98 US 145 (1879).

7 Ibid., 164.

8 Ibid., 166.

9 S.B. Gordon, *The Mormon Question: Polygamy and Constitutional Conflict in Nineteenth Century America* (Chapel Hill: North Carolina Press, 2012).

10 This issue was considered more recently by the Canadian Supreme Court in *Reference re: Section 293 of the Criminal Code of Canada* 2011 BCSC 1588. It decided that a prohibition was not a

precedent is in its strictness of the division between belief and practices and the refusal to protect the latter. Since the Court held that a government could clearly intervene if, for example, a religion claimed it had a duty to perform human sacrifices, it held that there can be no exemptions from laws regulating religious practice. Any form of balancing the importance of the act to the religion against the importance of the government interest is not considered.

Mormonism was a new and startlingly different religion, and it led to real fear of the challenge Utah could pose to the federal government if Mormons were permitted to control the state's government. Even so, the campaign against it was noteworthy. Following *Reynolds,* much greater infringements of rights were upheld on the basis that they did not affect religious belief, but only conduct. The Edmunds Act of 1887[11] denied the right to vote to any person who refused to state that they did not practise polygamy and were not married to a polygamist. A later Act[12] extended the meaning of polygamy to cover cohabitation, disincorporated the Mormon church and seized all its property. It also made it easier to gain convictions for adultery.[13]

The denial of the right to vote was challenged but upheld in *Murphy v Ramsey.*[14] This decision again rested on the conduct/belief distinction. It was held to be constitutional as the law explicitly stated that no person could be denied the vote because of his opinion of polygamy but only because of a refusal to disclaim particular conduct. Similar cases held that the Free Exercise Clause only gave protection against attempts 'to control the mental operations of persons'.[15] Eventually, faced with such pressure, the Mormons retracted their belief in religiously obligated polygamy, although there remain breakaway fundamentalist sects that still believe and practise it.

The action/belief distinction continued to be applied into the twentieth century. In *Minersville School District v Gobitis,*[16] decided in 1940, two Jehovah's Witness children refused to take a pledge of allegiance to the US flag as required in their public school, as they considered the pledge to be a form of idolatry and therefore contrary to their religious beliefs. The children were expelled for refusing to do so and challenged this as a violation of their free exercise rights. The Supreme Court, however, considered this to be a case about conduct, where the children were seeking an exception from a law that their school board had considered necessary to maintain national unity and cohesion. This aim was considered to be of fundamental importance by the Court, who also held it should be deferential in assessing whether or not a flag salute contributed to this aim. It therefore held there need be no exemption.

violation of the Charter. For opposing opinions on whether a prohibition would survive current US constitutional review see R. Vazquez, 'The Practice of Polygamy: Legitimate Free Exercise of Religion or Legitimate Public Menace?' (2001) 5 *NYU J Legis & Pub Pol'y* 225 and K. Berberick, 'Marrying into Heaven: The Constitutionality of Polygamy Bans Under the Free Exercise Clause' (2007) 44 *Willamette L Rev* 105. For nuanced accounts of polygamy from the perspective of women who practised it see A. Campbell, 'Bountiful Voices' (2009) 47 *Osgoode Hall LJ* 183.

11 Act of Mar 22, 1882, Ch. 47, § 8, 22 Stat. 30 (1882).

12 Edmunds–Tucker Act of Mar 3, 1887, Ch. 397, § 13, 17, 24 Stat. 635, 637, 638 (1887).

13 E. Harmer-Dionne, 'Once a Peculiar People: Cognitive Dissonance and the Suppression of Mormon Polygamy as a Case Study Negating the Belief-Action Distinction' (1998) 50 *Stan L Rev* 1295, 1327. See also W. Eskridge, 'A Jurisprudence of "Coming Out": Religion, Homosexuality, and Collisions of Liberty and Equality in American Public Law' (1997) 106 *Yale LJ* 2411.

14 114 US 15 (1885).

15 *Davis v Beason* 133 U.S. 333, 342 (1890).

16 310 U.S. 586 (1940).

Reynolds and *Gobitis* demonstrate the lack of protection which results from this distinction. It allows states to prohibit religious conduct for little or no reason, even 'for no reason other than the legislature's religious preference.'[17] The challenge the Gobitis children really posed to the interests of national security was extremely minimal, but they were still required to break a basic tenet of their religion. Such protection as the distinction grants is therefore fundamentally under-inclusive. It is particularly problematic because a state is likely to use its power to act against unpopular minority groups, thus encouraging further discrimination. Both the Mormons and the Jehovah's Witnesses faced heavy social discrimination and indeed, after *Gobitis* there was mob violence against the latter, which the authorities did not prevent.[18]

The kind of protection the belief/conduct distinction brings is in protection against mind control and against deliberate attempts to ensure internal conformity to religious orthodoxy. This is certainly a valuable right[19] but it is not sufficient. Acting on the basis of beliefs is the natural result of having them. The test is compatible with a great deal of unjustified, repressive government action.

Evidently a test based on such a distinction can be oppressive to individuals. It also fails to protect religious pluralism in society. This is partly because, as *Reynolds* demonstrates, coercion of religious practices can change belief. Faced with extreme state pressure, the Mormons renounced their belief in religiously mandated polygamy. Such a consequence is potentially problematic. As Harmer-Dionne puts it, there is a 'marked philosophical difference between theological developments that result from organic evolution and those that result from massive persecution and forced cessation of social customs and marital practices.'[20] Similarly, while it could be argued that a religious organisation could maintain a teaching that homosexuality was immoral ***and*** be required to abide by anti-discrimination norms, by, for example, being required to employ gay people as clergy, in practice maintaining such an internally inconsistent teaching would be subject to considerable pressure. In explaining this idea Harmer-Dionne makes reference to the idea of cognitive dissonance: it is psychologically difficult to maintain a situation where belief and action diverge, leading to pressure to change one or the other. A prohibition on permitting discrimination in practice may well change the underlying belief in its necessity.[21] Even though the distinction theoretically protects freedom of belief and merely affects the manifestation of beliefs, this distinction is less clear in practice.

A comparison of *Gobitis* with a case based on almost identical facts and decided only three years later demonstrates a further problem. In *West Virginia v Barnette*,[22] Jehovah's Witnesses challenged the West Virginia School Board's resolution making flag salutes compulsory in public schools. In contrast to *Gobitis*, the Supreme Court analysed the matter as a matter of belief or speech, rather than conduct. The challenge to the law was successful, and

17 T. McCoy, 'A Coherent Methodology for First Amendment Speech and Religion Clause Cases' (1995) 48 *Vand L Rev* 1335, 1345.

18 M. Nussbaum, *Liberty of Conscience* (New York: Basic Books, 2008) 211–12.

19 As Smith states, 'Victims of the Inquisition might have been profoundly grateful for something like an effective right or freedom to believe or disbelieve, free from legal investigations and sanctions'; S. Smith, 'Religious Freedom and its Enemies, or Why the *Smith* Decision May Be a Greater Loss Now Than it was Then' (2011) 32 *Cardozo L Rev* 2033, 2036.

20 Harmer-Dionne supra n.13, 1139.

21 C. Harper and B. Le Beau, 'The Social Adaptation of Marginal Religious Movements in America' (1993) 54 *Sociology of Religion* 171. However, the process is complex and some pressure may actually strengthen religious belief.

22 319 US 624 (1943).

Gobitis was overruled. The Court's decision is a ringing endorsement of free speech and opinion. It held that 'the compulsory flag salute and pledge requires affirmation of a belief and an attitude of mind'[23] and that 'compulsory unification of opinion achieves only the unanimity of the graveyard ... If there is any fixed star in our constitutional constellation, it is that no official, high or petty, can prescribe what shall be orthodox in politics, nationalism, religion, or other matters of opinion, or force citizens to confess by word or act their faith therein.'[24] The issue in these cases has therefore been transformed from a claim for an exemption from conduct required in order to promote national security in *Gobitis* to a claim to protect religious belief in *Barnette*. As a result, the burden in the latter case therefore appeared far more serious, and the relevance of the government interest correspondingly less. This is important because it demonstrates that 'the Court has wide latitude within the paradigm ... to identify the religious interest at issue as either belief or conduct.'[25] If the distinction is crucial, the arbitrariness of the enquiry is worrying.

This arbitrariness is partly because the distinction is too blunt, holding that belief and action are fully distinct concepts and furthermore that the protection of belief is always absolute. This is potentially misleading. Some beliefs may be considered incompatible with certain employment, for example, even if the person claims they will not affect their behaviour and there is no proof that they have in the past. Greenawalt gives an example of a person nominated for the head of the Environmental Protection Agency who believes that the Book of Revelation reveals that the world will end in twenty years, but who says this will have no effect on her job performance.[26] It would be entirely appropriate for the Senate to take this into account. Indeed, in *Hollon v Pierce*[27] a public school bus supervisor was held to have been constitutionally dismissed after he co-wrote 'a religious tract expressing threats, violence and retribution, and specifically referring to the burning of schools and the death of school children',[28] although he was found to be psychiatrically stable and there was no evidence he was going to take such action. It may be arguable too that particular beliefs relating to equality and non-discrimination may be relevant to particular employment, for example as a minister in a 'gay-affirming' Christian church.

The likely response to this argument is that while freedom of belief is an absolute right, there is no right to a particular job while holding a particular belief. However, the response needs to be more complex than this. It would presumably be regarded as an interference with freedom of belief, and not the more limited right to religious conduct, if all Muslims, for example, were prohibited from holding senior positions in government employment. Certainly in the US case of *Torcaso v Watkins*[29] it was held that a requirement that candidates for public office declare a belief in the existence of God was an interference with freedom of belief.[30] Either then, the meaning of 'belief' is extremely narrow and would not cover even broad discriminatory exclusions, or more complex decisions about the relevance of religious beliefs to employment are made in considering whether there is a violation of

23 Ibid., 633.
24 Ibid., 641–2.
25 Hamilton supra n.4, 724.
26 K. Greenawalt, *Religion and the Constitution Volume 1: Free Exercise and Fairness* (Princeton: Princeton UP, 2006) 44.
27 257 Cal App 2d 468 (1967).
28 Ibid., 479.
29 367 US 488 (1961).
30 Although the ECtHR held a similar law was an interference with the *manifestation* of belief in *Buscarini v San Marino* (2000) 30 EHRR 208.

religious freedom. Therefore, there cannot be a simple division between conduct and belief in this context.

A further argument against such a test is that the distinction between action and belief is discriminatory because it embodies a particular kind of Protestant belief. Hamilton argues that it comes from the distinction between faith and works made by St Paul, which was emphasised by reformation theologians who considered faith, and not works, to be crucial to religious salvation.[31] Indeed the approach of the US Supreme Court in the nineteenth century has been known as 'Republican Protestantism'.[32] This distinction has therefore been subject to criticism from other religious traditions; the Catholic theologian John Courtney Murray, for example, criticised the distinction as 'an irredeemable piece of sectarian dogmatism.'[33]

Merely because a distinction has religious roots does not automatically make it suspect and indeed it is probably impossible to separate the influence of Protestant thought from Western thought more generally, especially when referring to concepts of religious freedom, and particularly in countries where Protestantism has been the dominant religious tradition.[34] However, it is still problematic because it is easier for those religious traditions that privilege an internal and wholly private relationship with the divine above religious conduct to maintain this distinction between belief and action in favour of protecting the former but not the latter.

Nevertheless, this discriminatory aspect can be overstated. Given that almost all religions require some kind of external practice[35] the problem is more one of under-inclusivity rather than discrimination. Conduct is the normal result of belief. This approach does though have difficulty in comprehending religions which are *essentially* performative, that is, the religion centrally consists of performing certain actions, rather than individualistic reflection, since it assumes that belief is inevitably more important than conduct. Stahl argues peyote religions, particularly the Native American Church, are an example of such performative religions.[36] Peyote religions revolve around a sacred ceremony involving the use of peyote, a mild hallucinogen, but its importance goes beyond this since peyote is also considered an 'incarnation of God'.[37] Prohibiting peyote then is, he argues, akin to prohibiting the religion. Performative religions are also common in a different sense. Sociological research draws attention to the concept of 'lived religion', where what is important is religious tradition and custom, which may be engaged in for no more reflective reason than habit, but which is still internally seen as fundamentally religious.[38]

It might be suggested that the relevance of the distinction is that freedom of belief is absolute but freedom of conduct is not. This is often asserted in English and ECHR cases.[39] However, I am unconvinced that this is so, partly for the reasons explained above. Law and

31 Hamilton supra n.4. Berger also notes the connection between Protestant thought and an emphasis on belief rather than practice. See B. Berger, 'Law's Religion' in R. Moon (ed.), *Law and Religious Pluralism in Canada* (Vancouver: UBC Press, 2008) 284.
32 B. Gerard, 'Imagining the Past and Remembering the Future: The Supreme Court's History of the Establishment Clause' (1986) 18 *Con L R* 827.
33 J.C. Murray, 'Law or Prepossessions' (1949) 14 *Law and Contemp Probs* 23, 30.
34 With the important exception of Quebec.
35 As Hamilton accepts supra n.4.
36 R. Stahl, 'Carving Up Free Exercise: Dissociation and "Religion" in Supreme Court Jurisprudence' (2002) 5 *Rhetoric & Public Affairs* 439.
37 Ibid., 449.
38 W.F. Sullivan, *The Impossibility of Religious Freedom* (Princeton: Princeton UP, 2005).
39 See e.g. *R(Williamson) v Secretary of State for Education* [2005] 2 AC 246.

policies which affect religious actions also affect religious beliefs. Second, governments do in various circumstances try to influence religious and other beliefs directly, for example in combating 'Islamic extremism'.[40] Such policies can certainly be criticised but it would take a brave court to say that such policies are automatically illegitimate because their aim is to change beliefs. Third, as I have argued, particular beliefs can be required for particular employment. Given that the line between beliefs and actions is so blurred, any test which has such radical consequences, as appears to be the case with Art. 9 ECHR, seems unsatisfactory. Indeed, in every case which could have been interpreted as an interference with freedom of belief, the ECtHR has interpreted as an interference with the manifestation of belief instead, presumably so it can consider any potential justification.[41]

The above discussion has demonstrated the failure of the distinction in providing a mechanism for deciding cases where religious freedom conflicts with other rights or the public interest. This is not to say that the distinction is not of some use, but it fails as a full test of whether religious claims should be protected or not. It does not take account of the importance of religious freedom discussed in the Introduction, since it holds that, unless there is an attempt at 'mind control', interference with the right of freedom of religion on the basis of another right or a social interest will always be justified. Furthermore, the distinction is dominated by Protestant concepts and subject to manipulability. These latter two disadvantages may be acceptable if it is only a factor to be taken into account, but are problematic when this is the entire basis on which a decision is made.

The next possible test is based on a distinction between private and public spheres, a division which often runs alongside the action/belief distinction. While the protection only of religious belief is no longer considered appropriate in US law, the private/public distinction continues to have great relevance in this jurisdiction.

Public/private

The distinction between public and private is a fundamental one in modern society. It is therefore unsurprising that it has been suggested that there should be a clear dividing line on this basis when it comes to the protection of religious claims. Under this interpretation of religious freedom, society is divided into separate spheres of authority. Religion is confined to the private sphere, but in return the state undertakes not to interfere in its domain, apart from in narrowly defined situations of abuse. Collins argues that such an approach is central to the understanding of some actors in this context, including the ACLU and the Canadian Civil Liberties Association, who believe that 'religion [should be] thoroughly privatized so as to preserve both the liberty of individuals ... and the independence of the state from religion.'[42]

Such a division permits religious organisations and individuals to apply their own rules, including discriminatory rules, within the private sphere, subject only to minimal protection for individual rights, but no religious exemptions are made outside this. It has particular resonance in the US context since it fits into an understanding of a strict separation of church and state. Even though neither Canada nor the UK shares the same conception of

40 See Secretary of State for the Home Department, *Prevent Strategy* (HM Stationery Office, 2011).

41 E.g. *Buscarini* supra n.30.

42 D. Collins, 'Culture, Religion and Curriculum: Lessons from the "Three Books" Controversy in Surrey, BC' (2006) 50 *Can Geogr-Geogr Can* 342, 344.

this separation, the division between the two spheres is still an important element within public and legal thought in these jurisdictions.

The question of whether it is acceptable for citizens, legislators and officials to use religious beliefs in supporting and discussing political opinions is one which has given rise to a great deal of debate[43] but will not be discussed here. This section instead focuses on whether it should be permissible to live out religious beliefs in public life and the extent to which religion should be left unrestricted in the private sphere, in order to examine whether an approach which draws a division between the two is appropriate. In the context under discussion here, such a distinction would mean that religious individuals or organisations would not be able to discriminate in the public sphere, but that discrimination would be permitted in all cases in the private sphere.

Reference to the distinction between public and private in US law can be seen in Burger CJ's declaration in *Lemon v Kurtzman,*[44] the seminal case on the Establishment Clause of the First Amendment, that 'the constitution decrees that religion must be a private matter for the individual, the family, and the institutions of private choice.'[45] The distinction has also been relevant to ECHR case law, which has been adopted by English courts. In *Pichon and Sajous v France*[46] for example, the ECtHR held that pharmacists were not protected by Article 9 when they refused to sell contraceptives because they could manifest their beliefs outside the 'professional sphere'. The distinction is also relevant to Canadian law.[47]

The first question the distinction begs is in deciding what is 'public' and 'private'. The line between the two is highly contested. Collins argues that, 'in discussions of religious liberty and freedom of conscience, the term "private" is typically equated with the interests of individuals, families, and religious institutions, while "public" is usually synonymous with governmental authority.'[48] His reference to the 'interests of individuals' is potentially confusing, though, since it only refers to a person acting in an entirely individual capacity. More importantly, his description of public is incomplete as 'public' is often used to mean not only the state but also anything that is not 'private', including the commercial sector and non-religious employment.

In the same way, then, as the distinction between action and belief can be contested and different constructions of the distinction be the ground on which such decisions are fought, so can the distinction between public and private. In the Canadian case of *Chamberlain v Surrey School District No. 36,*[49] as mentioned in the Introduction, a school board decided not to approve three books for kindergarten children that presented gay parenting favourably, having taken into account the religious objections of some parents. These parents claimed the school would otherwise interfere with the private matter of teaching children about controversial moral issues. The opposing claim was made by a teacher, Chamberlain, who argued that the private matter of religious beliefs should not be allowed to influence decision-making in public schools, especially given that the British Columbia School Act stated

43 See e.g. R. Audi, *Religious Commitment and Secular Reason* (Cambridge: Cambridge UP, 2000); C. Eberle, *Religious Conviction in Liberal Politics* (Cambridge: Cambridge UP, 2002); K. Greenawalt, *Private Consciences and Public Reasons* (Oxford: Oxford UP, 1995).

44 403 US 602 (1971).

45 Ibid., 625.

46 App No. 49853/99 (2 Oct 2001).

47 See R. Moon, *Freedom of Conscience and Religion* (Toronto: Irwin Law, 2014) 60 (arguing that this distinction is central to the entire scheme of protection of religious rights in Canada).

48 Collins supra n.42, 344.

49 [2002] 4 SCR 710.

that schools must be on 'strictly secular and non-sectarian principles.'[50] The Canadian courts favoured the latter interpretation of the public/private division, although the exact meaning of public and private differed with each court decision.[51] The public/private distinction is therefore open to the same criticism of manipulability and vagueness as the action/belief distinction.

Even if an appropriate distinction between public and private can be made, a sharp distinction between the two, with its required privatisation of religious practice, gives rise to more fundamental problems. First, the private sphere is very small in the modern regulatory welfare state, particularly when employment is taken into account. Even those unusual religions that seek to distance themselves from wider society, such as the Hutterites or Amish, will interact with the public sphere at some point,[52] and thus will be subject to state control. For the vast majority of religious adherents, there is much greater interaction and conflicts can arise far more frequently.

Most importantly, once again as with the action/belief divide, the public/private distinction imposes a particular notion of religion which is at odds with the understanding many religious believers have of their religious obligations. As Stychin puts it, for many, 'in its essence, religion demands manifestation in the public sphere and to require otherwise is to undermine its core. For those of faith, to demand privatization is in practice to require exit from the public sphere.'[53] For many religious believers it may be nonsensical to attempt to divide religious experience into a privately religious and publicly non-religious identity in such a way. Religious beliefs are 'interwoven'[54] into their lives. The public nature of religion is simply inherent in much of the idea of what religion is. 'Religion inclines toward a total account of life, organizing, explaining and justifying all action. Therefore religions often generate elaborate systems of belief, institution and ritual applicable to all areas of life.'[55] Perry has pointed to the 'emotional (psychological) suffering' that can result from 'being legally forbidden to live a life of integrity'.[56] Being required to privatise religious belief may be experienced as false and hypocritical and as trivialising such beliefs.[57] Of course, this is not necessarily so for all believers and some may willingly and unproblematically divide their lives into such spheres. Evidently too, in some cases this will clearly be necessary to prevent a greater harm, but this is not necessarily so.

Such a person is therefore required to accept an ordering of the world which they do not accept,[58] with no justification or consideration of whether this is necessary to preserve other rights or the public interest. Furthermore, this division is not required for those who do not have such beliefs. Lupu therefore argues forthrightly that 'separationism is a matter of secular privilege' and amounts to the 'hegemony of secular ideology in the public square'.[59]

50 School Act R.S.B.C. 1996, c. 412.
51 Collins supra n.42.
52 E.g. *Alberta v Hutterian Brethren of Wilson Colony* [2009] 2 SCR 567; *United States v Lee* 455 U.S. 252 (1982).
53 C.F. Stychin, 'Faith in the Future: Sexuality, Religion and the Public Sphere' (2009) 29 *OJLS* 729, 734.
54 L. Underkuffler-Freund, 'The Separation of the Religious and the Secular: A Foundational Challenge to First Amendment Theory' (1995) 36 *Wm & Mary L Rev* 837, 843.
55 C. Cochran, *Religion in Public and Private Life* (New York: Routledge, 1990) 65.
56 M. Perry, *The Political Morality of Liberal Democracy* (Cambridge: Cambridge UP, 2010) 71.
57 E.g. S. Carter, *The Culture of Disbelief: How American Law and Politics Trivialize Religious Devotion* (New York: Basic Books, 1993); R. Trigg, *Religion in Public Life: Must Faith be Privatized?* (Oxford: Oxford UP, 2007).
58 R. Plant, 'Religion, Identity and Freedom of Expression' (2011) 17 *Res Publica* 7, 17.
59 I. Lupu, 'The Lingering Death of Separationism' (1994) 62 *Geo Wash L Rev* 230.

A further argument against a strict distinction is that it is discriminatory between different religions in a similar way to the distinction between action and belief. It is arguable that adherents of some religions, particularly what is called in US terms 'Mainline Protestantism', are better able to separate their identities between public and private than other religious groups because, as explained, they hold private religious belief to be of central religious importance. Belief, by itself, is intensely private and therefore religions which privilege belief above action are likely to have few problems with keeping religion as a private matter. However, as discussed before, to a greater or lesser extent, there are communal and social aspects to almost all religions. Religion is rarely *solely* private and internal as religions typically lay down rules of public behaviour.[60] Again the problem is more one of under-inclusivity than discrimination.

So far this discussion has focused on religion and the public sphere. The flip side of this distinction is the extent of religion's authority in the private sphere, in particular given our context, to what extent there should be protection against discrimination in private organisations. Horwitz, drawing on the approach of the nineteenth-century Dutch neo-Calvinist writer Kuyper, argues for an approach of 'sphere sovereignty'.[61] Kuyper argued that various non-state institutions, including churches, should largely be given autonomy within their own sphere, with the state responsible for ensuring the institutions do not encroach on each other's sphere and for protecting against abuses of power. Such an argument has also been historically present within British thought too, notably within the writing of the British pluralists.[62] Such an argument would therefore permit discrimination within the private sphere. Evidently there needs to be *some* human rights protection: violent or sexual abuse, for example, does not become any more acceptable because it takes place in a religious setting and indeed the vulnerability of victims may make it more serious. Minority groups within religious organisations can require protection, which they cannot gain merely by bringing their claims to the attention of the religious institution. However, laws, even those relating to human rights, protect a huge variety of state and societal interests of varying seriousness and it could be argued that the state should not intervene outside a very limited core of rights. Horwitz argues this is because 'the church's affairs are not the state's affairs' and more fundamentally because 'it simply has no jurisdiction to entertain these concerns.'[63]

This idea though is extremely problematic. Of course there is a difference between church and state affairs. However, in most cases, disputes are not directly between the state and a religious institution but between a religious institution and an individual who has sought the state's protection in some way.[64] It is unclear why the church should always win such disputes. Rather than enhancing religious freedom, it can merely be a 'tool to shield [religious] elites from accountability'.[65] The failure of the Catholic Church and other religious

60 R. McCrea, *European Law, Religion and the Public Order of the European Union* (Oxford: Oxford UP, 2010) 110–13.

61 P. Horwitz, 'Churches as First Amendment Institutions: Of Sovereignty and Spheres' (2009) 44 *Harv CR-CL L Rev* 79. See A. Kuyper, 'Sphere Sovereignty' in J.D. Beatt (ed.), *Abraham Kuyper: A Centennial Reader* (Grand Rapids: Eerdmans Publishing, 1998); J. Van der Vyver, 'Sphere Sovereignty of Religious Institutions: A Contemporary Calvinistic Theory of Church-State Relations' in G. Robbers (ed.), *Church Autonomy* (Bern: Peter Lang, 2001).

62 See J.N. Figgis, *Churches in the Modern State* (London: Longmans, Green & Co, 1913).

63 Horwitz supra n.61, 121.

64 R. Schragger and M. Schwartzman, 'Against Religious Institutionalism' (2013) 99 *Va L Rev* 917.

65 S. Baer, 'Privatizing Religion. Legal Groupism, No-Go-Areas, and the Public-Private-Ideology in Human Rights Politics' (2013) 20 *Constellations* 68, 70.

organisations to deal with child abuse acts as a potent reminder that such organisations can act in particularly abhorrent ways.[66]

While it is usually considered obvious that there can be no protection of a direct claim to abuse children for religious reasons, since that would fall within the limited core of rights protected,[67] there have been some successful US claims resisting government intervention because of fears of interference in private matters.[68] In *Gibson v Brewer*[69] a priest allegedly sexually abused a teenager. When his parents reported this to the diocese, it failed to take any action, and they then sued the priest and the diocese. The Minnesota Supreme Court struck out all claims relating to the diocese which did not rest on the intentional infliction of harm. It ruled that the parents could not sue for negligent supervision of the priest because it 'could not adjudicate the reasonableness of a church's supervision of a cleric' as 'this would create an excessive entanglement, inhibit religion, and result in the endorsement of one model of supervision'.[70] Similarly the parents could not bring a claim for negligent hiring as the 'ordination of a priest is a "quintessentially religious" matter'. In general terms this is true: it would be a great interference with the right of freedom of religion to force a particular leader on a religious institution.[71] However, it does not demonstrate why a church should necessarily not be liable for the harm perpetrated by the priest they have chosen.[72] This approach therefore raises great issues over the safeguarding of children, even if actual abuse is prohibited.

The issues of employment discrimination in religious organisations will be considered in more detail in Chapter 7. For the time being, it will be noted that an absolute right to dismiss religious employees at will cannot take into account opposing rights and interests, such as non-discrimination or the protection of children. Thus in the US case of *Hosanna Tabor v EEOC*,[73] which will be discussed at greater length, it was held that a 'called teacher' at a Lutheran school could not bring a retaliation claim after she was dismissed for raising a claim for disability discrimination, even though such discrimination was officially condemned by the religion. This was due to concern over state interference with the relationship between a

66 See generally M. Hamilton, *God vs. the Gavel: Religion and the Rule of Law* (Cambridge: Cambridge UP, 2005); T.J. Trotten, 'Shattering the Illusion: Child Sexual Abuse and Canadian Religious Institutions' (Waterloo, Ont: Wilfrid Laurier UP, 2002). In England and Wales 598 allegations of abuse by priests or others in the Catholic Church, of which 77 per cent were of sexual abuse, were reported to statutory authorities between 2003–12: *National Catholic Safeguarding Commission Annual Report 2013–4* (National Catholic Safeguarding Commission, 2014).

67 Although see *Khan v United Kingdom* App No. 11579/85 (7 Jul 1986); *R(Williamson)* supra n.39.

68 See Hamilton supra n.66.

69 952 S.W.2d 239 (Mo. 1997).

70 Ibid., 247. However, other state Supreme Courts have reached different conclusions: *Malicki v Doe*, 814 So.2d 347 (Fla. 2002); *Redwing v Catholic Bishop for Diocese of Memphis*, 363 S.W.3d 436 (Tenn. 2012); *Roman Catholic Diocese of Jackson v Morrison*, 905 So.2d 1213 (Miss. 2005). See J. O'Reilly and M. Chalmers, *The Clergy Sex Abuse Crisis and the Legal Responses* (Oxford: Oxford UP, 2014).

71 See *Kedroff v Saint Nicholas Cathedral* (1952) 344 US 94.

72 *Gibson* was not a case concerning vicarious liability for the priests' actions but a negligence claim against the diocese itself. The question of vicarious liability for sexual or other abuse committed by religious figures has been a difficult one for the courts in both Canada and England. See *John Doe v Bennett* [2004] S.C.J. No 17 (Canada). *E v English Province of Our Lady of Charity* [2013] Q.B. 722; *JGE v Diocese of Portsmouth*; *Maga v Trustees of the Birmingham Archdiocese of the Roman Catholic Church* [2010] All ER (D) 141 (England).

73 565 US __ (2012).

religion and its ministers. Since then, in *Weiter v Kurtz*[74] it has been held that a bookkeeper/receptionist at a Catholic church was prevented by the First Amendment from pursuing claims arising from her dismissal for telling parishioners that a priest who was awaiting trial for child abuse charges was being housed by the parish and to keep their children away from him. Since the case would involve analysis of the Archdiocese's administrative decisions regarding the treatment of priests accused of child abuse, it was held that the case could not be brought. It is highly questionable whether such a categorical rule really draws an appropriate balance between the protection of children and religious autonomy.

Even in cases where the motives are benign, excluding the private sphere from scrutiny is still unwarranted. As was discussed in the previous chapter, in *Yoder v Wisconsin*,[75] Amish parents wanted to remove their children from the last two legally required years of education since they believed it affected their ability to transmit their religion and distinctive way of life. The Supreme Court held the Amish were entitled to an exemption. Formally the case did not rest on a private/public distinction but rather on a strict scrutiny test, asking whether there was a compelling government interest in the policy. However, the private/public distinction is crucial to the case. The opposing interest considered is an entirely public one: the likelihood of the Amish to find employment, so they will not pose a drain on state resources, rather than 'private' issues such as the interests of the children. Even if the case was correctly decided (it is certainly arguable that it failed to give enough weight to the interests of children who wished to leave the Amish community, as many do), most would baulk at the idea that parents had unlimited power over their children. If the Amish had wanted to exclude their children from more than two years of public education, should this have been automatically permissible?

The most worrying exclusion of scrutiny of religious claims because of the division of public and private is the exclusion from child neglect laws for those who refuse medical care for their children, relying only on 'faith healing'. No fewer than 26 US states have exemptions for felonious child neglect, manslaughter, murder or other offences if parents fail to seek medical care for their children because of their religious beliefs,[76] although there are no such exemptions in Canada and the UK. Such religious practices have led to children's deaths that were easily preventable. The public/private distinction approach may then prevent an adult from wearing a religious headscarf in state employment, but permit such treatment of children. This cannot be justifiable.

A more fundamental argument can also be made that the very distinction legitimates oppression, since by its nature when something is designated as private, it is no longer a state responsibility but an individual one, and therefore does not require any state action.[77] This argument is particularly associated with feminist theories,[78] as in the famous slogan that 'the personal is the political', but is also an argument within critical legal theory[79] and queer theory.[80] Cobb, for example, writing from a queer-theory perspective, draws attention to the

74 No. 2011-CA-001058-MR (KY App., Dec. 14, 2012).

75 406 US 205 (1972).

76 Hamilton supra n.66, Ch. 2.

77 R. Gavison, 'Feminism and the Public/Private Distinction' (1992) 45 *Stan L Rev* 1, 19.

78 E.g. C. MacKinnon, *Toward a Feminist Theory of the State* (Cambridge, Mass: Harvard UP, 1989); F. Olsen, 'Constitutional Law: Feminist Critiques of the Public/Private Distinction' (1993) 10 *Const Comment* 319.

79 E.g. R. Mnookin, 'The Public/Private Dichotomy: Political Disagreement and Academic Repudiation' (1982) 130 *U Pa L Rev* 1429.

80 E.g. D. Richardson, 'Locating Sexualities: From Here to Normality' (2004) 7 *Sexualities* 391.

overemphasis given in British political and legal debates to potential discrimination against gay people in bed and breakfast accommodation, when it is intra-familial discrimination which is pervasive and most harmful, particularly to gay teenagers.[81] The particular harm of the public/private distinction lies in the fact that since this is viewed as a private problem, and not something that is capable of public or legal interference, it is rendered invisible or unproblematic.

This is not to say that there is no distinction between public and private or that such a distinction is irrelevant. Despite Cobb's criticism of the distinction and its consequence of making discrimination unseeable, discrimination by a parent against a legally adult child because she is gay is different from discrimination against gay people in state employment. Partly this is because of the effect of any state action. It seems unlikely that equality law could promote parental love or family reunification, but it can ensure that discrimination in employment is met with a legal monetary remedy.

In conclusion, the distinction between public and private is probably fundamental to contemporary Western society, even if what falls into each category is not objectively ascertainable.[82] To try to abandon such a distinction is therefore probably impossible even if it were desirable. Even those who have criticised this distinction for hiding oppression or making oppressive practices appear natural accept that some distinction is appropriate.[83] As with the belief/conduct distinction, it certainly has some value as a potential factor to be taken into account. However, it fails as a full test. This is partly because of its vagueness and potential manipulability, but mainly because such a test would lead to tolerating oppression in the private sphere, while simultaneously under-protecting religious claims in the public sphere.

Core/periphery

The third dichotomy that is sometimes proposed in considering how far to protect religious freedom is to distinguish between core religious activities, such as religious worship, and peripheral activities, such as demonstrations of public belief, whereby only core activities are protected. This argument can be seen in Buxton LJ's judgment in the Court of Appeal in *R(Williamson) v Secretary of State for Education and Employment*.[84] This was one of the first claims based on Art. 9 ECHR to be brought in the English courts following the Human Rights Act 1998, and the first time this provision had been considered in detail by an appellate court. The case involved parents and teachers at private Christian schools who claimed that corporal punishment was integral to their religious doctrines on the upbringing of children and that this therefore should be permitted at the schools which their children attended. However, Buxton LJ held that Article 9 only protected 'worship, proselytism and possibly … mandated religious "practice"' which was a 'clear, uniform and agreed requirement of the religion in question'.[85] Since the law prohibiting corporal punishment in schools only affected a peripheral rather than core right, he held that there was no interference with the parents' rights, although the House of Lords later overturned this reasoning.[86] Similarly,

81 N. Cobb, '"Gay Couple's Break Like Fawlty Towers": Dangerous Representations of Lesbian and Gay Oppression in an Era of "Progressive" Law Reform' (2009) 18 *Social & Legal Studies* 333.
82 A. Freeman and E. Mensch, 'The Public-Private Distinction in American Law and Life' (1987) 36 *Buff L Rev* 237.
83 Gavison supra n.77, 19.
84 [2003] QB 1300.
85 Ibid., 1315.
86 *R(Williamson) v Secretary of State for Education and Employment* [2005] 2 AC 246.

in the later case of *Ladele v Islington LBC*,[87] a case that will be discussed in detail in Chapter 6, it was held that when a registrar refused to perform civil partnerships because it conflicted with her Christian view of marriage, this did not affect her 'core' beliefs and she had no right to be accommodated in her refusal to perform them. Although this distinction was not the only reason for the decision, it was certainly an important factor in the Court of Appeal's judgment.[88]

Ahdar and Leigh argue that the distinction is inappropriate because it is extremely difficult to define the core beliefs of, for example, Christianity and this would in any case be a theological question.[89] However, some of this criticism is misplaced and their (predictably difficult) attempt to define the core of Christianity is not required, since the distinction is actually about religious *practices*. A minor change to a Christian liturgy may be at the periphery of a religious belief, but at the core of a religious practice since it involves religious worship. 'Core' then is really taken as a synonym for private religious belief and worship, which is assumed to be at the centre of all religions, as opposed to the 'non-core' of public manifestations of these beliefs. If this is accepted, though, the distinction then produces the same problems as the public/private distinction. A typical 'core' religious practice such as the protection of minor aspects of religious worship may be less important to an individual than a typically 'non-core' claim, such as proselytisation.

Alternatively, if it were the case that a real attempt was made to understand what the subjective core of religious activity was for each person, this would pose difficult questions of proof, not least because it may not be clear even to that person what the core of her religion is. This may be because a person's religious practices and beliefs may flow seamlessly from her religious understanding. Expert evidence is therefore likely to be demanded to provide more evidence on this point. The problem with this is that religious belief is often idiosyncratic, in that it is dependent on a person's own understanding of religious doctrines and authorities. Religious belief may vary vastly between people even within the same religious tradition. A person who deviates from the mainstream, for entirely sincere religious reasons, may therefore not be protected. As well as being likely to involve 'deeply theological questions, where courts have little expertise',[90] it could also impose religious orthodoxy, which is contrary to the purpose of religious freedom. In contrast to concerns raised elsewhere in this chapter, this may pose most problems for members of a majority religion because judges may feel more capable of adjudicating what is or is not a core belief for beliefs of which they have a cultural awareness. It may also pose major problems for religions with more amorphous beliefs, where identifying any 'core' practices will be difficult.

This is not to say that there are not relevant differences between different kinds of religious activities. Intuitively, there is a difference between a sermon condemning abortion and an employee wearing a badge at work with a picture of an aborted foetus, even if the latter is a manifestation of her religious beliefs.[91] Similarly, discrimination appears more acceptable in the context of permitting access to religious sacraments than it does to a charitable service

87 [2010] 1 WLR 955.

88 See also *Playfoot v Millais School Governing Body* [2007] EWHC 1698 (Admin) and the Employment Tribunal's decision in *Mba v London Borough of Merton* [2013] ICR 658. This held that a 'belief that Sunday should be a day of rest and worship upon which no paid employment was undertaken, whilst deeply held, is not a core component of the Christian faith', although this reasoning was rejected by the Court of Appeal [2013] EWCA Civ 1562.

89 Sandberg supra n.1, 168–9.

90 Ibid.

91 *Wilson v US West Communications* 58 F.3d 1337 (1995).

provided by a religion, such as a food bank, which, while motivated by religious beliefs, is not in itself a religious activity. As with the other tests considered so far, this is a relevant factor which should be taken into account. However, by itself it is too inflexible. An absolute division between core and peripheral beliefs should be rejected because of the difficulty in making such a distinction when religious beliefs can vary so considerably between individuals, and furthermore because some 'peripheral' practices may be extremely important to an individual.

Neutral laws of general applicability

The final test to be considered is the current constitutional approach taken in the US after the Supreme Court's decision in *Employment Division v Smith*,[92] the case involving a man who used peyote as part of a Native American religious ceremony, who as a result was dismissed from his employment and was unable to claim unemployment benefit because he had been dismissed for work-related misconduct. The Court held that neutral laws of general applicability, even if these affect religious practices, do not pose constitutional issues and therefore are not subject to strict scrutiny. Since the law prohibiting the use of peyote is neutral, that is not specifically aimed at any religious group, and generally applicable, that is it applies to everyone, the law is held to be constitutional, even if the use is for religious reasons.

The main problem with the Supreme Court's decision in *Smith* is that it permits interference with religious practices 'no matter how serious the interference, no matter how trivial the state's nonreligious objectives, and no matter how many alternative approaches were available to the state to pursue its objectives with less impact on religion',[93] since these are not required to be considered. It provides no justification to those affected by the interference with religious practices other than that the religion was not deliberately targeted, which may be of little comfort. It is indifferent to the fact that the law imposes a harsher burden on people such as Smith than on someone who uses peyote for merely recreational reasons.

It could be argued that the demands of equality require that Smith should be treated the same as others and he cannot have any 'special' rights because of his religious beliefs. That is, as everyone is prohibited from using peyote, equality demands that he too is prohibited from using it for whatever reason. This though is a cramped understanding of equality. Even formal equality only mandates the treating of like cases alike, which is not necessarily the same as treating everyone the same. There is a strong argument that Smith is not in a relevantly similar position to recreational drug users because the presumed anti-social effects of such drug use are less likely to occur in the tightly controlled circumstances of the Native American Church, and because the centrality of peyote to his religion means that abstinence would place a much greater burden on him than it would on others.

Indeed, the demands of equality may actually ***require*** exemptions from a generally applicable law. This type of argument has certainly been accepted by the ECtHR. It held in *Thlimmenos v Greece*[94] that 'the right not to be discriminated against … is violated when States without an objective and reasonable justification fail to treat differently persons whose situations are significantly different.' *Thlimmenos* involved a Jehovah's Witness who was

92 494 US 872 (1990).
93 McCoy supra n.17, 1346.
94 (2001) 31 EHRR 15.

prevented from becoming an accountant because of a criminal conviction resulting from his refusal to wear military uniform due to his religiously based pacifist views. The ECtHR held that the failure to treat this conviction as having no bearing on his suitability to be an accountant was a violation of his Art. 9 rights, taken with Art. 14, the right to non-discrimination. This is a good example of where a normally appropriate rule imposes an unjustifiable burden on a religious belief. *Smith* imposes formal equality at the expense of substantive equality. As Laycock argues, it means that 'a soldier who believes he must cover his head before an omnipresent God is constitutionally indistinguishable from a soldier who wants to wear a Budweiser gimme cap',[95] leading to, as he vividly puts it, 'the equality of universal suppression'.[96]

Scalia J's answer in *Smith* to this problem is that the proper course for those who are prevented from acting in accordance with their religious beliefs is to seek a legislative exemption. This is of course a possibility which should not be forgotten, but it is not sufficiently protective by itself.[97] The purpose of having legally enforceable constitutional rights is that individuals are not reliant on the will of the legislature to protect them.[98] Small, unpopular or new religions will find it more difficult to gain legislative exemptions, either through deliberate discrimination or, perhaps more likely, through ignorance of or indifference to them. Gaining an exemption through legislative means can potentially require far greater resources, both financial and in terms of political access, than bringing a court case. In any case, it cannot be raised as a defence to state action. Even Scalia J recognised this discriminatory effect, but he held that this is an 'unavoidable consequence of democratic government'.[99] In essence his conclusion is that 'minorities will always do worse in a democracy and there is nothing to be done about this.'[100] This seems both unfeeling and problematic from a fundamental rights perspective.

An inability to challenge restrictions unless it can be demonstrated that they are not generally applicable is also discriminatory for another reason. Those who have minority beliefs are likely to face more clashes because the majority, probably unthinkingly, creates structures to suit themselves.[101] For example, in all three jurisdictions, while a Christian employee is likely to have Christmas Day off since this is a public holiday, and therefore no clash between their religious obligation and their employment obligations arises, this is not so for a Jewish employee who wishes to have time off for Yom Kippur. They will be unable to challenge a generally applicable rule that everyone has to work on that day.

The approach in *Smith* only leaves a small category of acts open to challenge: those where there is a discriminatory motive and so the law is not neutral or generally applicable. This is unlikely to include many challenges to sexual orientation anti-discrimination rights since these will normally clearly be driven by a desire to protect gay rights, rather than to discriminate against those with particular religious views. However, the principle was found to

95 D. Laycock, 'The Remnants of Free Exercise' [1990] *Sup Ct Rev* 1, 11.

96 D. Laycock, 'The Religious Exemption Debate' (2009) 11 *Rutgers J L & Religion* 139, 173.

97 After the Supreme Court's decision, Oregonian law was changed in order to grant an exemption for religious use for peyote, but it seems unlikely that this legislative change would have happened without the publicity the court case brought.

98 This is still relevant even where, as in the UK system, the legislature retains the final word over the infringements of rights. At the very least, the courts have the power to force the legislature to consider whether or not to rectify a violation of a right.

99 *Smith* supra n.92, 890.

100 Nussbaum supra n.18, 119.

101 Ibid.

be violated in a different context in *Church of the Lukumi Babalu Aye v City of Hialeah*.[102] In this case, members of the Santeria religion, which requires certain ritualistic animal sacrifices, challenged a city ordinance which prohibited the killing of animals in a 'ritual or ceremony not for the primary purpose of food consumption'. The Supreme Court held the law was unconstitutional as it was clear that it was designed only to prevent these particular killings. This case raises a number of issues. First, it demonstrates the limited nature of the exception. This should be an easy case under the *Smith* test, but the claim had been rejected by both the District Court and Court of Appeals. There was considerable evidence that Hialeah was not motivated by concerns about animal cruelty, but rather by opposition to the Santeria religion. This can even be seen in the terms of the ordinance, which makes reference to a 'ritual' but then, presumably in an effort to exclude kosher or halal butchering, adds 'not for the primary purpose of food consumption'.

However, if the law had been more skilfully drafted, it would probably have been considered constitutional. If it had been based on the disposal of animal waste, for example, it may have been permissible without any consideration of the necessity of the law or the burden it placed on Santerians in living out their religion. In many situations it would be fairly easy to create a generally applicable law which would pass constitutional scrutiny. It has been said that 'a tax on wearing yarmulkes is a tax on Jews':[103] such blatant discrimination is therefore prohibited. However, it would be perfectly possible to have a rule forbidding any head coverings in federal employment. Although this would have a much more severe effect on Jewish men and Muslim women than others, this differential burden would not even be recognised and the need for such a rule would not be assessed. This is hardly a new problem, as the nineteenth-century English case of *Kruse v Johnson*[104] demonstrates. Byelaws prohibited singing in a public place within 50 yards of a dwelling house if asked to stop by a policeman or a resident. Whilst these laws were ostensibly aimed at noise pollution, they were in fact aimed at preventing the Salvation Army from holding outdoor services. Despite this being an important part of their religious practice, the laws were upheld without difficulty. The approach in *Smith* makes discrimination the only important factor in considering constitutionality. However, the actual effect on a religion may be the same whether the law is directed at it or if it is merely caught by a general rule.

The Court's judgment in *Smith* appears to be driven by a fear of anarchy to which, it is assumed, balancing the extent of the interference with the religious right against the justification for the policy will inevitably lead, notwithstanding the fact that a balancing approach had been used for the past 30 years. Scalia J argued that 'it is horrible to contemplate that federal judges will regularly balance against the importance of general laws the significance of religious practice' and thus 'it would require, for example, the same degree of "compelling state interest" to impede the practice of throwing rice at church weddings as to impede the practice of getting married in church'.[105] This seems to rest on a perplexing lack of faith in the ability of federal judges and a tenuous conclusion that religions would prefer not to have a judge decide the relative religious importance of these practices to being able to challenge a law forbidding church weddings at all. Balancing tests may require some intrusion into religious matters, but this may be a fair trade-off in return for greater religious protection. These problems and the benefits of balancing tests will be discussed in Chapter 5.

102 508 US 520 (1993).
103 *Bray v Alexandria Women's Health Clinic* 506 U.S. 263, 270 (1993).
104 [1898] 2 QB 91.
105 *Smith* supra n.92, 887.

An underlying feature of the approach in *Smith*, taken with subsequent developments in US law, is the reasserted distinction of the public/private distinction. *Smith* means the ability to challenge laws in the public domain is very limited, with an apparent aim of protecting private religion, since it does not lead to state assessment of religious belief. In doing so, though, it forces religion to be privatised when this may be quite contrary to the religion's precepts: a much larger interference with religious belief. This ironically undermines the very thing that Scalia J is so anxious to protect. Indeed, in another case he criticised the rest of the court for treating religion like 'some purely personal avocation that can be indulged entirely in secret, like pornography.'[106]

Although *Smith* denies religious exemptions in the public sphere, it does not govern the situation in the religious sphere. In *EEOC v Hosanna Tabor*,[107] the case concerning whether a religious minister is protected by discrimination laws, *Smith* was simply held to be irrelevant. Although some had argued that employment discrimination laws were neutral and general laws which should be applied to religious organisations under *Smith*,[108] this approach was firmly rejected. The Court held that *Smith* involved 'government regulation of only outward physical acts', whereas *Hosanna Tabor* involved 'interference with an internal church decision that affects the faith and mission of the church itself.'[109] It would therefore have been a violation of the First Amendment to allow a teacher, who was considered to be a minister by her church, to make a claim under disability discrimination law. In the private sphere, therefore, religions have much greater rights under US law, including rights to discriminate. The result of these decisions, then, is a reinvention of the public/private distinction, with all the problems this entails.

Hybrid rights?

The most incomprehensible part of the rule emanating from *Smith* is that the Court held that claims can be brought to protect 'hybrid rights'. The exact meaning of a hybrid right is unclear, but the idea is that free exercise combined with another right can give rise to a claim against a generally applicable law. In *Smith* Scalia J stated that cases that had been previously considered to purely involve free exercise claims were actually hybrid rights cases in that they involved a free exercise claim and another right. Thus when discussing *Yoder v Wisconsin*, Scalia J asserted that the case was not simply about free exercise, but also the rights of parents to control their children's education and thus gave rise to a hybrid right. A cynical explanation for the introduction of such a concept is that it was necessary to explain away previous cases where a violation of free exercise had been found. Even if this is not so, it is a very unclear concept.

That a right taken with another right can lead to a violation is not in itself an incoherent idea. Under the ECHR, for example, it is possible that there is no violation of a substantive right by itself, but there is a violation of that right taken with Article 14, the right to non-discrimination, as long as the claim falls within the 'ambit' of the substantive right. However, non-discrimination rights are different from other rights as they can only be measured

106 *Lee v Weisman* 505 U.S. 577, 645 (1992).

107 *Hosanna Tabor* supra n.73.

108 C.M. Corbin, 'Above the Law? The Constitutionality of the Ministerial Exemption from Antidiscrimination Law' (2007) 75 *Fordham L Rev* 1965.

109 *Hosanna Tabor* supra n.73, 15. Robinson argues that this distinction is crucial to understanding these cases: J. Robinson, 'Neither Ministerial nor an Exception: The Ministerial Exception in Light of *Hosanna-Tabor*' (2014) 37 *Harv J L & Pub Pol'y* 1151.

relationally, that is, with regard to how others are treated. While a member state may have discretion as to whether to grant a benefit or not, and therefore there is no violation of the substantive article, it does not have the right to grant the benefit unequally. Therefore, adding together the two rights can lead to a violation.

However, the problem with this idea of hybrid rights is that another right could almost always be considered to be implicated in the right of freedom of religion, particularly freedom of speech. This is a very broad principle in US law and the concept of expressive speech has for example been considered to include non-obscene commercial nude dancing.[110] Almost all religious practices must have some message, even if this is simply to identify a person as a member of a religion. If school pupils are protected in wearing black armbands to protest against the Vietnam War,[111] then it seems difficult to see why wearing a hijab, for example, could not be considered expressive speech. Smith's claim could also be reinvented as a free speech claim, indeed possibly political speech, and thus deserving of the highest degree of protection. It could be argued that the peyote ceremony was an expressive reassertion of a Native American way of life, in contrast to the discrimination and forced assimilation and Christianisation Smith had faced in his childhood.[112] Claims to discriminate could potentially also be re-invented as speech claims[113] and indeed will presumably always involve some kind of speech. Given, then, that cases can always be considered hybrid rights, the distinction is arbitrary. More fundamentally, it is simply unclear why two small infringements of different rights should add up to a violation when a great infringement of one does not. For these reasons, even if the generally applicable law rule is accepted, the hybrid rights idea cannot be.

In summary then, the approach in *Smith* too fails as a test. Whilst it is of course extremely problematic if a religion is deliberately targeted, this does not mean that a restriction is only problematic in this situation. Such an approach cannot protect religious freedom sufficiently, since it permits many invasions of religious rights without consideration as to whether this is justified.

Conclusion

This chapter has concluded that none of the tests expressed here are suitable for deciding when religious claims should be protected above other rights, such as non-discrimination, because they are variously under- or over-protective, do not take equality concerns seriously or give too much power to religious elites. Nevertheless, some of the insights they bring may be relevant in identifying differences in the circumstances and types of religious claims: that a case involves the private rather than public sphere, for example. Given, then, that none of these tests are appropriate by themselves, this evidently raises the question of how these claims should be dealt with.

110 *Barnes v Glen Theater Inc.* 501 US 560 (1991).
111 *Tinker v Des Moines Independent Community School District* 393 U.S. 503 (1969).
112 See Nussbaum supra n.18, 149–50.
113 See *Elane Photography v Willock* 309 P.3d 553 (N.M., 2013). Further discussed in Chapter 7.

4 Interference and justification

The previous chapter outlined four tests for deciding when the right of freedom of religion should be held to be violated. These tests all defined the right to religious freedom narrowly: the right to religious freedom was only engaged, for example, where a law was not neutral or generally applicable or only when it affected a matter defined as private rather than public. Under such approaches, most of the work done in deciding whether a right has been violated is in deciding whether the situation at issue falls within the category protected by the right. An alternative approach, though, would be to initially define the right broadly and then to consider whether the interference with the right was justified, given the extent to which, among other things, the rights of others were affected. This would require a two-stage test. This structure is strongly implied by many of the provisions of the ECHR and the Canadian Charter. For example, Art. 9 provides that:

1. Everyone has the right to freedom of thought, conscience and religion; this right includes freedom to change his religion or belief and freedom, either alone or in community with others and in public or private, to manifest his religion or belief, in worship, teaching, practice and observance.
2. Freedom to manifest one's religion or beliefs shall be subject only to such limitations as are prescribed by law and are necessary in a democratic society in the interests of public safety, for the protection of public order, health or morals, or for the protection of the rights and freedoms of others.

This clearly suggests there should be two stages to considering rights claims: first, a consideration of whether an act falls within the right 'to freedom of thought, conscience and religion', and second, whether a restriction on the manifestation of such beliefs is 'prescribed by law and necessary in a democratic society'. Under such an approach, rights can be defined broadly at the first stage, since success at this stage certainly does not guarantee the eventual success of the claim and does not necessarily imply the state has acted improperly. Such issues are only decided at the second stage, which will usually be by far the most important. At this stage the court considers whether the state has demonstrated sufficient justification for interfering with the right. However, as will be demonstrated later in this chapter, English courts and the ECtHR have sometimes been overly restrictive in considering whether the right to manifest religion has been interfered with, meaning that argument cannot proceed to the second stage.

Defining rights broadly

As will be further discussed in the next chapter, permitting rights to be defined broadly is advantageous. The main advantage relates to justification. If rights are defined narrowly, then there will be many situations where the state can restrict a person's freedom without having to justify or even explain why this is necessary, as was demonstrated in the previous chapter. By contrast, if rights are defined broadly, the majority of cases will be decided at the justification rather than interference stage. Since interferences with rights must always be justified, this approach makes the process of justification at the centre of rights adjudication.

The English case of *R(Begum) v Denbigh High School Governors*[1] illustrates the problem if a restrictive interpretation is given to the first part of the test. Begum claimed that she was under a religious obligation to wear a jilbab.[2] While her (state) school did have various school uniform options and allowed girls to wear a shalwar kameez,[3] jilbabs were not permitted and Begum was not allowed to attend school unless she wore the correct school uniform. She claimed that the school's actions violated her rights under Art. 9. The case reached the House of Lords, where a majority ruled the case out at the first stage of analysis, holding there was no interference with her Art. 9 rights. This was mainly because she could have attended a different school where she could have worn the jilbab.

Evidently, if a court finds there is no interference with a right then there is nothing for the state to have to justify. As Dyzenhaus points out, the position taken by the majority in *Begum* 'relieved [the school] of the burden of justification'.[4] It appeared that the school had in fact put a great deal of effort into consulting with parents as to appropriate dress for Muslim pupils, who constituted a majority of pupils at the school. There were concerns that allowing a more conservative style of dress would put pressure on other pupils to dress in the same way and would raise religious tensions. However, given that the Court stated that there was no interference with her rights, all of this was strictly irrelevant: the school could legally have not considered these issues at all. Given that Begum was clearly prevented from carrying out what she considered to be a religious obligation, and could only avoid this by incurring disruption to her education, this is highly unsatisfactory.

A general right to autonomy?

If justification is so important, this raises the question of how broadly human rights should be interpreted. From one perspective, the state should be able to provide justification in some form for all its activities which restrict its citizens' freedom of action: if it cannot, then this appears, at the very least, to amount to bad governance. On this basis, given that interferences with rights can potentially always be justified and as a matter of public policy we would want the state to be able to justify its actions, should rights not be defined as broadly as possible?

Kai Möller argues we should have a 'general right to autonomy', or in other words, 'a right to follow one's projects':[5] Since all autonomy interests would be included in this right,

1 [2007] 1 AC 100.
2 Described in the judgment as 'A long coat-like garment' ibid., 109.
3 Described in the judgment as 'A combination of the kameeze, a sleeveless smock-like dress with a square neckline, revealing the wearer's collar and tie, with the shalwar, loose trousers, tapering at the ankles' ibid., 108.
4 D. Dyzenhaus, 'Proportionality and Deference in a Culture of Justification' in G. Huscroft, B.W. Miller and G. Webber (eds), *Proportionality and the Rule of Law: Rights, Justification, Reasoning* (Cambridge: Cambridge UP, 2014).
5 Such a broad right would subsume all other rights beneath it, meaning that further rights provisions would strictly be unnecessary. However, as Möller argues, for ease of understanding it may be better to have specific rights such as expression or religion in order to give more information

it would include a (prima facie) right to take part in trivial or even immoral activities. Möller argues that there is no non-arbitrary way to create a threshold between acts which are perceived to be of specific importance and therefore receive constitutional protection, and those that do not, given that those that fall just under the threshold receive no protection, while those just above do. This minor normative difference should, he argues, not lead to such a great practical difference. He contends that the purpose of human rights is not to protect rights of a special kind of importance but rather to embody an 'attitude that takes [a person] seriously as a person with a life to live, and that will therefore deny her the ability to live her life in certain ways only when there are sufficiently strong reasons for this'.[6]

Such a wide interpretation of rights may seem surprising, but this idea is not wholly unprecedented. The German Federal Constitutional Court has held that Art. 2(1) of the Basic Law, which protects the right to freely develop one's personality, includes such trivial things as the right to feed pigeons in a park[7] and to ride horses in public woods.[8] An earlier draft of the right stated that 'Everyone can do as he pleases' but this was rejected only for 'linguistic reasons'.[9] Möller argues that even trivial activities such as pursuing hobbies are part of a person's self-conception and thus to interfere with a person's freedom to engage in them is to interfere with a person's autonomy. Thus the state should have an obligation to justify this infringement.[10]

Möller's argument in fact goes even further than this. He argues that the right to autonomy should extend beyond trivial activities to include even evil acts, so that it would be possible to talk of a right to murder or rape, although of course the state would always have sufficient justification to prohibit this when the second stage of analysis was considered. He argues that the relevant criterion at the interference stage is whether the activity enhances the autonomy of that person. The public interest and the rights of others should be only considered at the second stage of justification because to consider them earlier would lead to 'incoherence and structural confusion'.[11]

While such an approach is coherent and avoids the problem of gaps in legal protection, defining rights so widely is problematic. The most significant problem is that it loses the powerful connotations associated with the phrase 'human rights'. For this reason, among others, Grégoire Webber is a strong critic of such an approach. As he puts it, 'it remains an open question why one should dignify raping, torturing for pleasure, trafficking children, and enslaving a population' as cognizable "rights", even if qualified by "prima facie".'[12] He points out that Möller's approach 'does not award peremptory force to rights'[13] and thus, 'one may have conclusive reasons for acting *contrary* to the right'.[14]

as to the kind of things that are protected; K. Möller, *The Global Model of Constitutional Rights* (Oxford: Oxford UP, 2012) 88–90.

6 K. Möller, 'Proportionality and Rights Inflation' in Huscroft, Miller and Webber, supra n.4, 166.
7 BVerfGE 54, 143.
8 BVerfGE 39, 1, BVerfGE 88, 203.
9 Möller supra n.6, 159.
10 Ibid. See also M. Kumm, 'Who is Afraid of the Total Constitution? Constitutional Rights as Principles and the Constitutionalization of Private Law' (2006) 7 *German LJ* 341.
11 Möller supra n.6, 165.
12 G. Webber, 'On The Loss of Rights' in Huscroft, Miller and Webber, supra n.4, 143. See also G. Webber, *The Negotiable Constitution: On the Limitation of Rights* (Cambridge: Cambridge UP, 2009).
13 Webber, 'On The Loss of Rights' ibid., 132.
14 Ibid., 134.

We do not want to lose entirely the moral force behind the idea that human rights matter in the sense that they have some kind of special priority. While it should be possible to justify interferences with many rights, a right should not be made indistinguishable from other types of interest, otherwise it loses this moral force. If a person can show that there has been an interference with a right, this should give rise to a claim that, if possible and if consistent with others' rights, the state should act to alleviate the burden, and if it cannot, then our attitude should be that this involves a loss of some kind, even though this may be inevitable, an idea explained in more detail in the next chapter. There is no regret in forbidding someone to rape someone, even if this does affect a person's autonomy. On a more practical level, if a right is engaged, then the state has an obligation to respond by providing justification. This requires resources from the state and the courts, even if it is easy to justify the infringement of the right. While it demonstrates a serious flaw in the political process if the state is unable to justify its actions, legal action is not the only way to secure a person's interests. It is acceptable to only use the courts for more serious problems and leave other problems to be dealt with by the political arena.

A one-stage process?

Webber's argument, however, goes much further than these criticisms of a very broad definition of rights. He argues against the idea of a two-stage process at all, maintaining that you should refer to a 'right' only when all the contrary interests have been taken into account. In other words, you have a right only if it would be a *violation* for the state to act in a particular way. This means there would only be one stage in rights adjudication: specification of when a right exists. This would mean that the phrase the 'clash of rights' is unintelligible, apart from perhaps metaphorically.

Despite Webber's criticisms, it appears that his approach is fundamentally similar to the two-stage test, although this process is amalgamated into one stage.[15] A court still takes opposing interests to a claimed right into account and, once these have been considered, comes to an overall conclusion as to whether a person's rights have been violated. Take, for example, the issue of whether defamatory expression should be permitted. Under the two-stage approach, rights are defined broadly and so prohibiting this is an interference with the right of freedom of expression. At the second stage the rights and interests of others are taken into account and so the interference with freedom of expression will probably be justified.[16] Under Webber's approach there is simply one stage of specifying what is meant by freedom of expression. In considering this, the interests of others and the community as a whole are taken into account. The result under both approaches may therefore be identical and indeed the result of a similar process. Given this, it is clearer and more straightforward to hold that a person's right to freedom of expression has been interfered with, but that this is justified, rather than hold there is no relevant right to free expression at all. That person has clearly been prevented from expressing herself in the way she wishes.

In addition to being less transparent, Webber's approach also takes away the focus from the need for justification of rights, since the process of justification does not form its own stage but is merely considered when specifying the right. However, there appears to be little difference between what he refers to as specifying a right and considering justification for

15 Möller supra n.6.

16 Of course, many safeguards such as a prohibition of excessive damages, defences relating to discussion of public figures etc. may be required.

interferences with a right, although this second process is not carried out explicitly. It may be that this dispute therefore is primarily a linguistic one: a debate over whether something can be called a right when interferences with it can be justified, or whether this is the case only when a violation has been found and the state found to have committed a wrong. Webber is concerned that under a two-step process the word 'right' is used in two ways: as a prima facie right and as an actual right to act in a particular way. While there is the possibility of confusion between these two meanings, it does not appear that this is a widespread or major problem. In any case, if the concern is ease of understanding, the one-stage approach is more complex and opaque than the two-step approach advocated above.

There is another perhaps more subtle problem with Webber's approach. It means that by definition all rights are absolute, as opposed to there being a distinction between qualified rights, such as freedom of religion, and absolute rights like the right not to be tortured. The concept of a qualified right is, though, of value, as is the ability to distinguish between the two kinds of rights. Part of the strength of the right not to be tortured is in its absoluteness. The rights of others, for example, the rights of those who a terrorist has or is alleged to have killed, are irrelevant in considering whether a person has been tortured.[17] In comparison though, rights like freedom of expression and freedom of religion do not have this absolute character and the rights of others will always be relevant. Of course, there has to be specification as to what the right not to be tortured means, but that is not the same as the 'all things considered' justification process required for rights like freedom of religion.

To summarise the argument made so far then, there should be a two-stage process in analysing rights. Rights should be interpreted fairly broadly at the first stage, partly because otherwise the state is under no obligation to provide justification. However, Möller's argument that the definition of a right should include all autonomy interests is too broad. His approach has problems of 'fair labelling', since it includes within the definition of a right actions which cannot conceivably be permitted. It also loses the moral force behind the idea of a right and poses problems of practicality. With these parameters in mind, I will now move on to consider more precisely what should be included in the right to freedom of religion and to non-discrimination.

What should be included in the right to religious freedom?

Since society contains a multitude of religious and moral beliefs and practices, people will constantly be faced with practices with which they disagree and will in a myriad of ways be constrained from creating their ideal society. Not all of this should constitute an interference with rights for the reasons described above. It should be remembered that the current discussion is only about whether there is an interference with a right and does not consider whether any interference with the right can be justified.

Substantive limits?

The first question is whether there should be any substantive limit on what beliefs should be protected. This issue was raised in the English case of *R(Williamson) v Secretary of State for*

17 Although see A. Dershowitz, *Why Terrorism Works: Understanding the Threat, Responding to the Challenge* (Yale: Yale UP, 2002) Ch. 4; M. Kumm, 'What Do You Have in Virtue of Having a Constitutional Right? On the Place and Limits of the Proportionality Requirement' *New York University Public Law and Legal Theory Working Papers*, Paper 46 (2006), 1, 34–8.

Education and Employment.[18] The case involved parents who argued that the prohibition on corporal punishment in private schools violated their religious beliefs. The House of Lords and a majority of the Court of Appeal held that the parents' rights were engaged under Article 9.[19] Nevertheless, the House of Lords held that there were some substantive limits to Article 9(1). Drawing on the decision of the ECtHR in *Campbell and Cosans v UK,*[20] the House of Lords held that in order to be protected under Art. 9, a manifestation must be based on a belief[21] which is 'worthy of respect in a democratic society' and 'compatible with human dignity'. A belief that light corporal punishment administered in a loving environment was religiously required was held not to contravene this, although the prohibition on such punishment was ultimately justified because of the rights of the children.

However, limiting the scope of the right to freedom of religion at the first stage of consideration on these bases is potentially problematic. As Rix LJ argued in the Court of Appeal judgment in *Williamson*, 'religion is a controversial subject ... It is in part to guard against such controversy that the Convention guarantees religious freedom'.[22] Furthermore, of course, if the first stage is interpreted narrowly, then attention is taken away from the focus on justification for the infringement, rather than the preliminary question of the breadth of the right. In particular, the requirement to 'respect' these beliefs may be too high a bar. Religious beliefs may well be unpopular, perceived as odd or even dangerous, and not worthy of respect in the sense of positive approval, but should still be tolerated as part of a diverse society. As Lord Walker remarked in *Williamson*, 'the state should not show liberal tolerance only to tolerant liberals.'[23]

The tests discussed in *Williamson* originated in the context of interpreting the very different question of what counted as 'philosophical convictions' for the purpose of Protocol 1 Article 2 ECHR, which requires states to respect the rights of parents in ensuring that education and teaching is in conformity with their convictions. In contrast, Article 9 case law disclaims a role for assessing the respectability of religious beliefs. For example, in *Manoussakis v Greece* the ECtHR held that 'the right of freedom of religion as guaranteed under the Convention excludes any discretion on the part of the State to determine whether religious beliefs ... are legitimate.'[24]

Nevertheless, as we have seen, some acts should not be considered to be within the ambit of human rights and there should be some restrictions at the initial stage of defining the right. As Taylor argues, we should be able to reject some demands in a 'quick way', which 'cuts off all conversation from the start' rather than considers whether a right can be protected in practice.[25] It would be highly unsatisfactory, for the reasons given above, to say that there was a prima facie right to murder Salman Rushdie because of his authorship of *The Satanic Verses*[26] even if a person believed that to do so was a religious obligation, and

18 [2005] 2 AC 246.
19 See Ch 3. for the approach taken by Buxton LJ.
20 (1982) 4 EHRR 293
21 The right to freedom of belief is normally considered to be absolute and Lord Nicholls stated in *Williamson* that the criteria would only apply where the beliefs were manifested.
22 *R(Williamson) v Secretary of State for Education and Employment* [2003] QB 1300.
23 Supra n.18, 268.
24 (1995) 23 EHRR 387, para 47.
25 C. Taylor, 'Living with Difference' in A. Allen and M. Regan (eds), *Debating Democracy's Discontent: Essays on American Politics, Law, and Public Philosophy* (Oxford: Oxford UP, 1998) 219.
26 Taylor's example is the less clear-cut one of whether *calls* to kill Salman Rushdie can be outlawed as incitement to murder under this 'quick way'.

even given that the claim would clearly fail at the justification stage because of the rights of others.

Although the criterion of 'worthy of respect in a democratic society' is too restrictive, the requirement that a belief should be compatible with human dignity is more justifiable. Since the fundamental purpose of protecting rights, including freedom of religion, is to protect human dignity, they should not be used to undermine this purpose. Of course though, deciding what dignity means or requires is extremely contentious.[27] Care should be taken to ensure that the right is not too narrowly defined or that references to dignity are not used as a way of 'imposing a normative or ethical value onto individual behaviour or choice'.[28] As far as this relates to discriminatory beliefs, the requirement that a belief should be compatible with human dignity does not mean that individuals owe each other an obligation of equal respect, which the state owes to individuals, but should entail merely an idea of 'personhood': that all are worthy of inherent dignity simply because they are human. An individual is free to act in partisan ways. However, individuals should not be considered to have a right, even prima facie, to subject another person to violence, or to wholly exclude others from society merely because of their sexuality or beliefs. To do so would infringe a person's dignity and fundamentally ignore their basic rights.

A further requirement I will adopt, which is not discussed in *Williamson,* but which is connected to the requirement of being compatible with human dignity, is, as Taylor argues, that the belief must be compatible with reasonable co-existence in society with those who share different views. This is a demand of reciprocity. Otherwise the group claims a right to exist for itself, even though others oppose it, but refuses to accept that others should have this right. General acceptance of this idea is required for a liberal democracy to function and thus there is a need for limited containment of some views. However, this is not a requirement that groups must think that a state of co-existence is *desirable*. Sala gives the example of Jehovah's Witnesses who would, ideally, like everyone to be Jehovah's Witnesses, but since this is not the case, live peacefully in co-existence with others, although they seek to convert those around them.[29] This is acceptable. All that is excluded is the refusal to accept the situation of co-existence that *does* exist, given freedom of conscience and religion.

These two principles, of compatibility with human dignity and acceptance of a state of reasonable co-existence, will exclude calls to violence as well as some hate speech and some forms of discrimination from the ambit of the right to manifest religious beliefs.[30] However, the claim to discriminate may be limited. The reasoning behind it may be not that 'gay people should never receive this service because they, or their behaviour, should not be tolerated in any right-thinking society', but rather, 'I cannot in good conscience provide it, given that my beliefs place this obligation on me, although I understand others have different views'. As the English courts have suggested, such a claim is consistent with co-existence and with accepting that gay people are worthy of inherent dignity.[31]

27 See e.g. C. McCrudden, 'Human Dignity and Judicial Interpretation of Human Rights' (2008) 19 *EJIL* 655.

28 See the discussion of *S v Jordan* 6 SA 642 (CC) (2002) in E. Cameron, 'Moral Citizenship and Constitutional Protection' in C. McCrudden (ed.), *Understanding Human Dignity* (Oxford: Oxford UP, 2013).

29 R. Sala, 'The Place of Unreasonable People Beyond Rawls' (2013) 12 *European J of Political Theory* 253.

30 There may of course be other reasons not to prohibit hate speech.

31 E.g. *McFarlane v Relate Avon Ltd* [2010] EWCA Civ 880 at paras 18–19 and *Bull and Bull v Hall and Preddy* [2012] 1 WLR 2514, 2528.

How broad should the right be?

In considering the possible extent of this right, Kent Greenawalt draws useful distinctions between religiously compelled and religiously motivated acts, and between tests which require compliance with religious precepts to be legally impossible and those that merely make religious compliance more difficult.[32] These distinctions will form the basis of this discussion.[33]

At its strictest, it could be argued that for there to be an interference with a person's freedom of religion a religiously required act must be legally forbidden. The ECtHR has sometimes taken this approach. In *Cha'are Shalom Ve Tsedek v France*[34] for example, there was held to be no interference with religious rights where compliance with religious beliefs was not *impossible*. The applicant organisation was one of Ultra-Orthodox Jews who required meat certified as 'glatt' and not merely kosher. They were denied a licence to ritually slaughter animals on the grounds that there was a licensed slaughterer in the area, albeit one that only produced kosher meat. The ECtHR held there was no interference since glatt meat could be imported from Belgium and thus obtaining such meat was not legally forbidden.

This test would clearly exclude protection in situations such as *Lyng v Northwest Indian Cemetery Protective Association,* a US case.[35] The government wished to build a road and conduct logging on a sacred Native American site which would, as the Court noted, 'have devastating effects on traditional Indian practices'. This though would not be enough. They would still be able to practise their faith. It would not be outlawed in any way, simply practically difficult. There was no coercion.

Even in situations where a government more directly requires or prohibits certain behaviour, this test may not be met. In *Bowen v Roy,*[36] a Native American man believed that the maintenance of a social security number for his daughter 'robbed her of her spirit', but he could not receive social security benefits, including Medicaid, for her without it. This too did not involve an impossibility – he was under no obligation to claim those benefits, although they were in practice extremely important. Similarly, in the Canadian case of *Alberta v Hutterian Brethren of Wilson Colony,*[37] some Hutterites objected on religious grounds to being photographed. A new requirement that driving licences must have photographs was therefore contrary to their beliefs. But, again, even though not having a driving licence would make their rural farming existence very difficult, this would not be sufficient. An impossibility test would therefore allow severe burdens on belief, without requiring any justification to be given.[38]

The question of whether it remains strictly possible to comply with religious beliefs has also been considered relevant to whether an interference can be found in employment since an employee could resign and thus avoid the conflict. The ECtHR has found this issue surprisingly difficult. To take one example, in *Pichon and Sajous v France*[39] the Court held

32 K. Greenawalt, *Religion and the Constitution Volume 1: Free Exercise and Fairness* (Princeton: Princeton UP, 2006).

33 This section draws on my earlier article M. Pearson, 'Article 9 at a Crossroads: Interference Before and After *Eweida*' (2013) 13 *HRLR* 580.

34 9 BHRC 27 (2000).

35 485 US 439 (1988).

36 476 US 693 (1986).

37 [2009] 2 SCR 567.

38 The court actually found that there had been an interference with the Hutterites' rights but this was justified.

39 App No. 49853/99 (2 Oct 2001). See also *Kalaç v Turkey* (1997) 27 EHRR 552.

that requiring the applicant pharmacists to sell contraceptive pills did not interfere with their right to freedom of religion and thus their application was dismissed as manifestly ill-founded. However, the Court's reasoning was essentially a balancing process: women were entitled to access contraception with ease, the applicants were acting in the public sphere and they could manifest their beliefs in other ways. All of this is true and relevant, but as to whether the infringement of belief was justified, and not to the prior question of whether the right was infringed, which should have been answered affirmatively. The alternatives available to the pharmacists were to perform an act they were resolutely opposed to, or to resign. If resignation was always sufficient to protect rights then there should be no concern with dress codes, working hours or religious holidays, or perhaps even with religious harassment taking place within employment.

The British courts have in the past accepted and even extended the ECHR's reasoning. As has been outlined, in *R(Begum) v Denbigh High School Governors*[40] the majority of the House of Lords accepted that there was no interference where a pupil was not permitted to attend her school wearing a jilbab, because there were other schools she could have attended. Lord Bingham referred to *Cha'are Shalom Ve Tsedek* in his judgment and held that 'there remains a coherent and remarkably consistent body of authority which our domestic courts must take into account and which shows that interference is not easily established'.[41] Lord Hoffmann similarly held that since she chose the school knowing its uniform policies and she could have attended another school, there was no interference with her beliefs. As Lord Nicholls pointed out though, such an approach 'under-estimate[s] the disruption this would be likely to cause to her education' and places the school under no duty to 'explain and justify its decision'.[42]

More recently though the ECHR has appeared to change its approach, although the consequences of this decision have not yet been fully considered by UK domestic courts. In *Eweida v British Airways*[43] an employee was prevented from wearing a cross at work as a symbol of her Christian faith because this was contrary to British Airways' uniform policies. The Employment Appeal Tribunal and Court of Appeal held she had not been indirectly discriminated against because of her religion. She could not demonstrate that Christians as a group had been put at a disadvantage since wearing a cross is not a requirement of the Christian faith. It also held that there was no interference with Art. 9. The Court of Appeal quoted Lord Bingham in *Begum,* holding that 'The Strasbourg institutions have not been at all ready to find an interference with the right to manifest religious belief in practice or observance where a person has voluntarily accepted an employment or role which does not accommodate that practice or observance and there are other means open to the person to practise or observe his or her religion without undue hardship or inconvenience.' However, when this case was taken to the ECtHR in *Eweida v UK* the court reconsidered its approach. It held there had been a violation of Art. 9, even though it would have been open to her to resign and seek alternative employment. Issues regarding religious freedom within employment will be discussed in more detail in Chapter 6.

Although the clearest examples of a religious practice being made legally impossible are cases where a religion has ceremonies involving illegal drugs, such as the use of peyote in some Native American religions or cannabis in Rastafarianism, the test at its strictest also

40 Supra n.1. See also *Copsey v Devon Clays* [2005] IRLR 811.
41 *Begum,* 113–14.
42 *Begum,* 119.
43 [2010] EWCA Civ 80; [2010] ICR 89.

requires a religious compulsion. Such cases may fail since a judge could conclude that, while such ceremonies are an important part of the religion, there is no strict obligation to perform them. Not all religions have definite rules or doctrines, and some firmly reject hierarchy.[44] However, there may still be practices which are clearly part of the religion, even where there is no textual or other authority to which an adherent can point. A focus on religious obligation misses these practices.

Furthermore, defining what is merely religiously motivated rather than religiously required is difficult.[45] A compulsion requirement creates an impulse to 'dutify' every aspect of religion. This may be quite artificial. As Laycock puts it, 'it assumes that the exercise of religion consists only of obeying the rules ... all the affirmative communal and spiritual aspects of religion are assumed away ... for many believers the attempt to distinguish what is required from what grows organically out of the religious experience is an utterly alien question.'[46] It is probable that some religious practices are put in terms of duty because this is more likely to be accepted by a court.[47]

Even if there were a clear distinction between compulsion and motivation, religious duties may be less important to a believer than religiously motivated conduct. For example, most Christians do not think it is a religious requirement to attend Bible study groups, but for some it may be an important part of their religious practice. It would be nonsense to say that a law which made studying a sacred text with others a criminal offence did not interfere with their freedom of religion. It is therefore sufficient for an act to be religiously motivated.

However, to say that any act motivated by a sincere religious conviction, however indirect, is protected by the right is by itself too generous. It would include facts such as those arising in *Rushton v Nebraska Public Power District*.[48] Two employees of a nuclear power station refused drug testing, not because they were religiously opposed to it, but because the company's drug policy statement stated that alcoholism was a disease that could be treated. Contrary to this, they believed that alcoholism was not a disease but a sin. They therefore did not wish to affirm the policy. Including such a case would place weighty burdens on employers and the state in assessing these claims. It may encourage frivolous or spurious claims. Although the importance of the practice would be assessed at the justification stage, and therefore cases involving indirect unimportant interferences would be extremely unlikely to be ultimately successful, there is still benefit in excluding some cases via a threshold test.

An intermediate requirement is therefore appropriate. I will consider there to be an interference if an act is motivated by a sincere religious conviction, provided that there is a close connection between the act and the belief and there is more than a *de minimis* burden. This is very similar to the test put forward in *Arrowsmith v UK*[49] by the ECtHR, where it was held that an act must be 'intimately linked' to the belief it is manifesting. *Eweida v British Airways* may perhaps be difficult in this respect. Although Eweida wanted to wear a cross visible to others at work as a symbol of her Christian faith, she did not claim this was a strict religious obligation. However, given that it seemed to form part of a commitment to publicly demonstrating her faith, it should be included, as the ECtHR in fact held in *Eweida v UK*. An example which falls on the other side of the line is that of the refusal of some

44 See e.g. D. O'Brien, 'Chant Down Babylon: Freedom of Religion and the Rastafarian Challenge to Majoritarianism' (2002) 18 *J L & Religion* 219.
45 D. Laycock, 'The Remnants of Free Exercise' [1990] *Sup Ct Rev* 1.
46 Ibid., 24.
47 W.F. Sullivan, *The Impossibility of Religious Freedom* (Princeton: Princeton UP, 2005).
48 653 F. Supp. 1510 (D. Neb., 1987).
49 (1978) 19 DR 5.

Quakers to complete the 2011 British census form. They objected because the processing of the data was to be carried out by Lockheed Martin, a company that also manufactures military equipment, and it therefore conflicted with their pacifist views.[50] In this case the obligation to complete the census is too remote from the religious belief in pacifism.

What Lupu calls 'atmospheric burdens'[51] should also not be included. Living in a society that does not generally share your beliefs may make living according to their precepts more difficult, but this does not mean that the failure to change society to conform to your beliefs constitutes an interference with rights. Merely being aware that people have different views on a matter does not interfere with a right even if this causes offence. Therefore, for example, the mere existence of same-sex marriage cannot be an interference with religious rights. In the same way, mere exposure, without more, to religion or to anti-religious views is not an interference.[52]

Finally, although there should not be a strict rule preventing claims from being successful in employment, in truly voluntary situations no interference should be found. For example, if a person joins a university Christian Union, they cannot then complain that the society does not respect their atheist views by praying before each meeting. In this example the free choice to join and leave the society adequately protects freedom of religion.[53] As *Pichon and Sajous* illustrates though, most employment cannot be said to be truly voluntary, especially if circumstances change after an employee begins employment. However, in some circumstances, even in employment, there should not be considered to be an interference. For example, if a person willingly takes on a job when she is aware its *whole* nature conflicts with her conscience, for example the job is to provide Sunday cover or to work in an abortion clinic, she probably cannot accept it and subsequently claim an interference.

While there are therefore some substantive and practical limits on freedom of religion, in general this right should be interpreted broadly. In particular, the fact that the claim arises out of a person's employment should not by itself bar the claim.

What should the right to non-discrimination include?

In addition to prohibiting discrimination by the state itself, as discussed in the Introduction, the right also requires the state to provide legal protection against some kinds of discrimination by private actors.[54] Self-evidently, straightforward discrimination in access to material goods or services amounts to an interference, such as where a benefit is given to heterosexual couples but not to homosexual couples. The right is also interfered with if a gay person does not receive the same treatment even if she receives the same practical benefit. For example, if an official refuses to give a gay couple a wedding licence because of her beliefs but refers the application to a colleague, the couple's rights have still been infringed

50 'Pacifists and the Census Form', *The Guardian*, 30 Jan 2012, available at: http://www.guardian.co.uk/uk/2012/jan/30/pacifists-and-the-census-form <last accessed 20 July 2016>.

51 I. Lupu, 'Where Rights Begin: The Problem of Burdens on the Free Exercise of Religion' (1989) 102 *Harv L Rev* 933.

52 Other country-specific constitutional rules may be relevant though – exposure to religious teachings in state schools may not violate the right to religious freedom but may well violate rules about the separation of church and state.

53 See for opposing views on the efficacy of this right to exit, D. Borchers and A. Vitikainene (eds), *On Exit: Interdisciplinary Perspectives on the Right of Exit in Liberal Multicultural Societies* (Berlin: De Gruyter, 2012) and S. Moller Okin, '"Mistresses of Their Own Destiny": Group Rights, Gender, and Realistic Rights of Exit' (2002) 112 *Ethics* 205.

54 See e.g. *Vriend v Alberta* [1998] 1 SCR 493.

even if the licence is granted without delay.[55] The couple has not received equal treatment since they have not had the opportunity to have the licence granted by any available official, as a heterosexual couple would.

In the same way as atmospheric burdens against religion are not sufficient though, mere disapproval of homosexuality is not sufficient to constitute an interference with rights. It is not an interference to experience social disapprobation, although of course this may lead to sincere and understandable hurt. For example, it cannot be a violation of equality rights, without more, for there to be public and private disapproval of homosexuality or same-sex marriage. This does not mean that harassment or hate speech that is so pervasive that it prevents people from being able to live freely could not be an interference.[56]

However, in addition to protecting against interferences with the right per se, governments may also sometimes legitimately act to promote social harmony and tolerance, even if discriminatory attitudes have not reached the level of an interference with a right. As mentioned in the Introduction, there may be a desire to lessen cultural heterosexism and to promote equality as a matter of public policy. The state may seek to do this by such mechanisms as the Public Sector Equality Duty in British law.[57] This requires public authorities to have due regard for the need to eliminate discrimination, advance equality of opportunity and foster good relations between those who share a protected characteristic and those who do not. All of this is a legitimate purpose for government action, but to fail to do so is not in itself an infringement of a right. Not everything a government does or should do is in order to comply with a right.

There are important distinctions between a right and a public policy. Both can be used to justify infringements of rights. A requirement that all driving licences have a photograph on them even if this is contrary to a person's religious beliefs could, potentially, be outweighed by the public interest in requiring photographs. However, a right has more weight when balanced against another right compared to a public policy.[58] A second and clearer distinction is in the requirement of justification. If a right is infringed, then it must be justified. If the right of non-discrimination is interfered with, then the state has an obligation to demonstrate that this is justified. However, this is not the case if a state merely acts contrary to a policy of non-discrimination.

To summarise then, while the non-discrimination right can be breached if symbolic rather than practical harm is caused, there must be a specific act which is alleged to be discriminatory. However, the state can take broader action as a matter of policy.

Conclusion

At times in ECHR and English law, too much emphasis has been placed on considering whether there has been an interference with the right, rather than whether the state can demonstrate that they have suitable justification for acting in the way they did. This

55 Although not necessarily violated. These issues are discussed in more detail in Ch. 6.

56 In *97 Members of the Gldani Congregation of Jehovah's Witnesses v Georgia* (2008) 46 EHRR 30, a campaign of intimidation against Jehovah's Witnesses, which the authorities did very little to prevent, was held to be a violation of Art. 9. There would presumably have been an interference with Art. 8 (right to respect for private and family life) if this had been aimed at gay people.

57 Equality Act 2010 s.149.

58 M. Klatt and M. Meister, *The Constitutional Structure of Proportionality* (Oxford: Oxford UP, 2012) 26 and F. Schauer, 'Proportionality and the Question of Weight' in Huscroft, Miller and Webber supra n.4. This will be discussed in more detail in the next chapter.

argument, for a broad interpretation of rights, will be supported further in the next chapter. That chapter considers more precisely how to assess whether rights have been violated and how conflicts between rights should be addressed.

Scalia J in *Smith* was convinced that balancing approaches were doomed to turn into anarchy with everyone asserting a right to be free of laws with which they disagreed. It is to the question of balancing, and to a particular type of balancing test, proportionality, that the discussion now turns, and suggests that his fears are unfounded.

5 Proportionality

Chapter 3 concluded that none of the categorical tests outlined there were adequate to adjudicate the complexities of claims involving conflicts between freedom of religion and other rights, in particular the right of non-discrimination. The previous chapter identified that a two-stage process, which first considers whether there has been an interference with the right, and then considers whether this right was violated, was necessary. This chapter examines the second stage of this analysis and proposes proportionality as the best method of deciding whether a right has been violated.

Proportionality lays out a process for deciding cases as well as setting a standard of review. This chapter will first describe in some detail the different parts of the test and then will consider its advantages in the context of resolving conflicts between freedom of religion and non-discrimination. It will be argued that proportionality provides a coherent, principled and advantageous method for resolving these disputes. Throughout this section the problems described in the Introduction should be borne in mind: the difficulty of legislating and deciding cases in situations of social division. The chapter will end with a short description of whether and how proportionality is used in the Canadian, English and US legal systems in order to place the discussion of cases in later chapters in context.

Proportionality: an analysis

The idea of proportionality itself of course has a very long history. Proportionality as a legal doctrine, though, means far more than a general injunction to 'act proportionally'. Proportionality, in the specific sense referred to here, originated as a method of controlling government action in nineteenth-century Prussian administrative law and continued to be important in German law until the rise of the Nazis.[1] After the Second World War, despite no explicit mention of it in the German Basic Law, it became an important part of German constitutional law. Partly due to its use by the European Union and, to a lesser extent, the ECtHR, its use has spread to 'Continental Europe, including Eastern Europe, as well as Latin America, Canada, South Africa, Israel and New Zealand.'[2] Its use is such that it has been referred to as a 'post-war paradigm' of rights analysis.[3] It is notable that such acceptance does not extend to the USA, a situation that will be explored further below.

1 See for a history of proportionality: A. Barak, *Proportionality: Constitutional Rights and their Limitations* (Cambridge: Cambridge UP, 2012) Ch. 7.

2 M. Klatt and M. Meister, *The Constitutional Structure of Proportionality* (Oxford: Oxford UP, 2012) 2.

3 L. Weinrib, 'Postwar Paradigm and American Exceptionalism' in S. Choudhry (ed.), *The Migration of Constitutional Ideas* (Cambridge: Cambridge UP, 2006).

'Proportionality' as a legal test can take a number of forms and there are a number of differences between how it is used between jurisdictions, although all variations contain the same essential elements.[4] The test as set out by Alexy, an influential theorist in this area, in relation to German law is:[5]

1 Suitability: the aim must be capable of achieving the end desired.
2 Necessity: are there any less restrictive but equally effective means of achieving this aim?
3 Proportionality in the narrow sense, involving a balancing exercise.

The English courts have adopted proportionality as the appropriate test for some contexts, and although the test has not always been applied in precisely the same way,[6] all these elements are present. Thus a measure will be considered to be proportionate if:

1 The legislative objective is sufficiently important to justify limiting a fundamental right.
2 The measures designed to meet the legislative objective are rationally connected to it (which corresponds to the suitability part of Alexy's test).
3 The means used to impair the right or freedom are no more than is necessary to accomplish the objective[7] (which corresponds to the necessity part of Alexy's test).

To this, the House of Lords later added an overall consideration of whether the measure is proportionate, balancing the rights of the individual against the needs of society, thus incorporating the third part of Alexy's test.[8]

The Canadian test, though, is slightly different.[9] The test as laid down by the Supreme Court in *R v Oakes*[10] is:

1 There must be a substantial aim of 'sufficient importance to warrant overriding a constitutionality protected right … an objective [must] relate to concerns which are pressing and substantial'.
2 There must be a rational connection between the aim and the restriction of the right.
3 The means must be carefully designed to achieve the aim and should impair the right or freedom as little as possible.
4 Proportionality itself: does the objective justify the restrictions on the right?

Greater weight appears to be placed on the first step of legitimate aim than in Alexy's test. In its German incarnation, questions as to the appropriate balance between the rights and interests are left to the end of the process. The differences between these tests will be explored further below. However, despite the minor variations between the tests, they all

4 J. Bomhoff, 'Genealogies of Balancing as Discourse' (2010) 4 *Law & Ethics of Human Rights* 107.
5 R. Alexy, *A Theory of Constitutional Rights*, tr. J. Rivers (Oxford: Oxford UP, 2002).
6 See discussion in *R(Lumsdon) v Legal Services Board* [2016] AC 697 for the differences in use between cases involving EU law and those involving fundamental rights.
7 *De Freitas v Permanent Secretary of Ministry of Agriculture, Fisheries, Lands and Housing* [1999] 1 AC 69.
8 *Huang v Secretary of State for the Home Department* [2007] 2 AC 167.
9 D. Grimm, 'Proportionality in Canadian and German Constitutional Jurisprudence' (2007) 57 *U Toronto LJ* 383.
10 [1986] 1 SCR 103.

contain the same essential elements and so the various parts of the proportionality test will be referred to as legitimate aim; rational connection; no less restrictive means; and, finally, balancing. Each of these aspects will now be analysed in detail.

Legitimate aim

The first question under a proportionality test is whether there was a legitimate aim in infringing the right. If the aim was not legitimate then the right will have been violated. Some legitimate aims can be found explicitly in the constitution or other law granting the right. Thus under the ECHR, the right to manifest a religion or belief may be restricted on the basis of public safety, the protection of public order, health or morals,[11] or the protection of the rights and freedoms of others. Aims may also be implicit. In Canada, rights granted by the Charter may be subject to such reasonable limits prescribed by law as can be demonstrably justified in a free and democratic society. Whether something is a legitimate aim is a moral question which relies for answers on the constitutional or legal morality of a state and more generally on the morality inherent in a liberal democratic society.

The Canadian test as laid down in *Oakes* states that an objective must always be 'pressing and substantial'; a formulation which is not in the German or English model. It is far from clear why an objective must necessarily always be so. The interference may be minimal or unimportant.[12] Indeed, in later cases there appears to be a relaxation of the test, with an appreciation that the standard will vary according to the particular case. Trakman points out that the objective put forward was considered to meet this test in 97 per cent of the cases involving s.1 considered by the Supreme Court of Canada.[13] Despite the terms of the test then, the difference therefore seems to be 'merely semantic'.[14]

In many of the cases discussed in the next few chapters, finding a legitimate aim will be straightforward since the aim will be to protect a right of another party, whether this is non-discrimination or the right to manifest religious beliefs. In some cases, though, the aim will be not to directly protect a right, but for example, to promote equality or tolerance more generally. This can potentially still be legitimate since the aim is to provide a better environment for the protection of rights or to create a more harmonious society.[15] Public policy, as well as opposing rights, can potentially amount to justifications for infringing rights and, as discussed in the previous chapter, the public policy of preventing discrimination is broader than the right of non-discrimination.[16]

Tolerance, in the sense of putting up with behaviour or expression thought wrong or immoral, is an essential part of a liberal democratic society. However, this does not mean that it would be legitimate to require everyone to be 'inclusive' and 'non-judgemental'.[17] That there must be limits to this being a legitimate aim becomes clearer when it is considered that promoting tolerance is closely linked to preventing offence. In a pluralistic

11 The inclusion of morals on this list may be problematic though. This is discussed further below.
12 P. Blache, 'The Criteria of Justification under *Oakes:* Too Much Severity Generated Through Formalism' (1991) 20 *Man LJ* 437.
13 L. Trakman et al., '*R. v Oakes* 1986–1997: Back to the Drawing Board' (1998) 36 *Osgoode Hall LJ* 83, 95.
14 Grimm supra n.9, 389.
15 Barak supra n.1, Ch. 9.
16 To put it another way, there is a distinction between the 'sword' of the right of non-discrimination and the 'shield' of non-discrimination as public policy.
17 F. Furedi, *On Tolerance: A Defence of Moral Independence* (London: Continuum, 2011) 7.

multicultural society perhaps one of the few certainties is that almost any act could be potentially offensive to somebody.

There is an unjustified criticism sometimes made of proportionality that it is not sufficiently protective of rights because it permits offence to be used as a reason for outweighing a right. Cram criticises balancing tests, especially in the way they have been used by the ECtHR, because he argues they mean that everything, including offence, becomes 'eligible to be put on the scales'.[18] Similarly, Tsakyrakis points to the ECtHR's application of the proportionality test in *Otto-Preminger-Institut v Austria*,[19] where the court held that preventing religious offence was sufficient justification for interference with freedom of expression. *Otto Preminger* involved the seizure and confiscation of a film, *Das Liebeskonzil*, that was due to be shown in an art house cinema. The film was based on a nineteenth-century play which had been banned by the Austrian government and the author found guilty of 'crimes against religion'. In the words of the ECtHR the play 'portrays God the Father as old, infirm and ineffective, Jesus Christ as a "mummy's boy" of low intelligence and the Virgin Mary, who is obviously in charge, as an unprincipled wanton.' God, Jesus and Mary plot with the devil to create syphilis in order to punish humans for their immorality and the devil's daughter spreads the disease 'among those who represent worldly power, then to the court of the Pope, to the bishops, to the convents and monasteries and finally to the common people'. The majority of the ECtHR held that the interference with freedom of expression was justified on the basis of the rights of others. Three judges dissented, but they too held that the Austrian authorities had a legitimate aim in protecting the rights of others. They did though find the state's actions to be disproportionate, particularly as children were prohibited from seeing the film and those attending had warning of its subject matter.

However, as Kai Möller points out, proportionality should be judged according to its best possible version and not merely on how it has been assessed by a court on one occasion.[20] It is perfectly possible to accept proportionality as a test but to argue that it has been applied improperly in a particular case. Importantly, proportionality requires an aim to be *legitimate*. Not every aim that is put forward by a government must be accepted. In *Otto-Preminger-Institut* the real question therefore was whether the offence the showing of the film would have caused should have been sufficient to amount to a legitimate aim for the state's actions. Even given the majority's argument that the film was due to be shown in an area with a strongly Catholic population, there are strong reasons for arguing that it should not. Tsakyrakis correctly argues that, under the test identified by the ECtHR, if a majority of the Tyrolese hated Eskimos and felt 'violent feelings of moral indignation and uncontrollable fear' whenever Eskimo films are screened, these feelings would have to be taken into account if offence were sufficient.[21] It would mean that rights could be curtailed on the basis of 'the standards of some of the least tolerant, most easily outraged members of society.'[22] As the minority said in *Otto Preminger*, 'There is no point in guaranteeing [freedom of expression] only as long as it is used in accordance with accepted opinion.' Allowing expression to be prohibited

18 I. Cram, 'The Danish Cartoons, Offensive Expression, and Democratic Legitimacy' in I. Hare and J. Weinstein, *Extreme Speech and Democracy* (Oxford: Oxford UP, 2010) 316.

19 (1995) 19 EHRR 34.

20 Klatt and Meister also analyse the case from the perspective of proportionality. They come to the conclusion that there was a legitimate aim, but argue that the case fails at the proportionality stage: Klatt and Meister supra n.2.

21 S. Tsakyrakis, 'Proportionality: An Assault on Human Rights?' (2009) 7 *ICON* 468, 482.

22 Cram supra n.18, 322. See also J. Feinberg, *The Moral Limits of the Criminal Law – Volume 2: Offense to Others* (New York: Oxford UP, 1985) Ch. 9.

on the basis of offence prevents the public discussion of ideas, meaning that the marketplace of ideas cannot operate.[23] Given also that offence is so subjective and variable from one person to another because it depends on a person's emotional state, it is imprecise.

While Tsakyrakis is right to criticise the case, his argument is misconceived as a criticism of proportionality itself since it only demonstrates that offence should not be treated as a legitimate aim. The 'definitional generosity'[24] used to define rights under a proportionality approach does not, as Tsakyakris believes, require acceptance that freedom of religion must be defined so broadly so as to include a right not to be offended. Art. 9 certainly does not guarantee respect for religious feelings but only the right to believe and to manifest this belief. Mere criticism of beliefs, however deep the hurt caused, is not sufficient to interfere with this right. The ECtHR in *Otto Preminger* wrongly applied the proportionality test by not paying sufficient attention to the requirement of legitimate aim. The government's attempted justification should have been rejected at this point. However, this error does not affect the validity of the proportionality test itself.

Nevertheless, there may be good reason, partly in order to promote social harmony, to allow restrictions of some kinds of offensive acts (although of course any restriction would still have to pass the other elements of the proportionality test). There may be a legitimate aim in prohibiting some expression on the basis of the harm caused to others. Prohibiting actual attempts at intimidation of those who share particular beliefs or who have a particular sexual orientation is a legitimate aim. Not to do so may make the right of freedom of religion or to live in accordance with one's sexual orientation illusory.[25] Furthermore, there is potentially a legitimate state interest in prohibiting some kinds of discriminatory expression, even if it does not reach this level.[26]

An example of where there was a legitimate aim in prohibiting hate speech is *Vejdeland v Sweden*.[27] In that case, four men were convicted for placing leaflets in a school. The leaflets called homosexuality a 'deviant sexual proclivity' which had a 'morally destructive effect on the substance of society' and stated that homosexuals were responsible for the spread of HIV and AIDS and that 'homosexual lobby organisations' played down paedophilia and wanted to legalise it.

The difficulty, of course, is deciding what kinds of restriction are legitimate. Given that the concept of offence does not provide adequate guidance, because it is placed at too low a level and is subjective and variable, another criterion is required. Waldron argues for an approach which focuses on the idea of dignity, rather than offensiveness. He points out that hate speech is not merely offensive but 'attacks a shared sense of the basic elements of each person's status, dignity and reputation as a citizen or member of society in good standing.'[28] He argues this is more clearly understandable if we refer to such expression not as hate

23 See for discussion of this idea: E. Barendt, *Freedom of Speech*, 2nd ed. (Oxford: Oxford UP, 2005); S. Ingber, 'The Marketplace of Ideas: A Legitimizing Myth' (1984) *Duke LJ* 1; F. Schauer, *Free Speech: A Philosophical Enquiry* (Cambridge: Cambridge UP, 1982); P. Wragg, 'Mill's Dead Dogma: The Value of Truth to Free Speech Jurisprudence' [2013] *PL* 363.

24 Tsakyrakis, supra n.21, 482, 488.

25 *97 Members of the Gldani Congregation of Jehovah's Witnesses v Georgia* (2008) 46 EHRR 30; *Karaahmed v Bulgaria* [2015] ECHR 217; see *Identoba and Others v Georgia* (App No. 73235/12) (12 May 2015) and *M.C. and C.A. v Romania* (application no. 12060/12) (12 April 2015).

26 As discussed in Chapter 2, US law is the only jurisdiction discussed here which does not permit hate speech laws, on the basis that these are illegitimate viewpoint restrictions.

27 Application no. 1813/07 (9th Feb 2012).

28 J. Waldron, *The Harm in Hate Speech* (Cambridge, Mass: Harvard UP, 2012) 47.

speech, since this makes the problem appear to be the subjective emotion of the speaker rather than the effect it has on those it is aimed at, but instead to the idea of group libel and the protection of 'the basics of each person's reputation'. By focusing on fundamental obligations to individuals, rather than offence, Waldron's approach better encompasses the type of harm that is at issue. Although a vague concept, the protection of dignity is clearly relevant and important to the protection of human rights.[29]

The expression at issue in *Vejdeland* is evidently extremely offensive, particularly bearing in mind its unauthorised distribution in a non-public place and its intended teenage audience. But more importantly, it also undermined the dignity of gay people in a way in which the film at issue in *Otto-Preminger Institut* did not of Catholics. While differing opinions on whether or not something is immoral, even something as important as sexuality, do not intrinsically deny a person's dignity or good standing in society, the abusive statements in *Vejdeland* went far beyond this.

While preventing mere offence is not a legitimate aim and neither the right of freedom of religion or non-discrimination include a right not to be confronted with criticism, it should be noted that there may be other legitimate aims in some situations involving offensive speech or actions. Employers, for example, may have legitimate interests in controlling the actions of their employees at work in order to maintain efficiency or to promote their own ethos.

These restrictions on what counts as a legitimate aim protect both sides in this context to some degree. As the ECtHR said in *Dudgeon v UK*,[30] 'although members of the public who regard homosexuality as immoral may be shocked, offended or disturbed by the commission by others of private homosexual acts, this cannot on its own warrant the application of penal sanctions when it is consenting adults alone who are involved.'[31] Similarly, preventing all religiously based discussion or teaching opposed to homosexuality, same-sex sexual activity or legal rights for gay people in order to prevent offence would not be legitimate. As was held in relation to the Equality Act (Sexual Orientation) Regulations (Northern Ireland) 2006 in *Re Christian Institute*,[32] it is important to consider that such speech may involve the manifestation of a religious belief. The Court there held that there had been a failure to consider the danger that 'explanations of sincerely held doctrinal beliefs'[33] could breach the Regulations as they stood at the time.

The requirement of a legitimate aim also gives some protection against discrimination since 'a law whose only purpose is to discriminate is not for a proper purpose'.[34] This is particularly clear if the discrimination is on a constitutionally protected ground, but applies beyond this. An important word in the sentence quoted is 'only'. A law providing for affirmative action for marginalised ethnic minorities in jobs where they are under-represented discriminates on the basis of race, but is not designed for the purpose of discrimination. Its purposes are social inclusion, ameliorating historic injustices and so on. That a law's purpose is only to discriminate can be implicit in its terms. The US case of *Romer v Evans*[35] is such an example. An amendment to the Constitution of the State of Colorado prohibited all

29 See generally for a discussion of how the concept of dignity can be used in the discussion of human rights, C. McCrudden (ed), *Understanding Human Dignity* (Oxford: Oxford UP, 2013).
30 (1982) 4 EHRR 149.
31 Ibid., 167.
32 [2008] IRLR 36.
33 Ibid., para 40.
34 Barak supra n.1, 251.
35 517 US 620 (1996).

legislative, executive or judicial action which 'entitle[d] any person or class of persons to have or claim any minority status, quota preferences, protected status or claim of discrimination' on the basis of sexual orientation. Kennedy J held that 'laws of the kind now before us raise the inevitable inference that the disadvantage imposed is born of animosity toward the class of persons affected ... a desire to harm a politically unpopular group cannot constitute a *legitimate* governmental interest'.[36] Such a reason violates the principle of equal respect owed to all in a liberal democracy. This idea is sometimes referred to within US constitutional law as a prohibition on acting due to animus.[37]

This idea was applied more recently in *United States v Windsor*,[38] which, as discussed in Chapter 2, struck down the Defense of Marriage Act (DOMA), which had prohibited the recognition of same-sex marriages for any federal purpose. It was challenged by a woman who had to pay estate taxes on her wife's death which she would not have had to had she been married to a man, even though her marriage was legally recognised in the state, New York, that she was resident in. Kennedy J, giving the judgment of the Court, argued that, 'the purpose and practical effect of the law ... are to impose a disadvantage, a separate status, and so a stigma upon all who enter into same-sex marriages' and found that this purpose was the 'essence' of the statute. The act was found to be unconstitutional on this and other bases.

Steven Smith argues that this means that Justice Kennedy was accusing 'Congress – and, by implication, millions of Americans – of acting from pure malevolence' and by doing so aggravated the culture wars problem by making accusations 'normally associated with irresponsible and scurrilous pseudonymous comments on marginal political blogs'.[39] It is open to question whether Justice Kennedy was really suggesting that members of Congress or its supporters were acting purely as a result of malevolence.[40] However, it is understandable why the use of the word 'animus' or the phrase 'a bare desire to harm' may suggest this. It seems likely that the reason why many members of Congress voted for DOMA, and why it received public support, is because many had religious objections to defining marriage as being other than between a man and a woman. Saying that this is an illegitimate reason for the state to act does not equate to saying that anyone who believes this is bigoted or animated by hatred, rather than by a genuine concern for what they believe to be the best interests of individuals or society at large. This point is though more readily understandable and respectful if the terminology used is that of 'legitimate aim' rather than 'animus', because 'animus' has more negative and emotionally based connotations. 'Animus' also suggests that what is important is the subjective intent of those legislating. What really matters though is whether a valid aim can be put forward for the legislation, regardless of whether this was the actual intent of those legislating.[41]

36 Ibid. at 634 (emphasis in original).

37 See generally, D. Hellman, 'The Expressive Dimension of Equal Protection' (2000) 85 *Minn L Rev* 1.

38 570 US ___ (2013)

39 S. Smith, 'The Jurisprudence of Denigration' (2014) 48 *UC Davis LR* 675. But see A. Koppelman, 'Beyond Levels of Scrutiny: *Windsor* and "Bare Desire to Harm"' (2014) 64 *Case W Res L Rev* 1.

40 Although the dissenting judgment of Roberts CJ in *Windsor* suggests this.

41 See Möller's discussion of *Smith and Grady v UK* (2000) 29 EHRR 493 in 'Proportionality: Challenging the Critics' (2012) 10 *ICON* 709. However, in the cases dealing with Sunday closing laws it appears that Canadian courts would only consider the aim of the legislation at the time it was enacted, as Mary Anne Waldron points out in *Free to Believe: Rethinking Freedom of Conscience and Belief in Canada* (Toronto: University of Toronto Press, 2013). See *R v Big M Drug Mart Ltd* [1985] 1 SCR 295.

In considering what counts as a legitimate aim, further difficult questions arise over when it is legitimate to enforce morality, or what Perry has referred to as 'protecting moral truth'.[42] Notably, Art. 9 ECtHR refers to the protection of 'public morals' as a possible basis for the restriction of rights. This is though problematic. It is of course true that governments are motivated to act for moral reasons. The political answer that something must be prevented or done 'because this is wrong' is likely to be the case for a whole range of laws and policies from international development to laws prohibiting child pornography. In fact, it would be concerning if government action were not taken for moral purposes. Therefore, by their very nature governments constantly demonstrate moral values. As Greenawalt argues, by going to war a country rejects the religious view that all killing violates God's wishes and by providing higher education equally to men and women rejects the religious view that women should 'occupy themselves with domestic tasks'.[43] These principles may well be rejected explicitly as well, for example in state education. This, though, is not illegitimate for a number of reasons.

First, the government does not go to war in order to demonstrate the wrongness of a moral or religious view. As before, this discussion is only relevant if it *only* involves 'moral disagreements that do not implicate a legitimate governmental interest'.[44] If there are other reasons a government can point to, the fact that moral concerns are involved is irrelevant. For this reason, the restriction on enforcing morality is not applicable where actual harm would otherwise be caused. If harm will be directly or indirectly caused to another person, then preventing it will always be a legitimate aim. For example, sexual orientation discrimination might be outlawed because of a feeling that such discrimination is wrong. The reason why it is considered wrong is a moral reason: that homosexuality is a morally neutral trait, or at least that its wrongness is so minor that it does not justify discrimination. None of this, though, means that the state is impermissibly acting for moral reasons; the state acts to prevent harm caused by that discrimination. Second, in these kinds of situations the government action only places 'atmospheric burdens' on the belief. It does not coerce belief or behaviour. Atmospheric burdens are not sufficient to constitute an interference with a right. Finally, because this is simply an inevitable part of governing, it cannot be a violation.

However, the prohibition on acting to enforce morality does mean that the purpose of 'promoting a Christian way of life', for example, would be illegitimate.[45] This is another facet to the importance of the right to freedom of conscience. As Kumm puts it, 'it is not within the jurisdiction of public authorities to prescribe what the ultimate orientations and commitments of an individual should be.'[46] Preventing 'moral harm', that is the idea that certain behaviour is harmful to the 'moral health' of participants, would also not be a legitimate aim.

None of this means that religious exemptions to non-discrimination laws are necessarily illegitimate. Crucially they have the aim not of advancing religion: the type of religious belief in question is usually irrelevant. Instead their aim is to advance religious freedom, and therefore promote, rather than prevent, freedom of thought and conscience. Furthermore, this

42 M. Perry, *The Political Morality of Liberal Democracy* (Cambridge: Cambridge UP, 2010).

43 K. Greenawalt, 'Five Questions about Religion Judges are Afraid to Ask' in N. Rosenblum (ed.), *Obligations of Citizenship and Demands of Faith: Religious Accommodation in Pluralist Democracies* (Princeton: Princeton UP, 2000).

44 Perry supra n.42, 93.

45 M. Kumm, 'Political Liberalism and the Structure of Rights' in G. Pavlakos (ed.), *Law, Rights and Discourse* (Oxford: Hart Publishing, 2007) 142–6.

46 Ibid. Perry similarly argues that if the state were allowed to legislate on the basis of morality, it would take away the right to moral freedom; Perry supra n.42. See also R. Dworkin, 'Liberalism' in *A Matter of Principle* (Cambridge: Cambridge UP, 1985).

discussion does not mean that only precise tangible harms can be taken into account. The state can also legitimately aim to prevent symbolic harm. Take, for example, the situation where an employee objects to performing an aspect of their job for discriminatory reasons, such as providing a particular service to gay people, and seeks an exemption from doing so from their employer, as arose in the English cases of *Ladele*[47] and *McFarlane*.[48] If granting an exemption would not affect the service provided because the work would be rearranged among other employees, this causes no tangible harm. However, an employer would still have a legitimate aim in preventing such harm, beyond the practical disruption in rearranging work. This is because the employee is seeking to directly discriminate. Even where this does not cause practical harm, symbolic harm is caused in the denial of formal equality. Preventing symbolic harm can be a legitimate aim.

To summarise, in most situations there will be an obvious legitimate aim, in the present context usually protecting the rights of others. However, this should certainly not be considered a merely formal stage. It is illegitimate to act to prevent mere offence and to enforce morality where the rights of others are not affected.

Rational connection

The second part of the proportionality test is that of rational connection or suitability. This is a fairly weak factual test: is the measure capable of advancing the legitimate aim put forward for it?[49] It does not require that the measure completely fulfil the purpose or matter that another measure might fulfil the aim more efficiently. This is similar to rational basis review, which is the least searching of the types of review in US law. It only requires that a law is rationally related to a legitimate government purpose and is used when a fundamental right or suspect classification is not in issue. In some cases, there may be arguments between the parties as to whether or not a measure does in fact advance the aim. Some discretion will be given to the government but the amount is likely to depend on the nature of the policy question and the kind of uncertainty in question.[50]

In practice, cases are not likely to fail at this stage. A rare example of a case which did was *Benner v Canada (Secretary of State)*.[51] The citizenship rules for children born before 1977 meant that the child of a Canadian father or unmarried mother who was born abroad could acquire Canadian citizenship at birth. The child of a married Canadian mother had to apply for citizenship. This process included swearing an oath of allegiance and passing criminal and security checks. Benner had serious criminal convictions and was denied citizenship. The legitimate aim claimed was to help ensure the safety of Canadian citizens, which was clearly legitimate. However, this had no rational connection to a discriminatory policy: there was no reason why the children of Canadian mothers would pose more of a risk than the children of Canadian fathers.[52] While failure at this stage may be rare, it nevertheless has an important role in weeding out proffered justifications.

47 [2010] 1 WLR 955.
48 [2010] EWCA Civ 880.
49 R. Alexy, 'Constitutional Rights, Balancing and Rationality' (2003) 16 *Ratio Juris* 131.
50 Grimm supra n.9, 390.
51 [1997] 1 SCR 358.
52 This policy existed for historical reasons: originally only fathers could pass citizenship on to their children. The law was then amended to somewhat remedy this. However, as Kumm argues: 'traditions, conventions and preferences' cannot be used as legitimate aims unless they are linked to 'a plausible policy concern'. (M. Kumm, 'The Idea of Socratic Contestation and the Right to

No less restrictive means

The third issue is that of necessity or no less restrictive means. Canadian law diverts at this stage from the approach taken by many other jurisdictions which also use proportionality. Under the German approach, which has been extremely influential, a measure will be 'necessary' if there is no other measure which would impair the right to a lesser degree while equally fulfilling the conflicting purpose. Under the test laid down in Canadian law in *Oakes*, though, this is a more difficult hurdle. The question is whether the 'means is carefully designed to achieve the aim and to impair the right or freedom as little as possible'.[53]

This test is set at a high level and is where most cases have failed, rather than at the balancing stage, as is the case in Germany and those jurisdictions such as England which have followed it.[54] The question is whether this difference is advantageous. Under the *Oakes* test, the minimal impairment test includes some of the balancing considerations dealt with under the final proportionality test in other jurisdictions. It has therefore been criticised as 'evolv[ing] into a repository for under-articulated normative choices that should properly be explained under the proportional effects branch'.[55]

Davidov points to *Eldridge v British Columbia*[56] as an example of where the courts have used balancing considerations under cover of the minimal impairment test.[57] The case concerned the failure of the government to provide sign-language interpreters in hospitals, thus negatively affecting deaf patients' ability to access medical care. Whether this failure was justified by the, relatively small, cost to the government is a question of balancing. The Court, though, treated it as a question of minimal impairment. They held that the objective of 'controlling health care expenditures' could be protected even if sign-language interpreters were provided. This ducks the important point that the objective was not protected to the same extent: it evidently cost more to provide the interpreters than not. The real question is whether this cost is a sufficient reason to deny providing them.

Under the German form of the test, though, it is up to the state to decide what level of achievement of the purpose it wishes to attain.[58] If there is another measure which would interfere with the right less but not equally fulfil the purpose, then the measure will not fail this test.[59] Although it therefore requires consideration of hypothetical solutions, the

Justification: The Point of Rights-Based Proportionality Review' (2010) 4 *Law & Ethics of Human Rights* 141, 159). Security reasons were all that was left for the Canadian government.

53 [1986] 1 SCR 103, 139.

54 Trakman supra n.13.

55 Ibid., 102. Miller points out that only one Canadian case has been resolved at the overall balancing stage, suggesting the comparative importance of the no less restrictive means test: B. Miller, 'Proportionality's Blind Spot: "Neutrality" and Political Philosophy' in G. Huscroft, B.W. Miller and G. Webber (eds), *Proportionality and the Rule of Law: Rights, Justification, Reasoning* (Cambridge: Cambridge UP, 2014) 383.

56 [1997] 3 SCR 624.

57 G. Davidov, 'Separating Minimal Impairment from Balancing: A Comment on *R v Sharpe (B.C. C.A)*' (2000) 5 *Rev Const Stud* 195.

58 J. Rivers, 'Proportionality, Discretion and the Second Law of Balancing' in G. Pavlakos (ed.), *Law, Rights and Discourse* (Oxford: Hart Publishing, 2007).

59 Alexy, supra n.5, 397–401. However, Bilchitz argues that this test is too strict because it will usually be easy to think of an alternative which would be as effective but less restrictive of rights: D. Bilchitz 'Necessity and Proportionality: Towards a Balanced Approach' in *Reasoning Rights: Comparative Judicial Engagement* (Oxford: Hart Publishing, 2014). I am unconvinced that it is as easy as he argues, as the fact that in the majority of cases under the German model this stage is easily passed suggests.

distinctive part of the necessity test is that it examines whether there are less restrictive means for achieving the aim to the *same extent*. It is not about weighing up the pros and cons of different policies. Given this, it is best to keep the no less restrictive means test separate from the proportionality stage as occurs under the German approach. Often there are policies which would achieve the aim less well, but which create a lesser infringement of a right. Which one is chosen is a matter for the original decision-maker (although of course all policies must also be proportionate in the strict sense). This stage does not require a cost-benefit analysis of policies which affect the purpose to differing degrees. It therefore differs from a test of reasonable accommodation, which would require such an analysis in the consideration of whether any alternative less restrictive policies would be reasonable.[60] The existence of other policies which are not as effective, but are less rights-restrictive, may though be relevant for the final balancing test.

Under either formulation, this test is aimed at the problem of over-inclusivity. However, it does not prohibit over-inclusiveness if this is necessary to fulfil the purpose. If because of impossible difficulties of administration it is only possible to be under- or over-inclusive, over-inclusivity is permitted. For example, security measures at airports such as body and luggage scanners are aimed at preventing terrorist and other attacks. Since there is no way, a priori, to fully distinguish those who are intent on committing such acts from others, such a policy must be necessarily over-inclusive and there is no less restrictive means that can be used.

The no less restrictive means test is therefore an important part of the proportionality test, but it should be distinguished in purpose from the final balancing test. For that reason, the German rather than Canadian form of the test should be used.

Balancing

The balancing stage is usually the most important part of the proportionality test and refers to a precise mechanism for resolving conflicts of rights. Alexy gives a detailed analysis of how it should be carried out. The most important aspect of this is his Law of Balancing, which states that 'the greater the degree of non-satisfaction of, or detriment to, one principle, the greater must be the importance of satisfying the other.'[61] Thus the more a right is infringed, the more justification there must be for doing so.[62] Essentially then, the concept requires the extent and seriousness of the interference to be balanced against the importance of the conflicting interests and prohibits measures that impose a disproportionate burden.

Klatt and Meister, drawing on Alexy's work, argue that there are three stages to the balancing process. These are:

1. Establishing the degree of infringement with a right;
2. Establishing the importance of satisfying the competing right or public interest;
3. Establishing whether or not the importance of satisfying the competing right or interest justifies the infringement.[63]

60 For this reason, I would suggest that Erica Howard's argument that this part of the indirect discrimination test is the same as a reasonable accommodation test is mistaken, given that the test is more limited and has a different purpose. See E. Howard, 'Reasonable Accommodation of Religion and Other Discrimination Grounds in EU Law' (2013) *E L Rev* 360.

61 Alexy supra n.5, 102.

62 Rivers supra n.58.

63 Klatt and Meister, supra n.2, 57.

In establishing the degree of the infringement with the right, Alexy distinguishes between light, moderate and serious interferences. There is though, as he states, no necessary reason for a triadic scale, other than ease of use compared to a more complex one.[64] Therefore, while I will consider the degree of infringement of the right when discussing specific cases, I will not assign a precise category to the level of interference, because this is artificial as the categories really represent points on a sliding scale. The second stage requires assessment not only of the importance of the aim, but also how likely it is that the consequences sought to be avoided will result. In considering this, Alexy's Second Law of Balancing comes into play. This states that 'the more heavily an interference in a constitutional right weighs, the greater must be the certainty of its underlying premises'.[65] At the third stage, these two considerations are balanced against each other. Balancing in this context therefore clearly means 'ad hoc' rather than 'categorical balancing'.[66] That is, the enquiry is not about whether a right or principle is more important than another in general, but which right is more important in this specific context. For example, the right to life is generally considered more important than the right to respect for a family life, but it may not be in a specific situation. The balancing test therefore is only concerned with marginal benefits and disbenefits – the marginal decrease in the right compared to the marginal increase in the opposing interest or right.

While balancing is an essential part of the proportionality test, the metaphor of balancing should not be taken too far. Unlike the necessity test which is mainly factual, the balancing test is strongly normative.[67] There is no common metric against which the two interests are balanced. It is not like judging 'whether a particular line is longer than a particular rock is heavy'.[68] Rather, it is about assessing 'normative considerations of comparative importance.'[69]

We have now addressed each aspect of the proportionality test: legitimate aim, rational connection, no less restrictive means and proportionality itself. Each stage raises different issues and must be considered in turn. Only if a policy passes all four stages will it be considered proportionate. With this mind, we will now turn to the advantages of proportionality.

Proportionality and conflicts between freedom of religion and non-discrimination

There is a large and growing literature about the benefits or otherwise of proportionality.[70] The discussion here will primarily discuss its benefits for the present context of the relationship between freedom of religion and non-discrimination, although more general advantages of proportionality will also be considered.

64 Alexy supra n.5, 408.
65 Ibid., 418.
66 S. Evans and A. Stone Sweet, '*Balancing and Proportionality: A Distinctive Ethic?*', Paper given at VIIth World Congress of the International Association of Constitutional Law, Athens, 11–15 June 2007.
67 J. Rivers, 'Proportionality and Variable Intensity of Review' (2006) 65 *CLJ* 174.
68 Scalia J in *Bendix Autolite Corp. v Midwesco Enterprises* 486 US 888, 897 (1988).
69 Evans and Stone Sweet supra n.66, 4.
70 See in particular: D. Beatty, *The Ultimate Rule of Law* (Oxford: Oxford UP, 2004); Barak supra n.1; Möller supra n.5; G. Webber, *The Negotiable Constitution: On the Limitation of Rights* (Cambridge: Cambridge UP, 2009).

Conflicting claims

This discussion starts on the basis, as discussed in the Introduction, that both sides' claims have value, but also that this issue is often characterised by distrust and animosity, amounting in some cases to a 'culture war', where neither side is likely to give up its demands or to reach an accommodation.

Even if both sides' claims are legitimate, this of course does not mean that they should necessarily be accorded equal weight in a particular case. Even though there is legitimacy in the claim to live in accordance with one's religious beliefs, that does not necessarily mean that a service provider may discriminate when providing a general service which is not obviously 'sexualised'.[71] Similarly, the claim not to be discriminated against has value but will probably not be accepted where a religious organisation wants to discriminate in appointing its religious leaders. We are left therefore in a situation of opposing valuable but varying claims. What is clear is that views of the morality of homosexuality have changed and are continuing to change. Also in flux is the role of religion in society.[72]

The problem of drawing categorical tests which only protect non-discrimination or religious freedom rights in strictly defined categories, rather than on the particular circumstances of the situation, has already been demonstrated. In contrast, under proportionality, the aim is to 'optimise' rights: to give the greatest protection of a right that is compatible with the protection of other rights. Importantly, rights like non-discrimination or freedom of religion are not all or nothing rules, but rather are principles that can be satisfied to varying degrees. Given that these rights compete, neither can be applied fully. But where a decision is taken to protect one rather than the other, this does not mean either 'that the outweighed principle is invalid nor that it has to have an exception built into it'.[73] Rather, one right outweighs the other, according to its weight *in the particular circumstances.*

Proportionality is therefore ideally suited for deciding these cases. It can provide a structure within which to fairly adjudicate complex and variable decisions and also reduce tensions, thereby lessening the culture wars problem.

Proportionality as fact- and case-specific

One of the primary advantages of proportionality is that it is context-specific and fact-specific. The fact that these decisions are complex and variable means that a categorical rule is likely to fail to address the different nuances between them, as has been demonstrated. As both claims have value, it is not appropriate for one always to win over another. The question of whether freedom of religion is more important than freedom from discrimination is not one that can be answered in the abstract, but rather only in relation to a particular problem. As Samuels has pointed out, proportionality requires contexualised reasoning,

71 C.F. Stychin, 'Faith in the Future: Sexuality, Religion and the Public Sphere' (2009) 29 *OJLS* 729, 750.

72 The literature on this is vast. See e.g. G. Davie, 'Religion in Europe in the 21st Century: The Factors to Take into Account' (2006) 47 *European Journal of Sociology* 271; G. Davie, *Religion in Britain: A Persistent Paradox* (2nd ed.) (Oxford: Wiley-Blackwell, 2015); R. Sandberg, *Religion, Law and Society* (Cambridge: Cambridge UP, 2014); L. Woodhead and R. Catto (eds), *Religion and Change in Modern Britain* (Abingdon: Routledge, 2012).

73 Alexy supra n.5, 50.

which 'moves away from the idea of rights as individualistic fixed entitlements that trump other considerations.'[74]

The proportionality test is not about whether a right generally is more important than another as it only leads to a judgment for a particular fact situation.[75] Even then the enquiry is kept within strict bounds, since it only asks whether the marginal benefit of a particular measure is sufficient compared to the interference caused by the measure.[76] Such an approach not only highlights the actual dispute in issue, but this narrow focus also itself helps to reduce tension. Negotiation theory draws attention to the benefits of 'fractionating' conflicts. If conflicts over a large issue, here say the role and position of religion in society, can be broken down into smaller issues, progress is more likely.[77]

The opposite can also be true: too expansive a judgment can also spark severe tensions where these were manageable before. Nussbaum refers to an extreme example in the reaction to a case in India involving the rights of Muslim women to receive maintenance after divorce beyond the period of *iddat* recognised in Islamic law.[78] The Supreme Court judgment not only awarded the claimant maintenance but the (Hindu) Chief Justice interpreted Islamic sacred texts and criticised Islamic practices. This led to widespread protest, some violent, and its political use by Hindu fundamentalists to criticise Islam.[79] This is of course an unusual case, but the possibility of issues being used in such a way remains.

Part of the 'culture wars' problem is that one small decision becomes a marker for whether the courts, and by extension the whole of the governmental and political system, accepts or rejects an entire way of thinking. However, under proportionality, a case can stand for only its own facts and not as a symbol for an entire cultural disagreement. Beatty refers to an Israeli case, *Horev v Minister of Transportation,*[80] as a possible example of this.[81] The issue was whether traffic could be banned in an ultra-Orthodox street on the Sabbath. Barak J, who has subsequently written a great deal extra judicially about proportionality, used an extremely fact-specific proportionality analysis to resolve the case. He argued that if the street was closed all that would be required from non-religious residents was a two-minute detour, balanced against the right of the religious residents to tranquillity during prayer time. He did not permit closure on the whole of the Sabbath as had been sought. In analysing the conflict in this way, an issue that had resulted in a culture war was simplified to a much narrower, and more understandable choice. In this present context, since proportionality leads to a limited enquiry which does not involve repeated discussion of (much less judgment on) the morality of homosexuality or the morality of discriminatory religious beliefs

74 H. Samuels, 'Feminizing Human Rights Adjudication: Feminist Method and the Proportionality Principle' (2013) 21 *Fem Leg Stud* 39, 44. In making this point, she links proportionality to feminist methods of adjudication. See also B. Baines, 'Contextualism, Feminism and a Canadian Woman Judge' (2009) 17 *Fem Leg Stud* 27; K. Bartlett, 'Feminist Legal Methods' (1989) 103 *Harv L Rev* 829, particularly 849–63; R. Colker, 'Section 1, Contextuality and the Anti-Disadvantage Principle' (1992) 42 *U Toronto LJ* 77; S. Sherry, 'Civic Virtue and the Feminine Voice in Constitutional Adjudication' (1986) 72 *Va L Rev* 543.
75 R. Alexy, 'On Balancing and Subsumption' (2003) 16 *Ratio Juris* 433.
76 Barak supra n.1, 350–2.
77 M. Benjamin, *Splitting the Difference: Compromise and Integrity in Ethics and Politics* (Lawrence: University Press of Kansas, 1990).
78 *Mohd. Ahmed Khan v Shah Bano Begum* (1985) SCR (3) 844.
79 M. Nussbaum, *Women and Human Development: The Capabilities Approach* (Cambridge: Cambridge UP, 2000) Ch. 3.
80 [1997] IsrSC 51(4) 1.
81 Beatty supra n.70, 58–60.

generally, agreement is more likely.[82] Although certainly not suggesting that the law can or should necessarily resolve every problem, a Solomonic judgment, which looks in detail at the claims made, may in some cases be able to lessen tensions and resolve issues to some kind of satisfaction, although not the complete satisfaction, of the parties. By focusing on the narrow circumstances in each case it can challenge the recourse to rhetorical exaggeration that tends to dominate these cases. It is, as Barak puts it, 'balancing writ small'.[83]

Whilst not an example of a proportionality test, *Gay Rights Coalition v Georgetown University*[84] is an example of how certain kinds of judgments can help in reducing tensions. A gay and lesbian student society wished to receive official recognition at a Catholic university. This was opposed on the basis that it would endorse acts contrary to Catholic teaching. The deciding judgment separated the various elements of the society's claim and held the society's real need was for the practical benefits of recognition (such as access to university resources in the form of room bookings, a post box and so on), but that this could be achieved without university endorsement of their *message*. Thus Eskridge argues that the judge, by preventing the case from being dominated by arguments on the rights or wrongs of Catholic policy, allowed a compromise to be reached which benefited both sides.[85]

Of course disagreements still remained but this is in some way a benefit. The decision did not artificially end the debate by imposing a conclusion. Both sides could continue to express their different moral views through their policies and actions. After the case was decided, and after some extremely complicated political manoeuvring, the law was amended so that the non-discrimination law did not cover religious institutions such as Georgetown. Georgetown, however, still stuck to the terms of the agreements.[86] A workable compromise and dialogue must therefore have been established. It would be possible of course still to use the case as evidence of either the outdated homophobia of the Catholic Church, or of the overweening power of the liberal state, but this is more difficult when both parties are reconciled. As Paterson puts it, 'in reconciling the competing claims, the Court sought to accommodate both claims by way of an order carefully tailored to lessen the sum total of interest infringement such that the final result was as respectful of both interests as possible.'[87] While this case did not use a proportionality analysis, proportionality is inherently capable of ensuring such 'respectful' judgments result, since proportionality requires rights to be optimised where they conflict.[88] Thus the result is not that one right applies completely and another does not, but that there is conciliation between them, where both rights are protected as far as they can be without damaging the other.

I do not wish to hold this case out as an entirely unproblematic solution. It dates from 1979 and the District of Columbia was the first jurisdiction in the US to prohibit sexual orientation discrimination. As Eskridge notes (himself previously a gay academic at Georgetown), it could be seen as leading to a separate but equal situation, which potentially understates the hurt felt by

82 C. Sunstein, 'Incompletely Theorized Agreements' (1994) 108 *Harv L Rev* 1733.
83 A. Barak, 'Proportionality and Principled Balancing' (2010) 4 *Law & Ethics of Human Rights* 1, 8.
84 536 A.2d 1 (D.C., 1987).
85 W. Eskridge, 'A Jurisprudence of "Coming Out": Religion, Homosexuality, and Collisions of Liberty and Equality in American Public Law' (1997) 106 *Yale LJ* 2411.
86 L. Lacey, '*Gay Rights Coalition v Georgetown University*: Constitutional Values on a Collision Course' (1985) 64 *Or L Rev* 409. The law was recently repealed: Human Rights Amendment Act of 2014 B20–803.
87 H. Paterson, 'The Justifiability of Biblically Based Discrimination: Can Private Christian Schools Legally Refuse to Employ Gay Teachers?' (2001) 59 *U Toronto Fac L Rev* 59, 96.
88 Alexy supra n.5, 44–86.

gay students in being treated differently.[89] Nevertheless, it demonstrates how judgments can lessen social tensions when decided on 'minimal'[90] grounds.

Proportionality's case-specific nature also avoids some of the rhetorical problems associated with 'slippery slope' arguments. Without underestimating the power of particular cases to be controversial, what can make a controversy far more heated are the, real or imagined, consequences of that decision. Part of the reason why these cases can fall so easily into the narrative of 'culture wars' is because they are particularly characterised by rhetorical exaggeration. Thus, in the same way as *Horev* became not just a dispute about the use of one street, but an argument about the cultural and religious nature of Israel, so a conflict about the policies of one bed and breakfast business[91] becomes a symbolic high-level dispute about equality and the place of religion in the public sphere. However, if decisions are case-specific, based on the particular balancing of the relevant facts, there is less room for such arguments because the judgment will only decide the result for that particular case. Evidently these are controversial issues on which there is and should be considerable discussion. It is not suggested that proportionality, or indeed any legal test, should foreclose any of this debate in the public or political arenas. However, in a legal context, narrowing the debate can be beneficial.

Proportionality's fact-specific nature is also important because it allows subtle distinctions to be made between cases. Issues about the appropriate balance between religious liberty and non-discrimination are not straightforward and there is no advantage in artificially making them so. Proportionality can recognise this and provide answers tailored to the particular facts.

As well as being factually specific, proportionality is also factually contingent. This is relevant in ensuring that courts value and respect claimants, even if they ultimately lose. By factually contingent I mean that a decision is likely to depend on a number of factors. Importantly, this means that winners and losers are not created permanently – the result may always be different in another case. Stone Sweet and Mathews argue that balancing makes it clear to claimants and others that:

> (a) each party is pleading a constitutionally-legitimate norm … (b) that, a priori, the court holds each of these interests in equally high esteem; (c) that determining which value shall prevail is … a difficult judicial task involving complex policy considerations; and (d) that future cases … may well be decided differently.[92]

In deciding that both freedom of religion and freedom from discrimination are rights and therefore count in the balance, both sides are validated and feelings of exclusion can be lessened. The danger of a more categorical test or rule is that it not only creates 'all-out winners and losers' but also that it 'delegitimates [the losing side's] demands in principle, as against showing how they, alas, cannot be accommodated in practice, given other important such demands.'[93] It is the legal embodiment of that important word 'alas'.

89 W.N. Eskridge and G. Peller, 'The New Public Law Movement: Moderation as a Postmodern Cultural Form' (1990) 89 *Mich L Rev* 707.
90 C. Sunstein, *One Case at a Time: Judicial Minimalism on the Supreme Court* (Cambridge, Mass: Harvard UP, 1999).
91 As in *Hall v Bull* [2013] 1 WLR 3741.
92 A. Stone Sweet and J. Mathews, 'Proportionality Balancing and Global Constitutionalism' (2008) 47 *Colum J Transnat'l L* 73, 88.
93 C. Taylor, 'Living with Difference' in A. Allen and M. Regan (eds), *Debating Democracy's Discontent: Essays on American Politics, Law, and Public Philosophy* (Oxford: Oxford UP, 1998) 218.

That proportionality is a conciliatory and 'wounds-healing' form of argumentation[94] can be demonstrated in other aspects of the proportionality test as well as the balancing test. First, it permits a broad interpretation of interference. Although this is not strictly part of the proportionality test, the test relating to interference is closely linked to the test used to decide whether there is a violation of a right. If it is extremely difficult to justify any interference with a right, an interference will only be found in rare cases. Interference is then the most important hurdle that claimants will have to clear if they are to be successful. In contrast, the opportunity for interferences to be justified under proportionality means that a wide view of religious freedom and non-discrimination rights can be taken. Therefore, harm can be recognised in a greater number of situations than if there were a narrower approach to the definition of rights. The requirement of a legitimate aim is also relevant to proportionality's conciliatory nature since it ensures that these rights are only limited for appropriate reasons, thus preventing restrictions based on mere dislike and demonstrating that these rights are important. Finally, the least restrictive means test should be able to identify circumstances where a conflict can be avoided or lessened.

Proportionality's fact-specific nature is thus extremely important, for reasons of principle, and in its more practical effects in its ability to lessen tensions and to validate both sides' claims.

Proportionality as part of the culture of justification

Another great advantage of proportionality is that it requires the body that seeks to restrict rights to provide sufficient and suitable justification to those affected by these acts.[95] Proportionality thus inherently requires deliberation and justification.[96] This is part of the broader 'culture of justification' that characterises, or should characterise, a modern liberal democracy. What matters is not (or not only) *who* has the power to make a decision, as in a 'culture of authority', but *why* the decision was made.[97]

It is useful to draw on Calhoun's argument that we should think about the 'constitutional losers' in litigation.[98] While it is of course in the nature of a legal system that there will be winners and losers, and this is not in itself problematic, she argues that judges have obligations to the parties beyond deciding fairly who should win and lose and in particular that they have obligations to losing parties. Calhoun links this to the idea of 'constitutional stature', which all those who bring a rights case possess. Since they possess this constitutional stature, judges should not characterise constitutional losers as valueless or acting wrongly, but instead as 'worthy and respected proponents of non-frivolous constitutional arguments'.[99] Because the loser has this constitutional stature, it has both a right for the winner's claim to

94 W. Sadurski, '"Reasonableness" and Value Pluralism in Law and Politics' in G. Bongiovanni et al. (eds), *Reasonableness and Law* (Dordrecht: Springer, 2009) 140.

95 Kumm supra n.52. Although Chan has noted that courts sometimes reverse this burden of proof, this should, as she argues, be resisted, although the nature and extent of the evidence demanded will vary: C. Chan, 'Proportionality and Invariable Baseline Intensity of Review' (2013) 33 *LS* 1.

96 R. Alexy, 'Balancing, Constitutional Review, and Representation' (2005) 3 *ICON* 572. See also Samuels supra n.74 who argues that in doing so, proportionality has commonalities with feminist theory.

97 M. Cohen-Eliya and I. Porat, 'Proportionality and the Culture of Justification' (2011) 59 *Am J Compl L* 463.

98 E. Calhoun, *Losing Twice: Harms of Indifference in the Supreme Court* (Oxford: Oxford UP, 2012).

99 Ibid. at 4–5.

be justified in a way that is acceptable to a neutral third party[100] and for the third party to justify, and not merely enforce, their decision on the loser. To do otherwise would be to 'violate justices' obligations to citizens' and has the potential to cause 'outrage' among those who do not agree with the judgment, because they can correctly perceive that their claim is thought of as worthless.[101]

By requiring justification, proportionality preserves the interests of constitutional losers by requiring that the state justify why the right has been burdened. It means that both claims are assessed and taken seriously. In addition to the advantages relating to better decision making because of the requirement of providing reasons, such a requirement also treats both sides as *worthy* of justification and takes parties' concerns seriously and as legitimate.[102] Reason giving treats people with respect as capable of making and understanding rational arguments.

Although to some extent justification is inherent in the idea of judgment giving, proportionality is particularly intimately connected with it. It provides more opportunity to explain the problems with a rule or its application compared to categorical tests. For example, in the US, under *Employment Division v Smith,* which held that laws were only of constitutional concern under the Free Exercise Clause if they were not neutral or generally applicable, it would be sufficient to prove that a law was not aimed at any particular religious group. But this is not the core of the problem. A religionist could argue with some justification that whether or not the law was aimed at them is irrelevant to them: the problem is that they are being denied the opportunity to do something or are required to do something to which they have a religious objection. This core objection would be considered under a proportionality test, but not under the *Smith* test. Similarly, a blanket constitutional rule that forbade all state employees from demonstrating any religious belief in employment, because of a requirement of state secularism, does not provide any opportunity for religious people to challenge the rule or to receive justification for it. Indeed, since any challenge would be a challenge to, rather than under, a constitutional rule, as Taylor vividly puts it: 'they are not only being asked to make a sacrifice, they are being told they are barbarians even to see this as a sacrifice.'[103] Again, this affects a person's status as a constitutional loser.

Importantly, this consideration of the respective burdens and benefits of an act is based on a particular set of facts. It therefore provides an individualised decision since it considers the justifiability of the interference as it applies in each case. As Beatty argues, 'the theory behind proportionality is not intended to merely categorize a case into a group which solves the problem. Rather, proportionality is aimed at a constant review of the existence of a rational justification for the limitation imposed on the right, while taking into consideration each case's circumstances'.[104] It makes the burden or justification central to the process of deliberation. In this sense, proportionality is therefore connected to, although not the same as, the idea of reasonable accommodation in the sense that the requirement of individualised justification may lead to accommodation.[105] A general policy, such as a school uniform

100 R. Brown, 'Liberty: The New Equality' (2002) 77 *NYU L Rev* 1491, 1556.
101 Calhoun supra n.98.
102 C.f. Taylor supra n.93. It is not a coincidence that the obligation to give reasons is an important aspect of natural justice.
103 Taylor supra n.93, 216.
104 Beatty supra n.70, 459.
105 K. Henrard, 'The Effective Protection of the Freedom of Religion: The ECtHR's Variable Margin of Appreciation Regarding Religion-State Relations and the Rule of Law' in M. Foblets et al. (eds), *Belief, Law and Politics: What Future for a Secular Europe?* (Farnham: Ashgate, 2014) 164–6.

policy, may be entirely defensible. However, it may be a lot harder to show why the policy must be applied without an exception in a particular case.[106]

Deliberation and justification are also important in acting as a counter-majoritarian check. This is particularly relevant to the current issues under discussion. Both conservative religious groups and gay people can be politically unpopular. The history of gay people is one of oppression, with remaining inequality in many areas. Paradoxically, conservative religious organisations and individuals can also be unpopular, partly because of their wish to discriminate and apparent wish to undo hard-fought rights. Because religious belief may rely on revelation or adherence to authority, whether a written text or a religious hierarchy, it may be difficult for those who do not share such beliefs to understand. Furthermore, simply because both groups are likely to be minorities, and therefore their concerns may not be foremost in the minds of those making policies, a strong requirement of justification guards against the 'vice of thoughtlessness'.[107] Policies can overly restrict rights not because of any malice but because their impact has not been thought through or because those making policies over-estimate the importance of their goals merely because they are focused on them. Proportionality helps to guard against this danger.

The kind of justification given is also relevant. As suggested earlier, Kumm argues that the reasons given must be those that can be defended under Rawls' idea of public reason: the types of reasons the state uses to defend a policy should not rest on a 'comprehensive conception of the good', which is a reason relating to 'what it means to live a good, authentic life', but should instead rely on 'public reason'.[108] A public reason is a principle that citizens can affirm on the basis of a shared rationale and that can therefore be accepted even if they do not share the same conception of a 'good life'. Reasons should not be given that are 'based on their own exclusive "comprehensive" views (e.g. religious beliefs, or philosophical or moral views), that those with alternative world views cannot fully comprehend.'[109] As discussed above, it is not enough to prohibit behaviour merely because it is thought wrong. The requirement of public reason enables reciprocity and the possibility of dialogue between the parties since it provides a shared basis on which to talk.

The two advantages just outlined, that proportionality leads to factually specific conclusions and that it inherently requires justification, are those that are probably the most directly applicable to these cases. Proportionality also has many benefits which are relevant both to these situations and to a wider range of cases. The first is that it 'combines flexibility and structure'.[110] On the one hand, as described above, it responds flexibly to each case. On the other hand, though, this flexibility is not unconstrained. The test is structured. This structure creates a 'division of argumentative labour' which allows 'the parcelling of various opposing considerations'[111] and means that the reasoning is transparent. It requires judges

106 P. Bosset, 'Mainstreaming Religious Diversity in a Secular and Egalitarian State: The Road(s) Not Taken in *Leyla Sahin v. Turkey*' in E. Brems (ed.), *Diversity and European Human Rights: Rewriting Judgments of the ECHR* (Cambridge: Cambridge UP, 2013). Also see *Hall v Bull* [2013] 1 WLR 3741, 3754.

107 Kumm supra n.70, 163.

108 Kumm supra n.52.

109 P. Cumper and T. Lewis, '"Public Reason", Judicial Deference and the Right to Freedom of Religion and Belief under the Human Rights Act 1998' (2011) 22 *KLJ* 131, 135.

110 M. Cohen-Eliya and I. Porat, 'The Hidden Foreign Law Debate in *Heller*: The Proportionality Approach in American Constitutional Law' (2009) 46 *San Diego L Rev* 267, 380.

111 C. Panaccio, 'In Defence of Two-Step Balancing and Proportionality in Rights Adjudication' (2011) 24 *Can J L & Jurisprudence* 109, 120.

to 'show their working out'.[112] It requires judges to state precisely why they have reached the decisions they have, in a way which can be subsequently assessed.[113] However, despite these advantages, perhaps partly because of its rapid spread and the number and range of claims made in favour of it, proportionality has received a great deal of criticism.

Potential objections

Balancing has been criticised as being a process that takes place in an 'opaque black box',[114] where it is unclear what leads to the decision. Habermas has, for example, argued the process of weighing rights takes place 'either arbitrarily or unreflectively, according to customary standards and hierarchies.'[115] Such criticisms are unfair. To some extent, moral reasoning has to be impressionistic, especially given the time and resource constraints courts are under, but this is not a problem particularly related to proportionality. A judgment using proportionality should explain the reasons for assigning value to a particular interest or argument and for choosing one value over another. It is more transparent than many categorical tests where it may not be apparent why a case is placed in one category rather than another, particularly in hard cases.[116] Indeed, courts may not be clearly able to say why cases are placed in one category rather than another.[117]

In any case, balancing is often inherent in decision-making, even with categorisation. In deciding when rights should be protected, the rights will have to be balanced at some point, otherwise it would be impossible to say which right or interest is more important than another. For example, in US free speech law, the state is not normally permitted to restrict speech based on its viewpoint, no matter how offensive, but time, manner and place requirements are permitted.[118] This is based on an implicit balancing that freedom of speech is more important than the harm caused by hate speech. In considering categorisation, the court will have thought about an archetypal case or the particular case in question, but this ruling will be applied in many different contexts. However, in so doing the court is then denied the benefits of flexibility. Categorisation can thus lead to overly formalised rulings.

A different kind of argument is that proportionality makes it too easy to 'balance away' rights[119] or that it fails to protect rights because it does not treat them differently from other kinds of interest.[120] Webber has referred to this situation as 'the loss of rights', since, he argues, rights are reduced to 'defeasible interests, values or principles'.[121] It is true that under legal systems which use proportionality, rights tend to be widely drawn and, as can be seen from the structure of rights provisions under the Canadian Charter or the ECHR,

112 T. Poole, 'Tilting at Windmills? Truth and Illusion in "The Political Constitution"' (2007) 70 *Mod L Rev* 250, 268.
113 F. Coffin, 'Judicial Balancing: The Protean Scales of Justice' (1988) 63*NYU L Rev* 16, 25.
114 S. Gottlieb, 'The Paradox of Balancing Significant Interests' (1994) 45 *Hastings LJ* 825, 839.
115 J. Habermas, *Between Facts and Norms: Contributions to a Discourse Theory of Law and Democracy*, tr. W. Rehg (Malden, MA: Polity Press, 1996) 259.
116 As Chapter 3 demonstrated.
117 See Jackson's discussions of *R v Keegstra* [1990] 3 SCR 697 compared to *R.A.V. v St Paul* 505 US 377 (1992) in 'Ambivalent Resistance and Comparative Constitutionalism: Opening Up the Conversation on "Proportionality," Rights and Federalism' (1999) 1 *U Pa J Const L* 583.
118 See *Ward v Rock Against Racism* 491 US 781 (1989).
119 R. Dworkin, *Is Democracy Possible Here?* (Princeton: Princeton UP, 2006).
120 Tsakyrakis supra n.21.
121 G. Webber, 'On the Loss of Rights' in G. Huscroft, B.W. Miller and G. Webber (eds), *Proportionality and the Rule of Law: Rights, Justification, Reasoning* (Cambridge: Cambridge UP, 2014).

potentially defeated by public interest justifications. A 'right' in this sense may therefore look very different from Dworkin's idea of rights as trumps.[122] However, this does not mean that the idea of a right becomes meaningless. Greater weight can, and should, be given to rights than mere public interests.[123] Rights are also given priority over other interests in the sense that justification is required for their infringement and that only particular types of reasons will be sufficient to infringe them. As Schauer notes, rights automatically have greater weight than other kinds of interest, because of where the burden of proof lies.[124] We say, for example, that the right to freedom of expression must be interfered with no more than is necessary to protect public order, rather than public order must be interfered with no more than is necessary to protect freedom of expression. This 'asymmetry' demonstrates the presumption that freedom of expression is to be protected.[125]

A further criticism is that balancing is unprincipled or merely pragmatic.[126] Again this criticism is unjustified. Balancing is not an unprincipled process. If rights are not absolute (as neither non-discrimination nor freedom of religion is) then balancing them based on the particular circumstances at issue is the most principled a resolution could be.[127] The creation of a balance between them creates its own principle.[128] Having a wide interpretation of a right, with a narrower range of cases where that right is violated, is coherent. It is clearer to say that a measure interferes with, for example, freedom of speech, but that the interference is justified, rather than the act does not come under the category of protected speech at all.

A further criticism is that proportionality is too subjective and the results too dependent on the views of those hearing them because it does not provide sufficient guidance to judges as to how cases should be dealt with, thus giving judges too much discretion.[129] It is argued that this poses problems of legitimacy for courts.[130] Of course it is subjective to some degree, but the high requirement of justification, the structured decision-making process and the fact that these decisions are made with reference to the values immanent in the legal system mean that this problem is more than outweighed by its advantages.[131] Subjectivity is inherent in all kinds of judging, particularly in relation to constitutional issues, not just proportionality. This is particularly true in clash of rights cases where both rights are considered by the legal system to be prima facie valuable.

It could similarly be argued that proportionality is too administratively complex and uncertain. There are two issues here. First, the fear is that by giving rights to religious conduct, authorities will be paralysed by the number and extent of claims made. This seems

122 K. Möller, *The Global Model of Constitutional Rights* (Oxford: Oxford UP, 2012). Dworkin refers to rights as 'political trumps held by individuals': R. Dworkin, *Taking Rights Seriously* (Cambridge, Mass: Harvard UP, 1977) xi.

123 M. Klatt and M. Meister, 'Proportionality – A Benefit to Human Rights? Remarks on the ICON Controversy' (2012) 10 *ICON* 687, 690.

124 F. Schauer, 'Proportionality and the Question of Weight' in G. Huscroft, B.W. Miller and G. Webber (eds), *Proportionality and the Rule of Law: Rights, Justification, Reasoning* (Cambridge: Cambridge UP, 2014).

125 Ibid., 180

126 For example, Moon argues that it involves a pragmatic trade-off of interests rather than a principled reconciliation of rights: R. Moon, *Freedom of Conscience and Religion* (Toronto: Irwin Law, 2014).

127 R. Alexy supra n.5.

128 M. Minow, 'Is Pluralism an Ideal or a Compromise?' (2008) 40 *Conn L Rev* 1287.

129 F. Urbina, '"Balancing as Reasoning" and the Problems of Legally Unaided Adjudication: A reply to Kai Möller' (2014) 12 *ICON* 214.

130 Ibid.

131 Alexy supra n.5; Barak supra n.1, Ch 18; Beatty supra n.70.

unlikely. The American concept of strict scrutiny as applied in *Sherbert v Verner*,[132] a test which required greater justification than proportionality, did not create a flood of cases or make administration unwieldy.[133] It therefore seems unlikely that proportionality will cause major practical problems. Second, there is the fear that authorities will not know how cases will be decided and will have to 'second-guess' the court's decision. Evidently, those making decisions need to be able to act with a high degree of confidence. But proportionality analysis is not entirely freewheeling. Over time, decisions will build up which will show the main parameters for the rights. Some discretion will also be given to the original decision-maker.[134]

A different kind of criticism has been made that proportionality pretends to evade moral reasoning by creating 'the illusion of some kind of mechanical weighing of values'[135] and thus it 'depoliticises' rights.[136] It is true that some analyses of it may suggest this.[137] However as Möller demonstrates, the opposite is true: proportionality is centrally concerned with moral reasoning. The aim of the proportionality test is to provide a structured way of identifying and considering the relevant moral considerations. As should have been made clear by the discussion of balancing above, although the balancing stage does involve consideration of the weight of a right and its degree of infringement in a particular circumstance, these are the result of a process of moral reasoning. There is nothing mechanical about this process. It does not require a simple cost-benefit analysis.[138]

A further argument is that proportionality is impossible because it requires a court to compare incommensurables.[139] Moon, for example, refers to the 'myth of balancing', arguing that there is no principled way to balance 'public values' against 'spiritual beliefs or practices'.[140] However, many of the assertions that rights are incommensurable are at a superficial level.[141] While it may be difficult, although perhaps still not impossible, to say whether one right is more important than another in the abstract (for example is freedom of expression more important than freedom of property?), it is clearly possible to make arguments that one right is more important or is infringed more heavily than another in a particular situation. This is all that proportionality requires. It is unclear how any decision could be made as to whether or not a right should be held to be violated in a particular circumstance if this were not possible. Importantly, proportionality does not require all rights to be reduced

132 374 U.S. 398 (1963).
133 A. Adamczyk et al., 'Religious Regulation and the Courts: Documenting the Effects of *Smith* and RFRA' (2004) 46 *J Church & St* 237.
134 The issue of how and when this discretion will be exercised is complex and there are numerous points in the proportionality test at which deference could be exercised. See A. Brady, *Proportionality and Deference under the UK Human Rights Act: An Institutionally Sensitive Approach* (Cambridge: Cambridge UP, 2012); Chan supra n.95; and Rivers supra n.67.
135 Tsakyrakis supra n.21, 475. Similarly, Webber argues that it transforms questions of rights into 'management and mathematical measurements': G. Webber, 'Proportionality, Balancing, and the Cult of Constitutional Rights Scholarship' (2010) 23 *Can J L Jurisprudence* 179, 191.
136 Ibid. Webber.
137 Beatty makes this argument explicitly. Alexy does not make this point explicitly and does not, I think, mean to imply this, but his use of formulae may suggest that these questions can be resolved with a mathematical precision. However, other supporters of proportionality have clearly rebutted these arguments: see e.g. Cohen-Eliya and Porat supra n.97 and Möller supra n.122.
138 Möller supra n.41.
139 E.g. Tsakyrakis supra n.21.
140 Moon supra n.126, 133.
141 V. Da Silva, 'Comparing the Incommensurable: Constitutional Principles, Balancing and Rational Decision' (2011) 31 *OJLS* 273.

to a common metric.[142] It is only necessary to give rights an ordinal rather than a cardinal value.[143] This process is normative rather than mechanical.

Overall therefore, proportionality is advantageous for deciding these cases. Its fact-specific and justification-based nature make it possible to resolve these disputes in an atmosphere of mutual respect. It promotes an atmosphere of give and take and acknowledges the legitimacy of the interests of both sides. Most importantly, it engages in a process of rights maximisation, rather than necessarily perceiving disputes as winner takes all. Although, like any test, it has disadvantages, these are not so serious as to render it unsuitable.

Proportionality in the USA, England, and Canada

In order to place the discussion in the following chapters into context, I will now give an overview of how proportionality or proportionality-type arguments are used in the three jurisdictions. Both Canada and the UK have accepted that proportionality should be the appropriate test for cases claiming a violation of human rights.[144] Despite this it has not always been applied or always been applied strictly in the English context, as will become apparent in the next few chapters. There has been a tendency for the courts to argue that the proportionality test is not engaged because the right has not been interfered with. Thus in *Begum* there was held to be no interference with the claimant's religious rights when she was not permitted to wear a jilbab to school because she could have attended another school.

Proportionality in the human rights context was introduced as a result of the Human Rights Act 1998 in the UK. Proportionality-type tests have also become relevant not only for human rights cases, that is those involving challenges against state action through judicial review, but also between private parties in discrimination cases, for example in employment, largely as a result of the influence of EU law. To defend a claim of indirect discrimination, a policy, criterion or practice that puts persons who share a protected characteristic at a particular disadvantage must be a proportionate means of achieving a legitimate aim.[145] For example, in the case of *Ladele*,[146] a registrar claimed she had been indirectly discriminated against when her employer would not exempt her from performing civil partnerships. She had refused to perform them because of her Christian beliefs and thus argued that the employer's policy put people sharing her religious beliefs at a particular disadvantage and that the policy was disproportionate. The court however disagreed, as will be examined further in the next chapter.

Proportionality became widely used in Canada in response to the Canadian Charter of Rights and Freedoms in 1982. A proportionality test is used to assess whether there has been a violation of a Charter right, such as freedom of religion or non-discrimination. However, in claims alleging a violation of a human rights code, as with a discrimination claim brought against a private employer, a reasonable accommodation test is used instead. The test, known as *Meiorin*, contains three stages.[147] The employer must have adopted the standard

142 Möller supra n.41.

143 Klatt and Meister supra n.123.

144 See *R v Oakes* and, for the English context, e.g. *R(Daly) v Secretary of State for the Home Department* [2001] 2 AC 532; *Huang v Secretary of State for the Home Department* supra n.6. It has also been relevant to discrimination law, as a result of EU law.

145 See A. Baker, 'Proportionality and Employment Discrimination in the UK' (2008) 37 *ILJ* 305.

146 [2010] 1 WLR 955.

147 *British Columbia (Public Service Employee Relations Commission) v BCGSEU* [1999] 3 SCR 3. See G. Moon, 'From Equal Treatment to Appropriate Treatment: What Lessons Can Canadian

for a purpose rationally connected to the performance of the job; there must have been an honest and good faith belief that it was necessary; and the standard must be reasonably necessary to the accomplishment of that legitimate work-related purpose. In deciding whether it is reasonably necessary it must be shown that the employee could not be accommodated without imposing undue hardship. While the enquiry posed by this test is not the same as proportionality, there are some similarities in its requirements of legitimate aim, rational connection and overall balancing of the interests of employee and employer.[148]

The USA does not explicitly refer to proportionality in its constitutional law.[149] There is debate as to whether the US is 'exceptional'[150] in not using proportionality or whether proportionality is latent in its constitutional law.[151] It seems though that US constitutional law does not rely on one test or method of analysis. In certain contexts, there is little doubt that proportionality is not used. For example, in the context of state interference in the selection of religious employees (by laws prohibiting discrimination or other means) a categorical rather than proportionality test is used, forbidding interference with the religious institution's decision if the employee falls within the 'ministerial exception'. This is not to say that there is no balancing. This may occur for example in considering which category a case should be placed in, but this is likely only to concern specific issues rather than be an 'all things considered' proportionality test. For example, there may be balancing in deciding whether a job was mainly religious rather than secular in nature. However, once this balancing is completed and it is decided whether a person is a 'minister' or not, no further balancing takes place.

Nevertheless, there are some similarities between proportionality and aspects of US law. The US test of strict scrutiny, which requires the state to have a compelling government interest, and to have narrowly tailored the law to achieve that aim, bears some similarities to proportionality. While this test is no longer applied to all free exercise of religion cases, following *Employment Division v Smith*,[152] it will be relevant to cases decided under the Religious Freedom Restoration Act (RFRA). Proportionality and strict scrutiny both have a similar purpose: to permit government action where necessary in the public interest, but to examine the necessity of restrictions of rights rigorously.[153] Their basic two-step structure is also similar: both have a first stage considering whether the act restricts a right and a second considering whether there is sufficient justification for the restriction. Thus in *Yoder v Wisconsin*,[154] the case concerning whether Amish children could be withdrawn from school after the eighth grade, it was decided that the government's interest in ensuring that children had an extra year of schooling was not compelling compared to the Amish's interest in

Equality Law on Dignity and on Reasonable Accommodation Teach the United Kingdom?' (2006) 6 *EHRLR* 695.

148 For a comparison of proportionality and reasonable accommodation, see generally, P. Edge and L. Vickers, *Review of Equality and Human Rights Law Relating to Religion or Belief* (EHRC Research Report 97, 2016); Foblets et al. supra n.105.

149 Although there is some debate as to whether it should be used, see *District of Columbia v Heller* 554 US 570 (2008).

150 Weinrib supra n.3.

151 See I. Porat, 'Mapping the American Debate over Balancing' in Huscroft, Miller and Webber supra n.6; P. Yowell, 'Proportionality in United States Constitutional Law' in *Reasoning Rights: Comparative Judicial Engagement* (Oxford: Hart Publishing, 2014) (arguing that proportionality can be seen in *Lochner*-era cases).

152 494 US 872 (1990).

153 R. Fallon, 'Strict Judicial Scrutiny' (2006) 54 *UCLA* 1267.

154 406 US 205 (1972).

maintaining their community's way of life. This process is very similar to that which would take place under a proportionality analysis.[155] Under both the justification is weighed against the interference with the right.

Beyond these structural similarities, the tests have similar elements. The compelling government interest includes the idea of a legitimate aim. If the measure is for an impermissible purpose, such as straightforward discrimination against an unpopular minority religion, then it will be found unconstitutional. This is similar to the way the legitimate aim test functions. The idea of narrow tailoring, which is similar to the least restrictive means test, includes rationality and necessity tests.[156] It requires a 'proportionality-like judgment of whether marginal increments in the avoidance of risks or marginal reductions in the incidence of harms sufficiently justify infringements of fundamental rights in light of available, but typically less efficacious, alternatives'.[157] Finally, it contains some elements of overall balancing.

It has been suggested that strict scrutiny is not really a balancing test because once it has been decided that this is the appropriate test, the government will fail to justify the policy, leading to the aphorism that strict scrutiny is 'strict in theory and fatal in fact.'[158] Whatever the merits of this in other contexts,[159] it was never true in the free exercise context. An empirical study demonstrated the 'survival rate' of cases decided under strict scrutiny to be 59 per cent.[160] This rate was even higher when only exemptions from generally applicable laws were in issue, rather than laws claimed to be discriminatory.[161] An earlier study looking at Courts of Appeals judgments in the ten years before *Smith* found the survival rate to be 90 per cent.[162] More broadly, Sullivan and Frase point to cases where strict scrutiny has not been fatally strict, in contexts as diverse as the federal regulation of inter-state commerce and content-neutral restrictions of speech. They also draw attention to the use of 'intermediate scrutiny' and 'rational basis review with teeth': lower standards of review that nonetheless assess the legitimacy of government action based on balancing considerations.[163] There have been claims that the test applied under RFRA is more demanding than that under previous constitutional law, but it has not yet been applied in enough contexts for this to be clear.[164]

This does not mean though that these methods of review are the same as proportionality. As Fallon argues, strict scrutiny has a narrower focus, which does not lead to an 'all things considered' balancing analysis, as takes place under proportionality. The question is more about whether government action is appropriately targeted, rather than whether the action was proportionate. Cohen-Eliya and Porat also point to a more theoretical difference in

155 This does not mean that the same result would necessarily be reached under a proportionality test.
156 Cohen-Eliya and Porat supra n.110, 385–6.
157 Fallon supra n.153, 1336.
158 G. Gunther, 'In Search of Evolving Doctrine on a Changing Court: A Model for a Newer Equal Protection' (1972) 86 *Harv L Rev* 1, 8.
159 Such as prohibiting viewpoint speech discrimination by the state.
160 Although this study dates from after *Smith* it only considered cases decided with strict scrutiny, i.e. those cases unaffected by *Smith* and cases decided under RFRA.
161 A. Winkler, 'Fatal in Theory and Strict in Fact: An Empirical Analysis of Strict Scrutiny in the Federal Courts' (2006) 59 *Vand L Rev* 793.
162 J. Ryan, '*Smith* and the Religious Freedom Restoration Act: An Iconoclastic Assessment' (1992) 78 *Va L Rev* 1407.
163 E.T. Sullivan and R. Frase, *Proportionality Principles in American Law* (Oxford: Oxford UP, 2008) Ch. 4.
164 See Ginsburg J's dissent in *Burwell v Hobby Lobby* 573 U.S. ___ (2014); M. Hamilton, 'The Case for Evidence-Based Free Exercise Accommodation: Why the Religious Freedom Restoration Act is Bad Public Policy' (2015) 9 *Harv J L & Pub Pol* 129.

comparing the German use of proportionality-type tests to those in the US. While both countries use balancing, more opprobrium is attached to its use in the US. They argue this is because of a theoretical difference in its purpose. In the German model, proportionality is accepted as part of an 'organic conception of the state' based on 'reciprocal cooperation and trust amongst all state organs' where all interests should be optimised.[165] In the US by contrast, proportionality-type tests are more often seen as mere 'ad hocery': a way of enforcing political policy decisions, rather than a method of law.[166] Even if these arguments are wrong, it is certainly true that balancing and proportionality have a more residual role in the US than in, for example, Canada, with more use made of categorisation and excluded reasons for legislating.[167] The results of these differences will be explored in the following chapters.

Conclusion

This chapter has provided an analysis of proportionality and suggested its advantages for dealing with situations of moral disagreement and conflicts of rights, particularly regarding disputes about religious freedom and non-discrimination. The remainder of this book aims to provide an argument of how these cases are best resolved, basing this on a proportionality framework. It therefore has dual aims: arguing both for specific conclusions but also for a general framework. This means that it is of course possible to agree with the framework I argue for, but disagree about results in concrete cases. Given the expanding number of cases on these issues, I do not provide an entirely comprehensive analysis of the law in the three jurisdictions. Rather, cases are selected because they illustrate particular points or arguments. Sometimes cases are used as good examples of how proportionality can work. Sometimes different tests are used and I use proportionality to demonstrate how the case could have been decided or reasoned differently. Sometimes proportionality or proportionality-type tests are used but I nevertheless suggest how a proportionality analysis could also be used differently. The second part of this book now moves on to analyse how such an approach could work in four contexts: religious claims in secular employment, employment in religious organisations, and the provision of goods and services by religious individuals and by organisations.

165 Cohen-Eliya and Porat supra n.110, 390, also 'American Balancing and German Proportionality: The Historical Origins' (2010) 8 *ICON* 263 and *Proportionality and Constitutional Culture* (Cambridge: Cambridge UP, 2013).

166 J. Bomhoff, 'Lüth's 50th Anniversary: Some Comparative Observations on the German Foundations of Judicial Balancing' (2008) 9 *German LJ* 121.

167 Cohen-Eliya and Porat supra n.110.

6 Religious claims in secular employment

This chapter examines the right to manifest discriminatory religious beliefs within employment. Employees may seek exemptions from certain parts of their work on the grounds that they conflict with their religious beliefs, or may wish to express their discriminatory views in or outside the workplace. These actions may though infringe the right of service users or colleagues to be treated in a non-discriminatory way, as well as affect the interests of employers. This chapter will consider such cases, considering in particular whether registrars or those in similar jobs should be exempted from performing same-sex marriages if they have religious objections to doing so. It will draw on the approach explained in the previous chapter, arguing that applying a fact-specific proportionality test is the best way to resolve these types of cases. Even so, they are difficult to adjudicate. They involve complex moral issues and starkly raise the problem of how people with different views can live and work together.

Disputes around same-sex marriage

The existence of same-sex marriage/partnerships, although opposed by many religious organisations, is not itself a violation of religious freedom and indeed not to allow it is almost certainly a violation of anti-discrimination rights.[1] No state has required religious institutions to perform same-sex marriages and such a requirement would presumably violate constitutional or other religious freedom guarantees. Although this conflict is therefore not in issue, the creation of same-sex marriage or other legal partnerships does create new clashes between religious conscience and the obligation not to discriminate.

Disagreements have arisen over claims for exemptions made by state employees who have responsibility for performing civil marriages or partnerships. Some registrars or other public officials[2] have argued that due to their religious beliefs about the sanctity and special nature of marriage,[3] its extension to same-sex partners was illegitimate and morally wrong. They therefore maintained they could not in good conscience facilitate such unions. While

1 Canadian courts held the lack of same-sex marriage to be a violation of the Charter in *Halpern v Canada* 65 OR (3d) 161 and *Hendricks v Quebec* [2002] RJQ 2506. The US Supreme Court held it violated the Fourteenth Amendment's Due Process Clause in *Obergefell v Hodges* 576 US_____ (2015). The ECtHR held such decisions were within states' margin of appreciation in *Schalk and Kopf v Austria* (2011) 53 EHRR 20.

2 I will use this term to refer to all those who have the power to perform or register non-religious marriages or partnerships regardless of jurisdiction.

3 I will use the word 'marriage' to refer to all kinds of partnerships giving couples legal rights.

religious opposition should not by itself affect the existence of same-sex marriage,[4] such beliefs can form the basis of protection of religiously motivated behaviour. Evidently, though, such exemptions interfere with the right to non-discrimination.

These issues have been faced by the courts in the relevant jurisdictions on a number of occasions, albeit in slightly differing situations. Most give priority to the right not to be discriminated against above the right to freedom of religion.[5] In the English case of *Ladele v Islington LBC*,[6] a registrar refused to perform civil partnerships on the basis of her Christian beliefs. She was employed before the Civil Partnership Act 2004 was enacted. The Act required that a person be designated as a civil partnership registrar before they could register civil partnerships but Islington decided to designate all their registrars in order to share the new work equally.[7] Initially, Ladele managed to exchange her shifts with other employees when she was due to perform civil partnerships, but this became unacceptable to her employer, partly because of complaints made by her colleagues, and it held that this was a violation of Islington's non-discrimination policy, entitled 'Dignity for All'. Her line manager offered her the compromise of supervising simple signings of the register, rather than performing ceremonies, or the opportunity to change to other employment within the council, but these suggestions were unacceptable to her. With no resolution of the issue forthcoming, Ladele claimed she had been directly or indirectly discriminated against on the grounds of religion and eventually resigned. She succeeded at the Employment Tribunal but failed at the Employment Appeal Tribunal (EAT) and Court of Appeal. She then took her case to the ECtHR claiming that her treatment amounted to a breach of Article 14 taken with Article 9 but again failed.[8] Her request for a referral to the Grand Chamber was denied.

In the Canadian *Marriage Commissioners Case*,[9] a reference was made to the Saskatchewan High Court to decide whether an amendment to the Marriage Act 1995[10] to allow a marriage commissioner to refuse to solemnise a same-sex marriage would be constitutionally permissible. It was held that it was not. This followed earlier litigation brought by individual marriage commissioners under the Saskatchewan Human Rights Code. In one of these cases, *Nichols v M.J.*,[11] a gay couple complained to the Saskatchewan Human Rights Commission when a marriage commissioner had refused to perform their marriage. On appeal, the Saskatchewan Court of Queen's Bench held that the commissioner had no defence to the discrimination claim. Unlike British registrars, marriage commissioners are not employed by the state, but rather are licensed by the provincial authorities to perform marriages. In Saskatchewan the Marriage Unit maintains a list of marriage commissioners but couples then arrange for and pay a fixed fee to the commissioner directly.

In the US, especially following the Supreme Court's decision in *Obergefell v Hodges*[12] making same-sex marriage legal across the whole of the country, a number of claims have

4 Because of the obligation for restrictions of rights, including non-discrimination rights, to be defended on the basis of a public reason.
5 Some jurisdictions also have legislative exemptions e.g. 'Prince Edward Island: An Act to Amend the Marriage Act', 3d Sess., 62 Leg., 2005; Utah: SB0297S02 'Protections for Religious Expression and Beliefs about Marriage, Family, or Sexuality'.
6 [2009] ICR 387 [EAT], [2010] 1 WLR 955 [CA].
7 EAT judgment ibid. at 390.
8 (2013) 57 EHRR 8.
9 2011 SKCA 3.
10 S.S. 1995, c. M-4.1.
11 2009 SKQB 299.
12 576 US ___ (2015).

been filed by clerks who have refused to give marriage licences to same-sex couples. These include the case of Kim Davis, which became a media cause célèbre. Davis, an elected official, refused to issue marriage licences to *any* couples as a result of the Supreme Court's ruling and also refused to let her assistants issue them because her name would still appear on the licence. This led to two claims, the first brought by couples who were unable get licences in the county[13] and the second brought by Davis herself claiming that requiring her to issue licences violated her rights under the Kentucky Religious Freedom Act.[14] A preliminary injunction was issued, requiring her to issue the licences. She though refused to comply with it and as a result was jailed for contempt of court. Utah has a legislative exemption permitting clerks to recuse themselves from giving a licence, but there is an obligation to ensure a licence can be obtained.[15]

Also relevant are two cases which arose before the decision in *Obergefell*, decided under state rather than federal law. The first involved Vermont's civil union law (now repealed and replaced with same-sex marriage) where town clerks were required to issue a civil union licence or to appoint an assistant to do so.[16] In *Brady v Dean*[17] some town clerks argued that merely to appoint an assistant infringed their rights under the Vermont Constitution. This was rejected. However, in *Slater v Douglas County*[18] a clerk, who refused to process Declarations of Domestic Partnerships and whose request for accommodation was refused by her employer, was partly successful. She brought a claim alleging she had not been 'reasonably accommodated' by her employer, who responded by arguing that summary judgment should be awarded against her. This was denied and the case sent for trial by jury. Although a question for the jury, the judge strongly suggested it would have been possible to accommodate her without causing undue hardship: the office dealt with very few applications and these were not shared out equally among the staff. The case subsequently settled.[19]

I will now consider how these cases could have been dealt with under a proportionality test and provide a model for the resolution of such disputes by the courts. Before considering the proportionality test itself, the first issue is whether there has been any interference with the registrars' religious rights. Evidently, if there is no interference then there is nothing for the state to have to justify.

Interference

Some courts have found the question of whether there has been an interference to be a complex issue. As these claims arise within employment, on one understanding, since employees can resign, no further protection of their religious rights is necessary as they can thereby avoid the conflict between their conscience and their obligations. This idea,

13 *Miller v Davis*, No. 15-CV-44-DLB, 2015 WL 4866729 (E.D. Ky. Aug. 12, 2015).

14 Verified Third-Party Complaint of Defendant Kim Davis, *Miller v Davis*, No. 15-CV-44-DLB (E.D. Ky. Aug. 4, 2015). Her appeals to the 6th Circuit and the Supreme Court were refused. See R. Colker, 'Religious Accommodations for County Clerks?' (2015) 76 *Ohio State LJ* 87.

15 Utah S.B. 297.

16 18 V.S.A. § 5161. The newer marriage law does not have such a provision.

17 173 Vt. 542 (Vt. 2001).

18 743 F. Supp. 2d 1188 (2010).

19 'County Pays Off On Same-Sex Marriage Case', *The Roseburg Beacon*, 13 April 2011, available at: http://www.roseburgbeacon.com/home/2011/4/13/county-pays-off-on-same-sex-marria ge-case.html <last accessed 20 July 2016>.

sometimes known as the specific situation rule, was the approach of the European Commission of Human Rights,[20] and following it, English courts.[21] However, in the case of *Eweida, Chaplin, Ladele and McFarlane v UK*[22] (hereafter *Eweida v UK*), decided in 2013, the ECtHR reconsidered this idea. It held that it had been too strict in holding that there had not been an interference in these cases, and so the fact these situations took place within employment should merely be a factor to be taken into account.

The specific situation rule was unsatisfactory. That a person can resign is relevant to the balancing test and may ultimately be required, but such an approach prevented even the raising of the question of rights. As Gunn put it, it meant that the '"fundamental rights" of the European Convention are subject to a simple contractual waiver'.[23] Given that for most people their employment is an economic necessity, as well as providing important social benefits, employment is too important an area for religious freedom not to apply. A particular form of employment may also be particularly important to a claimant. Furthermore, these claims can involve only small parts of an employee's duties and any conflict between their obligations and their religious beliefs may have arisen only after they have begun employment.

The specific situation approach was not only itself a disproportionate rule but violated the important principle of providing justification. It could affect perceptions of the legitimacy of the decision because it did not demonstrate to claimants that their concerns were taken seriously by the courts or give them a full opportunity to tell their side of the story. These requirements are an important part of procedural justice, which radically affects claimants' opinion of the legal process.[24] As Stychin puts it, 'while proponents of freedom of religion may accept the need for balancing, they are more likely to advocate that it should be done openly as a majoritarian limitation on the exercise of the right, rather than *constitutively* in the definition of its scope.'[25] It excluded any attempt to find less intrusive measures which protected the rights and interests on both sides. It meant that any justification, no matter how unimportant the interest or how badly tailored the solution is, would suffice.

Other jurisdictions, including the US and Canada, have not adopted such a strict interpretation. In both these jurisdictions it has been largely unproblematic to suggest that religious freedom claims can be made relating to employment.[26] Thus in *Nichols*, the *Marriage Commissioners Case* and *Slater*, it was not in issue that the claimant's[27] rights had been affected. In *Brady v Dean*, although the claim failed because there was no 'substantial burden' on the town clerks' belief, this was not because the situation arose within employment, but because it was possible to appoint an assistant to issue civil union licences.

20 E.g. *Ahmad v United Kingdom* (1981) 4 EHRR 126; *Stedman v United Kingdom* (1997) 5 EHRLR 544.

21 E.g. *R(Begum) v Governors of Denbigh High School* [2007] 1 AC 100; *Copsey v WBB Devon Clays Ltd* [2005] ICR 1789, albeit with criticism.

22 (2013) 57 EHRR 8.

23 T.J. Gunn, 'Adjudicating Rights of Conscience under the European Convention on Human Rights' in J. Van der Vyver and J. Witte (eds), *Religious Human Rights in Global Perspective: Legal Perspectives* (The Hague: Martinus Nijhoff, 1996).

24 E. Brems and L. Lavrysen, 'Procedural Justice in Human Rights Adjudication: The European Court of Human Rights' (2013) 35 *Hum Rts Q* 176.

25 C.F. Stychin, 'Faith in the Future: Sexuality, Religion and the Public Sphere' (2009) 29 *OJLS* 729.

26 E.g. *Thomas v Review Board* 490 US 707 (1981) (USA); *Moore v British Columbia (Ministry of Social Services)* [1992] 17 CHRR D/426 (Canada).

27 For the sake of consistency I will refer to 'claimant' regardless of the jurisdiction.

The situation in *Davis* is more complex. It was held she had no claim under the Free Exercise Clause because the law was neutral and generally applicable under *Smith*. There was also held to be no claim under the free speech clause. The Court correctly doubted whether merely issuing a licence counted as speech at all, since it did not require her to condone same-sex marriage. It also held that her claim failed because she was not speaking as a private citizen but as part of her official duties. More problematically though, it also held that there was no violation of the Kentucky Religious Freedom Act, which is based on the federal RFRA. This applies to laws which are neutral and generically applicable since it only requires a 'substantial burden' on her belief. The court's discussion of this point was brief. It characterised the burden on her as merely being 'asked to signify that couples meet the legal requirements to marry'. This seems to understate Davis' involvement since she directly facilitated the legal marriage. The court also seemed to find relevant that she could exercise her Christian beliefs in other ways, such as 'attend[ing] church twice a week'. Although this would be relevant in considering the *extent* of the interference under the final balancing test it is irrelevant to the question of whether her right to religious freedom has been interfered with in the first place.

Davis though not only objected to issuing licences herself but refused to allow her assistants to do so either. As discussed in Chapter 4, a proportionality approach requires there to be a close connection between the belief and the act in order for there to be an interference with freedom of religion. Davis objected that having her name on the licence as the registrar for the county would imply that she endorsed the marriage. However, this is a very tenuous link and the mere appearance of her name on the licence is too remote from her belief about same-sex marriage to amount to an interference with her rights.

The correct approach then is to say that there was an interference with the registrars' rights where they were required to personally issue licences or perform marriages, since they were forced to choose between what they perceive as a religious obligation and their employment and there is a direct link between their actions and the marriage. This is not though the case in *Brady* or *Davis*, where the obligation to appoint or to allow an assistant to issue licences was too indirect to constitute an interference. Notwithstanding that the clerks might still consider that this involved them in an immoral act, not every burden on religious practice constitutes an interference with the right to freedom of religion.

Legitimate aim

Having decided that there is an interference, the first stage of the proportionality test proper is to decide whether there is a legitimate aim behind the refusal to grant an exemption. The clearest legitimate aim is preventing discrimination. Even in those cases such as *Ladele* where there would be no overall effect on the service provided, since services could be provided by other employees with little or no additional cost to the employer or inconvenience to service users, there is still a legitimate aim in providing a non-discriminatory service. This is not merely about avoiding 'bare offence',[28] which, as argued, does not amount to a legitimate aim. First, preventing discrimination itself is

28 As Hambler argues: A. Hambler, 'Recognising a Right to "Conscientiously Object" for Registrars whose Religious Beliefs are Incompatible with their Duty to Conduct Same-Sex Civil Partnerships' (2012) 7 *Religion and Human Rights* 157. See also I. Leigh and A. Hambler, 'Religious Symbols, Conscience and the Rights of Others' (2014) 3 *OJLR* 2.

legitimate. Gay couples are denied formal equality: they do not receive the same treatment from all public officials.[29] If it were not for the person's sexual orientation, the employee's duties would not have been rearranged. Even if the discrimination is not directly experienced, permitting it is stigmatising and hurtful and conveys the message that a person is not equal to others.[30] It therefore has real effects.

Second, although the employer does not necessarily take any view on the employee's objections, and certainly does not have to share them, the underlying argument of the employee is likely to be highly offensive to many. The employee is arguing that same-sex marriage or homosexual sexual activities, or perhaps even a homosexual orientation, are immoral. Employers have a legitimate aim in seeking to distance themselves from these views and to demonstrate that they think such views are unacceptable, although this does not mean that it will be proportionate to do so in all cases. Related aims are more prosaic but still legitimate, such as maintaining operational efficiency and aiming to prevent disquiet within the workplace.[31] In *Ladele* for example, there had been complaints from gay colleagues about her stance. Resolving the dispute had therefore become necessary.

A further potentially legitimate, although more problematic, aim is a broader objective to create an inclusive and welcoming space for all as a matter of public policy. Such a policy would not only include prohibitions against discrimination but go further, with the aim being to change people's attitudes. It is not a coincidence that Islington's anti-discrimination policy was called 'Dignity for All'. This is what could be called the 'cultural transformation' purpose of anti-discrimination law.[32] However, since this objective could justify severe interferences with moral autonomy, this needs to be interpreted restrictively in order to be legitimate.[33] Even leaving this aside though, this aspect of the proportionality test is met in these cases.

Rational connection

The second step in the proportionality analysis requires a rational connection between the legitimate aim and the action complained of. The connection between preventing a registrar from discriminating and the legitimate aims discussed is clear: it would mean for example that couples do not directly experience discrimination (where this is in issue), demonstrate that such discrimination is unacceptable and prevent the 'dignitary hurt'[34] arising from awareness of an exemption. This test is met in all the cases.

No less restrictive means

The no less restrictive means or necessity test aspect of the proportionality test asks what can be factually achieved:[35] is there an alternative which can maintain the 'amount' of freedom of religion, while increasing freedom from discrimination? In other words, is the restriction

29 B. MacDougall, 'Refusing to Officiate at Same-Sex Civil Marriages' (2006) 69 *Sask L Rev* 351.
30 S. Gilreath, 'Not a Moral Issue: Same-Sex Marriage and Religious Liberty' (2010) *U Ill L Rev* 205; A. Koppelman, *Antidiscrimination Law and Social Equality* (New Haven: Yale UP, 1996) 57–76.
31 Although the weight these aims are given will vary.
32 Koppelman supra n.30.
33 See previous chapter.
34 *Marriage Commissioners* supra n.9, para 107.
35 See previous chapter.

Pareto optimal?[36] The proposed amendment to the Saskatchewan Marriage Act in the *Marriage Commissioners Case* failed on the basis that it had not 'minimally impaired' the right, the Canadian equivalent of the no less restrictive means test.[37] Since the Saskatchewan system relied on couples contacting marriage commissioners themselves, the commissioner would directly tell a gay couple that he would not perform a ceremony. The Court therefore held that giving a right to refuse as the marriage system stood did not constitute the least impairment of the right to non-discrimination, since an alternative system could be devised where a same-sex couple would not be confronted with direct rejection. In this alternative system, couples could approach the Director of the Marriage Unit who would give them a list of marriage commissioners who were available and willing to perform the ceremony. Thus the couple would be unaware if a commissioner had objected. The proportionality and thus constitutionality of the legislative amendment therefore failed.

Within the English context though, the no less restrictive means test is met as the English registry system already uses a similar scheme to that suggested by the Saskatchewan Court of Appeal. Since a person applies to the local registry office as a whole rather than to a particular registrar, there is no replacement system available which could lessen the discriminatory effect of an exemption being given.

Greater concentration on this part of the test, not merely by courts when they eventually come to review these decisions but in a more general sense by all participants before this point, could move the discussion beyond the exemption and no exemption dilemma. The ECtHR in particular often tends to consider in an overall way whether the actions are justified rather than assessing each aspect of the test separately. Although this binary choice highlights the principles behind these cases, sometimes different practical solutions are available which can adequately protect rights on both sides. Failure to consider this stage carefully is therefore problematic.

Considering this part of the test separately can have beneficial effects. Minow draws attention to a resolution of a dispute in San Francisco.[38] The city proposed a policy that all its contractors must provide domestic partner benefits equal to those provided to spouses. The Catholic Church opposed this for its agencies on the basis that it required them to recognise domestic partnership as equivalent to marriage. This appeared to place the parties in deadlock. However, the Archbishop of San Francisco also stated that the Church approved of methods to ensure more had healthcare coverage. Thus an alternative policy was devised where a party would be compliant if they 'allow[ed] each employee to designate a legally domiciled member of the employee's household'.[39] This fulfilled San Francisco's aim of ensuring that gay employees, who could not legally marry at the time, received the same benefits as married employees to the same extent as the original policy, but interfered less with the Church's freedom of religion since it made the *type* of relationship irrelevant.[40] Although this part of the test will not necessarily make a difference to the conclusion in all cases, it is a valuable part of the proportionality test.

36 R. Alexy, *A Theory of Constitutional Rights*, tr. J. Rivers (Oxford: Oxford UP, 2002) 573.

37 As explained in the previous chapter, the Canadian test of minimal impairment is broader than the test of no less restrictive means used in the German model.

38 M. Minow, 'Should Religious Groups be Exempt from Civil Rights Laws?' (2007) 48 *BCL Rev* 781.

39 Ibid., 830.

40 C.f Stychin supra n.25 on similarities between queer and feminist theorists and religious arguments.

Balancing and justification

As *Ladele* and *Slater* pass the first three parts of the proportionality test the decision therefore comes down to the final balancing test. It might be argued that the balance should always come down on the side of the non-discrimination right on the basis that all discriminatory action denies respect and automatically assigns a less than equal worth and perhaps even less than human worth to those discriminated against. In other words, since protecting dignity is at the core of human rights protection, is it not almost always proportionate to prohibit discrimination?

As discussed in Chapter 4 though, the situation is more complex than this. Some discrimination certainly *does* deny the personhood of others, or in other words, the intrinsic respect granted to all merely by being human, but not every legally prohibited act of discrimination is necessarily a violation of human dignity.[41] The registrars' claims should not be rejected immediately on this basis. They did not act in a gratuitously offensive way. In *Nichols*, while the refusal to serve was undoubtedly hurtful, Nichols merely stated that he refused to marry the couple because it went against his beliefs. In *Ladele* the letter she wrote to her managers describing her position was described by the EAT as 'thoughtful and temperate'.[42] Not all discriminatory acts that involve criticism of homosexuality or same-sex marriage will be intrinsically unacceptable. There is also a difference between the obligations of a state and those of individuals. For a state to deny same-sex couples marriage or at least a functional equivalent to it is one thing; for an individual to refuse to perform it quite another. These cases therefore should rest on a fact-specific analysis of the rights involved in the particular case and not be immediately ruled out.

Indeed, those involved in these disputes may need to have 'moral recognition respect'[43] for those with opposing views. Having moral recognition respect for something means that the 'inappropriate consideration or weighing of that fact or feature would result in behaviour that is morally wrong'.[44] This form of respect is not necessarily, and indeed often will not be, about respect for opinions, which many think fundamentally wrong, but rather respect for individuals, including their religious identity. Taking *Ladele* as an example, even if her actual views are rejected, her dilemma, that of being forced to make a choice between her conscience and her employment obligations, is understandable. The argument that one has a duty to obey one's conscience is a morally coherent one.[45] Although opposed to civil partnerships, Ladele did not seek to prevent couples from entering into them, only to have no part in them. By exchanging her shifts with colleagues she aimed to resolve her dilemma.

Before considering what the appropriate balance of rights should be, more needs to be said about how the balancing stage should be carried out. As discussed in the previous chapter, much of the purpose of a proportionality analysis is about contesting the claims of public authorities and requiring them to demonstrate suitable justification for their actions.[46] Part of this suitability is about the kinds of reasons that should be given. The justification should go not only to the onlooker, but also to those who will be bound by it.[47] This does

41 M. Mahlmann, 'Six Antidotes to Dignity Fatigue in Ethics and Law' in C. McCrudden (ed.), *Understanding Human Dignity* (Oxford: Oxford UP, 2013) 610.

42 EAT judgment supra n.6, 406.

43 S. Darwall, 'Two Kinds of Respect' (1977) 88 *Ethics* 36.

44 Ibid, 41.

45 J.F. Childress, 'Appeals to Conscience' (1979) 89 *Ethics* 315.

46 M. Kumm, 'The Idea of Socratic Contestation and the Right to Justification: The Point of Rights-Based Proportionality Review' (2010) 4 *Law & Ethics of Human Rights* 141.

47 L. Swaine, *The Liberal Conscience* (New York: Columbia UP, 2006) Ch. 4.

not mean reasons have to be given that *will* be accepted by those who are bound by it. This may well be impossible. However, it means that arguments that a person's views are irrational or bigoted are not justificatory reasons. They express only a conclusion, not reasoning, and are not explicable unless the basis for judgment is shared. Such arguments are only likely to engender resentment and a greater sense of marginalisation.

Happily, there is rarely a breach of this principle in any of these cases even when the court considers the losing claim. For example, in denying the clerks' claim in *Brady v Dean,* the Court first relied on the duty of neutrality of public officials but more heavily on the accommodation already given to them as they were permitted to appoint an assistant to grant marriage licences for same-sex couples. In the Canadian cases, the courts denied an exemption based on a consideration of the duty of neutrality of public officials and the hurtful effect on gay couples if refused service. In *Ladele* it was the overarching importance of the non-discrimination policy to Islington Council that was significant. Indeed, at points Ladele even receives sympathy for her situation. Elias J for example in the Employment Appeal Tribunal stated that 'fundamental changes in social attitudes, particularly with respect to sexual orientation, are happening very fast and for some – and not only those with religious objections – they are genuinely perplexing'.[48] Although of course there can be disagreement as to the weight these arguments should be given, they provide a suitable type of reasoning. No mention is made in any of these cases of the central but contested moral claim that homosexuality must be accepted as a morally neutral trait. In none of these decisions were the registrars told that their beliefs are wrong, merely that they must bear the burden of their beliefs.

There is however a serious failure to characterise the non-discrimination right appropriately in the dissenting opinion given by Judges Vučinič and De Gaetano in the ECtHR in their discussion of *Ladele* in *Eweida v UK*. They held that there had been a violation of Article 14 taken with Article 9 in her case.[49] Rather than seeing this as a difficult question of conflicting rights though, they reduce the non-discrimination claim to mere pettiness, referring to the complaints made by Ladele's gay colleagues as 'back-stabbing', to Islington's policies as 'obsessive political correctness' and put 'gay rights' in quotation marks, as if these rights have no ECHR protection. This is highly unsatisfactory.

A second but related requirement regarding justification is that both sides should be permitted to have their concerns listened to and taken seriously by the decision-maker.[50] This is linked to a norm of promoting dialogue and deliberation and, as noted above, is an important part of procedural justice. Here the cases demonstrate a different, less satisfactory, picture. Ideally, such dialogue would take place informally when such issues are first raised. In *Ladele* this initial discussion was inadequate. Her managers seemed to have decided immediately that refusing to perform a civil partnership was 'an act of homophobia' and a breach of the Council's 'Dignity for All' policy and thus that no accommodation should

48 EAT judgment supra n.6, 412.

49 Ladele claimed there had been a breach of Art. 14, the right to non-discrimination, taken with Art. 9, because she was not treated differently from staff who did not have a conscientious objection to registering civil partnerships. Failure to treat a person differently when there is a relevant reason for doing so has been held to be a breach of Art. 14 by the ECtHR; see *Thlimmenos v Greece* (2001) 31 EHRR 411.

50 This idea of dialogue was used in G. Bouchard and C. Taylor, *Building the Future: A Time for Reconciliation* (Gouvernement du Quebec, 2008). As stated above, this is an important part of procedural justice: T. Tyler, 'Procedural Justice and the Courts' (2007) 44 *Ct Rev* 26.

even be considered.[51] At an earlier stage, the decision to designate her a civil partnership registrar without any consultation, despite her having raised objections and when there was no legal obligation to do so,[52] demonstrates a failure of dialogue. The Employment Appeal Tribunal and Court of Appeal however did not regard this as legally significant. Ladele's employer had suggested that she could supervise the simple signing of the register rather than perform civil partnership ceremonies. But this only raises further questions: to refuse to perform ceremonies is just as much discrimination as a refusal to perform civil partnerships at all, although presumably it will take place less often. Furthermore, this accommodation did not match her objection: she thought that all same-sex marriage or partnership, however created, was immoral.

This failure of dialogue is also apparent in the situation that arose in *Slater*. However, it was because of this that she is successful. The legal question in the US system, since this was a religious discrimination case brought against an employer and not a claim that her constitutional rights had been violated,[53] is whether she had been 'reasonably accommodated' up to the point of it causing undue hardship to her employer. While undue hardship has been interpreted very broadly by the US courts to include any more than a de minimis burden to the employer, at a minimum the employer must enquire as to what accommodation is sought and consider whether this accommodation would constitute an undue burden.[54] Since Slater's employer did not consider whether it would have been possible to distribute the work of registering domestic partnerships among the other staff, the court refused to give summary judgment against her and the claim was sent for trial. However, because this case was treated by the Court like any other claim to accommodate religious practices, and not conceptually as a clash of rights case, it underestimates the importance of the conflicting right of non-discrimination. It held only that 'so long as the registration is processed in a timely fashion the registrants have suffered no injury'.[55] Whilst acknowledging Slater's religious objections and the very small part of her job registering domestic partnerships comprised, the Court did not fully take into account the expressive harm suffered by same-sex couples when such an exemption is granted. Non-discrimination rights do not merely protect against the practical effects of discrimination, but aim to combat the stigmatic effect of discrimination and to increase a sense of inclusion, in particular in this case to challenge cultural heterosexism.

The requirements of justification and deliberation should also be fulfilled at the court stage as well as informally in the workplace. There are numerous problems in this regard in *Ladele*. Ladele's legal claim was that she had been indirectly discriminated against on the grounds of her religion. This requires there to be a policy, criterion or practice which put persons sharing a protected characteristic, in this case her religion, at a disadvantage and for this not to be a proportionate means of achieving a legitimate aim. In considering this, the court should take into account the demands of Art. 9.

51 M. Malik, 'Religious Freedom, Free Speech and Equality: Conflict or Cohesion?' (2011) 17 *Res Publica* 21.

52 Under the Civil Partnership Act 2004, registrars had to be specifically designated as civil partnership registrars. Islington had taken the decision to designate all its registrars. However, it was only under a legal obligation to provide enough civil partnership registrars to provide an efficient service: Civil Partnership Act 2004 s.29.

53 This case therefore differs from that of *Davis*. If this had been the case, she would have had to demonstrate that the policy was not neutral or generally applicable, unless state law gave a more extensive right.

54 *Brown v General Motors* 664 F.2d 292 (8th Cir. 1981).

55 Supra n.18, 1195.

These tests should have permitted her an opportunity to have her case fully considered. However, there are numerous problems with the decision. Firstly, she was curtailed in her ability to put forward her Article 9 case by the unnecessarily strict interpretation of interference that was current before the ECtHR's decision in *Eweida v UK*. After reviewing Strasbourg and domestic case law, the domestic courts essentially held that this only gives very limited rights to manifest beliefs in the public sphere. She therefore had no redress on this basis. Furthermore, the Court of Appeal's judgment also closed down her opportunity to explain and have taken seriously the harm caused to her by the refusal to exempt her because it accepted the argument that to do so would be unlawful because of the Equality Act (Sexual Orientation) Regulations 2007. This meant that refusing the claim was the only legally possible conclusion. The Regulations made it unlawful for a person 'concerned with the provision to the public or a section of the public of goods, facilities or services to discriminate, by refusing to provide a person with goods, facilities or services' on the grounds of their sexual orientation.[56] The Court of Appeal accepted the argument that this meant that not only the organisation as a whole, but also individual employees, are prohibited from discriminating by refusing to perform civil partnerships. Whilst it would have been possible not to designate her as a civil partnership registrar, once designated she would have to perform them. The Court of Appeal, like the EAT which had 'seen the force of this argument' but refused to decide it, showed obvious uneasiness with the possibility that their decision might upset locally worked out compromises whereby some councils had permitted registrars to opt out from performing civil partnerships, but it nevertheless accepted this reading of the Regulations. Such a result allows for a very limited scope for a fact-specific balancing of the two interests as part of a proportionality test.

At the Strasbourg level, although the ECtHR gave a much broader scope for Art. 9 rights within employment than it had before, making clear that such claims can be successful,[57] and argued that a proportionality approach is necessary, it holds that member states will have a great deal of discretion at the balancing stage.[58] Although this may be acceptable because of the lack of consensus in these situations in the member states and the ECtHR's role as a supervisory international court, it means that Ladele is not provided with much justification for the interference with her rights. More problematically, the court also took a very broad-brush approach to the question of proportionality, rather than considering each stage in turn. As argued in the previous chapter, the structured process of proportionality is advantageous compared to a vaguer balancing approach because it constrains judges' discretion and ensures that all relevant considerations are analysed in turn.[59]

In comparison, the justificatory process is far better realised in the Canadian case of *Nichols v M.J.*, which does clearly use a proportionality approach. This permits both sides to express their views, with M.J. clearly stating how the refusal of service affected him and the marriage commissioner stating his desire to follow his religious conscience and the value of his religion to him. However, as will be explored further below, the court applied an almost blanket rule that government officials cannot let their religious beliefs affect their

56 Reg 4(1), now Equality Act 2010 s.29.

57 As demonstrated by the finding of a violation in the conjoined case of *Eweida*.

58 This discretion is also evident in the Court's ready acceptance in the conjoined case of *Chaplin v Royal Devon & Exeter Hospital NHS Foundation Trust* that there were non-trivial health and safety concerns in preventing her wearing a cross at work as a nurse.

59 Hambler similarly criticises the decision for 'failing to conduct a full and adequate proportionality balancing exercise under either Article 9 or Article 14': A. Hambler, *Religious Expression in the Workplace and the Contested Role of Law* (Abingdon: Routledge, 2014) 90.

professional actions. This means that the analysis did not focus sufficiently on the actual facts of the case and therefore prevented full dialogue and consideration from taking place.

Balancing the rights

Under a proportionality test, these principles of justification and deliberation are fulfilled primarily through the application of a fact-specific contextual analysis at the balancing stage. This kind of test means that consideration of the harms caused to both parties are at the centre of the decision-making process and should permit both sides to fully explain the reasons for their actions. Given that the balancing stage involves a fact-specific analysis of all the issues in a particular case[60] the weight and the extent of the interference with each right must therefore be assessed. The greater the interference, the greater the justification that is required.[61]

Deciding the appropriate weight to give to each is not straightforward though. Beatty argues that the courts should simply rely on the facts and listen to what each side has to say about the effect on each of them.[62] But this subjective approach cannot be the whole answer. While in *Nichols* the claimant was 'crushed and devastated', others may have experienced the situation as a mere annoyance. This would suggest, absurdly, that an exemption could be given for some marriages but not for others. On the other side, cases can involve claims of 'dire consequences in an afterlife, perhaps for all eternity'.[63] If subjective effects are all that matter, even a catastrophic secular outcome could be potentially outweighed by a religious claim.[64] This difficulty, although real, is not insurmountable in this context. Since a person would presumably choose losing their employment over eternal damnation it is the secular effect, i.e. being forced to resign, which should be balanced. A person's subjective experiences are though relevant to show the depth of the dilemma that they face. As for those discriminated against, it is sufficient to consider that refusal of service *could* be highly distressing and corrosive of dignity.

A factor that must be weighed, which is mentioned repeatedly in the cases but not dealt with satisfactorily, is that these are state employees. There is obviously a public interest in having public employees perform all the obligations of their role. However, throughout these cases this factor was given a great deal of weight, so much so that there is almost an absolute bar on the employees being successful in their claims. Nichols was referred to as a 'public official acting as government'. The Marriage Commissioners 'are not private citizens ... rather they serve as agents of the Province' and are told to 'uphold the proud tradition of individual public officeholders'.[65] In *Brady v Dean* the Court stated that it was a 'highly questionable proposition that a public official ... can retain public office while refusing to perform a generally applicable duty of that office on religious grounds'.[66] In *Ladele* too it is emphasised that she was 'employed in a public job and was working for a public authority'.[67]

60 H. Loeb and D. Rosenberg, 'Fundamental Rights in Conflict: The Price of a Maturing Democracy' (2001) 77 *ND L Rev* 27.
61 R. Alexy, 'Balancing, Constitutional Review, and Representation' (2005) 3 *ICON* 572.
62 D. Beatty, *The Ultimate Rule of Law* (Oxford: Oxford UP, 2004) 70–2.
63 P. Cumper and T. Lewis, '"Public Reason", Judicial Deference and the Right to Freedom of Religion and Belief under the Human Rights Act 1998' (2011) 22 *KLJ* 131.
64 Ibid.
65 Supra n.9, paras 97–8.
66 Supra n.17 at 434.
67 CA judgment supra n.6, para 52.

Evidently the state can only work through, and enforce its policies by, its employees and office-holders but this does not mean that the duties of non-discrimination of a state are the same as the duties of an employee of the state. That a person is a state employee is relevant, but not conclusive. As Benson puts it, 'to say that someone has a public role … is relevant to the kind of review we bring to bear on the matter, but it cannot provide a complete answer that advantages one sort of claimant over another'.[68] Such an approach would treat all state employees, regardless of position or seniority, as the same. It also does not permit employees the chance to be rights holders and not rights violators[69] and risks reducing people to issues.[70]

In other contexts, both the US and Canada have in some cases given state employees religious exemptions from particular work, thus demonstrating that the interest in neutrality, as considered by that legal system, is not absolute. There is no necessary reason to suggest that an exemption has any endorsement, other than in a very limited sense, of the state. If, for example, an exemption was given to permit a person not to provide, or to assist in, abortions, this would not be taken as meaning that an employer thereby thought abortions were wrong, or even necessarily that they had sympathy for that view.[71] Similarly in *American Postal Worker's Union v Postmaster General*[72] it was held that some post office clerks had to be given an exemption from processing draft registration forms, but quite clearly the US state did not thereby adopt the view that pacifism was an imperative moral requirement. US courts have also rejected claims that religious accommodations breach the separation of church and state,[73] unless they provide an absolute religious veto.[74] State bodies have strong obligations of equality and non-discrimination, but their obligations to all their staff, including those with conservative religious opinions, should not be forgotten.[75] While as discussed in the next section, there are some employees where the interest in neutrality and non-discrimination is so strong that requests for exemptions must be rejected, this is not necessarily the case for all employees.

In addition to the nature of the role, a number of other factors must be examined. Considering *Ladele* first, on the one hand, she will lose her job if required to perform civil partnerships, which is a severe loss to her. Given also that the law had changed after she was employed, she was faced with a conflict she did not expect. On the other hand, other employment was open to her, perhaps even with the same employer. It was only her actions within employment that were affected and she, seemingly, remained free to oppose civil partnerships or same-sex marriage outside it. While Rivers argues that the Court of Appeal's

68 I. Benson, 'The Freedom of Conscience and Religion in Canada: Challenges and Opportunities' (2007) 21 *Emory Int'l L Rev* 111.

69 G. Trotter, 'The Right to Decline Performance of Same-Sex Civil Marriages: The Duty to Accommodate Public Servants' (2007) 70 *Sask L Rev* 365.

70 Baer argues that this often occurs when discussing religious practices: S. Baer, 'Privatizing Religion. Legal Groupism, No-Go-Areas and the Public-Private-Ideology in Human Rights Politics' (2013) 20 *Constellations* 68. See also L. Woodhead, 'Liberal Religion and Illiberal Secularism' in G. D'Costa et al. (eds), *Religion in a Liberal State* (Cambridge: Cambridge UP, 2013).

71 E.g. *Moore v British Columbia (Ministry of Social Services)* supra n.26 (employee given exemption from approving public funding for abortion cases).

72 781 F.2d 772 (9th Cir. 1986).

73 E.g. *EEOC v Ithaca Indus. Inc* 849 F.2d 116 (4th Cir. 1988). See J. Oleske, 'Federalism, Free Exercise and Title VII: Reconsidering Reasonable Accommodation' (2004) 6 *U Pa J Const L* 525.

74 *Estate of Thorton v Caldor* 472 US 703 (1985).

75 R. Sandberg, 'The Right to Discriminate' (2011) 13 *Ecc LJ* 157.

judgment in *Ladele* 'requires individuals to (pretend to) value what they do not value',[76] Ladele was not necessarily even required to be hypocritical – her approval of civil partnerships was never sought and was largely irrelevant. She was not required to value them or to believe such relationships to be equal to heterosexual marriage.

However, although the obligation of non-discrimination is a high one, the effect of the discrimination was negligible and would not have been directly experienced by gay couples.[77] Ladele is described as acting in a temperate way and only sought not to be involved in civil partnerships. Without ignoring the very real interests in non-discrimination, and although this is a borderline case, it was a disproportionate interference with her Art. 9 rights for her not to be permitted to refuse to perform civil partnerships. While it was a legitimate, and probably unavoidable, reading of the Regulations that they prohibited all employees, rather than merely the organisation as a whole, from providing a non-discriminatory service, this leads to a problematic result because it did not permit a proportionality analysis to be carried out. There was room within the Council's employment 'for both gay people and conservative Christians, both living out their life as they saw fit.'[78] This will be highly disagreeable to some, including some of her colleagues, but, as Stychin puts it, 'this is pluralism at the coalface, in which purity is foregone, solutions may not be pleasing to participants, and agreements are contingent and partial.'[79]

The application of a proportionality test therefore demonstrates that *Ladele* is a difficult case.[80] Even if my ultimate conclusion is disagreed with, it is still evident that a proportionality analysis gives both sides the opportunity to put forward their case and thus fulfils the principle of justification. It should be borne in mind that if there had been discussion and compromise at the beginning, this case might never have arisen since she may never have been designated a civil partnership registrar. There may still have been offence caused at the decision to have 'given in' to bigotry, but potentially the backlash would have been less and a 'reactive vicious circle'[81] avoided if Islington had sought volunteers rather than required Ladele and similarly placed employees to try to seek an exemption or to leave. There was no requirement to bring matters to a head.[82] Once she had been designated though, this dispute became much more intractable.

In *Slater v Douglas County,* even though the reasoning did understate the interest against discrimination, which may be because the Court used a reasonable accommodation rather than proportionality approach, and thus only really considered the practicality of accommodation, the Court nevertheless reached the correct decision. It highlighted the need for an 'interactive process' to assess the employee's objections and the hardship giving an exemption would cause. Processing Declarations of Domestic Partnership was a very small part of Slater's job: in the two years after the law came into force there were 37 applications, each taking about ten minutes to process, and five other clerks in her office. Furthermore,

76 J. Rivers, 'Promoting Religious Equality' (2012) 1 *Ox J Law & Religion* 386, 399.

77 Hambler also makes this point, although he suggests that the opposing interest is only one of offence; Hambler supra n. 59, 89–90.

78 A. Koppelman, 'You Can't Hurry Love: Why Antidiscrimination Protections for Gay People Should Have Religious Exemptions' (2006) 72 *Brook L Rev* 125, 142.

79 Stychin supra n.25, 755.

80 See for opposing opinions: R. McCrea, 'Religion in the Workplace: *Eweida and others v United Kingdom*' (2014) 77 *MLR* 277; R. Wintemute, 'Accommodating Religious Beliefs: Harm, Clothing or Symbols, and Refusals to Serve Others' (2014) 77 *MLR* 223.

81 Malik supra n.51.

82 P. Elias, 'Religious Discrimination: Conflicts and Compromises' (2012) 222 *EOR*. Elias J (as he then was) was the President of the EAT and gave the judgment in *Ladele.*

the applications were not divided evenly among the staff. Again the discrimination would be felt indirectly, and couples would probably be unaware of the accommodation given. In these circumstances, Slater was entitled to an exemption from having to perform this aspect of her work.

A proportionality analysis, though, produces a different result for the *Marriage Commissioners Case*. Even if the claim had not been rejected at the least restrictive means stage, permitting an exemption would not be proportionate. The directly felt discrimination prospective couples would have faced in this system, which would undoubtedly be felt by many as humiliating and unfair, changes the balance. This is not just a question of one or two extra phone calls.[83] In *Brady v Dean*, the claim was rejected on the basis that merely appointing an assistant did not 'substantially burden' the clerks' beliefs as it was too indirect. This is probably the correct decision. Even if not, to deny them any further exemptions was proportionate because otherwise the risk of couples not being able to enter into civil unions was too high. Such an exemption would entirely privilege the rights of those with religious objections to gay marriage above gay couples. This was not the reasoning given by the Court though which rested instead on concerns about the separation of church and state. However, as stated above, the conflation of the state and its employees is unwarranted and does not occur with other accommodations in other circumstances. The clerks should not have any further exemptions because of the effect on the rights of others, rather than because they are bringing their religious views into the workplace. It is even clearer that an exemption would be disproportionate in *Davis* where she sought to entirely prevent all couples from receiving marriage licences, even where there was an assistant willing to issue them. This would have such an effect on the couples' rights that it could make the right to marry illusory for those who could not easily go to another county to get a licence.

As these cases demonstrate, a proportionality test is highly nuanced and fact-sensitive, meaning that the results will be different in different cases. By requiring justification and balancing the rights, it can protect the rights of both parties.

Other 'conscientious objection' cases

While in some cases the registrars should therefore have been successful, there are some jobs where, due to the inherent obligations of the post, there is a much stronger interest in non-discrimination and neutrality. This does not mean that the proportionality test should not be applied or the possibility of dialogue and compromise should not be borne in mind. However, in these cases, prohibiting discrimination is likely to be proportionate. The first set of such cases involve jobs where the essence of the role is to be impartial, to treat all equally and to embody the state, and as a result such employees cannot be seen to take sides on social issues. This includes judges and those in similar positions. To have a public objection to homosexuality, whether religiously inspired or not, or to gay relationships or marriage, where legally recognised, violates these duties.

In the English case of *McClintock v Department of Constitutional Affairs*[84] a magistrate wished to be excused from officiating in cases where same-sex partners might adopt or foster children. This was refused, and he resigned from the family panel[85] and claimed he had been indirectly discriminated against contrary to the Employment Equality (Religion or Belief)

83 As Trotter seems to suggest supra n.69, 377.
84 [2008] IRLR 29.
85 He continued to hear criminal cases.

Regulations 2003.[86] That is, he claimed that he had been subject to a policy, that there were to be no exemptions, which would put persons sharing his religion at a particular disadvantage compared to others, and this was not a proportionate means of achieving a legitimate aim. The Employment Tribunal and the Employment Appeal Tribunal held his claim failed, but this was mainly because of the way the case was argued. McClintock wished to refuse to place children with same-sex couples, not strictly because of his religious views, but because he believed it was against children's best interests given the research available. Therefore, the Tribunal held, his objections did not constitute a religious or philosophical belief and so the claim failed at this early stage.

As Pitt states, this reasoning means that 'a stupid, but sincere belief, based on nothing at all, is within the scope of the protection, but an opinion based on logic and information is not.'[87] Nevertheless, whatever the merits or otherwise of this position, even if McClintock had passed this hurdle there still would have been adequate justification for refusing to accommodate him. The duty of neutrality and obligation to obey the law inherent in the role of a magistrate or judge meant that refusing to give an exemption is proportionate. This is regardless of how easy it would be practically to apply an exemption, or indeed the respectful basis on which these claims might be made.

In cases where a judge goes far beyond this and states his or her objection to homosexuality in vehement and hate-filled ways, which entirely undermines the dignity of those it is aimed against, there clearly should be no protection. Such a situation occurred in *Mississippi Commission on Judicial Performance v Wilkerson*.[88] Judge Wilkerson wrote a letter to a local paper identifying himself as a Christian and saying that 'homosexuals should be put in some kind of mental institute'. He also gave an interview to a local radio station repeating similar thoughts. The Judicial Performance Commission recommended that he should be removed from office but the Mississippi Supreme Court overturned that decision.

Since it is an American case, taking place in a state with no legal protection against sexual orientation discrimination, the reasoning is of necessity entirely different from a proportionality analysis. The Mississippi Supreme Court held he could not be sanctioned where he spoke on 'religious and political/public issue speech specially protected by the First Amendment' and where the 'forced concealment of views on political/public issues serves to further no compelling governmental, public or judicial interest'.[89] Evidently this case can only be understood within a strong First Amendment context which applies a strict scrutiny test stringently to restrictions on speech, and which is highly suspicious of viewpoint discrimination, that is, restrictions based on the content of the view put forward.[90] Under such an analysis, discriminatory speech, because it is likely to be political speech, is given the highest possible protection. A proportionality analysis would have asked a different question: were the restrictions on a person's expressive and religious freedoms proportionate? Viewpoint restrictions can be proportionate where necessary to protect the rights of others. The

86 Now incorporated into the Equality Act 2010.

87 G. Pitt, 'Keeping the Faith: Trends and Tensions in Religion or Belief Discrimination' (2011) 40 *ILJ* 384, 389.

88 876 So. 2d 1006 (Miss., 2004).

89 Ibid., 1009.

90 E. Kagan, 'Regulation of Hate Speech and Pornography After R.A.V.' (1993) 60 *U Chi L Rev* 873. For opposing views on the appropriateness of this doctrine see D. Bernstein, *You Can't Say That: The Growing Threat to Civil Liberties from Antidiscrimination Laws* (Washington D.C.: Cato Institute, 2003) and M. Matsuda et al., *Words that Wound: Critical Race Theory, Assaultive Speech and the First Amendment* (Boulder: Westview Press, 1993).

balancing process allows these issues to be seen as a true conflict and starts without a preconceived weight on either side. Freedom of expression is important, but so is protecting the rights of gay people and the state's interest in having, or at least being seen to have, an impartial judiciary. In refusing to permit this speech the state therefore has two legitimate aims.

It could be argued at the no less restrictive means stage of the proportionality test that the interest in non-discrimination could be met by Judge Wilkerson recusing himself in all cases where his prejudice might be in issue. Aside from any practical difficulties though, recusal would not meet the fundamental interest in having, and appearing to have, impartial judges to the same extent as dismissal. Given then that the initial stages of the test are met, the various interests have to be balanced. On one side, there is the interest in freedom of expression, and particularly the interest in allowing debate on political issues. On the other, there is the interest of minorities not to be denigrated and subjected to hate in public speech and the important public interest in having judges give, and be seen to give, equal treatment to all. Judges are aligned with the state, and intrinsically part of the mechanism of the state, in a way that registrars are not, and thus their interests have commensurably less weight. Therefore, if the test of proportionality had been applied, it would have been demonstrated that the right of non-discrimination outweighed the right to freedom of religion and expression, and therefore the subsequently overturned decision of the Judicial Performance Commission was the correct one.

A second type of public job where restricting discriminatory speech is likely to be proportionate is where the job is particularly tied to non-discrimination, beyond the general interest in non-discrimination relating to any public official. A further US case is relevant to this issue. In *Lumpkin v Brown*[91] a member of the San Francisco Human Rights Commission quoted the Bible in saying that gay people should be put to death and said he believed everything written in the Bible. He was dismissed. It was held he was entitled to state his opinions as a private citizen but he had no 'job security when he preaches homophobia while serving as a City official charged with the responsibility of "eliminat[ing] prejudice and discrimination."'[92] This is the correct analysis. When the purpose of a job is to promote non-discrimination, an employee should not be permitted to act directly against this objective.[93] Furthermore, the vehemence with which he expressed his views is also extremely relevant, because it interferes with the right of non-discrimination more severely, and forbidding such expression is a lesser interference with freedom of religion than if all types of discriminatory speech were prohibited.[94]

A further kind of employment where granting exemptions may be impermissible because of the nature of the role is that of counselling, although this is more complex than the previous examples given. Such roles raise distinct issues because of the importance of non-directive counselling and non-discrimination in their professional ethics. The role of the counsellor is

91 109 F.3d 1498 (9th Cir.).

92 Ibid., 1500.

93 See also *Dixon v University of Toledo* 702 F.3d 269 (6th Cir, 2012) where an Associate Vice President for Human Resources was dismissed because of the views she expressed in an article in a local paper. The article was in response to a column that had argued that the struggle for gay rights was the new civil rights struggle. In her article she argued that race and sexual orientation were not comparable because race was immutable but sexual orientation was not and referred to 'ex-gay' ministries to make her point. Her dismissal was upheld on the basis that she had responsibility for developing the university's diversity policies and her views were contrary to the policies she was required to develop.

94 See also *Kempling v BC College of Teachers* [2005] BCCA 327.

to work with the client's own beliefs, rather than to persuade a client to accept the counsellor's views. There are three relevant cases relating to these issues.[95] The US cases of *Ward v Polite*[96] and *Keeton v Anderson-Wiley*[97] concerned students taking counselling degrees who had religious objections to 'affirming' either same-sex relationships (in Ward's case) or 'homosexuality' more generally (in Keeton's case). Ward was removed from the course in her final year when she sought to avoid counselling a client about a same-sex relationship. Her university lost its claim for summary judgment against her, and the case subsequently settled. Keeton was required to take a 'remediation plan' after she 'continually voiced her condemnation of the homosexual "lifestyle" and her support of "conversion therapy" for GLBTQ clients based on her religious ideals'. She believed that 'sexual behavior is the result of personal choice for which individuals are accountable ... and that homosexuality is a "lifestyle," not a "state of being".'[98] Rather than completing the remediation plan, she instead claimed the university had breached her free exercise and free speech rights and sought an injunction to prevent it from dismissing her from the course if she did not comply. This was not granted.

In the English case of *McFarlane v Relate (Avon) Ltd*[99] a counsellor, while happy to provide relationship counselling, refused to provide sexual counselling to same-sex couples because he felt that this would require him to endorse sexual acts which were contrary to his religious beliefs. He was therefore dismissed and claimed this amounted to indirect religious discrimination. His claim was rejected by the Court of Appeal and he then sought redress in the ECtHR.[100] The ECtHR held that there was an interference with his manifestation of his beliefs, but that there was a wide margin of appreciation in deciding where to strike the balance between competing rights, and thus the interference was justified on the basis of the rights of others.

Both US courses used the American Counselling Association's (ACA) Code of Ethics. This requires counsellors to 'affirm' their clients' values, rather than to force their own values onto them, and not to discriminate on certain grounds including sexual orientation. It permitted, and in some cases required, referrals where a counsellor did not have relevant expertise or considered that they could not help the client. The British Association for Sexual and Relationship Therapy's Code of Ethics, which McFarlane was required to adhere to, had similar requirements.

It is probably unsurprising, given the vehemence and strength of her views, that Keeton lost her case. However, there were major problems in the court's reasoning. Since the university's policy of not allowing students' personal religious views to affect their counselling was considered to be neutral and generally applicable and therefore not open to challenge following *Employment Division v Smith*,[101] she had no claim that the university breached or even affected her free exercise rights. The case was therefore primarily decided as a free speech rather than free exercise case. The courts have held that, as a 'limited public forum', universities may impose some restrictions on the content of speech.[102] Under free speech

95 Also see *Walden v Centers for Disease Control and Prevention* 669 F.3d 1277 (11th Cir. 2012).
96 667 F.3d 727 (6th Cir. 2012). See for further discussion of this case M. Pearson, 'Religious Claims vs. Non-Discrimination Rights: Another Plea for Difficulty' (2013) 15 *Rutgers J of L & Relig* 47.
97 733 F. Supp. 2d 1368, (S.D. Ga. 2010), 664 F.3d 865 (11th Cir. 2011).
98 Ibid., 868.
99 [2010] IRLR 872.
100 (2013) 57 EHRR 8.
101 494 US 872 (1990).
102 See *Christian Legal Society v Martinez* 130 S. Ct. 2971 (2010).

law the question was therefore whether the university's policy was reasonable and viewpoint neutral; that is, the restrictions did not depend on the message being given. The Court held that both of these criteria were met. The university had a legitimate pedagogical aim as 'the entire mission of its counseling program is to produce ethical and effective counselors in accordance with the professional requirements of the ACA.'[103] These were the 'types of academic decisions that are subject to significant deference, not exacting constitutional scrutiny.'[104]

Keeton certainly had a strong speech element to her case and therefore consideration of free speech concerns was relevant. The Court was also right to give discretion to the university in considering the needs of their counselling programme. However, the assessment of her claims was still problematic. To ignore the free exercise element of her claim was unsatisfactory, since she not only wanted to speak, but to claim that it would be wrong for her to engage in affirming, as she saw it, immoral conduct. Even the analysis of her free speech claims is lacking because it used a weak standard of 'reasonableness'. It therefore failed to give her adequate justification for the interference with her rights.

The English case of *McFarlane* suffers from similar problems. His case was primarily ruled on the basis that the previous, and similar, case of *Ladele* was unsuccessful. Laws LJ, giving the Court of Appeal judgment, also makes a distinction between the right to hold and express religious beliefs and 'the substance and content of these beliefs' and appears to state that Article 9 'do[es] not, and should not, offer any protection whatever' of the latter. However, it is unclear how this relates to McFarlane's case. Article 9 of course protects the *manifestation* of beliefs, and not merely the right to hold such beliefs. McFarlane was not claiming that his religious beliefs should be incorporated into law: he was not claiming for example that same-sex marriage should be prohibited completely, he merely sought to manifest his beliefs. A consideration of whether the restrictions on the manifestation of his beliefs are justified was therefore required. Laws LJ also stated that 'there is no more room here than there was [in *Ladele*] for any balancing exercise in the name of proportionality.' This unhelpfully seems to suggest that proportionality is a pretence, or at least that it is not something to be encouraged. Even so, the case was in some ways respectful towards McFarlane's views. Laws LJ was keen to remark on the respectability of the religious views in question, stating that 'the judges have never, so far as I know, sought to equate the condemnation by some Christians of homosexuality on religious grounds with homophobia, or to regard that position as "disreputable". Nor have they likened Christians to bigots.'[105]

Despite this failure to fully assess many of the relevant factors by the courts in both cases, this does not mean that either of these cases should have been successful under a proportionality test. This is particularly evident in *Keeton*. Her attempt to infuse her professional obligations with her strong views meant the interests of her prospective clients, who were entitled to expect that counsellors would comply with the ethical obligations laid down by their professional body, were jeopardised. Moreover the university was, at present at least, only seeking to require her to perform additional tasks and engage in some reflection, rather than seeking to dismiss her from the course entirely.

Although McFarlane's objections were narrower his claim should still fail. The interests of his employer and clients were strong because discrimination violated core principles of his role and could affect his perhaps vulnerable clients. The applicable Code of Ethics stated that

103 Supra n.80, 876.
104 Ibid., 879.
105 Ibid., para 18.

counsellors must respect 'the autonomy and ultimate right to self-determination of clients and of others with whom clients may be involved. It is not appropriate for the therapist to impose a particular set of standards, values or ideals upon clients'. Non-discrimination and the creation of an inclusive environment for gay people were also essential parts of Relate's ethos. The particular facts also weaken McFarlane's case. Relate offered two different kinds of counselling: relationship counselling and psycho-sexual therapy. McFarlane appeared to object to providing any kind of sexual therapy to gay couples. Although it may have been possible to ensure he would not have to provide psycho-sexual therapy to same-sex couples, it would not have been possible to know in advance whether sexual issues would arise during relationship counselling. Permitting discrimination in that situation would be likely to cause significant disruption and harm to his clients. As for the psycho-sexual therapy, this problem only arose after McFarlane had decided to train for a diploma in this kind of counselling. This situation was therefore partly of his own making. Given these factors, the limited interference with the right of freedom of religion, and the greater interference with the right to non-discrimination, denying him an exemption was proportionate.

In *Ward* the Court of Appeals was sympathetic to her case and remanded it to the District Court for further consideration of the factual issues. As already noted, the case later settled.[106] As in *Keeton*, her claim was considered on two bases: free speech and free exercise. Again the Court did not use a proportionality-type test but rather considered, in relation to the free speech claim, whether the policy was reasonable and viewpoint neutral and, in relation to the free exercise issue, whether the policy was neutral and of general applicability.

The viewpoint-neutral policy the university sought to put forward was that there was a policy of not permitting students to refer clients. This argument was difficult to make though, because the ACA did permit referrals where this was in the client's best interests.[107] The Court's approach meant that the case was entirely focused on the nature of the policy rather than either of the interests at stake, leading to unsatisfactory reasoning. The problem is that there is nothing necessarily suspect in not having an absolute policy. There is, for example, a difference between referring a client who is seeking bereavement counselling from a student who has recently suffered a bereavement[108] and referrals for discriminatory reasons in terms of their effect on clients' rights and interests. Although certainly the Court is right in that, 'at some point, an exception-ridden policy takes on the appearance and reality of a system of individualized exemptions, the antithesis of a neutral and generally applicable policy and just the kind of state action that must run the gauntlet of strict scrutiny', there is no necessary reason why there should only be assessment of the justifiability of the policy in these situations or why these situations are necessarily the most problematic. In any case, it is not entirely clear why it was so readily assumed that the policy failed strict scrutiny,[109] given the strength of the interest in non-discrimination and compliance with professional ethics.

106 L. Jones, 'Christian Counselor Bias Case Settled Out of Court', World on Campus, 13 Dec 2012, available at: http://www.worldoncampus.com/2012/12/christian_counselor_discrimination_case_settled_out_of_court <last accessed 20 July 2016>.

107 There was therefore a factual disagreement, which is why the case was remanded to the District Court.

108 An example given in the case.

109 The Court stated, 'the university does not argue that its actions can withstand strict scrutiny, and we agree. Whatever interest the university served by expelling Ward, it falls short of compelling.' Supra n.96, 740.

Certainly there seemed to be a higher standard than usual in free exercise cases in considering this.

A proportionality enquiry would have dealt with this case far better. It would have meant that the discussion would not have focused entirely on the rule's generally applicable nature. If the rule were discriminatory – if, for example, it permitted those of non-Christian beliefs or those whose objections were not based on religious beliefs to refer clients because they were gay – then this would have been an additional problem, but even if not, it would not have meant that the policy was unproblematic. The Court argued that 'allowing a referral would be in the best interest of Ward (who could counsel someone she is better able to assist) and the client (who would receive treatment from a counsellor better suited to discuss his relationship issues).'[110] This may be persuasive if only the short term is considered. However, it ignores the wider interest the university and the ACA have in promoting particular ways their accredited counsellors should act. The Code of Ethics is not, and nor should it be, viewpoint neutral. Discrimination is inconsistent with the type of counselling required. Therefore, the university should have been permitted to prevent Ward from discriminating.

This does not mean that Ward's treatment was entirely fair. The formal review to decide whether she should be dismissed from the course, at least in the way it is represented by the Court, was questionable. It appeared to focus more on her religious beliefs than on her behaviour and professional obligations, with one professor stating in his evidence that he took her 'on a little bit of a theological bout'[111] and another telling her that she was 'selectively using her religious beliefs in order to rationalize her discrimination against one group of people'.[112] Of course, discussion of different moral and religious beliefs is good and, indeed, probably essential if a pluralistic society is to function, but it was not appropriate for this context. This is first because her professors were in a position of power. Second, it gives the appearance of bias, leading to some basis for an allegation of religious discrimination, even if there were sound reasons for the university's decision. Third, and more substantively, if possible, decision-makers should avoid judging people's deepest moral convictions (unless these have to be rejected on the basis that they deny the basic dignity of all human beings and so are completely incompatible with the protection of human rights) and decide disputes on low-level rather than high-level reasoning.[113] Here that means that the review should have been based on what is required to comply with the relevant code of ethics, rather than the 'truth' about the morality of same-sex relationships according to Christianity, a subject of deep complexity even for the most eminent theologians. This is connected to the principle, discussed above, that the reasons that should be given are those which can be accepted by participants. Providing low-level rather than high-level reasoning would avoid challenging her deepest moral beliefs, respect her as a moral and reasoning agent, help realise mutual respect and reduce the cost of disagreements for participants.[114] Deciding greater controversies may do nothing other than create a sense of marginalisation in the losing side and make it more difficult to compromise in the future.[115]

In conclusion then, the Court was correct in saying that denying Ward a referral because 'her conflict arose from religious convictions is not a good answer; that her conflict arose

110 Ibid.
111 Ibid., 738.
112 Ibid., 737.
113 C. Sunstein, *Designing Democracy: What Constitutions Do* (Oxford: Oxford UP, 2001).
114 C. Sunstein, 'Incompletely Theorized Agreements' (1994) 108 *Harv L Rev* 1733.
115 W. Eskridge, 'Pluralism and Distrust: How Courts Can Support Democracy by Lowering the Stakes of Politics' (2004) 114 *Yale LJ* 1279.

from religious convictions for which the department at times showed little tolerance is a worse answer'.[116] She may have an understandable sense of anger and discrimination. Nevertheless, a proportionality analysis demonstrates there are sufficient reasons why she, Keeton and McFarlane should not have been permitted to discriminate.

Discriminatory religious expression and the workplace

Some religious employees may not experience conscientious dilemmas between their employment obligations and their faith, but may find themselves in conflict with employment rules when they express discriminatory views in or outside the workplace. As I have previously argued, speech that does not accept the personhood or basic dignity of others can be prohibited, and this is particularly true in employment, where employers have obligations to protect their other employees from harassment and harm.

In the English case of *Apelogun-Gabriels v London Borough of Lambeth*,[117] the claimant distributed a document to his colleagues with extracts from the Bible. The first headings on this document were 'sexual activity between members of the same sex is universally condemned' and 'male homosexuality is forbidden by law and punished by death'. He was dismissed and lost his claim for religious discrimination. The decision itself is the correct one. The interests of his colleagues not to be faced with such material, together with the interests of the employer in maintaining a non-discriminatory workplace, clearly outweighed the limited interference with the claimant's right to expression, given the combination of the extreme nature of the views expressed and the fact that this material was given to employees who had not sought it. Dismissal was therefore proportionate.[118]

The Employment Tribunal rejected his claims that he had been directly or indirectly discriminated against. It seems clear that there was no direct religious discrimination: he would have been dismissed for disseminating such views at work even if they were not related to his Christian beliefs. His claim of indirect discrimination was rejected on the basis that there was no provision, criterion or practice that put Christians, including him, at a particular disadvantage compared to others. However, there is certainly an argument that a prima facie case of indirect religious discrimination can be made out although this can be justified on the basis that the employer's actions were a proportionate means of achieving a legitimate aim. A policy preventing the dissemination of material giving a negative view of homosexuality is likely to disadvantage employees who share similar religious views to Apelogun-Gabriels, whether this group is defined as members of his church, the Celestial Church of God, or more widely as members of prophetic African-based churches or merely conservative Christians, in that it prevents them from sharing their religious beliefs on this matter at work. Again this case shows the tendency of the English courts to exclude claims at an early stage of analysis, thereby meaning that there is no full justificatory process.

In a similar US case, *Peterson v Hewlett-Packard Co.,*[119] Peterson objected to a series of posters put up around the office as part of a workplace diversity campaign. In response he put up Biblical passages in his work cubicle, including an extract saying 'If a man also lie with mankind, as he lieth with a woman, both of them have committed an abomination;

116 Supra n.96, 737.

117 ET 2301976/05. See also *Haye v London Borough of Lewisham* ET 2301852/2009.

118 Although Hambler argues that whilst some disciplinary action was necessary, dismissal was overly harsh. Hambler supra n.59.

119 358 F.3d (9th Cir., 2004).

they shall surely be put to death; their blood shall be put upon them'. Peterson said the posters were intended to be hurtful, so that 'gays and lesbians would repent'. He refused to remove them whilst the diversity posters remained. After unfruitful discussions Peterson was dismissed. The Ninth Circuit held that he had not been discriminated against on the ground of his religious belief and that in any case accommodating him would have caused his employer undue hardship because it would have affected the company's right to promote diversity.

Koppelman wonders whether, although Hewlett-Packard was within its rights to dismiss him, this was the best resolution given that Peterson had worked there without incident for 21 years.[120] I disagree. Peterson's comments were hurtful and explicitly intended to be so. Quite correctly there had been a process of dialogue, with Hewlett-Packard holding no fewer than four meetings with him, but Peterson was unwilling to change. Eventually matters had to be concluded and dismissal was the only solution. The effect on gay colleagues who would be regularly confronted with the posters would be quite severe. This was only a limited interference with his freedom of religion. He was not being asked to perform an act that directly went against his conscience: he was merely restricted in the way that he expressed his beliefs whilst at work. As a proportionality test would have demonstrated, not all the burden should be on his gay colleagues or his employer.

A more complex English case is *R(Raabe) v Secretary of State for the Home Department.*[121] Raabe, a GP, was appointed as a member of the Advisory Council on the Misuse of Drugs (ACMD). Six years before his appointment he had co-authored a short paper entitled '"Gay Marriage" and Homosexuality: Some Medical Comments', which argued against the introduction of same-sex marriage in Canada. It argued that gay men were extremely sexually promiscuous and engaged in risky sexual practices, that they tended to have short relationships and that this posed a risk for children brought up by gay people and, most controversially, that there was a link between homosexuality and paedophilia. It stated that 'there is an overlap between the "gay movement" and the movement to make paedophilia acceptable' and that 'the prevalence of paedophilia among homosexuals is about 10–25 times higher than heterosexuals'. It also argued that it was possible for some gay people to change their sexual orientation by 'reparative therapy'. The Home Office became aware of the paper after Raabe had been appointed and it was the subject of media attention. He was then dismissed.

This was not an employment case, but rather concerned appointment to a post where the government normally has considerable discretion in appointing and dismissing members. As a result, the Court did not use a proportionality test, instead reviewing the case on the less intensive bases of whether the decision was irrational or irrelevant considerations had been taken into account. However, proportionality should have been considered on the basis that there was an interference with his Convention rights. It is true that there was no interference with his freedom of religion since, as the Court held, while he was motivated by his religious views, he was not manifesting them. This was because the paper purported to be a neutral scientific paper rather than a religious tract, not mentioning any religious precepts at all. It was not Raabe's opposition to same-sex marriage per se which was the issue. As discussed in Chapter 4, for there to be an interference with the right of religious freedom, there has to be a close link between the religious belief and the objected-to act and it is more than

120 Koppelman supra n.78.
121 [2013] EWHC 1736 (Admin).

arguable that this did not exist here. However, it was an interference with his freedom of expression and therefore a proportionality test should have been applied on this basis.

Nevertheless, applying this test would not have affected the outcome of the decision since a combination of factors would have made his dismissal proportionate. The paper was extremely offensive, particularly in its linking of homosexuality with paedophilia. Although presented as a scientific document, the paper was not a summary of peer-reviewed studies but a polemic against gay people. Although the paper was not recent, Raabe refused to distance himself from the views it contained. As a result, other members of the ACMD had threatened to resign if he were not dismissed. There had recently been a number of high-profile resignations in the organisation and the Home Office was anxious that more should not follow. It was also considered important for the ACMD to have the support of gay people because research had identified that there were particular patterns of drug misuse among some gay people. The government therefore had legitimate aims in ensuring the smooth running of the organisation and in ensuring that its pronouncements were seen as authoritative. There were no other less restrictive means short of dismissing Raabe which could have been taken which would have fulfilled these aims, and given the unusual circumstances and the very offensive nature of the paper, the dismissal was proportionate.

While this dismissal was proportionate, the question arises as to whether employers should be able to restrict a broader range of expression, which while it may be discriminatory, could not in any sense be described as hate speech. In a further English case, *Smith v Trafford Housing Trust*,[122] a Housing Manager, who had listed his employment on his Facebook page, put a link on Facebook to a news article entitled 'Gay church "marriages" set to get the go-ahead', with the comment 'an equality too far'. After a colleague posted 'does this mean you don't approve?' he replied:

> 'No not really, I don't understand why people who have no faith and don't believe in Christ would want to get hitched in church the bible is quite specific that marriage is for men and women if the state wants to offer civil marriage to same sex then that is up to the state; but the state shouldn't impose it's [sic] rules on places of faith and conscience.'

Because of these comments he was demoted to a non-managerial position with a 40 per cent reduction in pay. It was considered that the comments 'had the potential to cause offence' and 'could be seriously prejudicial to the reputation of the Trust' and that he had committed a serious breach of its Equal Opportunities Policy. He claimed that the Trust had committed a breach of contract in demoting him.

In deciding the case, the High Court did not use a proportionality analysis, since the case focused on the terms of the employment contract and whether there had been a breach of contract. As a result, it did not directly consider his rights to freedom of expression or religion. However, the Court took a 'principled and sensible approach',[123] identified the factors that would be relevant to this discussion and reached the correct conclusion. It held that in demoting him, Trafford Housing Trust had breached his contract of employment.[124] The judge said that he had come 'without difficulty' to the conclusion that 'his moderate

122 [2012] EWHC 3221 (Ch).

123 D. McGoldrick, 'The Limits of Freedom of Expression on *Facebook* and Social Networking Sites: A UK Perspective' (2013) 13 *HRLR* 125.

124 He made no claim that he had been unfairly dismissed.

expression of his particular views about gay marriage in church, on his personal Facebook wall at a weekend out of working hours, could not sensibly lead any reasonable reader to think the worst of the Trust for having employed him as a manager' and thus he did not bring the Trust into disrepute. It was held that his expression of his views could not 'objectively be described as judgmental, disrespectful or liable to cause discomfort, embarrassment or upset.' The subject of gay marriage is an important matter of public interest and debate which should not be entirely restricted purely on the ground it might cause offence, as this would highly restrict the right to freedom of expression. It should be accepted that such discussion, particularly in an out of work context, is permissible.

Proportionality and belief

It has been demonstrated so far that a proportionality analysis is capable of providing nuanced and fact-specific decisions in a way which categorical tests, which always prioritise one right over another, in particular circumstances do not. As we have also seen, it may be proportionate to restrict speech and deny exemptions for specific types of employees. In all employment, the rights of others and the public interest will always have to be considered. Is it proportionate, though, not only to prevent employees from obtaining exemptions from part of their duties and restricting their speech, but also to require them to advance the conception of equality promoted by their employer?

As argued earlier, it is certainly not necessarily a violation to be required to hold particular beliefs for a particular job; for example it is obviously not a violation of freedom of belief for a priest to be required to hold official Roman Catholic beliefs. This is also the same for some secular jobs, for example an animal welfare charity could require its employees to have a commitment to animal welfare.[125] The question for current purposes is whether an employer can require some of its employees to hold a particular conception of equality, or act to encourage particular conceptions of this idea. Normally, of course, it will not seek to do so, being more concerned with actions rather than belief.

Where a state may seek to do this is where the purpose of the employment is at least partly to care for and to inculcate beliefs in children. The aims here are twofold: first to advance children's well-being, perhaps by promoting messages of inclusion, and second to exert a 'moderate hegemony'[126] over children's beliefs. The two are of course linked.

Such a policy was in issue for foster parents in the English case of *R(Johns) v Derby City Council*.[127] The Johns wished to be approved as foster parents but were Pentecostal Christians who believed that homosexuality was wrong. They felt they could not 'lie' to a foster child and tell her the opposite. While the council thought they were 'kind and hospitable people' who would take their caring responsibilities seriously, and indeed the Johns had previously been foster parents, their views posed a problem for their application. Without a final decision having been made, the couple sought a declaration that 'adhering to a traditional code of sexual ethics' did not make a person an unsuitable foster parent. The council sought an alternative declaration that a fostering service provider 'may be'[128] acting lawfully if it

125 See A. Motilla, 'The Right to Discriminate: Exceptions to the General Prohibition' in M. Hill (ed.), *Religion and Discrimination Law in the European Union* (Trier: Institute for European Constitutional Law, 2012).

126 S. Macedo, 'Transformative Constitutionalism and the Case of Religion: Defending the Moderate Hegemony of Liberalism' (1998) 26 *Pol Theory* 56.

127 [2011] HRLR 20.

128 Originally this was 'would be'. This was changed during the hearing.

decides not to approve a prospective foster carer who 'evinces antipathy, objection to, or disapproval of, homosexuality and same-sex relationships and an inability to respect, value and demonstrate positive attitudes towards homosexuality and same-sex relationships.'

Ensuring the best interests of the child is the most important aspect of foster parenting. This does not mean that rights are not relevant: a status-based bar on adopting or fostering could certainly be a violation,[129] but where there are relevant reasons to believe that a person's beliefs are potentially harmful to a child, then preventing this is a legitimate aim for the purposes of the proportionality enquiry. As the Court put it, 'this is not a prying intervention into mere belief' but an investigation of their probable treatment of a child.[130]

In the event, the Court declined to give a declaration but suggested that opinions on homosexuality *may* be taken into account. This is unobjectionable, although perhaps rather meaningless. If a couple is to be given the responsibility of caring for a child who is under the state's care, then they have to be deemed to be suitable parents based on the available evidence as to what promotes child welfare. The state could point to evidence that children raised by parents who were disapproving of homosexuality had greater problems in adulthood if they were gay. Given this, the interference with the Johns' rights is justified on the basis of the rights of the child. However, this is not to say that the council was necessarily right to prevent the Johns from becoming foster parents nor that there might have been no way around this problem, by, for example, using them as short-term relief foster parents. Whether a person is suitable to be a foster parent relies on a great deal of information and expert opinion and is therefore impossible to state in the abstract. Nevertheless, it is clearly proportionate to assess a person's view of homosexuality and to take this into account on a fact-specific basis.

It should be highlighted though that this is an unusual case. Normally it will not be proportionate to even consider an employee's view of homosexuality, as opposed to merely requiring certain behaviour, because this is an intrusive interference into a person's religious freedom, which is generally not justified by the employer's interest in a non-discriminatory workforce. In the US case of *Buonanno v AT&T Broadband*[131] for example, an employee was dismissed because he refused to sign an equality statement which required him to 'value the differences between employees'. He refused because he believed this required him to value the 'sinful' state of homosexuality and to value other religions as equal to Christianity. However, he stated he would never discriminate against colleagues and valued individuals in themselves. There was nothing particular about his employment, which involved scheduling jobs for technicians, that required him to have particular beliefs about homosexuality or non-Christian beliefs. It is doubtful whether requiring him to have such beliefs was even a legitimate aim. In general, people should be free to develop and hold whatever beliefs they choose. It was certainly disproportionate and bore little relation to the needs of his employer. Although the court did not use a proportionality enquiry, Buonanno rightly was successful in his religious discrimination claim on the basis that his employer had not reasonably accommodated his objections.

129 A bar on unmarried couples adopting was held to be a violation of Art. 8 and Art. 14 in *Re P* [2009] 1 AC 173.

130 supra n.127, para 97. A case which does appear to show such a 'prying intervention' is *Re A* [2015] EWFC 11 where social services considered that a father was unsuitable to care for his child partly because of his earlier involvement in the far-right English Defence League.

131 313 F.Supp.2d 1069 (D. Colo., 2004).

Conclusion

This chapter has argued that an approach based on a proportionality test, which focuses on providing full and appropriate justification to the parties, is the best way of deciding these employment cases. In contrast, many of the English and American cases rule out the claims at an early stage, meaning that such justification is lacking. There are few straightforward or absolute answers in this context. Employees do have (limited) rights to manifest their beliefs within employment and thus their claims should be taken seriously. This should include a right to put their case forward and to have their interests directly assessed by a decision-maker. For this reason, it may be permissible even for state employees to discriminate, and I have argued that registrars should be exempted by their employers from performing same-sex marriages if this is practical and if the discrimination would not be directly experienced. In other cases, though, such as foster parenting, the employer has a sufficient interest not only in preventing discrimination, but also in trying to ensure particular attitudes are expressed relating to sexuality. The vehemence of the speech or practice and the extent to which it undermines the dignity of others will also be relevant.

Whether or not a person has a 'right to discriminate'[132] therefore depends on many factors and a fact-specific enquiry. Such an approach will not fully satisfy either side. This is inevitable though where no-one has the absolute right to live out their lives or to have society ordered entirely as they wish and where similar questions of identity and liberty exist on both sides.[133] The next chapter considers this question from perhaps an opposite perspective: if secular institutions can be required to accommodate those who disagree with the organisation's non-discriminatory ethos, when (if at all) can a religious organisation be required to employ gay people, if it believes that this is contrary to the organisation's purpose?

132 Sandberg supra n.75.
133 C. Feldblum, 'Moral Conflict and Liberty: Gay Rights and Religion' (2006) 72 *Brook L Rev* 61.

7 Discrimination and religious employment

The conflict between non-discrimination obligations and freedom of religion does not only arise in secular employment. Many religious organisations may wish to require that their staff comply with religious rules relating to sexuality, which may conflict with laws prohibiting sexual orientation discrimination in employment. This chapter addresses whether religious institutions, including religious bodies such as churches, as well as religious educational establishments and social service providers, can be required not to discriminate against gay people in employment.[1] Of course, it should always be remembered that many will not wish to: sometimes because they have no theological objections to homosexuality, or more narrowly because they do not consider it necessary for the particular position in question.[2] Very often these may be contested issues within religious organisations. As before, these issues will be considered through the framework of proportionality, bearing in mind the importance of dialogue and justification. In many situations, particularly in the US, the law, either through legislation or case law, takes a categorical approach to these issues, excluding certain classes of employees from discrimination law coverage, rather than balancing the two rights against each other given the specific employment in question.

From a legal perspective, a major problem in analysing these issues is considering what is meant by different kinds of discrimination. Religious organisations are generally permitted greater rights to discriminate on the basis of religion than they are on the basis of other characteristics such as gender. This leads to a problem in how to characterise sexual orientation discrimination. If same-sex sexual activity is not permitted by the religion, but an employee still considers herself a member of that religion and believes its other precepts, should discrimination against her be considered discrimination on the grounds of religion, because she is not compliant with religious rules (which may be legally permitted), or discrimination on the grounds of sexual orientation (which may not be)? Furthermore, what if an employee is discriminated against because of her status as a gay person, rather than for any particular behaviour?

These are difficult questions. Religion is evidently a matter not only of belief but also of practice. A religion may find it difficult to define a person as a member unless they follow religious rules. It also goes to the heart of religious autonomy for a religion to be able to define its own criteria for membership. On the other hand, merely because someone is gay

1 As in the previous chapter I do not use 'employment' in any technical sense: many religious ministers may not be 'employees'. I use the term to cover any situation where a person, on an ongoing rather than one-off basis, performs work and receives payment.

2 For a range of views different religious institutions have taken see P. Dickey Young, 'Two by Two: Religion, Sexuality and Diversity in Canada' in L. Beaman and P. Beyer (eds), *Religion and Diversity in Canada* (Leiden: Martinus Nijhoff, 2008).

and belongs to a discriminatory[3] religious organisation does not necessarily mean that the religion itself does not define that person as a member, albeit a failing one, or mean that they cannot perform religious aspects of the job. Of course a person is likely to self-define as a member of that religion and denying this may be extremely hurtful. These issues will be considered throughout the discussion that follows. A hard and fast rule will not be given, but rather I will consider the question of whether sexual orientation discrimination is proportionate in particular circumstances.

This chapter will address when discrimination should be permitted in relation to religious ministers, teachers at religious schools, employees of faith-based social service organisations and employees with no religious function. It will then consider the idea of 'islands of exclusivity': that is, whether it is proportionate for some organisations to be allowed to ensure that *all* their staff believe and follow its religious precepts. Of course, in many situations no conflicts between perceived religious need and the law will arise at all, or can be dealt with informally. In other cases the issue will be fiercely contested.

Collective religious freedom

In the previous chapter I argued that individual religious freedom should be given priority above the right not to be discriminated against in some situations. The present context involves the slightly different issue of collective religious freedom. I have previously argued[4] that individual religious freedom should be protected largely in order to protect conscience and to allow the development of moral autonomy. Collective religious freedom may be required in order to safeguard these individual rights of conscience. In our present context, for example, a leader of a religious organisation may argue that it goes against his[5] conscience, and against his understanding of its religious precepts, to employ someone who is gay.

Only recognising individual rights to religious conscience, though, would exclude much of what is significant about religious practice. Maintaining collective religious freedom provides the structure and support for individual religious belief to thrive and the continuation of doctrine and thought over time. Groups provide the context for 'personal expression, development and fulfilment'.[6] Permitting the formation of exclusive groups allows them to provide 'a source of ideas', an opportunity to 'learn and stimulate learning' and 'provide comfort in both an emotional and material sense'.[7] Religious organisations also act as mediating institutions: that is, as organisations that stand between the individual and the state, protecting individuals from the state's interference.[8]

An important part of collective religious freedom, and indeed the right of freedom of association generally, is the right to disassociate, or to exclude those who are in disagreement with the group. This can be as important as being allowed to associate at all in terms

3 As always, by discriminatory, I mean differential treatment on the basis of a protected characteristic such as sexual orientation or sex.

4 See Ch. 1.

5 I use 'his' deliberately here given that the leaders of religious organisations tend to be male.

6 F.M. Gedicks, 'Toward a Constitutional Jurisprudence of Religious Group Rights' (1989) 99 *Wisconsin LR* 100, 116.

7 C. Boyle, 'A Human Right to Group Self-Identification? Reflections on *Nixon v. Vancouver Rape Relief*' (2011) 23 *Can J Women & L* 488, 509.

8 B. Hafen, 'Institutional Autonomy in Public, Private, and Church-Related Schools' (1988) 3 *Notre Dame J L Ethics & Pub Pol'y* 405.

of defining or maintaining an organisation's message or purpose.[9] Without it, a group loses the 'authority to define and to control the terms of its own existence ... The group's vision of itself, its ability freely to tell and retell its narrative story is destroyed'.[10] Therefore religious organisations require some degree of autonomy over their membership and message, or in other words, the 'power of a community for self-government under its own law'.[11] In some ways, permitting religious organisations to discriminate by requiring members and employees to adhere to religious precepts is comparable to permitting any political or moral organisation to only have employees that agree with the organisation's message.[12]

Many religions have strict rules about sexual morality. Therefore, religious bodies may seek to exclude gay people from certain positions within their organisation in order to maintain a coherent message on these matters and to exclude those who they believe are acting immorally. It would be difficult for a church to maintain its teaching that all sexual activity outside heterosexual marriage is wrong, if those responsible for spreading this message do not agree. There may well also be a role model element. As Supreme Court Justice Alito put it, 'When it comes to the expression and inculcation of religious doctrine, there can be no doubt that the messenger matters'.[13] Even if the position does not involve disseminating the faith, the mere inclusion of those who disagree with a religious precept undermines the message. Employees also represent and are the 'public face' of the institution.[14]

Balanced against these interests though, is the right not to be discriminated against, and possibly also the individual right to freedom of religion. The denial of employment because a person is gay obviously has important practical economic and social disbenefits for that person, especially when patterns of discrimination exist.[15] This may be particularly so for jobs not immediately thought of as religious in nature. For more centrally religious employment, such as clergy, there may also be an additional argument: that of the individual's right to freedom of religion which, it could be argued, is infringed where a person is prevented, because of the institution's rules on sexuality, from taking up a religious vocation that they believe they should fulfil. This issue is further discussed below. In all cases, allowing discrimination increases exclusion within the organisation, causing hurt to those affected and making the needs and wishes of gay people less likely to be heard. As explained in the Introduction, there is also a public interest in non-discrimination, which is a widely shared 'fundamental moral value'.[16] Permitting religious organisations to discriminate also has repercussions outside the religious context, even if the exemptions are narrowly interpreted, since they demonstrate to all that such discrimination may be tolerable in some situations.[17]

9 W.P. Marshall, 'Discrimination and the Right of Association' (1986) 81 *Nw U L Rev* 68.
10 Gedicks supra n.6.
11 J. Rivers, *The Law of Organized Religions: Between Establishment and Secularism* (Oxford: Oxford UP, 2010) 333.
12 C.H. Esbeck, 'Charitable Choice and the Critics' (2000) 57 *NYU Ann Surv Am L* 17, 22.
13 *Hosanna-Tabor Evangelical Lutheran Church and School v EEOC* 565 US ____ (2012).
14 P. Taylor, 'The Costs of Denying Religious Organizations the Right to Staff on a Religious Basis When They Join Federal Social Service Efforts' (2002) 12 *Geo Mason U CR LJ* 159.
15 P. Brest, 'The Supreme Court 1975 Term Foreword: In Defense of the Antidiscrimination Principle' (1976) 90 *Harv L Rev* 1.
16 Ibid., 5.
17 Of course, it does not show that these policies are necessarily *approved* of in any way. However, it does show that they are *tolerable,* which other kinds of discrimination may not be. For example, race discrimination is not permitted even in the selection of religious ministers in English law, seemingly on the assumption that to do so would be entirely unacceptable (although see the difficulties that may arise following *R(E) v Governing Body of JFS* [2010] 2 AC 728). In the US, the state may

Types of religious activities

In an important article, Bagni proposed an approach which resembled 'three concentric circles revolving around an epicenter'.[18] Under his model, the 'spiritual epicentre' of a church should be regulated only if there is 'the most compelling government interest'. The closer the church's activities are to the purely secular world, the more regulation it should receive. His four categories, decreasing in religiosity, are:

1 'Spiritual epicentre';
2 'Church-sponsored community activities';
3 Church's secular business activities and relationships with employees with no religious functions;
4 Totally secular activities.

There would be inevitable definitional problems in deciding, for example, what the 'spiritual epicentre' includes, especially if a religion asserts that all its activities are spiritual in nature. However, this approach should not be taken as having four entirely distinct categories; rather there is a sliding scale between spiritual and secular activity, with totally secular activities by religious organisations treated the same as those carried out by secular organisations.

It is important to distinguish between employment related to different kinds of religious activities as part of the proportionality enquiry: the greater the interference with the right to religious freedom, the greater the justification required.[19] The interference with religious autonomy is much less and the interference with the right to non-discrimination greater where the employment in question is as a cleaner rather than as a minister, for example. However, Bagni's approach only focuses on religious freedom and not on the non-discrimination right. Under a proportionality test, additional questions need to be asked: is there a legitimate aim for permitting the discrimination and, even if a religious organisation is pervasively religious, is this a sufficient reason to allow it to discriminate, when balanced against the interference with the non-discrimination right? With these issues in mind I will now turn to different types of religious employment.

Religious ministers

How should discrimination law apply to the 'spiritual epicentre' of religious activities? Specifically, how should the courts approach the question of whether and when it is permissible for religious institutions to discriminate in selecting clergy or other religious ministers?[20] As before, in answering this question I will apply a proportionality approach,

constitutionally remove an education charity's tax exempt status if it discriminates on the basis of race, even if the institution believes this is religiously required (*Bob Jones University v US* 461 US 574 [1983]), but the state has not taken such action relating to sex or sexual orientation discrimination and it is open to question whether this would be constitutionally permissible.

18 B. Bagni, 'Discrimination in the Name of the Lord: A Critical Evaluation of Discrimination by Religious Organizations' (1979) 79 *Colum L Rev* 1514, 1539.

19 This is part of Alexy's First Law of Balancing, discussed in Ch. 5.

20 I have adopted the phrase 'religious ministers' from US law. The inadequacies of this phrase will be immediately apparent given how very few religious organisations use this expression and how its use in everyday speech largely refers only to not merely Christian, but Protestant religious leaders. Whilst there are significant problems in deciding who exactly counts as a religious minister, I will adopt the definition used in each jurisdiction for current purposes.

with its four-fold enquiry of legitimate aim, rational connection, no less restrictive means and balancing.

Legitimate aim

As always, the first part of the proportionality test requires there to be a legitimate aim. There would appear to be two possible legitimate aims in permitting a religious organisation to apply discriminatory rules in choosing a minister, and thus interfering with the right of non-discrimination. These correspond to the benefits of collective religious freedom discussed above. The first, based on conscience, is about relieving the burden on organisations (and thereby their members) when they are required to act in ways with which they do not agree. It is a legitimate aim to allow an organisation to act in accordance with its religious beliefs as this protects religious conscience. I will refer to this as the 'conscientious objection' argument. The second legitimate aim is based on the autonomy of religious organisations, and is potentially broader. This recognises that the ability to choose religious leaders in accordance with religious beliefs, and without interference, is at the core of collective religious rights. As Laycock puts it, 'when the state interferes with the autonomy of a church, and particularly when it interferes with the allocation of authority and influence within a church, it interferes with the very process of forming the religion as it will exist in the future.'[21] I will refer to this as the 'autonomy' argument.

Rational connection and no less restrictive means

It might be argued that there is a rational connection to protecting institutions' religious rights *only* where the religion discriminates in order to comply with its religious teachings. However, while what I have described as the 'conscientious objection' aim only has a rational connection to permitting discrimination where the discrimination is religiously mandated, meaning that the religion would otherwise be forced to act against its beliefs, the 'autonomy' aim applies whatever the reason for dismissal or refusal to employ.[22] That is, it applies whether or not a person is dismissed on the basis of a religious rule. Whilst the interference with religious autonomy is evidently much greater where the discrimination is religiously mandated, any regulation of the selection of a religious minister interferes with the religion's autonomy. Therefore, only a policy of complete non-interference, which permits religious organisations to be as capricious as they wish in employment decisions relating to religious ministers, will fulfil the autonomy aim to the same extent. Thus the rational connection test and the no less restrictive means parts of the proportionality test are met even where the discrimination is not religiously mandated. The important issue therefore is one of balancing the interests.

Balancing the interests

In deciding the appropriate balance between freedom of religion and non-discrimination in this context, the first question is whether discrimination in employment by religious

21 D. Laycock, 'Toward a General Theory of the Religion Clauses: The Case of Church Labor Relations and the Right to Church Autonomy' (1981) 81 *Colum L Rev* 1373, 1391.

22 Therefore, it is not right to say that there is no reason to permit the discrimination where it is not religiously required as Corbin seems to suggest, in 'Above the Law? The Constitutionality of the Ministerial Exemption from Antidiscrimination Law' (2007) 75 *Fordham L Rev* 2031.

institutions should be permitted in any circumstances. To put this another way: will the interference with the right to religious freedom always be outweighed by the interference with the right of non-interference? Such an argument is made by Rutherford.[23] She has argued that discrimination should be forbidden even for centrally religious roles such as clergy. Her first, jurisdiction-specific, argument is that equality is the 'primary constitutional value' in the US constitution. This is unpersuasive. All kinds of social and economic inequality are seen as perfectly acceptable and perhaps even mandated by the constitution.[24] If there is a primary constitutional value, rather than a collection of sometimes competing values, this could easily be liberty. Presumptively, this would seem to permit such discrimination.

More generally, Rutherford argues that prohibiting discrimination would enhance the 'free exercise' of religious groups, as discrimination leads to the 'exclusion of viewpoints of disfavored groups from religious dialogue'.[25] While free exercise, or the manifestation of individual religious belief, is undeniably extremely important, it is unclear why this necessarily means that religious institutions have to change their practices to comply with some of their members' religious beliefs, even if they would otherwise be excluded from power within the organisation. Religious people always have the possibility of joining a different religious organisation more in accordance with their views, or, if enough disagree and there is the will to do it, to divide, as many religious institutions have done.[26] Of course, leaving a religious group is not without cost, perhaps severe, to the believer, for whom their religion may be the overwhelming link to their community. However, it is not clear why the opposite would not also be true: that forcing religious organisations to change would be a violation of the rights of members who agreed with the original policy. In fact, this would be a greater violation: believers who did not agree with the change would have no choice but to accept a religious institution that did not comply with their beliefs. Finally, Rutherford argues that creating an incentive to change one's faith, by only providing the right to change religion, violates the Free Exercise Clause.[27] Given that the state constantly and inevitably influences religious belief, this is difficult to accept.[28]

This does not mean there are no arguments for prohibiting discrimination in the selection of religious ministers. In addition to the general disadvantages of discrimination discussed in the first chapter, it would be important in breaking down entrenched patterns of discrimination in often non-democratic and change-resistant organisations, which have greater resources than an individual believer.[29] Equality is an important value in all three legal

23 J. Rutherford, 'Equality as the Primary Constitutional Value: The Case for Applying Employment Discrimination Laws to Religion' (1996) 81 *Cornell L Rev* 1049. See also H. Skjeie, 'Religious Exemptions to Equality' (2007) 10 *Critical Review of International Social and Political Philosophy* 471.

24 See e.g. C. Sheppard, 'Equality Rights and Institutional Change: Insights from Canada and the United States' (1998) 15 *Ariz J Int'l & Comp L* 143.

25 Rutherford supra n.23, 1086.

26 For example, the Anglican Church in North America is a breakaway group from the Episcopal Church in America and the Anglican Church of Canada which opposes the ordination of gay people.

27 Rutherford supra n.23, 1087.

28 See Ch. 3 and R. Finke and L. Iannacone, 'Supply-Side Explanations for Religious Change' [1993] 527 *Annals Am Acad Pol & Soc Sci* 27; W.P. Marshall and D.C. Blomgren, 'Regulating Religious Organizations Under the Establishment Clause' (1986) 47 *Ohio State LJ* 293, 310: 'Although [religion] can and should be free from government coercion, it cannot be insulated from government action that might affect religious values.'

29 F.M. Gedicks, 'Narrative Pluralism and Doctrinal Incoherence in *Hosanna-Tabor*' (2013) 64 *Mercer L Rev* 405.

systems in issue. However, a complete policy of non-discrimination has received little support, with all three jurisdictions permitting some discrimination in this area. Even challenges to discriminatory policies in this context have been rare. An American woman did challenge the Roman Catholic Church's prohibition on female priests but this was, unsurprisingly, firmly rejected.[30] This was the correct decision. Permitting some discrimination in this area must be justifiable. Not to permit this would be a great interference with freedom of religion and would severely constrain religious organisations from formulating their own doctrines. What is less clear is whether discrimination should be permitted in all circumstances.

The US and Britain[31] take contrasting approaches on this issue. I will therefore outline three possibilities: the first the very broad discretion given under US law, the second the narrower situation under British law, and finally a more restrictive approach which would only allow religious institutions to discriminate in appointing religious ministers where they could specifically demonstrate this was necessary to uphold their religious mission. As will be explained further below, the British approach permits discrimination where the employment[32] is 'for the purposes of an organised religion', where the discrimination is either 'necessary to comply with the doctrine of the religion' or if, 'because of the nature of the employment and the context in which it is carried out', it is necessary to discriminate 'to avoid conflicting with the strongly held religious convictions of a significant number of the religion's followers'.[33] If the discrimination does not fall within either of these categories then discrimination is not permitted. In contrast, under US law, religious organisations have complete discretion in choosing their religious ministers, even where discrimination is not based on religious rules. There is little law specifically on this point in Canada. Rather than having specific rules on discrimination relating to religious ministers, Canadian law tends simply to provide generally that there is a defence to employment discrimination if being of a particular religion or of a particular sexual orientation etc. is a bona fide occupational requirement. This kind of test is explored further below.

In the US, Title VII of the Civil Rights Act of 1964, which grants rights not to be discriminated against in employment, excludes religious organisations from its ambit in relation to their religious activities for religious discrimination,[34] but for no other form of discrimination. The question therefore arose as to whether it was constitutional to prohibit discrimination on other grounds such as sex. This was first considered by the Fifth Circuit Court of Appeals in *McClure v Salvation Army*.[35] McClure was an officer in the Salvation Army. After she complained that she received lower pay than her male equivalents she was dismissed. The Salvation Army put forward no theological argument for the difference in pay. The Court held that Title VII could not constitutionally be applied to ministers. It held that the 'relationship between a church and its ministers was its lifeblood'[36] and 'the minister is the chief instrument by which the church seeks to fulfil its purpose'.[37] Thus the Court should not intervene, 'otherwise there would be intrusion in matters of internal organisation

30 *Rockwell v Roman Catholic Archdiocese of Boston* 2002 WL 31432673 (D.N.H. 2002).
31 The law applies to Scotland as well as England and Wales.
32 Strictly if there is a contract of employment or a contract personally to do work: Equality Act 2010 s.83.
33 Equality Act 2010 Sch 9 para 2.
34 42 U.S.C. § 2000e.
35 460 F.2d 553 (5th Cir., 1972).
36 Ibid., 558.
37 Ibid., 559.

which are matters of singular ecclesiastical concern'.[38] This has become known as the ministerial exception.

EEOC v Hosanna-Tabor[39] is a more recent restatement and reaffirmation of this principle by the Supreme Court. Perich was a 'called' teacher at a Lutheran private school. Her official title was 'Minister of Religion, Commissioned': a position seen by the Lutheran church as distinct from either an ordained pastor or an ordinary member of the church.[40] However, the main part of her job was teaching secular subjects. While there may be doubt therefore as to whether she should qualify as a 'minister' at all, that is not the important question for present purposes.

Perich became ill with narcolepsy. Following disability leave the school, having concerns about her health, would not permit her to return to work and asked her to resign. She refused and advised she would sue for disability discrimination. She was then dismissed, as the school considered their relationship to be 'damaged beyond repair' and because she did not follow the 'Biblical chain of command'. This was a religious policy which held that all disputes should be decided within the auspices of the church and not by secular courts. Perich filed a claim of discrimination, on the basis that she had suffered 'retaliation' after asserting a claim of disability discrimination, contrary to the Americans with Disabilities Act.[41]

Evidently, the discrimination, if proved, was not religiously required. However, the Supreme Court's view was that the reason for her dismissal was irrelevant. The purpose of the ministerial exception was 'not to safeguard a church's decision to fire a minister only when it is made for a religious reason. The exception instead ensures that the authority to select and control who will minister to the faithful … is the church's alone.'[42] The American approach then is almost a jurisdictional one: if a person is a minister, then the church will have a defence to a discrimination claim in the secular courts. This is particularly important when it is considered that 'minister' has been interpreted broadly. The Fifth Circuit Court of Appeals has held that a Music Director at a church was a 'minister', although he had no religious training and his only role was to play the piano during services. The Court argued that because he 'performed an important function during the service … he played a role in furthering the mission of the church and conveying its message to its congregants'.[43] The expansion of 'minister' to cover teachers at religious schools even in religious institutions that do not have a concept of 'called minister' will be discussed further below.

The British approach is different. Although there was some doubt initially as to whether religious ministers were covered by discrimination law, *Percy v Church of Scotland*[44] held that a religious minister could at least in some cases sue for sex discrimination as, while not

38 Ibid., 560.
39 Supra n.13.
40 D. Laycock, '*Hosanna-Tabor* and the Ministerial Exception' (2012) 35 *Harv J L & Pub Pol'y* 840.
41 42 U.S.C. § 12101.
42 Supra n.13, 698.
43 *Cannata v Catholic Diocese of Austin* Case No. 11–51151 (5th Cir., Oct 24, 2012) 18. Although see *Davis v Baltimore Hebrew Congregation* 985 F.Supp.2d 701 (D. Md 2013) (ministerial exception did not apply to facilities manager at synagogue) and *McCallum v Billy Graham Evangelist Association* 824 F.Supp.2d 644 (W.D.N.C. 2011) (ministerial exception did not apply to race discrimination claim brought by administrative assistant). See R.B. Levinson, 'Gender Equality vs. Religious Autonomy: Suing Religious Employers for Sexual Harassment after *Hosanna-Tabor*' (2015) 11 *Stanford J C R & CL* 89.
44 [2006] 2 AC 28.

an employee,[45] she had a contract personally to execute work. Percy argued she had been constructively dismissed after it was alleged she had had an affair with a married elder and complained that a man would not have been dismissed for similar reasons. The relevant exemption in the legislation allows an employer to impose a requirement to be of a particular sex, including not to be transgender, or a requirement related to sexual orientation or marital status where the employment is 'for the purposes of an organised religion' if the 'compliance' or 'non conflict' principles are engaged. The compliance principle applies where discrimination is 'necessary to comply with the doctrine of the religion'.[46] The non-conflict principle applies where 'because of the nature of the employment and the context in which it is carried out' it is necessary to discriminate 'to avoid conflicting with the strongly held religious convictions of a significant number of the religion's followers'.[47] The alleged discrimination did not fall within any of these exemptions.

Only one case has arisen under the organised religion provision in relation to sexual orientation and it went no further than an Employment Tribunal. In *Reaney v Hereford Diocesan Board of Finance*,[48] Reaney was gay and had applied for the post of Diocesan Youth Officer. The official church position was that while gay people could become clergy[49] they would have to remain celibate. Despite Reaney's assurance that he would remain so, the Bishop of Hereford refused to offer him the post. He sued for sexual orientation discrimination and won on the basis that he met the church's condition relating to homosexuality and there were no reasonable grounds for the Bishop to disbelieve him.

A contrasting case, *Pemberton v Inwood, Acting Bishop of Southwell and Nottingham*,[50] considered the very similar provisions relating to qualifying bodies, rather than employers. Pemberton worked as a chaplain, employed by the NHS, and required an Extra Parochial Ministry Licence to be given by the Bishop in order to take up a new post. This was denied because he had married his male partner. He sued the Bishop, claiming that his actions were a violation of the Equality Act 2010. It was though held that the Bishop was covered by the compliance part of the exemption because Pemberton had clearly acted in contravention of the Church's teachings. Organised religions will therefore have some, although not unlimited, discretion under British law in applying discriminatory employment rules.

US and British approaches compared

Evidently, requiring the discrimination to be for a religious reason is a greater interference with religious freedom than if discrimination is always permissible. Whether the organisation has complied with its own rules will have to be assessed in each case. There are normally strong presumptions against interfering in religious disputes because of the lack of

45 See also *Sharpe v The Bishop of Worcester* [2015] EWCA Civ 399, although see *Moore v President of the Methodist Conference* [2013] 2 AC 163 and for ECHR law, *Nagy v Hungary* [2015] ECHR 1051. For a history of when in English law a religious minister has been considered to be an employee in law see P. Edge, 'Judicial Crafting of a Ministerial Exception: The UK Experience' (2015) 4 *OJLR* 244.

46 Equality Act 2010 Sch 9 para 2(5).

47 Equality Act 2010 Sch 9 para 2(6).

48 ET Case No. 1602844/2006.

49 Reaney was not ordained and the post could be performed by clergy or laity. However, candidates had to state that they complied with the Church's teachings on sexuality as they were considered to be 'ministers of the gospel'. The Tribunal held it was one of the small number of non-clergy posts which were 'for the purposes of an organised religion'.

50 [2015] ET 2600962/2014.

competence of the court in assessing such matters, the possibility of cases becoming extremely complex and contested, and the lack of state interest in deciding them.[51]

Balanced against the right to religious autonomy though is the right not to be discriminated against. This right is underprotected by the US ministerial exception. It is obvious that the effect of such discrimination can be severe. To some extent, of course, this will happen if discrimination is permitted at all, but any element of surprise and unfairness in these situations presumably increases feelings of hurt and exclusion quite sharply. Furthermore, as Hamilton argues, to give an exemption 'where [the religious organisation's] actions were not dictated by religious belief, but rather expediency or a desire for secrecy, is to invite misbehaviour'.[52] As previously outlined, providing justification is an important part of the requirements of natural justice and may result in an unfavourable decision being more acceptable to those affected. Since the religious organisation is under no obligation to explain why the employee has been dismissed under the US approach, it does not take seriously enough the individual's right to justification. Even if the exemption is not used cynically, the very act of requiring religions to state their position may lead to a reassessment of policy in some cases, partly because of the internal and external dialogue this necessitates.[53] The ministerial exception as interpreted in *Hosanna-Tabor* is extremely broad. In argument, counsel for the school argued that the court should be prohibited from hearing all cases where a minister was dismissed, even if, for example, they were dismissed for reporting child abuse allegations.[54] Certainly a claim cannot be brought for race discrimination, even if this is against the tenets of the church.[55] Gedicks has rightly called it a 'constitutional right on steroids'.[56]

Laycock argues that a case-by-case analysis of whether discrimination is religiously required would be practically unworkable.[57] However, determining whether or not discrimination is religiously approved will normally be fairly straightforward. In many cases the organisation's views will be set out in a formal document.[58] Significantly, this enquiry is not a centrality enquiry: the importance of the discriminatory rule in the religion's theology is irrelevant. What matters is whether or not the rule exists. It may be harder to establish the content of a religious policy in non-hierarchical institutions, where there is no central authority. However, this is not an insuperable problem. A 'rule' could for example be as vague as that it is up to each congregation to decide its own policy. Furthermore, under the British approach, identifying 'true' religious doctrine is unnecessary, since the exemption also applies where discrimination is necessary to avoid offending the religious feelings of a significant number of the religion's followers. Such an exemption is justifiable and proportionate. There is often division and doubt within religious institutions on these issues. Different sections of a religious membership may have different views on what is religiously required and be able to provide theological reasons for their views. Secular courts are not well placed to decide religious matters, both as a matter of expertise and as a matter of

51 See e.g. *Baba Jeet Singh Ji Maharaj v Eastern Media Group* [2011] EWCA Civ 139.

52 M. Hamilton, *God vs. the Gavel: Religion and the Rule of Law* (Cambridge: Cambridge UP, 2005) 196.

53 K. Greenawalt, *Religion and the Constitution Volume 1: Free Exercise and Fairness* (Princeton: Princeton UP, 2006) 382.

54 Gedicks supra n.29. See also *Weishuhn v Catholic Diocese of Lansing* 756 N.W.2d 483 (2008).

55 *Young v Northern Illinois Conference of United Methodist Church* 21 F.3d 184 (1994).

56 Gedicks supra n.29, 429.

57 Supra n.21.

58 As was the case in *Pemberton,* supra n.50.

authority. It is therefore important that any approach does not require a court to decide religious disputes, but leaves this as a matter to be resolved internally.

US courts fear that if there is greater scrutiny of religious decisions, courts will inevitably be drawn into deciding religious questions in cases of disputed facts where the church claims dismissal is for religious reasons, such as disagreements over services[59] or the content of sermons.[60] However, this is not the case. In *Percy* for example, it would have been quite possible for the church to demonstrate that male ministers were dismissed because they had affairs, without deciding any religious matters. In many cases no non-discriminatory reason is put forward at all. This is not to say that it does not involve any entanglement in religious matters. Where a minister argues she was dismissed for a discriminatory reason but the organisation argues it was because she failed to live up to religious standards, there will have to be some enquiry into religious matters, but this will be limited: the enquiry will only be to assess whether the religious reason is a pretext. In order to avoid considering religious questions, this may lead to a more truncated assessment than would take place in an ordinary discrimination case, but this does not mean that no assessment can ever take place. The decision in *Hosanna-Tabor* therefore disproportionately interferes with the employee's right of non-discrimination.

The ECtHR too does not categorically exclude such claims but instead balances the rights of the employee and employer. This has not led to the rights of religious organisations being overly restricted, although it should be noted that most cases do not consider the position of clergy, but rather other employees. While under ECHR law it appears there must be some oversight of the employment situation of organised religions, religious autonomy is still an important consideration. It is therefore very unlikely to be a violation where clergy are dismissed because of disagreements over religious doctrine.[61]

In *Fernandez Martinez v Spain*[62] the applicant was ordained as a priest but later applied to the Vatican for dispensation from the obligation of celibacy and then married. His contract as a teacher of Catholic religion at a state school was not renewed after a newspaper article was published which stated that he was a member of the Movement for Optional Celibacy. He claimed that this was a violation of Art. 8, the right to respect for private and family life, and Art. 14, non-discrimination. Drawing on previous cases,[63] the Grand Chamber held that the state had positive obligations to ensure that Art. 8 was protected from interference between private parties and that the rights of the two parties needed to be balanced. It therefore did not adopt the hands-off approach taken by US courts. However, the Court protected the Catholic Church's rights sufficiently by drawing attention to the importance of religious autonomy and the state's duty of religious neutrality. The majority of the Court ultimately held that there was no violation of his rights.

It should be remembered that this discussion is only relevant where the interference is for a legitimate aim, here non-discrimination. If the interference with the right to religious autonomy is not for a legitimate aim it cannot be proportionate. The ECHR case of *Hasan*

59 *Tomic v Catholic Diocese of Peoria* 442 F.3d 1036 (7th Cir., 2006).

60 Supra n.55.

61 See *Williamson v UK* App No. 27008/95 (17 May 1995) and *Sindicatul Pastorul cel Bun v Romania* [2014] IRLR 49.

62 [2014] ECHR 615.

63 *Obst and Schüth v Germany* (2011) 52 EHRR 32. Both employees were dismissed for adultery. Obst was a senior public relations employee of the Mormon Church and Schüth was a church organist in a Catholic church. The Court found a violation in the second but not the first case, demonstrating the fact-specific nature of the Court's enquiry.

v Bulgaria[64] provides an example. A dispute had arisen over the election of the Chief Mufti of Bulgarian Muslims. The government replaced one candidate, who appeared to have the support of Bulgarian Muslims, with the previous incumbent who had collaborated with the Communist government. This was impermissible, because the government's purported aim of ensuring civil peace did not seem plausible. The action appeared to be taken for the purpose of favouring the government's preferred candidate.

As always, merely because the approach suggested here permits some legal intervention, this does not mean that legal solutions should necessarily be pursued. With good advice and discussion, the litigation in *Hosanna-Tabor* could probably have been avoided. Hosanna-Tabor had paid Perich's salary while she was on sick leave for much longer than was legally required. They also had a fairly strong case that permitting her to come back in the middle of the school year when a replacement teacher had been hired would have placed them under undue hardship as they tried to maintain continuity in teaching.[65] Nevertheless, it would not have posed a great risk to religious freedom to have required Hosanna-Tabor to pay damages to Perich in her claim that she had been retaliated against for asserting a claim of disability discrimination. This would still leave religious organisations free to create their own rules on, for example, sexual morality, even if, and in fact particularly importantly if, these are 'practices that the larger society condemns'.[66] Religious organisations are free to apply any policy they wish relating to employment of ministers and sexual orientation. At worst therefore, they will only be forced to adhere to their own rules. This rule thus deters hypocrisy.[67]

Is the British approach too broad?

A third possibility is that allowing discrimination relating to religious ministers wherever this is mandated by religious rules is too broad. Rather, a religious institution should have to specifically demonstrate the necessity of applying discriminatory rules in each case. While the law as originally contained in the Employment Equality (Sexual Orientation) Regulations 2003 did not have a proportionality test, when the law was incorporated into the Equality Act the initial version of the Bill added an explicit proportionality test so that it would have had to be demonstrated that the discrimination was a 'proportionate means' of complying with the non-conflict or compliance principle. This addition was removed as the Bill went through Parliament.[68] The failure to include an explicit proportionality test had previously been the subject of a legal challenge to the Employment Equality Regulations in *R(Amicus) v Secretary of State for Trade and Industry*,[69] on the basis that the Regulations did not comply with the EU Directive they were intended to incorporate into domestic law.[70] The British exemptions do not appear in the Directive, which only allows a derogation from the principle of equal treatment where it is a 'genuine and determining occupational

64 (2002) 34 EHRR 55.
65 Laycock supra n.40.
66 S. Carter, *The Culture of Disbelief: How American Law and Politics Trivialize Religious Devotion* (New York: Basic Books, 1993) 34.
67 G.S. Buchanan, 'The Power of Government to Regulate Class Discrimination by Religious Entities: A Study in Conflicting Values' (1994) 43 *Emory LJ* 1189.
68 P. Johnson and R.M. Vanderbeck, *Law, Religion and Homosexuality* (Abingdon: Routledge, 2014) 121.
69 [2004] EWHC 860 (Admin).
70 Council Directive 2000/78/EC.

requirement' to be of a particular sexual orientation.[71] However, the court in *Amicus* accepted that the exemptions complied with the Directive as the criteria were 'tightly drawn and are to be construed strictly'.[72]

Given the importance to collective religious freedom of being able to select religious ministers in accordance with religious precepts, it is difficult to see how the Regulations, as far as they related to religious ministers, could not be proportionate. Although the British law is expressed as a rule, it can also be seen as a working out of the requirements of proportionality in a particular situation. The exemptions therefore draw an appropriate balance between the interests of society and employees in non-discrimination and the interests of the religious institution in protecting its autonomy and conscience and a narrower approach is unnecessary.

Biblical chain of command

So far I have argued that it is proportionate to allow religious institutions to discriminate in dismissing or selecting religious ministers in some circumstances. However, the decision to dismiss may be based on a different religious rule particularly in Fundamentalist[73] Protestant churches: the failure of the minister to subject herself to the religious institution and, by involving secular authorities in religious matters, breaking the Biblical 'chain of command'.[74] In *Hosanna-Tabor* itself this precept was irrelevant to the Supreme Court's decision: the school would have had the right to dismiss Perich for any reason, but if the ministerial exception is narrowed, this rule could become crucial. The rule may be just as important to the religion, being Biblically based, and resonating with other religious concepts, such as a rule forbidding women ministers, for example. Preventing religious organisations from applying this rule may therefore be a great interference with its autonomy and conscience.

Considering this under a proportionality enquiry, there is a legitimate aim of protecting religious autonomy by allowing religious organisations to operate in accordance with this belief. There is also no less restrictive means of achieving this aim than allowing dismissal in all circumstances. However, this does not necessarily mean that such an approach is proportionate. Evidently, such a policy greatly affects the right to non-discrimination, increasing the number of situations where there is no recourse against discrimination. Most importantly though, it deeply affects the right to justification.[75] It means that a person may be treated extremely badly, both by secular standards and according to the rules of the religion itself, but be prevented from having any opportunity to challenge this. It can be used entirely cynically. Religious ministers, like any employees, can be extremely vulnerable vis-à-vis their employer. For these reasons when the interests are balanced, the right to religious autonomy, although potentially deeply affected, is outweighed by these concerns in this context. Non-compliance with the 'Biblical chain of command' by making complaints about discrimination to secular authorities should not be sufficient reason for dismissal.

71 See E. Svensson, 'Religious Ethos, Bond of Loyalty, and Proportionality – Translating the "Ministerial Exception" into "European"' (2015) 4 *OJLR* 224.

72 Supra n.69, para 103.

73 See for meaning C. Pasquinelli, 'Fundamentalisms' (1998) 5 *Constellations* 10.

74 As in *Dayton Christian Schools v Ohio Civil Rights Commission* 766 F.2d 932 (6th Cir., 1985); 477 US 619 (1986).

75 C.f. I. Leigh, 'Balancing Religious Autonomy and Other Human Rights under the European Convention' (2012) 1 *OJLR* 109.

Religious ministers: conclusion

A blanket rule that always allows discrimination in the selection and dismissal of ministers is disproportionate. It 'protects unjustified discrimination and administrative blunders by a congregation'.[76] Instead a case-by-case assessment should be undertaken in deciding whether discrimination is religiously required.[77] Whilst the British approach does not use proportionality explicitly, to permit a religious organisation to discriminate if it demonstrates either that the discrimination is doctrinally mandated or that it is needed to avoid offending a significant number of followers is proportionate. It draws an appropriate balance between the interests. Too close scrutiny in these centrally religious matters would be a violation of the right to religious freedom given the effect on religious autonomy this would have.

The rest of this chapter is devoted to the more difficult subject of religious employment aside from religious ministers. There may be great differences between the religious roles such employees perform, even if the role, such as a teacher at a religious school, is formally the same. For this reason, proportionality's fact-specific nature is very useful and relevant to this context.

Teachers

Teachers in religiously based institutions have a dual aspect to their employment. In Bagni's schema, discussed at the beginning of this chapter, they occupy a position overlapping the first category, the spiritual epicentre of a religion, and the second category, church-sponsored community activities. On the one hand they are responsible for passing on religious teachings, what Buchanan calls its 'mind-training function'.[78] One of the main purposes of religious institutions, including religious schools, is to 'train, persuade, or otherwise influence' those who hear their messages.[79] This function is not confined to the teaching of religious subjects. Schools may try to present religious messages in secular subjects and in other activities. Teachers may also be expected to be role models, demonstrating how to live a religiously acceptable life. If a religion wishes to pass on the message that homosexuality is unacceptable, this message will be undermined if those giving the message are gay. A school may also wish to preserve its strictly religious character and define itself in opposition to secular society. This raises issues of religious autonomy similar to those discussed above in reference to religious ministers. The rights of parents to educate their children in line with their beliefs are also relevant. They may argue that the school should provide an environment which does not undermine the moral messages they wish to pass on to their children.[80] Finally, it is also possible that, as in *Hosanna-Tabor,* teaching is seen as part of wider ministry, and a teacher is therefore an important part of a religious community.

On the other hand, much of the work of a teacher at a religious school will be indistinguishable from that of teachers at non-religious schools or from those teachers who are not expected to disseminate religious teachings. The religious interest may therefore be

76 Gedicks supra n.29.

77 See for a similar argument J. Vartanian, 'Confessions of the Church: Discriminatory Practices by Religious Employers and Justifications for a More Narrow Ministerial Exception' (2009) *U Tol L Rev* 40.

78 Supra n.67, 1225.

79 Ibid., 1240.

80 R. Ahdar and I. Leigh, *Religious Freedom in the Liberal State,* 2nd ed. (Oxford: Oxford UP, 2013) 248–50.

minor. In contrast, the interest in non-discrimination can be great. Religious schools can make up a sizeable proportion of the overall employment market for teachers. Teachers may be attracted to work in private schools for reasons entirely unconnected to their religious ethos, such as better resources and smaller classes, which may be a problem where the majority of private schools are religious.[81] If, rather than refuse such employment, gay teachers decide to closet themselves then this 'stunts and often destroys the mental health of the suppressor. It impedes the development of self-esteem as well as a person's ability to build meaningful relationships.'[82] A discriminatory policy may also lead to intrusive and personal questioning.[83]

Such a policy can also have negative effects on gay students, leading to a greater sense of isolation. This is particularly important given that gay teenagers are at greater risk of depression and suicide.[84] Furthermore, as with all discrimination it has a societal effect, sending out a general message that gay people are less worthy of respect, even to those not directly affected by the policy. In Canada and the UK, this discrimination may occur in state schools directly funded by the state. Even in private schools, in all three jurisdictions it is likely that the school will be tax exempt, which functions as a state subsidy. The relevant interests in these areas can therefore be extremely complex. I will first outline the approaches in each jurisdiction and then consider how these cases could be dealt with under a proportionality enquiry.

English approach

The English approach is fairly complicated. Whether it is permissible to discriminate on the basis of *religion* depends on the type of school. If it is a foundation or voluntary controlled school with a religious character, the school may reserve up to a fifth of its teaching posts as requiring a particular religious view.[85] These are both types of state schools. In voluntary controlled schools the land and buildings are controlled by the church, but the local authority provides funding, employs the staff and controls admission. Foundation schools are controlled by an elected governing body, which employs the staff and controls admissions. Voluntary aided and private schools listed as schools with a religious ethos may discriminate for all their teaching staff,[86] as may free schools and academies if they are registered as having a religious character.[87] Again voluntary aided, free schools and academies are all state schools, but their method of funding and state control differs. In a voluntary aided school, the land and buildings are controlled by the church and the governing body employs the staff and controls admission but the school is funded by the local authority. Free schools and academies

81 S. Brandenburg, 'Alternatives to Employment Discrimination at Private Religious Schools' (1999) *Ann Surv Am L* 335. She points out that 90 per cent of private schools in the US are religiously affiliated.
82 H. Paterson, 'The Justifiability of Biblically Based Discrimination: Can Private Christian Schools Legally Refuse to Employ Gay Teachers?' (2001) 59 *U Toronto Fac L Rev* 59, 84. See also C. Yarel, 'Where are the Civil Rights for Gay and Lesbian Teachers?' (1997) 24 *Human Rights* 22.
83 Brandenburg supra n.81.
84 B. Mustanski and R.T. Liu, 'A Longitudinal Study of Predictors of Suicide Attempts Among Lesbian, Gay, Bisexual, and Transgender Youth' (2013) 42 *Arch Sex Behav* 437.
85 School Standards and Framework Act 1998 s.58. See L. Vickers, 'Religious Discrimination and Schools: The Employment of Teachers and the Public Sector Duty in Law' in M. Hunter-Henin (ed.), *Law, Religious Freedoms and Education in Europe* (Farnham: Ashgate, 2012).
86 School Standards and Framework Act 1998 s.60.
87 School Standards and Framework Act 1998 s.124A.

are state funded but can be set up by any interested party such as teachers, parents or businesses and are not controlled by the local authority. They do not have to follow the national curriculum.

The legislation only gives rights to discriminate on the ground of religion and not on other protected characteristics. However, s.60(5)(b) of the School Standards and Framework Act 1998 states that 'regard may be had, in connection with the termination of the employment or engagement of any teacher at the school, to any conduct on his part which is incompatible with the precepts, or with the upholding of the tenets, of the religion or religious denomination so specified'. This may suggest that a teacher could be dismissed for, for example, being in a same-sex relationship if this was forbidden by the religion, although not for her sexual orientation per se, even if she otherwise were a member of the religion and compliant with its religious rules. However, in *O'Neill v Governors of St Thomas More RCVA Upper School*,[88] a case which predates the School Standards and Framework Act, it was held to be unlawful sex discrimination to dismiss a religious studies teacher at a Catholic school who had become pregnant by a priest. The Employment Appeal Tribunal rejected the argument that she had been dismissed only because she had breached religious precepts since her pregnancy was an important factor in the dismissal and this was therefore unlawful.

If requirements regarding religious behaviour under the School Standards and Framework Act permit discriminatory rules relating to sexual behaviour, these are then potentially extremely wide exceptions and go far beyond what many schools require to fulfil their religious purposes. Over 35 per cent of state schools in England have a religious character.[89] The particular religious role of teachers may vary widely between, and even within, schools. There are many schools where the religious ethos is merely nominal.

There is no explicit exemption for sexual orientation discrimination at religious schools in the Equality Act 2010, although there is a general exception if a requirement relating to sexual orientation is an 'occupational requirement' and it is 'proportionate to apply that requirement in the present case'.[90] This, however, as stated above, was considered in *Amicus*[91] to be a very narrow exemption, and it was suggested that it would not cover a science teacher at a Catholic school. Some schools have, however, relied on this provision to discriminate on the grounds of sexual orientation for some of their teachers that are more directly connected to the dissemination of religious principles. For example, the policy of the Diocesan Schools Commission in the Archdiocese of Birmingham is that head teachers, deputy head teachers, co-ordinators or heads of Religious Education and other 'key leadership posts which directly affect the Catholic mission of a school' must be 'practising and committed Catholics'. 'Maintaining a partnership of intimacy with another person, outside of a form of marriage approved by the Church and which would, at least in the public forum, carry the presumption from their public behaviour of this being a non-chaste relationship' is considered to contravene this.[92]

88 [1996] IRLR 372.

89 R. Long and P. Bolton, *Faith Schools: FAQs* (House of Commons Library Briefing Paper Number 06972, 14 Oct 2015). This includes many of the schools set up under the academies and free schools programmes.

90 Equality Act 2010 Sch 9.

91 Supra n.69.

92 M. Stock, 'Catholic Schools and the Definition of a "Practising Catholic"' (Diocesan Schools Commission, Archdiocese of Birmingham, 2009), available at: http://www.bdes.org.uk/uploads/7/2/8/5/72851667/catholic_schools_and_the_definition_of_a_'practising_catholic'_april_2016.pdf <last accessed 20 July 2016>.

Overall it is unclear how broad these exceptions are. The exceptions in the School Standards and Framework Act 1998 particularly, potentially leave gay, and certainly leave non-religious, teachers vulnerable to discrimination and may lead to arbitrary decisions. This situation is therefore unsatisfactory.

US approach

American law is even more complex than English law. As sexual orientation discrimination is not prohibited at federal but only at state level, legislative exemptions for religious organisations vary by state, but some simply exclude religious schools from their ambit.[93] Importantly, there are also constitutional restrictions based on the First Amendment on the extent to which states may prohibit sexual orientation or other kinds of discrimination in religious schools, and this section will primarily address this constitutional issue. As there are few cases dealing with sexual orientation discrimination specifically, I will also discuss cases involving other grounds of discrimination.

The first constitutional bar on prohibiting discrimination comes from the ministerial exception which will apply to teachers in some contexts. *Hosanna-Tabor* declined to give a test for when a person would be considered a minister, but considered that a person's title and the functions they performed, including whether they had responsibility for teaching the faith, were relevant. Some subsequent case law has considered some teachers at religious schools to be 'ministers' if they have a religious role, even if the religion does not have a concept of 'called teacher' as in the Lutheran Church. The particular importance of this is that if a teacher is considered to be a minister then, as discussed above, she can be dismissed for any reason at all, without any kind of balancing or other limits.

A teacher of religious subjects is likely to be considered a 'minister'. In *Weishuhn v Catholic Diocese of Lansing*[94] a teacher of mathematics and religion, who was also responsible for planning masses at the school and for preparing her students for confirmation, was not protected from dismissal under the Whistleblowers' Protection Act for raising child abuse claims and could not bring a sex discrimination claim, because her role was 'primarily religious'. Not all teachers at religious schools though will be held to be ministers. In *Dias v Archdiocese of Cincinnati*[95] a non-Catholic teacher was dismissed after she became pregnant by artificial insemination and she claimed that this amounted to pregnancy discrimination. Despite the school's attempt to portray her as a role model, it was held that she was not a 'minister' because she was not involved in teaching, and indeed as a non-Catholic was not permitted to teach, Catholic doctrine.[96]

93 E.g. Minnesota allows 'any religious association … that is not organized for private profit, or any institution organized for educational purposes that is operated … by a religious association … that is not organized for private profit' to discriminate on the grounds of sexual orientation: Minn. Stat. 363A.26 (Supp. 2003); New Mexico's law does not 'bar any religious or denominational institution or organization that is operated, supervised or controlled by or that is operated in connection with a religious or denominational organization from imposing discriminatory employment … practices that are based upon sexual orientation' NMSA § 28-1-9C.

94 supra n.54.

95 114 Fair Empl.Prac.Cas (BNA) 1316 (S.D. Ohio, 2012).

96 Since then the Archdiocese has amended all its teachers' contracts to explicitly state that this, and other matters related to abortion, pre-marital sex and homosexuality will violate the morals clause and be grounds for dismissal. The contract is now also headed 'Teacher-Minister'. WLWT, 'Archdiocese of Cincinnati Expands Morals Clause in Teacher Contracts', available at: http://www.wlwt.com/news/archdiocese-of-cincinnati-expands-moral-clause-in-teacher-contracts/24846662 <last accessed 22 July 2016>.

Requiring teachers like Weishuhn, who have clearly religious roles, to adhere to religious rules even if these are discriminatory may well be justified in a particular case because of the importance of collective religious freedom. Permitting such discrimination ensures a consistent message is given in teaching the tenets of the religion, provides role models, and allows a religious community to be organised around particular values. However, discrimination should not be accepted where it is not for a religious reason. The ministerial exception leaves teachers vulnerable to dismissal when this is not needed to protect an institution's religious mission or teachings.

The crucial effect the distinction between ministerial and non-ministerial employees gives rise to is illustrated most starkly in the cases of *Kant* and *Kirby v Lexington Theological Seminary*.[97] These cases arose out of the same facts, and although they were not formally joined by the Kentucky Supreme Court, judgment was given on the same day. Both Kant and Kirby were tenured professors at the Seminary which was affiliated to the Christian Church (Disciples of Christ). They were dismissed following severe budgetary constraints on the Seminary. Both claimed that this was a breach of contract and Kirby also alleged race discrimination. The Seminary's principal source of funding was from the Church, which it was required to work in partnership with in a 'Covenant relationship'. Kirby was a member of the Christian Methodist Episcopal Church, a separate church from the Disciples of Christ, but one with which it was in an official ecumenical relationship Kant was Jewish.

The court held that Kirby was a minister but Kant was not. Relevant factors were that Kirby taught Christian Social Ethics and 'participated in chapel services, convocations, faculty retreats and other religious events', including preaching and serving communion and had acted as a representative of the Seminary. In contrast, Kant was an Associate Professor of the History of Religion and while he attended some chapel services did not take communion or in any way hold himself out to be Christian. Rather surprisingly, the Kentucky Court of Appeals had held that Kant was a minister, despite being of a different religion to his employer, having an academic rather than spiritual role and not taking part in any explicitly religious activities, but this decision was sensibly reversed by the Kentucky Supreme Court.

The Court rightly rejected a categorical rule as to whether or not a seminary professor was a minister. Religious freedom is more heavily implicated in the dismissal of Kirby than Kant and recognition of this is defensible. Less defensible is the effect that designation as a religious minister has on Kirby's claim. The Disciples of Christ claimed no theological reason for race discrimination but the ministerial exception still provided them with a defence. While in considering whether or not the employees were 'ministers' the court considered factors that would be relevant under a fact-specific proportionality test, in particular the exact nature of the role and the extent to which it was academic or spiritual, the consequence of this designation led to disproportionate results. Oddly, the Kentucky Supreme Court held in *Kirby* that the ministerial exception only prevented him bringing a claim for race discrimination and that he could still bring a claim for breach of contract. This was because the obligations in the contract rested on a voluntary commitment by the Seminary. Whether this is really on all fours with *Hosanna-Tabor* is perhaps open to doubt, but more importantly does not explain why Kirby has no claim for racial discrimination. As this is explicitly condemned by the religion, this condemnation would appear also to be a voluntary action taken by the religious institution.

In addition to the ministerial exemption, earlier case law demonstrates that First Amendment concerns may provide a defence to claims involving religiously prohibited conduct

97 2012-SC-000502-DG, 2014 and 2012-SC-000519-DG (Ky. April 17, 2014).

brought by teachers even in non-ministerial cases, under the ecclesiastical abstention doctrine. This is a broader doctrine than the ministerial exemption and forbids court interference in religious decisions. In *Little v Wuerl*[98] a non-Catholic teacher at a Catholic school divorced and remarried. The Court held the school could dismiss her for not following the canonical process required to have her first marriage annulled and this did not breach the prohibition on religious discrimination. It considered that applying non-discrimination laws to the school would 'arguably' infringe its free exercise rights and that 'attempting to forbid religious discrimination against non-minister employees where the position involved has any religious significance is uniformly recognized as constitutionally suspect, if not forbidden'.[99] It therefore held that Title VII of the Civil Rights Act of 1964, which prohibits religious discrimination, did not apply in this context.

It is questionable though whether merely because a job has some religious significance it should then be automatically permissible to discriminate, especially where the school did not think it necessary for a teacher to be a member of the religion at all. The decision is also odd in that the Court held it could not make a determination as to whether Little rejected the teachings or doctrines of the Catholic Church. However, quite obviously, simply by not being Catholic, Little had rejected some of the Catholic Church's teachings. This was not the issue. The question should have been whether in these circumstances the school's interest in discrimination on the grounds of marital status was sufficient to outweigh the interest in non-discrimination. The judgment thus overstated the effect on religious autonomy.

In other cases, though, courts have held that applying discrimination law to teachers even in pervasively religious schools does not pose constitutional problems. Thus in *EEOC v Fremont Christian Schools*[100] it was impermissible for a religious school to provide health insurance coverage to married male but not female teachers, on the basis that they were the head of the household.[101] The extent to which the doctrine forbids bringing discrimination claims where there is some religious basis to the discrimination is therefore uncertain.

To summarise, under *Hosanna-Tabor* it appears that if a teacher teaches explicitly religious subjects or is directly involved in spreading the organisation's religious message then she will be designated a minister and cannot make a discrimination claim, no matter how remotely this discrimination is connected to a religious aim. It is unclear how much further this exemption applies. In deciding whether a person is a minister there seems to be some kind of balancing approach, but the factors to be taken into account are unclear and the balancing is not carried out openly, occasionally giving rise to somewhat Delphic pronouncements. Battaglia rightly criticises this case law for 'mask[ing] judicial judgments regarding burdens and interests' and failing to 'articulate those implicit judgments leading to the conclusory characterization' as to whether or not a person is a minister.[102] In addition these cases understate the interest in non-discrimination because of the drastic consequence of finding a person to be a minister. In further cases, a teacher may not be a minister, but will not be protected by discrimination laws if they have not complied with religious rules; an exception which also arises out of the First Amendment, but which is not as absolute as that under the

98 929 F.2d 944 (3rd Cir., 1991).
99 Ibid., 948.
100 781 F.2d 1362 (9th Cir., 1986).
101 See also *Dole v Shenandoah Baptist Church* 99 F.2d 1389 (4th Cir., 1990).
102 J. Battaglia, 'Religion, Sexual Orientation and Self-Realization: First Amendment Principles and Anti-Discrimination Laws' (1999) 76 *U Det Mercy L Rev* 190, 378.

ministerial exception. This may though still underestimate the importance of the right to non-discrimination.

Canadian approach

In contrast to that of the US and England, Canada's approach is clearly a balancing one, although in common with the other jurisdictions, religious schools may sometimes discriminate in order to ensure their employees' compliance with religious precepts. Although there is some variation in the law between jurisdictions, the usual approach is to use a BFOR (bona fide occupational requirement) model. This permits discrimination where it is a bona fide occupational requirement that the person is, for example, of a particular religion, and this requirement is a proportionate means of achieving a legitimate aim. This is therefore very similar to a proportionality enquiry.

In *Caldwell v St Thomas Aquinas High School*[103] the Canadian Supreme Court held that a school had a BFOR, and so it was not illegal marital status discrimination to dismiss a Catholic teacher at a state denominational school because she married a divorced man in a civil ceremony. The school did employ some non-Catholic teachers where suitably qualified Catholic teachers could not be found, but these teachers were expected to support the school's religious approach and to abide by the practices of their own religion. In deciding that compliance with religious rules constituted a BFOR, the Court stated that the purpose of the school was to impart a Catholic way of life to its students. The religious aspect of the school 'lies at its very heart and colours all its activities and programs'.[104] Teachers were expected to act as role models and had to be able to credibly espouse Catholic doctrine. The Court therefore considered that there existed 'the rare circumstances'[105] in which religious conformance was a bona fide qualification. The school's interest in maintaining the religious behaviour of its Catholic staff was obviously higher than its non-Catholic staff, and this is recognised. Even so, the Court may have been overly deferential to the school in assessing its interest, in that it is open to question whether it would really have affected the school's interest greatly if it had had to accept an 'imperfect' role model in *Caldwell*.

Proportionality approach

The religious autonomy that is appropriate in selecting and dismissing religious ministers is not appropriate for teachers because of the less fundamentally religious nature of their employment and the fact that their role, status in the religion and the religious nature of their workplace varies widely. Nevertheless, at the heart of these cases is an unavoidable dilemma. Either some schools will be forced to employ those who do not agree or comply with the school's religious message, or teachers will be left vulnerable to discriminatory dismissals. In settling this dispute, it is not sufficient to classify certain schools as able to discriminate or to exempt all religious schools from discrimination law. It is not necessary, for example, for all voluntary aided schools or for all private schools with a religious ethos to be able to discriminate for all their teaching posts, as they can under English law, in order to

103 [1984] 2 RCS 603.
104 Ibid., 624.
105 Ibid., 625.

maintain the level of religious ethos that they require. The 'religious intensity'[106] of schools varies greatly.[107] The English approach allows schools to discriminate where they could not demonstrate the need for teachers to follow religious rules. This denies the importance of fact-specific judgments and does not provide justification to those to whom the discrimination affects. It therefore unjustifiably privileges one right above another.

An alternative to the kinds of categorical tests used in the US or England is to use a BFOR approach as used in Canada.[108] This essentially incorporates the proportionality enquiry. It focuses on the particular need for discrimination in the particular circumstances and balances the interests at stake. In this enquiry, the first question is whether there is a legitimate aim in permitting such discrimination. This will generally be easy to find, unless the stated reason for dismissal is clearly a pretext. The religious organisation is likely to have legitimate interests in protecting its religious conscience and in protecting the religious autonomy of the school.

The next test, a rational connection between the discrimination and protecting religious conscience or autonomy, will also normally be easy to pass. This is not explicitly mentioned in the BFOR test, but as any discrimination must be proportionate, it is an essential part of it. Similarly, it is important to consider whether the approach taken is the least restrictive means of achieving the aim. It is conceivable that there could be some resolution of the dispute if, for example, instead of being dismissed, an employee is moved from teaching religious subjects to only secular ones.

Normally though the decision will depend on whether the policy is 'proportionate' in the strict sense. Although this requires a fact-specific enquiry, some factors are likely to be generally relevant in deciding these cases. The first and most important factor is the pervasive religiousness of the school or other workplace. Relevant to this is how strong its links are to a church or other religious body. Control over admission may be relevant if the school only accepts children of one faith. This might not though be conclusive. An evangelical Christian school may argue that it is religiously obligated to encourage as many people as possible to hear its religious message and a Catholic school in a deprived inner-city area may see providing education to those particularly in need, regardless of their religion, as part of its religious mission. The schools may though require strict codes of behaviour and belief for their employees.

Araujo argues that 'to have some external, secular institution … dictate what is the "essence" of a private school and what constitutes its "central mission" places [the institution] in a peculiar position for which its expertise can claim no competence'.[109] However, if a school's right to freedom of religion is in conflict with another right such as non-discrimination, a secular authority must decide the appropriate balance between them. This weighing of competing rights is an important *legal* and not religious question: although religious institutions may have opinions as to where the balance should be struck, that does not automatically make it a religious question. A holistic enquiry into whether the school's religiosity is merely nominal or all-encompassing is a suitable objective factor for ascertaining the boundaries of these rights.

106 Laycock supra n.40, 1403.

107 See C. Evans and B. Gaze, 'Discrimination by Religious Schools: Views from the Coal Face' (2010) 34 *MULR* 392.

108 And for some religious employment in Britain. See the discussion of social service employees below.

109 R. Araujo, '"The Harvest is Plentiful, but the Laborers are Few": Hiring Practices and Religiously Affiliated Universities' (1996) 30 *U Rich L Rev* 713, 751.

The second factor is the religiousness of the post. Even if a school has a religious mission, this does not necessarily mean that it should be permitted to discriminate with regard to all its teachers. It is clearly easier to demonstrate that it is a requirement that a teacher of religion belongs to a religion and complies with religious rules, as compared to a teacher of only secular subjects. Nevertheless, the school may wish the religious ethos to be infused throughout teaching and extracurricular activities. The degree of religiousness should not be assessed formulaically. The proportion of time a person spends 'doing religion' is relevant, but only as part of the enquiry. Facts such as that a person only spends 10.6 per cent of their time teaching and supervising religious activities should not be decisive.[110]

A third important factor is whether the religious rule has been brought to the attention of the teacher, as failed to occur in cases such as *Dias*.[111] This allows teachers to take up employment in full knowledge of what is expected from them and provides some protection against arbitrary enforcement of rules. It also has a more intangible benefit in that it demonstrates respect to prospective employees because it shows that the organisation recognises it can only enforce its beliefs on those who are willing to accept its authority. A related factor is whether the rule has been applied consistently. This is relevant because it demonstrates the importance of the rule to the religion. If an organisation has not previously considered the rule vital, presumptively it makes it difficult for it to claim that a further dispensation would be a great interference with its religious interest. It is likely therefore to be outweighed by the opposing interest, unless good reason can be shown.

This does not mean that different standards of behaviour could not be required for different types of employees. Care should also be taken not to place religious organisations in a double bind when it comes to consistency. Since it is necessary to consider the importance of a rule on a case-by-case basis, it could be suggested that having one exception will not undermine the school's interests. However, if a rule is not applied to all this may then be used to undermine the claim that the rule is necessary at all.[112] Therefore the requirement of consistency should not be seen as absolute. A school may well be able to show its interest in maintaining some religiously compliant staff but not others.[113]

There is also a more general requirement of consistency. If gay sexual activities or relationships are the only behaviour prohibited, this looks less like an effort to maintain religious exclusivity and more like mere homophobia.[114] If employees have been dismissed for breaking other religious codes, or are at least required to uphold them, it makes it more likely that the dismissal is justified. Some cases have highlighted the importance of these factors. Cases involving pre-marital pregnancy have for example highlighted the importance of applying a rule forbidding pre-marital sex equally to men and women, otherwise this is simply unlawful sex discrimination.[115]

110 See discussion of *Clapper v Chesapeake Conference of Seventh-Day Adventists* No. 97–2648, 1998 WL 904528 (4th Cir., Dec. 29, 1998) in L. Fisher, 'A Miscarriage of Justice: Pregnancy Discrimination in Sectarian Schools' (2010) 16 *Wash & Lee JCR Soc Just* 529. This type of approach was rejected in *Hosanna-Tabor*.

111 See also *Trehar v Brightway Ctr* 2015-Ohio-4144 (youth camp prevented from dismissing employee for living with her boyfriend when president of organisation was previously aware of this).

112 A. Esau, '"Islands of Exclusivity" Revisited: Religious Organizations, Employment Discrimination and *Heintz v Christian Horizons*' (2009) 15 *Canadian Lab & Emp LJ* 389.

113 *Pime v Loyola University of Chicago* 585 F. Supp. 435 (N.D. Ill., 1984).

114 C.f. *Brown v Dade Christian Schools* 556 F.2d 310 (5th Cir., 1977).

115 E.g. *Dolter v Walhert High School* 483 F. Supp. 266, 271 (N.D. Iowa, 1980); *Vigars v Valley Christian Ctr* 805 F. Supp 802 (N.D. Cal., 1992).

It should be remembered that the BFOR approach requires some loss to both rights. Even if an exception to a discrimination provision were to be made out in particular cases, deciding this would still involve some interference with religious practices. There may be a chilling effect where organisations amend their practices to avoid the risk of litigation, even if this would ultimately not be required if assessed by the courts. On the other side, the lack of a clear prohibition of discrimination at religious schools may make gay employees vulnerable as they may be unsure whether such discrimination is illegal. Nevertheless, a case-by-case proportionality approach is the best way to take full account of the conflicting rights. Whilst it could be argued that a proportionality approach is too complex and administratively difficult, a categorical approach is hardly straightforward, as the numerous cases both before and after *Hosanna-Tabor* demonstrate, and may too demand a great deal of evidence to be put forward. As stated before, a proportionality approach is not a question of vaguely balancing the rights with no other guidance, but a defined process. At the balancing stage sufficient guidance should be provided by the factors I have described above. Proportionality therefore provides a better method of resolving these situations than a categorical rule.

Social service organisations

Religious institutions are greatly involved in a wide provision of social services: from healthcare provision, to services for homeless people, to care of people with disabilities. They may receive quite extensive government funding, and in some sectors a significant proportion may be run by religious organisations.[116] The services they provide may be quite indistinguishable from secular services. On the other hand, the work may be seen as a vital part of a religion's mission and indeed as a kind of religious practice in itself.[117] In some cases the organisation may only provide a benefit for co-religionists. Alternatively, it may be part of outreach work or perhaps include an element of proselytisation to service users. Like teachers, although to a lesser extent, employees may be required to act as role models. In order to maintain a religious atmosphere, the organisation may argue that it is vital that the work is carried out by co-religionists, which they might argue includes adherence to religious precepts in non-work life. Again, I will argue that a BFOR approach, which requires a proportionality analysis, is the best way to deal with these cases, given the very wide range of circumstances in which these cases can arise. I will consider the approach of each jurisdiction and suggest how a proportionality approach would have made a difference.

British approach

In British law[118] organisations with a religious ethos may discriminate based on religion if this is an occupational requirement and a proportionate means of achieving a legitimate aim, having regard to that ethos and the nature or context of the work.[119] There is also a general exception for all organisations if being of a particular sexual orientation, or indeed having any other protected characteristic, is a genuine occupational requirement having regard to the nature or context of the work.[120] The religious ethos exception has though been defined

116 See S. Monsma, *When Sacred and Secular Mix: Religious Nonprofit Organizations and Public Money* (London: Rowman & Littlefield, 1996) 7–10.
117 Ibid., 50–1.
118 This law applies to Scotland as well as England and Wales.
119 Equality Act 2010 Sch 9 para 4.
120 Equality Act 2010 Sch 9 para 1.

fairly narrowly.[121] *Hender v Prospects*[122] involved a charity which provided housing and day care facilities for people with learning disabilities. Prospects wished to give strong preference to Christians even when selecting gardeners, cooks, cleaners, maintenance assistants and relief workers[123] and to appoint only Christians to all other roles[124] even though many of these positions involved no religious role at all and some little direct involvement with service users. This policy was challenged by a non-Christian support worker who was not promoted because of her lack of Christian faith. The organisation was largely publicly funded and most service users were not Christian.

The Tribunal held that there must be something specifically religious about the particular job for the exemption to apply. The fact that some religious tasks had to be carried out in order to maintain the organisation's Christian ethos was not determinative. The case correctly identified the need for a fact-specific enquiry. Prospects' policy failed to give Hender sufficient justification for the discrimination she faced. The Tribunal's decision was therefore correct, as this was a disproportionate interference with her right of non-discrimination.

Given the very limited amount of case law on the religious ethos provision, it is difficult to assess generally whether tribunals are drawing a suitable balance between the two rights, but the structure of the enquiry is appropriate. There are no cases as to whether such an organisation may additionally discriminate on the grounds of sexual orientation and not merely religion, but it is likely that such an argument would not receive much support.[125] This is likely to be justifiable in most cases but as always a fact-specific enquiry is needed.

US approach

As in previous contexts, the law in the US differs from state to state. Not all states prohibit sexual orientation discrimination in employment and most of those that do exclude religious organisations entirely from such laws, at least for their non-commercial activities. This leaves gay employees extremely vulnerable to discrimination. Thus in *Thorson v Billy Graham Evangelistic Association*[126] a mail room supervisor could be dismissed because she was gay, because sending out religious materials was part of the organisation's religious function. Some states prevent religious or other discrimination as a condition of receiving state funding, but religious discrimination is permitted where the use of federal funds is involved.[127] Thus in *Lown v Salvation Army*[128] it was held that even in government funded programmes open to the public, it was constitutionally permissible for the Salvation Army to discriminate in hiring and dismissing its workers on religious grounds. While President Obama issued an Executive Order in July 2014 providing that contractors with the federal government may not discriminate on the grounds of sexual orientation and gender identity, religious

121 Although see *Muhammed v The Leprosy Mission International* ET 2303459/0989, 16 December 2009 (Employment Tribunal).
122 ET Case No. 2902090/2006.
123 Although they did not state that this was an occupational requirement for these posts.
124 Hender was employed before these rules were applied strictly, but they meant she could not be promoted from her current position.
125 And this may well be prohibited under EU law: L. Vickers, 'Religion and Belief Discrimination in Employment Under the Employment Equality Directive: A Comparative Analysis' (2015) *European Equality Law Review* 25, 33–4.
126 687 N.W. 2d 652 (2004).
127 M. McClellan, 'Faith and Federalism: Do Charitable Choice Provisions Preempt State Nondiscrimination Employment Laws?' (2004) 61 *Wash & Lee L Rev* 1437.
128 393 F Supp 2d 223 (S.D. N.Y., 2005).

organisations may still select only members of their religion.[129] Whether this allows religious organisations to select or dismiss employees on the basis of discriminatory religious rules is unclear.

Some claimants have attempted to bring *religious* discrimination claims where there is no legal protection against sexual orientation discrimination. Such arguments have not fared well. This is partly because the cases do not fit easily into such a claim, but also because the employer's claim to maintain religious conformity is valued extremely highly. Thus in *Pedreira v Kentucky Baptist Homes for Children*[130] a lesbian therapist could be dismissed from her job in a children's home because her 'lifestyle' was not in accordance with its 'Christian core values'. Her claim of religious discrimination was rejected by the Court on the basis that she did not 'allege that her sexual orientation is premised on her religious beliefs or lack thereof.'[131]

There was a similar result in *Hall v Baptist Memorial Health Care Corp.*[132] There a gay woman employed as a 'student services specialist' at a Southern Baptist college 'permeated with religious overtones',[133] which trained medical staff as part of its Christian outreach mission, was dismissed. Her job involved organising student societies' activities and ensuring that they complied with Baptist teachings. She also had a role in counselling students. This is not a straightforward case of sexual orientation discrimination though because she was dismissed only after she became a lay minister at a church that encouraged gay membership and taught that there was no inconsistency between Christianity and homosexuality. Southern Baptists though saw a 'homosexual lifestyle' as 'an abomination in the eyes of God'.[134] She was offered a transfer of position, but refused and was dismissed because there was a 'conflict of interest'. The Court held that since she publicly opposed an important aspect of Southern Baptist teaching she could be dismissed. It argued there was no religious discrimination because any person who publicly opposed an aspect of the college's teaching would have been dismissed, whether this was for religious reasons or not.

This argument is though unsatisfactory: she was dismissed because she held different opinions about a religious matter from her employer and because of her involvement in a different church. It is better to separate the question of whether there is religious discrimination from the question of whether the discrimination was justified, as could be done under a proportionality approach. This could accept that she had been discriminated against because of her religious beliefs but then consider the argument that such discrimination was proportionate.[135]

If this case had been considered under a proportionality enquiry, the college could claim it had a strong interest in freedom of religion because of the nature of her job and the importance to the college of maintaining a clear religious identity and message. Evidently there is a greater religious interest where an employee actively and publicly opposes a religious precept, rather than simply failing to abide by it. However, the court might have overstated how public Hall's opinions were. Courts should be careful not to see public

129 Executive Order 13672. See I. Lupu, 'Moving Targets: *Obergefell*, *Hobby Lobby*, and the Future of LGBT Rights' (2015) 7 *Ala CR & CL L Rev* 1, 24–5.
130 579 F.3d 722, 725 (6th Cir., 2009).
131 Ibid., 728
132 215 F. 3d 618 (6th Cir., 2000).
133 Ibid., 625.
134 Ibid., 622.
135 As the ECtHR did for example in the case of *Siebenhaar v Germany* (App No 18136/02) 3rd April 2011.

openness about being gay as 'activism', in a way which would seem bizarre if a person was heterosexual. However, the decision would be appropriate if the college had dismissed an employee in a similar role for a non-private disagreement with another major tenet of the religion. The college's claim was fairly narrowly defined: it related only to certain employees and was not claimed merely because she was gay or because of her membership in a different church.

A proportionality approach could therefore have dealt with these two cases in a principled way which paid due attention to the needs of religious organisations, but also to that of non-discrimination. An obvious problem with both *Hall* and *Pedreira* is that since non-discrimination on the grounds of sexual orientation is not a legally recognised interest it is necessarily undervalued. Since neither Tennessee or Kentucky prohibit sexual orientation discrimination, these cases have to be forced into unsuitable causes of action. Furthermore, a proportionality analysis could apply a more contextual approach, which would take into account the need for some religious organisations to discriminate in some circumstances and could recognise relevant differences between different roles.

Canadian approach

As in the US, the approach in Canada differs according to the province, but most have a BFOR approach.[136] *Heintz v Christian Horizons*[137] is a good illustration of these issues. It involved a care worker at an evangelical Christian home in Ontario for children with severe learning difficulties. When she began, she signed a Lifestyle and Morality statement that forbade, among other things, 'homosexual relationships'. After several years working there she came out as a lesbian and began a relationship. Once it became apparent that she would be dismissed, she resigned. She remained a committed Christian. She was successful in her claim for sexual orientation discrimination.

Slightly unusually, Ontario's law is not a simple BFOR but also requires the organisation to be 'primarily engaged in serving the interests of persons identified by their creed' as well as the discrimination to be 'a reasonable and bona fide qualification because of the nature of the employment'.[138] At first instance, the Ontario Human Rights Tribunal held that since Christian Horizons provided services regardless of the service users' religion, it could not benefit from the exemption, regardless of the fact the work was intended as an outward manifestation of Christian belief. The Ontario Divisional Court held that such a narrow focus could not have been meant by the legislature, as otherwise this would ignore 'the long history of assistance to the disadvantaged offered by religious groups in Canada, which have not imposed a requirement of religious membership or adherence on recipients'.[139] It also held it would infringe the right of freedom of religion under the Charter. Whether this is right as a matter of statutory interpretation is a matter for debate. On a Charter or proportionality analysis this though seems correct: whether the service is provided to co-religionists or the public should be a relevant factor, but not necessarily decisive. Otherwise a religious organisation that provides some services to the public could not choose even the head of the organisation on religious grounds, even if the organisation was entirely privately funded.[140]

136 G. Demeyere, 'Discrimination in Employment by Religious Organizations: Exemptions, Defences, and the Lockean Concept of Toleration' (2010) 15 *Canadian Lab & Emp LJ* 435.

137 [2008] 63 CHRR 12 (Ontario Human Rights Commission); *Ontario Human Rights Commission v Christian Horizons* 2010 ONSC 2105 (Divisional Court).

138 S.24(1)(a) Ontario Human Rights Code.

139 supra n.137, para 67.

140 Esau supra n.112.

However, the court held that in these particular circumstances the discrimination was not a BFOR. As the Employment Tribunal held in the British case of *Hender v Prospects,* the Divisional Court argued that Christian Horizons had not considered whether the particular employment required such discrimination. It held that the requirement 'must not just flow automatically from the religious ethos of Christian Horizons … There is no evidence that anyone … ever considered whether the prohibition on same-sex relationships was necessary for the effective performance of the job of support worker in a home where there is no proselytizing and where residents are not required to be Evangelical Christians.'[141]

This point is important. It is the converse of what is required by secular employers for their religious staff: given the importance of the right not to be discriminated against, it must be asked whether it is possible to accommodate the other. It could, though, be doubted whether the failure to consider this issue was as drastic as it seemed to the Court. There had been some consideration of whether the policy was necessary since the Lifestyle and Morality policy arose out of consultation with the organisation's employees. As Esau argues, there is no reason in principle why the fact that the policy originated from employees rather than the leadership should necessarily matter.[142] Nevertheless, without an examination of whether there should have been different policies for certain positions, the important requirement of fact-specific consideration was not fulfilled. Requiring this is not entirely unproblematic. Inevitably a focus on particular roles within an organisation places pressure on Christian Horizons and similar bodies to secularise themselves. It makes it very difficult to create a large outward facing body which is pervasively religious. However, this may have to be the price that is paid in order to provide sufficient protection for non-discrimination rights.

Permitting Christian Horizons to discriminate against Heintz would have had severe practical effects for gay people seeking employment in this field. It 'operate[d] over 180 residential homes across Ontario, ha[d] over 2500 employees and provide[d] care and support to approximately 1400 individuals with developmental disabilities' and was the largest provider of residential services in the province.[143] In providing this care and support, it was funded almost exclusively by the Ontario Ministry of Community and Social Services.[144] It was therefore conceivably 'quasi-governmental in nature'.[145] The interest in non-discrimination was thus very great.

Christian Horizons' religious interests were also fairly weak. It originally grew out of the desire of Evangelical parents to provide family-type, Christian settings for the provision of care to disabled adults and children. However, by the time this case arose, it had expanded to provide care regardless of religious background, and the religious element of care was diluted, although evidently still present. In these circumstances, the interest in having all employees abide by strict religious rules was fairly small. Given this, the result was correct. Certainly, this case demonstrates the 'ambiguous embrace'[146] of government funding.

Even if it had been proportionate for Christian Horizons to dismiss Heintz, there was also a major failing in the requirement of mutual respect in the way this was carried out. After

141 Supra n.137, para 90.
142 Esau supra n.112.
143 Although, as Esau points out, this only constituted 2 per cent of people with developmental disabilities who were supported through government funding.
144 Supra n.137, para 2.
145 B. MacDougall and D. Short, 'Religion-based Claims for Impinging on Queer Citizenship' (2010) *Dalhousie LJ* 133, 141.
146 C. Glenn, *The Ambiguous Embrace: Government and Faith Based Schools and Social Agencies* (Princeton: Princeton UP, 2000).

her relationship became known, she continued to work there for five months. This was a 'disaster'.[147] Her performance reviews, previously positive, became very critical. A colleague made allegations of abuse against her, which were investigated without consideration of whether they were motivated by homophobia. This was unacceptable. Even if an organisation has a right to dismiss an employee, it does not have unlimited discretion in the way this is carried out.[148]

In summary, a proportionality approach, perhaps based on a bona fide occupational requirement model, is the best way of dealing with the very wide range of employment and types of institutions that exist within the religious social service sector. Although not entirely without loss to both rights, such an approach allows the particular circumstances of the employment to be taken into account, requires justification to be given to both sides and balances both rights.

Secular function employees

In contrast to many of the situations discussed so far, where staff do not have any religious functions at all, the religious interest is very small and the non-discrimination right correspondingly great. In Bagni's schema, discussed at the beginning of the chapter, these jobs fall within his third category as they are 'far removed from the spiritual epicenter of the church'.[149] Whilst Canada and Britain do not permit discrimination in this context, in the US it has been held constitutional to exclude all employees of religious organisations from discrimination laws and some, unusual, cases *require* such discrimination to be permitted. In *Corporation of Presiding Bishop v Amos,*[150] a building engineer was dismissed from his employment at a Mormon-owned non-profit gym that was open to the public because he failed to keep his Temple Recommend, a document showing that he complied with the tenets of the Mormon faith. The relevant law[151] simply excluded religious organisations from its remit as it related to religious discrimination. Amos sued on the basis that the law infringed the Establishment Clause as it provided an unconstitutional benefit to religion. The Supreme Court held that it did not and that permitting such discrimination was constitutional.

This left open the question of whether state or federal governments *may* legislate to prevent such discrimination. In some later cases the constitutional rights of religious organisations to discriminate have been held to extend far beyond the core of religious employment. It has been held constitutionally *required* to allow discrimination for religiously based reasons when a lesbian sports journalist was dismissed from a church newspaper in *Madsen v Erwin.*[152] The Massachusetts Supreme Court held that 'requiring the defendants to pay damages to maintain their religious belief would constitute a substantial burden on the defendants' rights' and any assessment would involve the court in a review of 'an essentially ecclesiastical procedure'.[153] However, in a similar case there was

147 Esau supra n.112, 394.
148 C.f. *Logan v Salvation Army* 10 Misc 3d 756 (N.Y., 2005): 'Those limited exemptions for religious organizations are a far cry from letting them harass their employees and treat the employees in an odiously discriminatory manner during their employment, and to use derogatory expressions toward the employees'.
149 Supra n.18.
150 483 US 327 (1987).
151 Title VII of the Civil Rights Act of 1964 § 702.
152 481 N.E. 2d 1160 (1985).
153 Ibid., 1166.

held to be no First Amendment defence where a married female editorial secretary for a religious magazine did not receive allowances paid to married male employees.[154]

Some have argued that discrimination should be permitted in situations like *Amos*. Gedicks has argued that to force the Mormon Church to retain a religiously unacceptable employee and to use religious tithes to pay for his salary would 'have undermined the sacrifice narrative that is so prominent both in Mormon history and in contemporary Mormon life ... it would be forced to dilute ... the powerful concept that tithing is the sacred means by which Mormons build the Kingdom of God.'[155]

However, merely because there is some impact on a religious right does not mean that a religious institution should necessarily be permitted to discriminate. As a proportionality approach would demonstrate, where there is no religious aspect to the employment at all, being forbidden to discriminate interferes very lightly with a religion's interest in propagating and maintaining its faith, even if there are religious motivations for the discrimination. Permitting such discrimination could amount to severe pressure on employees to comply with a religion out of economic necessity.[156] Furthermore, the interest is not simply an individual one. Society generally also has a strong interest in non-discrimination, to avoid patterns of inequality and ensure that opportunities are available for all. A proportionality analysis would have balanced the interests and demonstrated that such an exemption is disproportionate.

Even in the context of US law, the interest in religious autonomy and deference to religious organisations seen in *Madsen* also does not sit well with other cases. Only in a very loose way was the employer required to 'pay damages to maintain their religious beliefs'. They could certainly 'maintain their religious beliefs' but they could not require that *this* employee abide by them. Fears that permitting secular function employees to bring discrimination claims would lead to entanglement with religious matters are overstated. The Court did not have to decide a religious issue.

Islands of exclusivity?

The analysis has so far assumed that it is possible to distinguish between the importance of various positions and that it is always far more important to a religion to have, for example, the leader of an organisation abide by religious precepts than a secretary. It is possible though that in some cases this assumption cannot be made. Some organisations are so pervasively religious that the only way of protecting their religious rights is for them to be able to create an 'island of exclusivity'.[157] To require them to prove the religiousness of each job may radically alter and misunderstand the nature of the religious organisation. This is not an argument that a proportionality or BFOR approach is wrong in these cases but that an 'occupational requirement' should not always necessarily be interpreted narrowly.

The Canadian case of *Schroen v Steinbach Bible College*[158] illustrates this point. The college was a small Mennonite college offering degrees in Mennonite scholarship and pastoral

154 676 F.2d 1272 (9th Cir., 1982). See also *Whitney v Greater New York Corp. of Seventh-Day Adventists 401* F. Supp 1363 (N.Y. 1975).

155 Gedicks supra n.6, 114. Although see supra n.29 for his later, very different, views on this topic.

156 N. Rosenblum, '*Amos*: Religious Autonomy and the Moral Uses of Pluralism' in N. Rosenblum (ed.), *Obligations of Citizenship and Demands of Faith: Religious Accommodation in Pluralist Democracies* (Princeton: Princeton UP, 2000).

157 A. Esau, '"Islands of Exclusivity": Religious Organizations and Employment Discrimination' (1999) 33 *UBC Law Rev* 719.

158 [1999] 35 CHRR D/1 (Man. Bd. Adj.).

training to about 75 students. It described itself as 'an evangelical Anabaptist college equipping servant leaders for Church ministries'. Schroen was given the post of accounting clerk on the understanding she was a Mennonite. In fact, she had been brought up Mennonite, but subsequently converted to Mormonism. When this was discovered she was dismissed. The difference between the two is quite radical and indeed Mennonites view Mormonism as a kind of 'false cult'.[159] The Manitoba Human Rights Commission eventually[160] held that hiring a co-religionist was a BFOR. In doing so, it reached the right decision. This is a highly unusual case. Employment here is to be equated with membership of a religion. The organisation was small and privately funded and had the purpose of training future religious ministers in an exclusivist religion. The state interest in preventing discrimination was therefore very small and the interest in religious freedom great.

Esau has argued though that a BFOR approach does not sufficiently protect religious organisations and is too demanding. There were religious aspects to Schroen's job. All staff were expected to be available to students and each other for religious discussions and prayer. However, the important aspect of this case was not just that she had to perform religious duties, but that every element of her work was meant to be infused with Mennonite beliefs. Can a proportionality or BFOR test adequately take account of this?

Schroen's claim of religious discrimination of course failed. The criticism Esau therefore makes is not of the result but the process by which such a decision was reached. In particular he criticises the BFOR test because of its intrusiveness and contextual nature, which he argues does not adequately protect religious institutions. He argues that 'to force an exclusivist communitarian religious organization, like that of Steinbach Bible College, to accept people of incompatible faiths into the community is a direct assault on the religion of the employer at its very core'.[161] That a proportionality or BFOR test is intrusive cannot be denied. It requires organisations to defend their policies and is likely to require detailed evidence. However, not to assess the situation in some detail does not treat the right of non-discrimination in itself as an important right. The employee of a religious organisation has a right, just as religionists have in secular employment, to an individualised assessment of whether her right has been violated. Neither right should be treated as merely an exception to each other but as rights that are a priori equal. Therefore, providing a wider exception than a BFOR is unnecessary.

So far, of course, this discussion merely demonstrates that it may be a BFOR for a person to be of a particular religion. But what if the issue in *Schroen* was that she was gay, although a practising Mennonite? Steinbach College listed 'homosexual relationships', among many other things, as prohibited for its staff. However, a gay Mennonite could still perform religious tasks, lead prayer meetings and so on, in a way in which a Mormon could not. This though takes an instrumental rather than organic view of employment which is inappropriate for such an organisation.[162] The college did not want to create an organisation where its employees only paid lip service to religious rules, but a community of, and adhering to, a particular, and strict, faith. Perhaps the best question to ask is whether, to the college, its 'exclusivist communitarian religious organization' with its 'close, tight, focused and interactive culture'[163] would be jeopardized by the forced inclusion of someone whom they did

159 Esau supra n.157, 720.
160 It took more than five years for the investigation to be concluded. This cannot be defended.
161 Esau supra n.157, 733.
162 Ibid., 720.
163 *Schroen* supra n.158, para 61.

not consider a compliant member of their religion.[164] If this is so, then it would have been proportionate to dismiss her.

Conclusion

There are several approaches in evidence in this area of law. Both Canada and Britain have incorporated the requirement of proportionality into assessments of discrimination in religious social service organisations and Canada has also done so in relation to religious schools. Rivers argues that the British law is characterised by 'narrowly drafted exceptions narrowly interpreted by an unsympathetic judiciary'.[165] However, a proportionality approach, on which the British approach is generally based, does give religious organisations the autonomy needed to live out their religious mission. Compared to a categorical approach, 'this nuanced approach may ultimately prove better equipped to navigate the complexities of a world in which both religious and equality rights are taken seriously and given their due.'[166] However, although the BFOR approach is a good way to address the proportionality enquiry in this context, care must be taken that not too much is demanded from religious organisations. Intangible concerns, such as maintaining a religious ethos, may be as relevant and as worthy of protection as tangible ones such as the specific religious role performed by an employee.

In other situations, though, categorical tests are used which give too much discretion to religious authorities. This is particularly evident in the American doctrine of the ministerial exception. This is understandable within a system that has as a constitutional priority the separation of church and state, but it means that the value of non-discrimination is understated, or even discounted. There is a valid fear of becoming embroiled in religious disputes, but a narrower approach would not necessarily lead to this.

Throughout this chapter it has been demonstrated that proportionality can sufficiently recognise and protect collective religious freedom, as it can individual religious freedom, whilst also protecting non-discrimination rights. Proportionality identifies relevant differences between situations, allowing differences between roles even with the same job titles to be taken into account, rather than imposing a 'one size fits all' approach. It is also more coherent and intuitively easier to understand and to apply than many of the other tests and categorisations used in this area of law. So far, therefore, it has been demonstrated that proportionality is a useful concept in considering employment claims. The next chapter moves on to develop this approach outside the employment context.

164 Gedicks supra n.6.
165 J. Rivers, 'Law, Religion and Gender Equality' (2007) 9 *Ecc LJ* 24, 52.
166 C. Evans and A. Hood, 'Religious Autonomy and Labour Law: A Comparison of the Jurisprudence of the United States and the European Court of Human Rights' (2012) 1 *OJLR* 81, 107.

8 Religious organisations and services

I have so far demonstrated that it may be proportionate to allow religious organisations to maintain their distinctive nature and to comply with the doctrines of their religion when hiring their staff, even if this results in discrimination. Religious organisations may also wish to place restrictions on who they provide services to, for a number of reasons. Some organisations may provide some services only to members of their religion. This may be because the service is either seen as a benefit of membership or because it involves a religious practice and is thus only for those who abide by its religious tenets. Given potentially discriminatory rules of membership, this may constitute sexual orientation discrimination. Religious organisations may also provide extensive services to the general public, some of which may receive state funding, but may claim that for reasons of conscience they cannot serve, for example, gay people in some contexts. Religious organisations may also claim some control over the use to which their property is put. As can be seen, the number and range of circumstances where conflicts can arise is large and diverse. It will be argued that, as in the employment context, proportionality is a valuable method of resolving these varied conflicts where each right may be affected to very different extents depending on the context.

Religious activities

The religious interest is at its strongest where there is a claim for inclusion into core religious activities such as religious worship. This will normally be a claim to be included in an organisation's membership. As was described in the previous chapter, the ability to associate is valuable, in part because associations provide a source of comfort and meaning for their members. A right of association must include a right to refuse to associate. As White puts it, 'individuals are hardly free to associate in pursuit of some shared set of beliefs about the good life and/or good society unless they are also free to exclude from this specific association those who do not share their distinctive beliefs'.[1] They must be allowed to protect themselves against those who would 'corrupt or undermine pursuit of these purposes.'[2] To tell a religious group who they must accept as members violates the core of its religious freedom.

This analysis does not presuppose a monolithic view of religious belief. It is extremely unlikely that within all but the most tightly controlled organisations there will be no dissent on doctrinal or organisational matters. The relationship between religious doctrine and members' beliefs is likely to be a complex one. However, it should still be within the

1 S. White, 'Freedom of Association and the Right to Exclude' (1997) 4 *J Pol Phil* 373, 377.
2 Ibid., 380.

religious organisation's power to decide ultimately who can be a member and on what terms. Whilst such an interference with religious freedom would be severe, in contrast the state interest in preventing such discrimination would be limited. While a person may take employment in a religious organisation for non-religious reasons, such as economic pressure, there is likely to be a freer choice in joining and leaving such organisations as a member, and thus the right to non-discrimination is affected less severely. Of course, leaving the right to exit as the only recourse against intra-group discrimination may well cause harm to those excluded, but this does not mean the state should necessarily act to prevent it.[3]

In fact, none of the jurisdictions under discussion here would consider claims over religious membership or taking part in religious worship. Evidently, all discrimination law is limited in scope: thus for example it is not prohibited to discriminate on any basis in forming personal relationships. While there are variations in the three jurisdictions as to whether and when membership organisations are permitted to discriminate, all accept that permitting discrimination on any ground is sometimes appropriate. Thus, under federal US law only 'public accommodations' are covered by discrimination law, excluding private contexts. Most states also have exclusions for private clubs and there would undoubtedly be constitutional problems if there were an attempt to apply anti-discrimination laws to, for example, attendance at a religious service.[4] Under English law there is an explicit exception for religious organisations where the discrimination relates to 'membership of the organisation',[5] and the law does not cover religious worship at all. Even legal challenges to such discriminatory policies are rare. One such challenge was *Parry v Vine Christian Centre,*[6] where a transgender woman claimed she should be allowed to attend the women's prayer meeting, but was unsuccessful. In Canada, discrimination laws vary by province, but all are similar to the Canadian Human Rights Act which forbids discrimination in an 'accommodation, service or facility customarily available to the public'.[7] It is unlikely that access to religious worship would be included within this. A religious organisation may open its doors to all who are interested in hearing the religious message and becoming members, but that does not necessarily thereby make it 'public'. In any case, there is also an exception if there is a bona fide and reasonable justification for the discrimination.

Situations that do not fall into the archetype of religious worship at specific times at a place specifically dedicated to this purpose may though cause greater difficulty for religious organisations. Two cases have been brought in the US as a result of the Nation of Islam's policy of having sex-segregated religious services. This policy extended to lectures given by its leader, Louis Farrakhan, which were open to members and non-members. In the first, *Donaldson v Farrakhan,*[8] a woman sued after she was prevented from attending a meeting.

3 On this 'right to exit' see D. Borchers and A. Vitikainene (eds), *On Exit: Interdisciplinary Perspectives on the Right of Exit in Liberal Multicultural Societies* (Berlin: De Gruyter, 2012) and S. M. Okin, '"Mistresses of Their Own Destiny": Group Rights, Gender, and Realistic Rights of Exit' (2002) 112 *Ethics* 205.

4 K. Francart, 'No Dogs Allowed: Freedom of Association v Forced Inclusion. Anti-Discrimination Statutes and the Applicability to Private Organizations' (2000) 17 *TM Cooley L Rev* 273.

5 Equality Act 2010 Sch 23 para 2.

6 Bridgend County Court, BG 101748, 15 February 2002, referred to in R. Ahdar and I. Leigh, *Religious Freedom in the Liberal State,* 2nd ed. (Oxford: Oxford UP, 2013). The case predated the prohibition of transgender discrimination but the claimant sued on the basis of sex discrimination.

7 Canadian Human Rights Act R.S.C., 1985, c. H-6 s.14.

8 436 Mass. 94 (2002).

In the second, *City of Cleveland v Nation of Islam*,[9] the Nation of Islam challenged a refusal to allow it to hire a convention centre because of its discriminatory policies. In both cases, it was held that the municipally owned theatres hired by the organisation were not places of 'public accommodation' in this context and that even if they were, enforcing the law in this situation would have violated the First Amendment.

Rosenblum disagrees with this reasoning, arguing that discrimination law should have applied.[10] She contends that permitting women to attend would only have had a minimal impact on the organisation's message, particularly given that the purpose was to reach a broad audience. She points out that this would have left alternatives open to Farrakhan, in that he could have decided to only invite selected men or to hold the event in an alternative venue.[11] However, these alternatives would have greatly affected the ability to spread the religious message to non-members. Rosenblum's more general argument is also problematic. In pointing out that 'the government would be just as concerned about discriminatory admission to a basketball game or bake sale' and thus the restriction is content-neutral, she does not thereby make her case that 'universal application of the public accommodations law is preferable to a scheme in which municipal or state authorities or courts assess the constitutional rights of each applicant in an ad hoc manner'.[12] Of course, the authorities would be concerned about such discriminatory admission, but that does not mean that the situations are analogous. The opposing interest to non-discrimination when the issue is admission to a basketball game is likely to be minimal at best, but is much greater where the issue is access to a core religious activity. It is precisely because the opposing interest to non-discrimination is likely to vary that a fact-specific analysis is necessary. It is principled to hold that in some cases it might be proportionate to permit such discrimination depending on the weight of the conflicting right.

If a proportionality analysis had been applied, it would have demonstrated that permitting discrimination was proportionate in the circumstances, as the courts in fact held, albeit using different reasoning. In *Donaldson* the state, by allowing such discrimination, had a legitimate aim of protecting the Nation of Islam's right of freedom of religion by allowing it to choose who attended its religious events. In *City of Cleveland*, the state had a legitimate aim in protecting the rights of others in preventing discrimination taking place on its property. In both cases such legitimate aims had a rational connection to the action taken. There were also no less restrictive means that could have been taken to protect either the right of freedom of religion in *Donaldson* or the right of non-discrimination in *City of Cleveland* to the same extent. The question would thus come down to the final balancing stage. Of importance here is that the Nation of Islam believes in different religious roles for men and women. The message to be given, therefore, differed according to the audience. While it was not an act of worship in its strictest sense, although the lecture was to take place at a time traditionally used for men's worship, it had a religious purpose. Merely because it sought to reach a wider audience than its existing membership does not necessarily negate its rights to control access to its religious events.

9 922 F.Supp. 56 (1995). See also *Southgate v United African Movement* 1997 WL 1051933 (N.Y.C. Com. Hum. Rts., June 30 1997) where it was held that a black separatist movement unlawfully discriminated when it refused to permit a white journalist to attend a publicly advertised speech.

10 L. Rosenblum, 'Equal Access or Free Speech: The Constitutionality of Public Accommodations Law' (1997) 72 *NYU L Rev* 1243.

11 Although many other venues would, on her argument, still be public accommodations.

12 Rosenblum supra n.10, 1280.

A proportionality test is therefore protective of core religious rights. Even though there may undoubtedly be understandable anger and distress caused by a discriminatory policy, this does not mean that it will be permissible to 'disturb the intimacy'[13] of a religious organisation and require it to change its rules on membership and access to religious activities. Beyond this core case though, matters become more complex.

University societies

One context where the right to exclude certain groups from membership of a religious organisation is far less clear involves university religious societies. Many universities have policies prohibiting religious, sex and sexual orientation discrimination for membership and leadership positions in university-affiliated societies. This may cause problems for some religious groups.

In the UK, associations, including student societies, may confine membership to those who share a protected characteristic, such as religion.[14] Religious organisations are also protected by the exemption described above, permitting them to discriminate in membership.[15] However, some Student Unions may require societies affiliated to them not to discriminate. As a result, controversy has arisen in several universities.[16] For example, Exeter University Evangelical Christian Union threatened legal action when it was suspended from its Students' Guild because it required its committee members to sign a doctrinal basis of belief[17] and thereby clearly discriminated on the basis of religion. Ultimately, this dispute was resolved and it re-joined the Guild.[18] At other universities, Christian Unions have chosen not to formally affiliate with Student Unions so they do not have to comply with non-discrimination and other policies.[19] None of these conflicts have reached the courts. In Canada, as religious organisations, student societies may legally limit their membership, either on the basis that to do so is a bona fide and reasonable justification or based on specific exemptions for religious associations,[20] but again universities may also wish to impose their own policies.[21]

In the US, this issue reached the Supreme Court in *Christian Legal Society v Martinez*.[22] In order to receive 'Registered Student Organization' (RSO) status at Hastings College of the Law, organisations had to comply with the university's non-discrimination policy. This forbade discrimination on the grounds of, inter alia, religion and sexual orientation, and was

13 I. Lupu, 'Free Exercise Exemption and Religious Institutions: The Case of Employment Discrimination' (1987) 67 *BU L Rev* 391.
14 Equality Act 2010 Sch 16 para 1.
15 Equality Act 2010 Sch 23 para 2.
16 D. Lister and R. Gledhill, 'Students Sue over Christian Rights at Colleges' *The Times* 16 Nov 2006, 1.
17 One which would not be acceptable to many Christians.
18 Christian Concern, 'Exeter Evangelical Christian Union', 12 Dec 2007, available at: http://www.christianconcern.com/our-concerns/universities/exeter-evangelical-christian-union <last accessed 20 July 2016>
19 Ekklesia, *United We Stand: A Report on Current Conflicts between Christian Unions and Students' Unions* (London: Ekklesia, 2006).
20 See e.g. British Columbia Human Rights Code s.41; Newfoundland Human Rights Act 2010 C. H.-13.1 s.11(3)(d) and (e); Alberta Human Rights Act 2000 C.H.25.5 s.11.
21 C.f. *Gray v UBC Students' Union* 2008 BCSC 1530.
22 561 US 661 (2010). *Alpha Delta Chi-Delta Chapter v Reed* 648 F.3d 790 (9th Cir., 2011) raises a similar point.

apparently interpreted as an 'all-comers' policy: RSOs had to permit 'any student to participate, become a member, or seek leadership positions, regardless of her status or beliefs'.[23] However, the Christian Legal Society (CLS) required members and officers to abide by a 'statement of faith', which as well as requiring specific Christian views, required them not to engage in any sexual activity outside heterosexual marriage, although it permitted anyone to attend its meetings. As a result, it was denied RSO status.

The Supreme Court, albeit with a strong dissent, held that the university's policy was permissible. The Court characterised the issue as being one of access to a 'limited public forum' and so the test under American free speech jurisprudence was whether the restriction was 'reasonable and viewpoint neutral'. The majority characterised the university as 'dangling the carrot of subsidy, not wielding the stick of prohibition' and thus the policy did not require strict scrutiny.[24] It held that the proffered justification of ensuring the 'leadership, educational and social opportunities'[25] afforded by RSOs were available to all students meant the policy was a reasonable one. Merely because the policy affected some groups more than others did not mean that the policy was not viewpoint neutral.

This is a deferential form of review and there are many problems in the Court's reasoning. First, the dissent persuasively argued that the evidence did not demonstrate that there was an 'all-comers' policy, but rather that other organisations at the university were permitted to control their membership by reference to the organisation's purposes, including one which was permitted to only admit students of Hispanic origin as voting members. These exceptions may of course be justifiable under a proportionality test, but they demonstrate severe difficulties in finding that the policy was viewpoint neutral. Second, in assessing reasonableness, the majority was deferential in assuming that the aim of increasing leadership and social opportunities could actually be achieved by such a policy. CLS was only one of many societies at Hastings and was created for a particular purpose. Having a pluralistic range of societies, aimed at different groups of students and requiring different interests and beliefs, could have increased rather than reduced leadership and social opportunities. The fit between the goal and the policy is therefore not a close one,[26] which would have been an important consideration under a proportionality test.

Nice argues though that '*Martinez* enhances liberty, making space for an individual to embrace any religious ideology regardless of his or her sexual orientation'.[27] This is true, but the problem is that CLS wished to espouse a particular conservative, evangelical, Protestant form of Christianity, rather than be open to anyone who identified as Christian. Nice's statement is therefore problematic: particular views on sexuality *were* relevant to this group's ideology and so its religious message could not be accepted 'regardless' of sexual orientation. An enforced change would have altered the religious ideology. It should be noted that the university also prohibited societies from discriminating on the basis of religion and therefore the society could not have prevented an atheist from becoming a member or even running for a leadership position. Although this may 'enhance liberty, making space for an individual to embrace any religious ideology regardless of his or her' *religious beliefs*, this comes at the

23 Ibid., 2982.
24 Ibid., 683.
25 Ibid., 688.
26 A. Brownstein and V. Amar, 'Reviewing Associational Freedom Claims in a Limited Public Forum: An Extension of the Distinction Between Debate-Dampening and Debate-Distorting State Action' (2011) 38 *Hastings Const LQ* 505.
27 J. Nice, 'How Equality Constitutes Liberty: The Alignment of *CLS v. Martinez*' (2011) 38 *Hastings Const LQ* 631, 672.

cost of lessening the coherence and purpose of the organisation. There was nothing to prevent those who do not agree with such an interpretation of Christianity, as of course many do not, forming their own society.[28] Finally, the court did not consider the right of freedom of association separately from the right of freedom of speech in a limited public forum. This seems a serious problem. As Bhagwat puts it, 'the primary burden imposed by Hastings was not on CLS' ability to communicate; rather, it was on its ability to select its members'.[29] Whether or not the policy was viewpoint neutral is not the crux of the problem.

The various interests in this case would have been far better considered under a proportionality analysis. The university put forward as justification the ensuring of access to leadership and social activities. Although a legitimate aim, the university's actions were not the least restrictive means of achieving this since having a range of societies centred on different viewpoints could protect this interest to the same extent. A more persuasive way of formulating the university's aim would be to say that it had an interest in preventing discrimination on certain grounds on its campus and distancing itself from CLS' discriminatory message because such discrimination affected its students' sense of self-worth and inclusion.

Being an RSO, though, had many practical consequences. It permitted an organisation to book rooms, use newsletters and bulletin boards and participate in a yearly students' fair. The majority of the Court held that being allowed access to these official methods of communication was not necessary because CLS could use 'electronic media and social networking sites'.[30] This is of course true, but ignored the problem of how the society could easily recruit new members at the university or hold events without such access. The distinction between subsidy and prohibition, which was at the basis of the majority judgment, is slight when this is taken into account. Although the majority stated that the university had asserted it would permit CLS to book rooms and hold activities, the minority pointed to the difficulties CLS had in fact faced in attempting to do so. An informal policy was therefore not satisfactory.

Given that the case cannot be resolved at any earlier stage of analysis, the interests must be balanced. The university's policy deeply affected the rights of the organisation. Conversely, permitting the organisation to operate would have a limited effect on non-CLS member students: membership was entirely voluntary, and students could attend events without being a member. Nevertheless, the university did still have an interest in demonstrating its disapproval of CLS' policy. A fact-specific proportionality analysis could though pay attention to the fact that being an RSO brought with it a bundle of benefits. An alternative to preventing CLS from being an RSO at all would be to refuse to give CLS the *status* of being an RSO, but still grant it some of the benefits. This is a similar analysis to the Georgetown University case described in Chapter 5, where a gay rights organisation wanted to receive official recognition in a Catholic university. Allowing Hastings to, for example, deny CLS the right to use the university's name or logo and of course to describe itself as an RSO permits it to distance itself from the discriminatory message. The symbolic aspect of

28 There may be a problem in its nomenclature though: 'Evangelical Christian Union' may be better than 'Christian Union' to highlight that it only advanced a particular understanding of Christianity. See Ekklesia report supra n.19.

29 A. Bhagwat, 'Associations and Forums: Situating *CLS v. Martinez*' (2011) 38 *Hastings Const LQ* 543, 553. Luther also points out that students joined the society because they were 'actively looking to mingle with those who share a common ideology', rather than to engage in 'the robust spread of ideas': R. Luther, 'Marketplace of Ideas 2.0: Excluding Viewpoints to Include Individuals' (2011) 38 *Hastings Const LQ* 673, 681.

30 Supra n.22, 691.

CLS' policy is small if this distinction between status and support is made. It is not noticeably greater than the symbolic exclusion caused by general knowledge of some religions' views on sexuality. Although CLS' policy may have very real effects on students' well-being, this may simply have to be tolerated. In any case, even if this conclusion is disagreed with, a proportionality analysis does far better justice to these issues than the approach of the US Supreme Court.

Educational contexts

Religion's role in education goes far beyond student societies. Many religious institutions run schools and, particularly in the US, colleges and universities. Some of these organisations require that students follow at least some religious rules, and may also insist that they are members of a particular religion. In some fairly rare cases in the US and Canada, university students may be prohibited from having same-sex relationships or any sexual activity outside heterosexual marriage.[31] The university may argue that the point of the institution is not merely or even primarily to teach secular subjects but rather to inculcate religious virtues. For example, Bob Jones University, a private Fundamentalist American University, sees its mission as 'growing Christ-like character that is scripturally disciplined, others-serving, God-loving, Christ-proclaiming and focused above'.[32]

Bingham argues that private religious universities engage in 'expressive association' and if they permit a gay student to attend, when this is in opposition to their beliefs, then this may give a contradictory message.[33] In principle such an argument could be accepted. As explained in the previous chapter, it may be proportionate, especially where an organisation is attempting to create a community of believers, to permit religious organisations to discriminate in hiring their staff. Similar considerations, such as the religiosity of the institution and whether the rule has been brought to the student's attention, should apply where the rules are applied to students. However, given that there is likely to be less coercion on students than teachers to join these organisations and thus be subject to these rules (because students are likely to have a greater range of choices about where to attend university compared to employment opportunities), less should be demanded to justify the discrimination. If this assumption is not justified, because, for example, there are particular benefits in education at a religious university, or because a large number of universities have religious entry requirements and thus access to university education for all students is compromised, then this should be a crucial factor.

The present legal structure in all three jurisdictions permits religious discrimination in education in some contexts. English law permits schools[34] with a religious ethos to discriminate on

31 See *TWU v BCCT* [2001] 1 SCR 772. In the US, see e.g. Brigham Young University's behaviour code, available at: https://policy.byu.edu/view/index.php?p=26 <last accessed 25 July 2016>.

32 Bob Jones University, *University Creed and Mission,* available at: http://www.bju.edu/about/creed-mission.php <last accessed 25 July 2016>.

33 T. Bingham, 'Discrimination in Education: Public Versus Private Universities' (2007) 36 *J L & Educ* 273.

34 And other designated institutions with a religious ethos (Equality Act 2010 Sch 12 para 5). Only Catholic Sixth Form Colleges have been designated. It is also permissible to discriminate for vocational courses if such discrimination is an occupational requirement for the intended employment, e.g. a Catholic seminary may only accept men (Equality Act 2010 Sch 9 para 4). The issue only has limited practical importance in the UK because of the lack of private religious universities, although there might be an issue in religious schools.

the ground of religion in admissions.[35] In addition, where the purpose of an organisation is to advance a religion or belief or to teach the practice or principles of a religion or belief, discrimination relating to membership of the organisation or its provision of goods, facilities or services is permitted on the grounds of religion or sexual orientation. This exemption applies as long as the main purpose of the organisation is not commercial.[36] In Canada again this varies by province, since as private institutions the Charter will not apply to them, but religious institutions will usually be exempted in this context. For example, in British Columbia, a non-profit charitable, educational or religious organisation or corporation that has as 'primary purpose the promotion of the interests and welfare of an identifiable group or class of persons characterized by ... religion', may 'grant a preference to members of the identifiable group'.[37] Discrimination is also permitted in the provision of services on any ground if there is a 'bona fide and reasonable justification'.[38]

In the US, as always, the exemptions relating to sexual orientation discrimination vary by state, but religious educational institutions will usually be at least partly exempted.[39] There would also be clear First Amendment problems in applying non-discrimination policies to admissions to religious universities.[40] For comparison, federal legislation relating to sex discrimination in universities, Title IX of the Civil Rights Act of 1964, exempts educational institutions controlled by religious organisations if the application of the non-discrimination requirement 'would not be consistent with the religious tenets of such organisation'.[41] This applies to universities which receive any form of public funding, which includes most private universities.[42] Universities which do not receive any public funding at all are not covered by the legislation at all.

Sometimes it is accepted that the university may lawfully discriminate, but as a consequence of discriminating it is subjected to disadvantage, which the university may then seek to challenge. This issue arose in *British Columbia College of Teachers v Trinity Western University*,[43] decided in 2001, and more recently in *TWU v Nova Scotia Barristers' Society*,[44] *TWU v Law Society of Upper Canada*,[45] and *TWU v The Law Society of British Columbia*[46] in litigation which is still ongoing. TWU is a private university, associated with the Evangelical Free Church of Canada. All students and staff have to accept the TWU Community Standards which forbid 'practices that are Biblically condemned', including 'sexual sins including ...

35 Equality Act 2010 Sch 11 para 5.
36 Equality Act 2010 Sch 23 para 2.
37 British Columbia Human Rights Code [RSBC 1996] c.210 s. 41.
38 British Columbia Human Rights Code [RSBC 1996] c.210 s. 8.
39 New Jersey's law for example exempts 'any educational facility operated or maintained by a bona fide religious or sectarian institution'. *N.J. Stat. Ann*, § 10:5-l.
40 C.f. *Boy Scouts v Dale* 530 US 640 (2000) Although see *Bob Jones v US* 461 US 574 (1983).
41 20 US Code § 1681(a)(3).
42 Since public funding includes grants given to students to enable them to pay for tuition.
43 [2001] 1 SCR 772.
44 2015 NSSC 25.
45 2015 OSSC 4250.
46 2015 BCSC 2326. As this decision primarily relates to the decision-making process of the Law Society and is currently being appealed, I will not discuss it further here. For comments on these cases see: E. Craig, 'The Case for the Federation of Law Societies Rejecting Trinity Western University's Proposed Law Degree Program' (2013) 25 *CJWL* 148; D. Newman, 'On the Trinity Western University Controversy: An Argument for a Christian Law School in Canada (2013) 22 *Const Forum* 1.

homosexual behaviour'. In both cases it was accepted that the discrimination was lawful under British Columbian law.[47] Rather, the issue was whether its degrees had to be accepted by professional regulatory bodies.

The first case related to TWU's education degree. When the course was set up in 1985 the last year of the course had to be spent at another university, as appears to be standard practice for new courses. In 1995 TWU applied to have control over the fifth year, but this was denied by the British Columbia College of Teachers (BCCT) on the grounds that it would not be in the public interest to allow teacher education to be wholly controlled by a university which had discriminatory policies. The second case arose as TWU wished to set up a School of Law. While the Federation of Law Societies approved it, many provincial law societies have reached different decisions.[48] Whether these decisions were lawful is currently being challenged in the courts: while Nova Scotia's Barristers' Society's refusal to approve it was successfully challenged by TWU, the Ontario Divisional Court decided the case the other way. This decision is, at the time of writing, being appealed, and it seems likely the issue will end up being heard by the Supreme Court of Canada.

In the earlier dispute about teacher education, the Supreme Court of Canada held in favour of TWU, holding that BCCT could not refuse to accredit the course. The majority, not applying the standard Canadian proportionality test strictly, but weighing the factors generally, held that BCCT did not weigh the relevant rights in its assessment and had neglected to consider the importance of freedom of religion and the place of private institutions in Canadian society and its constitution. The Court held that when a university had a right to discriminate in its selection policies it would then be strange if exercising that right submitted it to detriment.[49] There was no evidence to suggest that graduates of TWU would discriminate or have a detrimental effect in public schools. Furthermore, personal rules of conduct could generally be adopted provided they did not interfere with rights of others. However, L'Heureux-Dubé J dissented. For her, this was not a human rights matter but a case about providing the best possible educational environment for public school students. TWU's graduates could still become teachers and the detriment of one year at a different university was not very severe. Given the strong need for teachers to be sensitive to the concerns of gay students, it was reasonable, she argued, to require students at a university which condemned homosexual behaviour to experience life at another university.

Assuming for present purposes that it was proportionate to allow TWU to apply such rules to its students, while the majority of the Supreme Court dealt with the main arguments and reached the correct decision, applying a proportionality analysis more strictly would have sharpened the reasoning. The legitimate aim here was to provide a discrimination-free public education system. But as the majority saw it, requiring TWU students to spend a year at another university would not have done much to change ingrained beliefs, even if there had been evidence that they did or would discriminate in their employment. The connection between the two, although sufficient to pass the rational connection test, was fairly tenuous.

47 As a private institution the Charter did not apply to it, and as a religious institution it appeared to be exempted from British Columbia's human rights law.

48 So far, it has received accreditation from the Law Societies of Saskatchewan, Alberta, New Brunswick and British Columbia (where the school is based), but has been rejected by Nova Scotia and Ontario.

49 This does not necessarily follow – it may be tolerable for a discriminatory organisation to exist, but only if it receives no state support of any kind e.g. *Bob Jones University v United States*, 461 US 574 (1983) (a religious university which earlier banned black students, and then forbade inter-racial dating, could be denied tax exemption).

The policy was both under-inclusive and over-inclusive. It was over-inclusive because it assumed that all TWU students would discriminate, unless required to attend another university. It was under-inclusive because it still permitted students with objections to same-sex sexual behaviour to become teachers. The badly tailored nature of the restriction raises doubts about whether it can be proportionate.[50]

If the aim is to protect against discriminatory behaviour, then the likelihood of this arising must be considered, as this is relevant to the proportionality test.[51] That the students would discriminate is assumed only because of their attendance at a particular university. Although students were required to sign the Community Standards, it is possible that they may not necessarily have agreed with them but have merely agreed to uphold (or even pretended to uphold) the rules for the duration of their degree. Second, even if the trainee teachers were opposed to homosexuality, that does not mean that they would necessarily have sought to spread discrimination against their students or their colleagues. Indeed, the Standards themselves stated that respect should be shown to everyone. Possibly, as Gonthier J put it in *Chamberlain v Surrey School District No. 36,* 'adults in Canadian society who think that homosexual behaviour is immoral can still be staunchly committed to non-discrimination'.[52] Furthermore, if a teacher did discriminate or vehemently expressed discriminatory ideas when qualified then appropriate action could be taken because of the rights of others, irrespective of whether they were a former TWU student or not.[53]

Alternatively, it could be argued that what was needed was not only non-discrimination but also the positive affirmation of gay students. Moon argues that 'if sexual-orientation equality is to be affirmed in the public schools, teachers must do more than simply refrain from direct acts of discrimination … A teacher should be excluded from the schools if he has indicated in his public statements or actions that he regards homosexuality as sinful or objectionable, even though there is no evidence that he has directly discriminated against gays and lesbians in the classroom'.[54] This though would require a far more expansive and intrusive policy that would in turn raise serious problems of proportionality, given the extensive interference this would involve with a teacher's freedom of religion and out-of-work expression.[55]

In the more recent case of *TWU v NSBS,*[56] NSBS refused to accept TWU's law degree for the purpose of allowing graduates to practise law in Nova Scotia, again because of its Community Covenant. NSBS's argument was slightly different from BCCT's. It did not argue that its graduates were more likely to discriminate, but rather that 'accepting a law degree from the institution would amount to condoning discrimination'.[57] The Nova Scotia

50 See A. Stone Sweet and J. Mathews, 'All Things in Proportion? American Rights Doctrine and the Problem of Balancing' (2011) 60 *Emory LJ* 797.

51 Alexy's Second or Epistemic Law of Balancing states, 'The more intensive an interference in a constitutional right is, the greater must be the certainty of its underlying premises'. R. Alexy, *A Theory of Constitutional Rights,* tr. J. Rivers (Oxford: Oxford UP, 2002) 419.

52 [2002] 4 SCR 710, para 127.

53 E.g. *Kempling v British Columbia College of Teachers* [2005] 255 DLR (4th) 169.

54 R. Moon, *Freedom of Conscience and Religion* (Toronto: Irwin Law, 2014) 80–1.

55 Moon does however draw the line at 'a serious probe into the individual's thought or attitudes about sexual orientation' because 'this might involve too great an invasion into her personal sphere' (ibid., 80) but this nevertheless appears to undervalue the right of freedom of expression and conscience. For greater discussion of these issues see M. Pearson, 'Offensive Expression and the Workplace' (2014) *ILJ* 429.

56 2015 NSSC 25.

57 *TWU v NSBS,* para 194.

Supreme Court applied a proportionality analysis on the basis that requiring TWU to change its Community Covenant in order to have its degree accepted was an interference with its freedom of religion under the Charter.

As the Court showed, a proportionality test clarifies the relevant issues. The interest NSBS advanced was limited since it was fairly remote from the act of discrimination. It was 'not about anyone being discriminated against in Nova Scotia but about the profound sense of hurt that people feel when witnessing discrimination elsewhere[58] and the compounding of that hurt by the NSBS being seen as approving of it.'[59] The Court pointed out there would be no question that a Catholic lawyer would be prevented from practising, even though she would belong to a religious institution that prohibits same-sex marriage and sexual activity outside heterosexual marriage. While such a situation involves individual religious freedom rather than the collective freedom that TWU was claiming, the Court highlighted the importance for evangelical Christians of being able to belong to an institution which allows them to live out their faith and therefore the significance of the interference with religious freedom in this situation. As in *BCCT* therefore, it found that the interest in non-discrimination on these particular facts was fairly minimal, and was outweighed by the interest in freedom of religion.

However, the Ontario Court decided the proportionality analysis the other way. In contrast to the Nova Scotian court, it perceived the interference with the discrimination right to be quite extensive, because it focused not on whether the Law Society would be condoning the university's policies, but on the practical effect on the right to an equal opportunity to become a lawyer. Since gay students could only attend the university by denying their sexual identity and therefore at great personal cost, they therefore would have fewer opportunities to be accepted on a university course, given that acceptance onto these courses is competitive.[60] The Court therefore held that the interference with TWU's rights were outweighed on the basis that 'TWU can hold and promote its beliefs without acting in a manner that coerces others into forsaking their true beliefs in order to have an equal opportunity to a legal education'.[61]

While it reaches a different decision from the Nova Scotia court, this is because the practical effect of non-equal access to a profession is a far greater interference of the right to non-discrimination than the weaker and more remote harm of condoning discriminatory conduct argued in the Nova Scotian case. The extent to which TWU's policy would make access unequal is an empirical question. While these opposing conclusions do show that a proportionality analysis is not always straightforward, they do show that the proportionality test requires the careful identification of specific harms: to simply identify an interference with the right to non-discrimination is not enough.

Of course, even if BCCT or NSBS were required to accept TWU's course in this situation, this does not mean that in all cases a university should be free from detriment because of its discriminatory policies: this requires a fact-specific assessment. The answer may be quite different where the detriment involves, for example, access to public funding rather than licencing.

58 TWU is based in British Columbia.

59 *TWU v NSBS*, para 209.

60 Of course, this argument applies just as strongly to *religious* as well as sexual orientation discrimination and so the effects of this decision may be broader.

61 Supra n.45, para 117.

Hall v Powers

Even if an institution does not have such prohibitive rules on membership as BCCT it may refuse to offer services, understood broadly, where this might be seen as endorsing same-sex relationships or falsely demonstrating that such relationships are equal in the eyes of the religion. This was the argument in a Canadian case that received an enormous amount of media coverage and attracted extremely heated debate. The issue in *Hall v Powers*[62] was whether a student at a Catholic high school could take his boyfriend to his prom. The school refused to permit him on the basis that it would contravene its religious teachings and be seen as an endorsement of same-sex relationships. Hall won an interlocutory injunction, granted on the day of the prom, to permit the couple to attend together. The case was discontinued (contrary to the wishes of the school) before a full trial. The Court held that since the school was publicly funded and had 'establish[ed] and implement[ed] policies of general application', it was subject to the Charter and, in particular, to the equal protection right of students under s.15.[63] However, it considered that, since it was a Catholic separate school, the interference with Hall's right was potentially justified because of its right to manage the school in accordance with Catholic beliefs. The Court ultimately found though that this was not sufficient justification for its actions.

Although the Court did apply a proportionality test, the main basis of the decision is unfortunately flawed because it rests on the Court's own interpretation of Catholic doctrine. Evidently, there is a great diversity of views within the Catholic tradition as to the morality or otherwise of same-sex relationships, and, even if same-sex relationships are seen as sinful, then as to the appropriate pastoral reaction. To highlight this in a judgment is not therefore wrong. However, the Court used this uncertainty to argue that there was no religious reason why Hall could not attend the prom with his boyfriend. As it pointed out, there is an inconsistency in the Church's reasoning: it was not automatically assumed that opposite-sex dancing would lead to any sexual behaviour not permitted by the church or seen as sexual behaviour in itself, but the same activity by a same-sex couple is seen as intrinsically sexual.[64] This criticism is valid, but requiring religious teachings to be internally consistent is not the Court's responsibility. Religious teachings are 'not always susceptible to lucid exposition, or still less, rational justification'.[65] The court overstepped its role. It is not legitimate for a secular court to argue that there is no religious reason for a policy when the religious authority could point to a large body of thought within the Church which supported its point of view.

Whilst there are criticisms that can be made of the way proportionality was applied here, the judgment is certainly not entirely flawed and does demonstrate some benefits of the proportionality test. In Chapter 6 I argued that, where possible, judgments should embody mutual respect, and ultimate moral questions should be left aside providing space for individuals and organisations to 'define [their] own concept of existence, of meaning, of the universe.'[66] The judgment draws attention to this idea, stating that 'Mr. Hall has a duty to accord to others who do not share his orientation the respect that they, with their religious

62 [2002] 213 DLR (4th) 308.

63 Ibid., para 16.

64 J.A. Russ, 'Shall We Dance? Gay Equality and Religious Exemptions at Private Californian High School Proms' (1988) 42 *NYL Sch L Rev* 71.

65 *R(Williamson and Others) v Secretary of State for Education and Employment* [2005] 2 AC 246, 259.

66 Kennedy J, *Planned Parenthood v Casey* 505 U.S. 833 (1992).

values and beliefs, are due. Conversely … the principal and the Board have a duty to accord to Mr. Hall the respect that he is due'.[67] The judgment therefore attempts to reduce antagonism between the parties by pointing out that there is something of value in both sides' perspectives that is worthy of protection. It also places the dispute in context as part of an ongoing relationship.

Considering a proportionality enquiry more precisely, the school has the legitimate aims of protecting its religious conscience and its autonomy in the running of its schools. By forbidding Hall to attend with his boyfriend there was also a rational connection to this aim. As a less restrictive means of restricting Hall's rights, the school had suggested a compromise whereby a female friend of Hall's could take his boyfriend as her 'date', meaning that both could attend. However, this was unacceptable to Hall and evidently did not protect his right to non-discrimination to the same extent.

Considering the balancing stage, even on the most favourable reading to the Church, the religious interest was limited. The reason the school gave for forbidding Hall's boyfriend to attend was that 'interaction at a prom between romantic partners is a form of sexual activity and that, if permission were granted to Mr Hall to attend the prom with his boyfriend as a same-sex couple, this would be seen both as an endorsement and condonation of conduct which is contrary to Catholic church teachings.'[68] Even on the interpretation of religious doctrine put forward by the Catholic Church, though, this endorsement would have been rather remote. Of more importance is that 'the prom in question is not part of a religious service (such as a mass), is not part of the religious education component of the Board's activity, is not held on school property, and is not educational in nature.'[69] Significantly though, the discussion about the particular nature of the activity misses the stronger aspect of the school's claim, an aspect that careful application of the proportionality test could have foregrounded. Hall was still a student at the school and therefore subject to its control as to what constituted appropriate behaviour based on its religious beliefs. As Schneiderman puts it, 'this was a claim not merely about "same sex dancing" but also about the autonomy of the church to regulate the conduct of its members enrolled in its schools.'[70]

There are two entirely different ways of looking at the importance of this dispute. On one hand it is merely about one social occasion with no religious significance, which is not closely related to the Catholic Church's message or core religious activities. On the other, Hall's demand could be interpreted as a challenge to the Catholic Church's whole position on same-sex relationships and a challenge to its perceived inability to respond, at minimum, compassionately towards gay people particularly in schools. Hall can be seen as a role model to other gay students, leading them to challenge their schools' homophobic and heterosexist policies. Combine this with a new, more vocal, attitude amongst gay students[71] and it is unsurprising that the Church vehemently opposed Hall's claim. If this is so, then the case

67 Supra n.62, para 60.

68 Supra n.62, para 4.

69 Supra n.62, para 26.

70 D. Schneiderman, 'Associational Rights, Religion and the Charter' in R. Moon (ed.), *Law and Religious Pluralism in Canada* (Vancouver: UBC Press, 2008) 75.

71 A. Grace and K. Wells, 'The Marc Hall Prom Predicament: Queer Individual Rights v. Institutional Church Rights in Canadian Public Education' (2005) 28 *Canadian Journal of Education* 237, 239: 'Many making up today's queer student body are vocal, visible, and proud. They are making their schools key sites in their struggles for social justice and cultural recognition and respect.'

can be perceived as no longer a claim at the peripheries of Catholic teaching, but rather as a challenge to its centre.

This second way of seeing it, though, is unpersuasive. The 'slippery slope' argument is unconvincing because one decision does not lead inexorably to any future decisions. Even if Hall's success were to make other students more likely to challenge teachings on sexuality in denominational schools, these claims could be dealt with on their own merits. Furthermore, whether and in what way the case is likely to change public opinion is difficult to predict and in any event should not be relevant to the Court's decision. As previously stated, proportionality is 'balancing writ small'.[72] Therefore Hall's challenge should not be seen as a challenge to the core of Catholic rights and the interference with the Church's rights is therefore slight, although certainly existent.

The difficulty is, of course, in deciding ultimately where the burden of tolerance lies. The interests on both sides are limited: whether or not Hall could bring his boyfriend to the prom would not necessarily affect the Catholic Church's teachings on sexuality or even the school's ability to control or disseminate its religious message. Similarly, although undoubtedly extremely hurtful, the discrimination was only symbolic, and only related to one evening, although the psychological effects of such discrimination may well of course be experienced well beyond this. The most persuasive factor is the school's interest in religious autonomy in controlling the behaviour of students at the school. The timing of the issue is also important. This was a liminal moment for Hall. He was about to leave the school. From then on the amount of direct control the Catholic Church would have over him would be of his own choosing. For these reasons, although the Court's decision is more than understandable, it is questionable whether it reached the right decision. However, a proportionality analysis, which pays careful attention to all the interests in the case, demonstrates how finely balanced the interests in this case are.

Non-members and services

In addition to claims that involve the control of members of a religious organisation, claims may also be made by outsiders who wish to use some service run by a religious organisation for primarily secular rather than religious reasons. In comparison to the previous examples, the interests of those challenging the religious organisation's policy are likely to be higher because they do not claim inclusion into an organisation but merely the provision of a service on equal terms.

English law permits religious organisations to discriminate in the 'provision of goods, facilities or services in the course of activities undertaken by the organisation' or 'the use or disposal of premises owned or controlled by the organisation' on the grounds of religion or sexual orientation in some circumstances.[73] If the restriction relates to religious discrimination this restriction must be imposed 'because of the purpose of the organisation' or to 'avoid causing offence, on grounds of the religion or belief to which the organisation relates, to persons of that religion or belief'.[74] For sexual orientation discrimination it must be imposed 'because it is necessary to comply with the doctrine of the organisation' or to avoid conflict with 'the strongly held religious convictions of a significant number of the religion's

72 A. Barak, 'Proportionality and Principled Balancing' (2010) 4 *Law & Ethics of Human Rights* 1, 8.
73 Equality Act 2010 Sch 23 para. 2(3).
74 Equality Act 2010 Sch 23 para. 2(6).

followers'.[75] However this exemption does not apply if the service is provided on behalf of a public authority and under the terms of a contract between the organisation and the public authority.

Canada's law varies by province but normally discrimination is permitted where this is a bona fide qualification. Nova Scotia, for example, permits discrimination in the access to services or facilities where this is a bona fide qualification or 'a reasonable limit prescribed by law as can be demonstrably justified in a free and democratic society'.[76] In the US, state discrimination laws apply to public accommodations, and so in some situations religious organisations will not be covered at all by discrimination law.[77] Numerous states also have specific exemptions relating to same-sex weddings or marriages.[78] The First Amendment may also be relevant. Applying discrimination law to a religious organisation may contravene the Free Exercise Clause as it interferes with the religious organisation's autonomy,[79] or the Establishment Clause, on the basis that it requires an unconstitutional entanglement with religion.[80]

Hiring of religious organisation-owned premises

One basic dispute is whether religious organisations can deny the use of their premises to organisations with which they disagree. It is not enough to say that a religious organisation can avoid any conflict by not renting out their property. It may well be used to spread general awareness of the religion or be an important source of income which is relied on to fulfil the religious mission. As has been highlighted before, merely because a conflict is avoidable does not mean that there is no interference with the right.[81] Indeed, one of the advantages of proportionality is that interference can be defined broadly because it allows justification to be fully considered.

There are of course different kinds of property. A church has a greater claim over the use of sacred places, such as a chapel, than it does to premises used mainly as a source of income, not used for religious purposes and rented out to all-comers. As always, the greater the interference with the religious right, the greater the justification required, and vice versa.[82] At the secular end of this continuum is the American case of *Bernstein and Paster v Ocean Grove Camp Meeting Association*[83] (OGCMA). Ocean Grove is a resort owned by a Methodist organisation, which has its roots in the nineteenth-century camp meeting revival

75 Equality Act 2010 Sch 23 para. 2(7).
76 Nova Scotia Human Rights Act s.6(f) R.S., c. 214, s.1.
77 E.g. New York's law states that a religious corporation will not be held to be a provider of public accommodation: N.Y. Admin Code § 8–102.9. In *Wazeerud-Din v Goodwill Home and Missions, Inc.*, 737 A.2d 683 (N.J. Super. AD, 1999) an addiction therapy programme run by a religious organisation which used religious teaching and worship was held not to be a public accommodation under New Jersey law.
78 See N. Tebbe, 'Religion and Marriage Equality Statutes' (2015) 9 *Harv Law & Pol Rev* 25.
79 Presumably *Hosanna-Tabor v EEOC* 565 US ___ (2012) rather than *Employment Division v Smith* 494 US 872 (1990) would govern this issue because it relates to an internal matter of the religious organisation.
80 *Lemon v Kurtzman* 403 US 602 (1971).
81 See discussion of specific situation rule in Ch. 6.
82 This is Alexy's First Law of Balancing. See Ch. 5.
83 OAL Dkt. No. CRT 6145–09 (N.J. Office of Administrative Law, 2008). See M. Pearson, 'Religious Claims vs. Non-Discrimination Rights: Another Plea for Difficulty' (2013) 15 *Rutgers J of L & Relig* 47.

movement.[84] On the resort was the Boardwalk Pavilion, which was used for religious services and concerts but which could also be hired out for weddings. When not in use it was freely open to the public. A lesbian couple, Bernstein and Paster, tried to book the Pavilion for their wedding but were refused on the basis that the Methodist Church did not approve of same-sex marriage.

The administrative law judge found that the Pavilion was a place of public accommodation at the time, and so therefore OGCMA was covered by New Jersey's discrimination law. Furthermore, since there was no targeting of religious practice, there was no free exercise defence under the approach in *Employment Division v Smith*.[85] This reasoning though is unsatisfactory. As previously argued,[86] the fact that religious practice is not specifically targeted does not mean that interferences with freedom of religion are necessarily acceptable. Such an approach does not provide fact-specific justification to the parties and does not take into account the value of religious freedom and conscience.

A proportionality approach would have resolved these issues far better, although it would not necessarily have reached a different conclusion. OGCMA had legitimate aims in protecting its institutional conscience and in preserving autonomy over its spaces. Prohibiting same-sex marriage had a rational connection to these aims, and it appears that there was no less restrictive means of resolving the dispute. The decision must therefore come down to the final balancing test.

In assessing the importance of the opposing interests at this balancing stage, much depends on whether the Pavilion is characterised as a public or private space. I do not wish to use this distinction to set up a false dichotomy between public and private or to suggest that whether the discrimination is permissible or impermissible is coterminous with this distinction. However, ascertaining the character of the Pavilion is relevant in deciding the level of interference with OGCMA's right. On the one hand, Bold characterises the Pavilion as private, arguing that 'if the public sees religious institutions such as the Methodist pavilion owners allowing same-sex civil commitment ceremonies on their premises, casual observers may erroneously think the Methodist church has changed its historic stance against same-sex marriage.'[87] He also suggests that a ceremony would have received a great deal of media interest. This analysis makes the mere ownership of a place crucial. On this argument, it follows that a religious organisation may prevent a use which it does not agree with on any premises it owns, no matter how attenuated its link. This dramatically reduces the protection given by the anti-discrimination norm. It also fails to appreciate that the Pavilion was at least a partly public place. Although used for religious worship, it was not a church and was open to everyone. Non-Methodist and non-religious weddings had taken place there with no indication that the Church thereby endorsed them. Importantly also, OGCMA received a tax exemption for the Pavilion on the basis that it was open to the public.

In contrast to Bold, Lupu and Tuttle depict the Pavilion as public. They argue that 'Bernstein and Paster asked to use a facility that was not specifically identified with Methodist worship, that ordinary observers would see as public space, and that had been available

84 T.W. Messenger, *Holy Leisure: Recreation and Religion in God's Square Mile* (Philadelphia: Temple UP, 2000).
85 94 US 872 (1990).
86 See Ch 3.
87 F. Bold, 'Vows to Collide: The Burgeoning Conflict between Religious Institutions and Same-Sex Marriage Antidiscrimination Laws' (2009) 158 *U Pa L Rev* 179, 202.

for rental by anyone willing to pay the fee.'[88] This analysis is more appropriate than Bold's. Although OGCMA is a religiously based organisation, this does not thereby make the property it owns necessarily religious. Given the particular circumstances and use to which the Pavilion was put, the religious interest is fairly small. The risk of confusion between the Methodist Church's precepts and the actions it permits on some of its property therefore appears remote. Perhaps the fears concerning people erroneously thinking that the Methodist Church endorsed same-sex weddings could be met by having a sign saying that any activity taking place there did not necessarily represent the views of the Methodist Church.[89]

Of course, none of this means that OGCMA necessarily had to allow anyone to use the Pavilion. Their obligation was only not to discriminate, not to actively provide places for same-sex weddings. OGCMA could use it only as a religious space if it so wished and indeed did so after the case was brought, with it then being classified for tax purposes as a religious space rather than a public one. Thus the laws on non-discrimination in public accommodations did not apply to it. Another lesbian couple later tried to make a complaint to the Human Rights Tribunal, but this was rejected on the basis there was no cause of action.[90] The choice OGCMA was put to was therefore not a disproportionate one. However, a proportionality approach would recognise that it had some religious interest in the control of its property, which the approach under *Employment Division v Smith* does not, as it is only concerned with situations where religious practices are deliberately targeted.

In other cases, the religious organisation has a stronger claim. *Dignity Twin Cities v Newman Center & Chapel*[91] is a US case at the other end of the spectrum. Dignity is a national organisation of LGBT Catholics who press for change within the Catholic Church on matters relating to sexuality as well as acting as a support group. A chapter of this organisation had rented a chapel and meeting rooms owned by the Roman Catholic Archdiocese of St Paul and Minneapolis for a number of years. However, the Archdiocese then reconsidered its policy and decided it would permit it to hire the premises only if it signed a document affirming the Church's teachings on homosexuality, which it refused to do. Dignity then made a complaint to the Minneapolis Commission on Civil Rights which initially rejected the claim for a lack of jurisdiction. The Commission Appeals Board held though that there was a violation of Dignity's civil rights, except in so far as this related to the chapel. However, the Minnesota Court of Appeals overturned this decision on the basis that the entire relationship between the two parties was a religious one. It held that deciding the case would involve excessive state entanglement in church affairs and would infringe the Church's free exercise rights.

The decision is short and is primarily based on the concern that it would create excessive state entanglement and thus violate the Establishment Clause, an argument which is jurisdiction-specific. Nevertheless, it reached the correct decision. As the Court pointed out, 'Dignity's sole reason for using the facility was for worship and involvement in the Catholic tradition … They utilized the facility because of its religious identity.'[92] As a proportionality approach could have identified, in the specific context of this case there was little difference

88 I. Lupu and R. Tuttle, 'Same-Sex Equality and Religious Freedom' (2010) 5 *Nw J L & Soc Pol'y* 274, 285.

89 While relevant, this would not amount to a less restrictive alternative under the third stage of the proportionality test, as it does not protect OGCMA's interest in its religious autonomy to the same extent as being able to fully control what events took place on its property.

90 Lupu and Tuttle, supra n.88.

91 472 N.W.2d 355 (Minn. Ct. App., 1991).

92 Ibid., 357.

between using the Chapel and using the rest of the Center. Whilst in other cases there may have been a less restrictive means of preserving the Newman Center's rights by differentiating between different parts of the Center, it was here not an adequate response to the Center's concerns. Dignity was using the whole Center as a religious venue. Although the case certainly involved discrimination, this was primarily an internal religious dispute and it would have been inappropriate for it to have been resolved by an external body. Dignity's aim is to challenge the Catholic Church's doctrines on homosexuality. Of course, within every religious organisation there is dissent, but this does not mean that a religious leadership must provide facilities to allow it to take place. The fact that non-religious groups, such as Weight Watchers and the Alliance for Sustainable Agriculture, used the premises (although Dignity was the only one to use the Chapel) did not negate this. In contrast to Dignity, these relationships involved purely secular business relationships. The Center's religious interest was therefore greater than Dignity's. Dignity could continue its work in another venue.

The Canadian case of *Smith v Knights of Columbus*[93] falls between the two cases just outlined in terms of the importance of the religious right. A lesbian couple booked a hall run by the Knights of Columbus, a Catholic fraternal organisation, owned by the Archdiocese of Vancouver, for their wedding reception. The hall was on the same piece of land as a chapel and a parish school and was primarily used for parish activities, but could be hired for other events. It was advertised via a sign outside which had no indication of its religious character. Unfortunately, the events that then unfolded were characterised by confusion and misunderstanding on both sides. The couple did not realise the hall was owned by the Catholic Church or who the Knights of Columbus were. The manager of the hall did not realise the wedding was to be between two women. When this was discovered, and apparently on the misapprehension that a wedding rather than a wedding reception was to take place there, the Knights of Columbus cancelled the booking.

The couple complained to the British Columbia Human Rights Tribunal. The question was whether the Knights' religious beliefs constituted a 'bona fide and reasonable justification' for the discrimination: a very similar enquiry to a proportionality test. The Tribunal held that it was not enough that the Archdiocese owned the hall, especially since there was no warning given of any restriction on its use. It therefore correctly rejected an absolute rule which would nullify any non-discrimination obligation of the Archdiocese, including a limited obligation to consider whether such discrimination was necessary for its religious purposes. Oddly though, the Tribunal also stated that a 'person cannot be compelled to act in a manner that conflicts with [his/her] belief.'[94] This is evidently too wide. More relevantly, it held that the Knights did have the right to restrict the use in the circumstances, but it 'could have taken additional steps that would have recognized the inherent dignity of the complainants and their right to be free from discrimination'.[95]

Quite clearly, the situation that arose was not the least restrictive means of interfering with the couple's rights while preserving the Knights' rights. The Knights could have provided more information to the couple as to the ownership and management of the hall before the booking was taken, without this infringing their rights at all. In fact, this would have greatly reduced the likelihood of conflict. The couple said that had they known this they would not have tried to make a booking because of the Catholic Church's position on

93 2005 BCHRT 544.
94 Ibid., para 108
95 Ibid., para 123.

gay marriage. To take a booking and then cancel it is also likely to cause more distress than if the booking had not been taken at all. Even in cancelling the booking the Knights could have done more to protect the couple's interests while still acting in accordance with their beliefs. As the Tribunal suggested, it 'could have taken steps such as meeting with the complainants to explain the situation, formally apologizing, immediately offering to reimburse the complainants for any expenses they had incurred and, perhaps offering assistance in finding another solution.'[96] The confusion as to whether there was to be a wedding reception or a wedding itself also meant that the situation was not given the consideration by the Knights it deserved, even though the organisation later said they did not distinguish between the two and had religious objections to holding a wedding reception. Given all these factors, the couple's claim should have been successful, as indeed it was. The case demonstrates how the proportionality test requires the consideration of alternative solutions to resolve disputes and rights to be interfered with as minimally as possible.

Moon though criticises the case because, he argues, forbidding discrimination in this context did not restrict the organisation's religious practices, although he agrees with the ultimate result.[97] However, the organisation does have a legitimate interest in ensuring that activities taking place on the property it owns and uses for at least quasi-religious purposes are in accordance with its religious principles. Chapter 4 demonstrated the problems with deciding cases at the interference rather than justification stage in terms of the coherent analysis of the issues and the importance to the parties of having their claims fully considered. Rather than automatically rejecting the Knights' claim, the Tribunal was right to consider the claim in detail. There is a coherent conscience claim in these situations. Defining freedom of religion broadly, as a proportionality analysis permits, allows these concerns to be heard.

These three cases demonstrate that a religious organisation's right to control the use of their premises is not absolute, even if there are religious objections to the activity taking place. Nevertheless, in all these cases the religious organisation's claim should be taken seriously and assessed. It should not be rejected a priori on the basis that it can solve this dilemma by not offering the property for hire at all, although of course that is relevant, and may in the end be the best solution. Furthermore, the opposing interest of non-discrimination should also be recognised as important. Doing this takes the conflict of rights seriously and demonstrates a conciliatory form of reasoning.

English law

There has so far been no legal challenge to a refusal to hire out religious-owned property under English law. Under the Equality Act 2010, a religious organisation may discriminate on the grounds of sexual orientation regarding the 'use or disposal of premises owned or controlled' by a religious organisation where this is necessary either to comply with the doctrine of the organisation or 'to avoid conflict with the strongly held convictions of a significant number of the members of the religion or belief'.[98] This exemption does not apply where the organisation's 'sole or main purpose is commercial'.[99]

96 Ibid., para 124.
97 Moon supra n.54.
98 Sch 23 para 2.
99 Sch 23 para 2(2).

The EHRC's guidance states, however, that a religious organisation may discriminate 'provided it does not normally hire out its premises for payment'.[100] Under this interpretation, this could mean that if a religious organisation hired out its church for some purposes, such as concerts of religious music, this would be enough to mean it could not subsequently discriminate, even if all the previous events had been consistent with its religious mission. It is doubtful whether the EHRC's analysis is correct. A restriction on discrimination in purely commercial activities is likely to be justifiable, as will be discussed in the next chapter, but the Act does not say that a non-commercial organisation cannot hire out its premises for payment and the income used to support the organisation's non-commercial aims. The EHRC's stance would be very restrictive. However, the contrary reading also raises difficulties, because it seems to propose an absolute right to discriminate. There is nothing to prevent gay organisations alone from being singled out where the organisation otherwise hires its premises out to all-comers, since there is no proportionality test. This is therefore problematic.

Services provided to the general public

Religious organisations' interactions with wider society go well beyond hiring out premises. Religious organisations also provide a number of welfare services, which may receive state funding, and in some cases would otherwise be provided by the state, such as health care, addiction counselling or care of children or vulnerable adults. In some cases, religious organisations may argue that due to reasons of conscience they cannot provide a particular service to gay people. Many practical and symbolic issues arise out of these restrictions. The first practical issue is whether a service can still be easily accessed even if refused by a religious organisation. In most cases, but certainly not all,[101] the religious provider is likely to only be one provider among many and a person can choose to use another service. Indeed, permitting religious providers may increase choice since some people may prefer to use specifically religious services. It may therefore fit into policies of welfare pluralism, which aim to encourage competition and choice in the provision of services.[102] Furthermore, if large and well-established charities refuse to provide services unless they have an exemption there may be an impact on services if this is denied.

Although these practical issues are important, symbolic harms are more likely to motivate disagreement. These symbolic harms can be characterised either as the loss to dignity caused by state-sponsored discrimination[103] or, alternatively, as 'concerning the extent to which the

100 Equality and Human Rights Commission, *Your Rights to Equality from Voluntary and Community Sector Organisations (Including Charities and Religion or Belief Organisations)* (Manchester: EHRC, 2011) 21.

101 E.g. as Clark explains, in some cases the only healthcare available in a particular area may be controlled by a religious organisation; B.R. Clark, 'When Free Exercise Exemptions Undermine Religious Liberty and the Liberty of Conscience: A Case Study of the Catholic Hospital Conflict' (2003) 82 *Or L Rev* 625, 629.

102 See for the UK context, e.g. National Council for Voluntary Organisations, *Faith and Voluntary Action: An Overview of Current Evidence and Debates* (London: NCVO, 2007); J. Rees, 'Public Sector Commissioning and the Third Sector: Old Wine in New Bottles' (2014) 29 *Public Policy and Administration* 45. For the US see e.g. W. Bielefeld and W.S. Cleveland, 'Faith-Based Organizations as Service Providers and their Relationship to Government' (2013) 42 *Nonprofit and Voluntary Sector* 468, and for Canada e.g. J. Rekart, *Public Funds, Private Provision: The Role of the Voluntary Sector* (Vancouver: UBC Press, 2011).

103 R. Wintemute, 'Religion vs. Sexual Orientation: A Clash of Human Rights?' (2002) *Journal of Law & Equality* 125.

discourse of equality and gay rights trumps the sincerely held faith-based views of a minority.'[104] In England, these issues have arisen most controversially over whether Catholic adoption agencies can refuse to place children with gay couples. In many ways the controversy is not surprising. Any issue about the best environment for raising children, including either fear of children remaining in care when suitable parents are available or which challenges 'the heterosexual family as the "gold standard" of parenting'[105] is bound to be controversial. Although practical issues of ensuring adequate access to adoption services were relevant in this debate, as Stychin argues, given that gay couples could adopt through state or non-Catholic agencies (and it seems unlikely that many would want to adopt *only* through Catholic agencies), the true issue was its symbolic significance.[106]

In this heated debate, the adoption agencies could be characterised as bigots, ignoring the best interests of children in care for the sake of dogma.[107] Those arguing against an exemption could also be characterised as ignoring the best interests of children in forcing 'unsuitable' parents onto vulnerable children and as forcing a minority to 'either violate their clear Church doctrine, or ignore their religious vocation'.[108] In England this dispute led to an extremely long, but unsuccessful, legal battle by one adoption agency, Catholic Care (Diocese of Leeds) (hereafter Catholic Care), to gain an exemption. This issue has also led to extensive debates in a number of states in America, most notably in Illinois and Massachusetts.[109] In contrast, in Canada private adoption agencies may discriminate on religious grounds, although many of course do not choose to do so, and this has not so far been noticeably controversial.

In England, voluntary adoption agencies do not care for children in care themselves or arrange direct placements between birth and adoptive parents, but instead recruit and assess potential adoptive parents and provide support and training. The local authority is responsible for matching children with prospective parents approved by these agencies. Alternatively, potential adopters can apply directly to the local authority. As a concession, religious voluntary adoption agencies were granted an exemption from the prohibition of sexual orientation discrimination until December 2008, under a temporary exemption from the Equality Act (Sexual Orientation) Regulations 2007. They could not bring themselves

104 C.F. Stychin, 'Faith in Rights: The Struggle Over Same-Sex Adoption in the United Kingdom' (2008) 17 *Const F* 7, 8.

105 Ibid., 8.

106 Ibid. See also C.F. Stychin, 'Pluralism, Equality and the Challenge of Faith Based Services' (2014) 1 *JICL* 141.

107 E.g. National Secular Society, 'Catholic Adoption Agency Loses Fight Over Gay Adoption', 3 Nov 2012, available at: http://www.secularism.org.uk/news/2012/11/catholic-adoption-agency-loses-fight-over-gay-adoption <last accessed 25 July 2016>.

108 C.T. Rutledge, 'Caught in the Crossfire: How Catholic Charities of Boston was Victim to the Clash Between Gay Rights and Religious Freedom' (2008) 15 *Duke J Gender L & Pol'y* 297, 299.

109 In both states discrimination was prohibited. Illinois' prohibition was a consequence of the Illinois Religious Freedom Protection and Civil Union Act 750 ILCS 75, meaning that civil unions had to be treated as equivalent to marriage. As a result, the state refused to continue to contract with charities that discriminated. A case challenging this decision failed: *Catholic Charities of the Diocese of Springfield v State of Illinois* 2011-MR-254 (7th Cir., Aug 18, 2011). Massachusetts' law on public accommodations does not contain any religious exemptions. Catholic Charities of Boston did place children with same-sex couples but when this became publicly known, the Catholic Church refused to allow adoptions to continue that were not in line with its teachings. The charity therefore withdrew from providing adoptions in order to comply with the law. It did not seek to challenge the law. See M. Minow, 'Should Religious Groups Be Exempt from Civil Rights Laws?' (2007) 48 *BCL Rev* 781.

under the exemption allowing religious organisations to discriminate in the provision of services in defined circumstances because this does not apply where the service was publicly funded and provided under a contract.[110]

In order to continue to provide services, which it refused to do without an exemption, Catholic Care attempted to bring itself under another permanent exemption, now s.193 of the Equality Act 2010 which provides that:[111]

1 A person does not contravene this Act only by restricting the provision of benefits to persons who share a protected characteristic if –

 a the person acts in pursuance of a charitable instrument, and
 b the provision of the benefits is within subsection (2).

2 The provision of benefits is within this subsection if it is –

 a proportionate means of achieving a legitimate aim, or
 b for the purpose of preventing or compensating for a disadvantage linked to the protected characteristic.

This is essentially a legislatively mandated proportionality enquiry. Catholic Care wanted to change its Memorandum of Association to say that it only provided adoption services to married heterosexual couples. To do this it needed the permission of the Charity Commission of England and Wales and this could only be given if Catholic Care's work fell under the exemption in s.193. This litigation was extremely lengthy. The Charity Commission originally refused permission to make the required change in November 2008. Catholic Care appealed to the Charity Tribunal in June 2009,[112] which upheld this decision. This was further appealed to the High Court,[113] which held the change could potentially be lawful and sent the decision back for reconsideration by the Charity Commission. The Charity Commission again refused permission.[114] Catholic Care appealed this decision to the First-Tier Tribunal (Charity)[115] and subsequently to the Upper Tribunal (Tax and Chancery Chamber).[116] Both of these appeals were unsuccessful.

110 Sch 23 para 2. If the adoption agency was not publicly funded this would not violate discrimination law; however, this is not a practical option for adoption agencies given the way the adoption system operates in Britain.

111 The law at the beginning of the dispute until 1 October 2010 was as follows: *Reg 18(1) Nothing in these Regulations shall make it unlawful for a person to provide benefits only to persons of a particular sexual orientation if – (a) he acts in pursuance of a charitable instrument, and (b) the restriction of benefits to persons of that sexual orientation is imposed by reason of or on the grounds of the provisions of the charitable instrument (2) Nothing in these Regulations shall make it unlawful for the Charity Commission for England and Wales … to exercise a function in relation to a charity in a manner which appears to the commission or to the holder to be expedient in the interests of the charity, having regard to the provisions of the charitable instrument.* See D. Morris, A. Morris and J. Sigafoos, 'Adopting (In)Equality in the UK: The Equality Act 2010 and its Impact on Charities' (2016) 38 *Journal of Social Welfare and Family Law* 14.

112 *Father Hudson's Society and another v Charity Commission* [2009] PTSR 1125.

113 *Catholic Care (Diocese of Leeds) v Charity Commission for England and Wales* [2010] EWHC 520.

114 Decision of the Charity Commission of England and Wales, 21 July 2010.

115 [2011] Eq LR 597. The First-Tier Tribunal (Charity) and Upper Tribunal (Tax and Chancery Chamber) have taken over the responsibility of the Charity Tribunal and, in this respect, the High Court, following the coming into force of the Tribunals Courts and Enforcement Act 2007.

116 [2012] UKUT 395 (TCC).

In Scotland, interpreting the same legislation, the Office of the Scottish Charity Regulator (OSCR), the equivalent of the Charity Commission, initially gave permission for a Catholic adoption agency, St Margaret's Children and Family Care Society, to change its constitution to allow it to provide services in accordance with the teachings of the Catholic Church and to give preference to married Catholic couples. This situation continued for a number of years, but the OSCR reconsidered its decision in January 2013, following a complaint from the National Secular Society. However, the Scottish Charity Appeals Panel overturned this decision in January 2014.[117] Importantly though, the charity did not have a blanket policy prohibiting gay people from becoming adoptive parents. Rather, it only gave preference to those who wished to adopt within the framework of Catholic teaching on the family, and the interests of the adopted child were always considered to be paramount. Thus the Panel considered that the discrimination was indirect rather than direct, and therefore there was greater scope under the law to justify it.[118] Even given these distinctions though, there are inconsistencies between the Scottish and English decisions.[119]

The issue at the heart of the English dispute was whether Catholic Care could demonstrate that providing adoption services only to married heterosexual couples was a proportionate means of achieving a legitimate aim. The justification put forward did not rely on the religious rights of the agency. Although there could be an argument that the work of a Catholic adoption agency was a direct outworking of its religious mission and therefore interference in the way it was run was a violation of its religious rights,[120] this argument was, at the time, doomed to failure on account of the very narrow interpretation of Art. 9 that had been given by the British courts.[121] As the courts had held that there is no interference where a person is required to choose between their employment and following their religious conscience, it would have been strange to hold there is an interference where a religious charity could run its services in the way in which it wishes, given that it could alter the services it provided or withdraw entirely from providing services at all. The Court of Appeal's suggestion in *Ladele v Islington LBC*,[122] that interference would not normally be found where the service took place in the public sphere, also would have made finding an interference in these circumstances difficult. Although the test for interference is now broader after the ECtHR's decision in *Eweida v UK*,[123] and so the fact that the activity is voluntary does not necessarily exclude the claim, to be successful the claim must go beyond a mere licence to provide these services. In order to continue its service, Catholic Care would have to contract with the state. Essentially then, Catholic Care would have had to argue that there was an obligation to require the state to fund a particular activity by a particular organisation because of its religious nature. This would place such a burden on the state that it cannot be accepted.

An American case is instructive on the point. The Illinois Circuit Court concluded in the factually very similar case of *Catholic Charities of the Diocese of Springfield v State of Illinois*[124] that there is no legally cognisable interest in requiring the state to contract with a

117 App 2/13 (31 Jan 2013).
118 Under English law, indirect discrimination can always be justified on the basis that it is a proportionate means of achieving a legitimate aim. For direct discrimination to be justified it must fall into an explicit exemption.
119 See Morris, Morris and Sigafoos supra n.111.
120 Such an argument was accepted by the Scottish Charity Appeals Panel.
121 See Ch. 6.
122 [2010] 1 WLR 955.
123 (2013) 57 EHHR 8.
124 Case No. 2011-MR-254 (August 18, 2011).

particular contractor. Catholic Charities had contracted annually with the state for forty years to provide foster care and adoption services. In 2011 the state refused to renew its contract because the charity would not provide these services to unmarried cohabiting couples, including to those in civil unions. The Court held that since there was no legally recognised protected property interest in the renewal of its contracts, Catholic Charities had no claim when it was not renewed.

The justification Catholic Care instead advanced was based on the interests of children in care. The charity specialised in finding placements for 'hard to place children', which included older children, sibling groups and children with disabilities. It placed about ten children per year. The funding it received from the local authority for each child it placed was not sufficient payment for the work it did, leading to a shortfall of about £13,000 per placement. It therefore relied on charitable donations to make up the difference. These largely came through the auspices of the Catholic Church. The Church stated that if the charity did not have an exemption it would no longer be operating in accordance with Catholic principles and it could therefore no longer support it. Since this income stream would no longer be available, the charity would have to close and its capacity and expertise would be lost. The High Court held that this could in theory constitute justification but subsequently both the First-Tier Tribunal (Charity) and the Upper Tribunal (Tax and Chancery Chamber) held that this justification was not in practice made out. The charity failed to demonstrate that it would affect to any great extent the interests of children in care, since there was no evidence that more children would be adopted if it remained open. There therefore did not exist the 'convincing and weighty reasons' required for discrimination based on sexual orientation by ECHR law.[125]

It may seem surprising that the closure of an adoption agency has no effect on the number of children adopted. As explained in the judgments, this was mainly because of the complexities of the adoption system and its funding. Voluntary adoption agencies are paid an 'inter-agency fee' by the local authority for each placement they make. However, because this is more expensive than placing children through the local authority itself, local authorities are reluctant to use such agencies.[126] Although if Catholic Care closed this would reduce the number of routes by which an adopter could be approved, a greater number of potential adopters registered with voluntary adoption agencies did not necessarily mean that more children would be adopted. Furthermore, as the Upper Tribunal pointed out, local authorities did not seem to have experienced greater problems in finding adopters since Catholic Care stopped providing adoption services in 2008, as they had simply made more use of other agencies. Although voluntary adoption agencies have higher success rates than local authorities, Catholic Care's success rate was comparable to other voluntary agencies. There was therefore no *particular* benefit of Catholic Care continuing to provide services.

Refusing to permit it to discriminate was therefore the appropriate conclusion. An attention to the facts actually demonstrates that many of the reasonable fears caused by the 'forced' closure of an adoption agency were misplaced, as it relates to the current English experience. Whether an exemption was granted or not would seem to have little effect on the needs of children in care. This further demonstrates the lack of practical importance of

125 *EB v France* (2008) 47 EHHR 509.

126 J. Fink, A. De Jong and M. Langan, 'New Challenges or Different Opportunities? Voluntary Adoption Agencies and the Shifting Terrain of Child Care Services' (2011) 15 *Voluntary Sector Review* 177; J. Selwyn, *Adoption and the Inter-agency Fee* (Department for Children, Schools and Families, 2009).

the issue and could potentially lower some of the tension caused by refusing an exemption. Nevertheless, there are problems with the judgments and decisions. They are strongly influenced by the Court of Appeal's judgment in *Ladele,* which had been interpreted to mean that there is an absolute rule that it is impermissible to rely on discriminatory religious ideas in the public sphere. In the Charity Commission's decision there is perhaps also an implied lack of respect towards the religious actors in the case. It asserts that the views of Catholic donors who do not wish to donate to a charity that does not follow the Catholic Church's teachings on the family cannot be relevant because these views are discriminatory. The Upper Tribunal, which held that the attitude of donors had a 'legitimate place in a pluralist, tolerant and broadminded society', though corrected this problem.[127] These judgments are also very clear on the importance of non-discrimination, repeatedly holding that very weighty reasons must be given for discrimination.

Although this was the correct legal decision, this leaves open the question of whether the government was necessarily right not to grant an exemption as a matter of policy. Practical concerns could have been met by notice requirements to prospective adopters that only heterosexual married couples would be accepted and an obligation to refer to other agencies if approached.[128] Of course symbolic issues would still remain. There is the danger that the state would be seen as approving the view that gay couples are not suitable adopters. However, as was discussed in Chapter 6 in relation to registrars who do not wish to perform same-sex marriages, there is no reason in principle why this view should be ascribed to the state merely because an exemption is given. Rather it would only demonstrate, as McIlroy argues, that 'these positions were merely tolerated, in the proper sense of the word, that is to say that they were exceptions made to positions of which the government disapproved, but given on the principled ground that there was no imperative *raison d'état* why those conscientious objections should be overridden.'[129] Nevertheless, this argument still involves an acceptance that these are views that can be tolerated and that ending discrimination against gay people is not an 'imperative *raison d'état*'. An exemption can therefore undermine gay people's dignity since 'people are harmed in respect of their civil status if they are refused a service that is available to all other citizens.'[130]

There is also a strong argument that if charities are to be given public money then the state can decide the terms on which the services are provided. The government may have a number of purposes alongside the practical provision of a service, which may include non-discrimination and inclusivity. This may have a heavy impact on some charities, but the argument might be that if they cannot provide the service on the basis the government wishes, they should withdraw from providing it.[131] On the other hand, an exemption can fulfil a symbolic role in favour of religious conscience, as well as against gay people. It may symbolically demonstrate that the work of religious charities is valued and that religious beliefs are given a space within an accommodationist and pluralist society and thus reduce (whether well-founded or not) fears of marginalisation.

127 Supra n.116, para 45.
128 R.F. Wilson, 'A Matter of Conviction: Moral Clashes over Same-Sex Adoption' (2008) 22 *BYU J Pub L* 475.
129 D. McIlroy, 'Legislation in a Context of Moral Disagreement: The Case of the Sexual Orientation Regulations' (2007) 159 *Law & Just – Christian L Rev* 114, 127.
130 R. Plant, 'Religion, Identity and Freedom of Expression' (2011) 17 *Res Publica* 7, 15.
131 M. Malik, 'Religious Freedom, Free Speech and Equality: Conflict or Cohesion?' (2011) 17 *Res Publica* 21, 37.

We should be careful, however, not to create false dichotomies. There does not necessarily have to be an either/or situation where the only options are no exemption and the closure of adoption agencies or an exemption and discrimination. A closer look at the situation arising after the legislation in fact demonstrates this. Although some did stop their adoption placement service, ultimately most organisations found a way to reconcile their religious message with the law.[132] Religious agencies run by the Church of England, although initially opposed to the legislation,[133] decided that they could comply with it without compromising their religious mission. This was also the case for one Catholic charity, Nugent Care, which continues to provide adoption services and has maintained its official religious links.[134]

In other cases, the situation is more complex. Although the Roman Catholic Bishop of Lancaster strongly opposed the legislation and demanded the charity in his diocese, Catholic Caring Services, sever its links with the Church if it decided to comply with it,[135] this did not lead to the organisation's closure and indeed it took over the work of another Catholic adoption agency that had felt forced to close. It did, however, rename itself Caritas Care, and the Bishop resigned as a trustee.[136] One of its charitable objects remains though, 'to further the general charitable works of the Roman Catholic Church'.[137] The Catholic Children's Society, now renamed Faith in Families, has similarly severed its formal links with the Catholic Church but continues to exist.[138] Father Hudson's Society, which originally sought an exemption alongside Catholic Care, dealt with the legislation by hiving off its adoption work into a separate charity, Adoption Focus.[139] Whilst Father Hudson's Society is still run as a Catholic charity, Adoption Focus is not.

This variety of reactions to such legislation is reflected in other jurisdictions. In Massachusetts, Illinois and Washington, D.C., Catholic charities have stopped placing children for adoption. However, such laws have not necessarily meant the entire closure of religious adoption agencies. In San Francisco, Catholic Charities no longer directly places children with adopters but 'joined with a non-profit organization that manages an Internet database of children available for adoption, and assists with adoption referrals to any prospective parent, including gays and lesbians.'[140] In Massachusetts, Catholic Charities of Boston transferred its adoption staff and caseload to a private agency.[141]

The various responses to the legislation have been highlighted because they indicate that it is possible to achieve solutions whereby, most importantly, children's needs are met, but where also the interests in non-discrimination of prospective adopters and society, and the interests of religious organisations and their staff can be also protected. Too often this topic

132 Fink, De Jong and Langan supra n.126; T. Philpot, 'Keeping the Faith', *Community Care,* 22 January 2009, 18.

133 BBC News, 'Churches Unite over Adoption Row', 24 January 2007, available at: http://news.bbc.co.uk/1/hi/uk_politics/6293115.stm <last accessed 25 July 2016>.

134 See Charity Commission, 'Nugent Care', available at: http://beta.charitycommission.gov.uk/charity-details/?regid=222930&subid=0 <last accessed 25 July 2016>; Philpot supra n.132.

135 R. Butt, 'Bishop Hits Out at Adoption Agency over Gay Couples Rule', *The Guardian* 21 Dec 2008.

136 L. Dodd, 'Fractured Relationship' *The Tablet* 19th Jan 2013, 7.

137 Charity Commission, 'Caritas Care', available at: http://apps.charitycommission.gov.uk/Showcharity/RegisterOfCharities/CharityFramework.aspx?RegisteredCharityNumber=326021&SubsidiaryNumber=0 <last accessed 25 July 2016>.

138 Philpot supra n.132.

139 Ofsted, *Adoption Focus: Inspection Report for Voluntary Adoption Agency* (Ofsted, 2013) 3.

140 Minow supra n.109, 843.

141 Ibid.

was merely used as a 'banner' where the discourse was 'reduced to simplistic all-or-nothing positions' rather than a discussion which took as its basis 'the equal worth of each person and tolerance for different ways of life'.[142] However, this does not necessarily support the idea of an exemption. In many cases the actual result is not far off what would have happened if there had been an exemption with a referral requirement: religious organisations are cooperatively working with and referring to non-religious agencies and in many cases this has included the transfer of staff.

Conclusion

Many of the court decisions and pieces of legislation discussed in this chapter are justifiable. They demonstrate respect to both parties by recognising the difficult nature of these decisions and weighing the particular interests at issue. Nevertheless, it has been demonstrated that those cases which use a proportionality, or at least a balancing, test are best able to account for and weigh the different interests. In assessing these conflicts this approach has rejected any absolute right to discriminate, although it has suggested that discrimination should be permitted in relation to religious membership and worship.

In considering these issues, the courts have rarely suggested that because the religious organisation has a choice as to whether it provides the service, there is no real conflict between religious precepts and the law. This idea is though apparent in the next issue to be considered: religious individuals and the provision of services.

142 Ibid., 843.

9 The secular marketplace and religious claims

This final substantive chapter addresses the question of whether individuals can discriminate in providing services. A desire to control who may receive services is not just limited to religious organisations. Religious individuals may also claim that their freedom of religion is breached when they, or the businesses they run, are required, as they see it, to facilitate or aid acts contrary to their beliefs, such as those relating to same-sex marriage. A florist may refuse to provide flowers for a gay couple's wedding, saying that, 'As a born-again Christian, I must respect my conscience before God and have no part in this matter.'[1] A landlord may refuse to rent a flat to a gay couple because he believes that 'same-sex relationships are "unnatural and against nature" and "the Bible warns against being associated with such wickedness"'.[2] A bed and breakfast business may refuse to allow a gay couple to share a room on the basis that 'monogamous heterosexual marriage is the form of partnership uniquely intended for sexual relations'.[3] This area raises some very complex issues, including the extent of religious rights and the question of whether businesses can have rights to manifest religious beliefs, as well as the central question of whether and how to balance conflicting rights. As before, it will be demonstrated that proportionality provides a workable and nuanced method of deciding these cases.

None of the jurisdictions provide general explicit legislative exemptions in the provision of commercial services.[4] Therefore claims will normally have to be made on the basis that there has been a violation of constitutional or human rights provisions. Such claims are though likely to face difficulties even at the preliminary stage of finding a mere *interference* with the right to freedom of religion. Given this, I will first consider how the three jurisdictions have addressed this issue and how it should be addressed by a proportionality approach. I will then go on to consider how these cases should be solved in the context of general commercial services, housing, and bed and breakfast accommodation. The range of situations where conflicts can arise is immense as is, correspondingly, the potential width of any

1 CBC News, 'Florist Refuses to Outfit Same-Sex Wedding', 16 Mar 2011, available at: http://www.cbc.ca/news/canada/new-brunswick/florist-refuses-to-outfit-same-sex-couple-s-wedding-1.1026447 <last accessed 25 July 2016>.
2 *Robertson and Anthony v Goertzen* 2010 NTHRAP 1 (5th September 2010).
3 *Black and Morgan v Wilkinson* [2013] 1 WLR 2490.
4 Although attempts to include such provisions have been made in various US states. See I. Lupu, 'Moving Targets: *Obergefell*, *Hobby Lobby*, and the Future of LGBT Rights' (2015) 7 *Ala CR & CL L Rev* 1. For letters to legislatures written by various law scholars with a statutory proposal see: T. Berg, 'Memos/Letters on Religious Liberty and Same-Sex Marriage', 2 August 2009, available at: http://mirrorofjustice.blogs.com/mirrorofjustice/2009/08/memosletters-on-religious-liberty-and-samesex-marriage.html <last accessed 25 July 2016>.

religious exemption. For this reason, among others, it may be more difficult to claim an exemption here than in other contexts.

Interference

England

The question of whether there is an interference with the right of freedom of religion where a person claims they are religiously obliged to refuse to provide a service can be a particularly difficult one. As previously outlined, until the ECtHR's decision in *Eweida v UK*,[5] in the employment context English law relied on the 'specific situation rule'. This held that if a person could avoid a conflict by resigning their employment or taking similar action then there was no interference with the right. However, this principle was never as straightforwardly accepted in the present context as it was in the employment sphere, even though it could be argued that a person could give up their business and find alternative employment in the same way.

The first case to consider these issues in depth was *Bull v Hall and Preddy*,[6] which reached the Supreme Court in 2013.[7] The owners of a bed and breakfast business refused to let a same-sex couple in a civil partnership stay in a double room because they felt this would be condoning sexual activity outside opposite-sex marriage and thus contravened their beliefs. They would have allowed them to stay in a twin bedded room had one been available. The Supreme Court accepted that the Bulls' rights under Article 9 were engaged, although this may have been because the assumption was not challenged in the appeal. Baroness Hale stated that the Court of Appeal had reached the same conclusion. However, this is slightly open to doubt. Rather, the Court of Appeal gave two substantive judgments, which appear to reach different conclusions as to whether there was an interference, with the third judge agreeing with both judgments.[8] Rafferty LJ's judgment appears to adopt the specific situation rule and so there would be no interference with freedom of religion where a conscientious dilemma could be avoided by resignation or similar conduct. She quotes approvingly the Court of Appeal's discussion in *Ladele v Islington LBC*[9] of the ECtHR case, *Pichon and Sajous v France*,[10] which held that there was no interference with pharmacists' rights under Article 9 where they were fined for refusing to supply contraception because they could manifest their beliefs outside a professional context. However, since she runs this issue together with that of whether 'the limitations are necessary in a democratic society for the protection of the rights and freedoms of others', whether she actually adopts the specific situation rule is unclear. Since she concludes that, 'to the extent to which the Regulations limit the manifestation of the Appellants' religious beliefs, the limitations are necessary',[11] she avoids the important question of whether there is an interference. The concurring judgment of Morritt LJ did, however, hold that there was an interference with the Bulls' religious beliefs.

5 [2013] 57 EHRR 8.
6 [2013] UKSC 73.
7 A similar case, *Black and Morgan v Wilkinson* supra n.3, was decided by the Court of Appeal a few months before this.
8 [2012] 1 WLR 2514.
9 [2010] 1 WLR 955.
10 App no. 49853/99 (2 Oct 2001).
11 supra n.8, 2531.

In any case, the Supreme Court was right to treat the two issues of interference and justification separately. Whether a right has been infringed is an analytically separate question from whether this infringement is justified. Moreover, as has been argued throughout, even where a claim must fail because of the importance of a conflicting right, it is important to acknowledge the loss caused by the interference with the right.[12] Separating the two issues of interference and justification can help to do this. An interference should have been found in *Bull* because there is a clear link between the owners' belief, that sexual activity outside heterosexual marriage is immoral and that they would be facilitating it by providing accommodation, and their act in refusing to let same-sex couples stay. If this were not the case, the dilemma they face between being asked either to violate their conscience or to give up their business, which may be very difficult financially, would be given no legal weight or recognition.

Canada

In Canada, under a proportionality test, it seems to be recognised that there is an interference in similar circumstances. In *Ontario (Human Rights Commission) v Brockie,*[13] a printer refused to print stationery for the Canadian Gay and Lesbian Archives, a non-profit organisation, because he believed 'that homosexual conduct is sinful and, in the furtherance of that belief, he must not assist in the dissemination of information intended to spread the acceptance of a gay or lesbian lifestyle.'[14] Although he did not object to serving gay customers and had indeed provided services to 'a commercial organization which produces underwear marketed to the gay male population',[15] he felt that this was too direct a link and therefore violated his conscience. This was conceded to be an interference with his rights. By being able to recognise this, proportionality can demonstrate respect to religious claimants by acknowledging their dilemma, thus illustrating its conciliatory and 'wounds-healing'[16] nature.

USA

Compared to the straightforwardness of this conclusion under a proportionality test, the question of whether a religious freedom right is engaged under US law in this context is very complex and may have to be considered under a number of legal tests. First, it could be argued there is an infringement of a person's free exercise rights. However, since the Supreme Court's decision in *Employment Division v Smith*[17] that laws could only be challenged on this basis where they were not neutral or generally applicable, this is a limited right. Evidently, the vast majority of anti-discrimination laws will be neutral and generally applicable, in that they prohibit everyone from discriminating on particular grounds, and do not target those who believe they should discriminate for certain religious reasons.

However, *Smith* does permit challenges where a 'hybrid' right is infringed. As explained previously,[18] this is where the Free Exercise Clause is considered 'in conjunction with other

12 See Ch. 4.
13 [2002] 222 DLR (4th) 174.
14 Ibid., para 3.
15 Ibid., para 15.
16 W. Sadurski, '"Reasonableness" and Value Pluralism in Law and Politics' in G. Bongiovanni et al. (eds), *Reasonableness and Law* (Dordrecht: Springer, 2009) 140.
17 494 US 872 (1990).
18 Ch. 3.

constitutional protections, such as freedom of speech and of the press.'[19] What this means in practice is unclear. This concept has been the subject of much academic criticism[20] and indeed, 'one circuit court of appeals has categorically declined to apply the hybrid rights doctrine, citing its unworkability, and several other federal appellate and trial courts have criticized it.'[21] It has been interpreted as meaning that there must be a 'colourable' or 'conjoined' claim regarding another right,[22] although this does not make its meaning much clearer. Nevertheless, it has been found to be relevant in some cases in this context.

In *Thomas v Anchorage Equal Rights Commission*[23] a landlord claimed that being required to rent property to unmarried couples infringed his free exercise rights. The Ninth Circuit Court of Appeals held the claim was sufficiently associated with freedom of speech to make the claim a hybrid claim under *Employment Division v Smith,* since landlords were also forbidden to state that they preferred not to rent to unmarried couples. A compelling interest therefore had to be demonstrated. The case demonstrates the flawed and arbitrary nature of the hybrid right exception. Whether or not the landlord could state that he preferred not to rent to unmarried couples is only a peripheral concern. The real issue is not what he can say, but what he can do. It is also far from clear why an additional small interest of a different kind should make a case subject to strict scrutiny, while a great interference with one right does not require any justification.

The second route by which it is possible to claim that a right has been infringed is to bring a claim under the federal Religious Freedom Restoration Act (RFRA). As previously discussed, this reinstated the test under constitutional law before *Smith* and therefore requires a compelling state interest to be demonstrated when there is a substantial burden on religious belief. However, it has limited coverage. Cases can only be brought against the state and not in disputes between private parties. It was also held in *City of Boerne v Flores*[24] that it could only constitutionally apply to federal, rather than state, action. Since prohibitions against sexual orientation discrimination are, apart from rare exceptions,[25] state rather than federal laws, it only has limited relevance to this area of law. Some states do have a state RFRA, or have equivalent protection in the state constitution. These provide similar protection to the federal RFRA, but apply to state rather than federal law. While they could be used to challenge state anti-discrimination legislation, these too do not apply in disputes between private parties.[26]

Under US law, therefore, it may be very difficult to have a religious claim recognised as even infringing a right. For example, in *Elane Photography LLC v Willock,*[27] summary

19 Supra n.17, 881.

20 See e.g. K. Greenawalt, 'Quo Vadis: The Status and Prospects of "Tests" under the Religion Clauses' (1995) *Sup Ct Rev* 323; D. Laycock, 'The Remnants of Free Exercise' (1990) *Sup Ct Rev* 1; Harvard Law Review Board, 'The Best of a Bad Lot: Compromise and Hybrid Religious Exemptions' (2010) 123 *Harv L Rev* 1494.

21 S. Aden and L. Strang, 'When a "Rule" Doesn't Rule: The Failure of the *Oregon Employment Division v. Smith* "Hybrid Rights Exception"' (2003) 108 *Penn St L Rev* 573.

22 Ibid.

23 165 F.3d 692 (9th Cir, 1999).

24 521 US 507 (1997).

25 E.g. federal government employees: Executive Order 13087 of May 28, 1998. While same-sex marriage is required by the constitution, *Obergefell v Hodges* 576 US ____ (2015) the decision does not prohibit discrimination outside this context.

26 Indiana's RFRA does apply to private parties, but following widespread opposition to the Bill it does not cover anti-discrimination laws. See Lupu supra n.4.

27 284 P.3d 428 (N.M.App, 2012), 309 P.3d 53 (N.M. 2013). See for further discussion of this case, M. Pearson, 'Religious Claims vs. Non-Discrimination Rights: Another Plea for Difficulty' (2013) 15 *Rutgers J of L & Relig* 47.

judgment was granted against a photography company which refused to photograph a same-sex couple's commitment ceremony because the owners believed that same-sex marriage was immoral. The owners, the Huguenins, had no claim under the Free Exercise clause because the law prohibiting discrimination in public accommodations did not 'selectively burden any religion or religious belief'.[28] They had no claim under either the New Mexico RFRA or the federal RFRA, because the other party was a private individual. The Huguenins therefore had no opportunity to raise their claims at all and so the harm caused to them was not recognised. They were essentially told that they have suffered no injury even though they have been put to a difficult conscientious dilemma (although of course this may well be justified).

Even if the RFRA applies, there have been further difficulties in establishing that being prohibited from discriminating in providing such services constitutes a substantial burden on a person's free exercise right. In *Smith v Fair Employment and Housing Commission*,[29] a woman refused to rent an apartment to an unmarried couple because she believed that sex outside marriage was immoral and 'that God will judge her if she permits people to engage in sex outside of marriage in her rental units and that if she does so, she will be prevented from meeting her deceased husband in the hereafter.'[30] The Court though held there was no substantial burden on her religious beliefs because the law only made compliance more expensive and 'investment in rental units [is not] the only available income-producing use of her capital'.[31] She could therefore 'avoid the burden on her religious exercise without violating her beliefs or threatening her livelihood.'[32]

This is a similar analysis to the 'specific situation' rule in ECHR, and following it, English law, and like that rule, it is severely restrictive. First, as a practical matter it is perhaps questionable whether other forms of livelihood were easily available to an elderly woman whose income was based on the rent from four properties. On a more principled basis, as O'Neil puts it, 'the potential impact is much deeper than simply making adherence to faith more expensive. Suggesting that rental property owners could find other lucrative investments has a callous ring, quite at variance with *Sherbert*'s solicitude for the conscientious Sabbatarian.[33] *Sherbert v Verner*[34] was a Supreme Court case which held that a woman's free exercise right was substantially burdened where she lost her job because, as a Seventh-Day Adventist, she refused to work on Saturdays, and was then denied unemployment benefit on the basis that she failed to accept suitable work without good cause. This was recognised even though she was not directly prevented from practising her religion, but rather it was only made 'more expensive'.

Smith v Fair Employment and Housing Commission fails to take seriously rights of conscience. No justification is required to be given for acts which may place significant burdens on Smith's ability to live in accordance with her beliefs. As Lin puts it, it is surprising to say that a person's right of freedom of religion is not burdened in a situation where she is 'preclude[d] entirely … from engaging in a particular type of commercial activity on the

28 Ibid., para 37.
29 12 Cal. 4th 1143 (Cal., 1996).
30 Ibid., 1194.
31 Ibid., 1175.
32 Ibid.
33 R. O'Neil, 'Religious Freedom and Nondiscrimination: State RFRA Laws Versus Civil Rights' (1999) 32 *UC Davis L Rev* 785.
34 374 US 398 (1963).

basis of [her] religious convictions'[35] unless she violates her conscience. Of course, this is not to say that she should not ultimately have to bear this burden, but the Court's approach excludes this cost entirely from consideration.

Indeed, the extremely limited nature of religious freedom rights under US law is demonstrated by the fact that religious claimants have put forward often artificial arguments in an attempt to have a case decided under a more beneficial test. In *Elane Photography* the argument was made that the photography had an expressive element, and therefore the Huguenins' freedom of speech was violated because they would thereby be forced to demonstrate that they approved of same-sex marriage. This argument was advanced because, in contrast to free exercise cases, an interference with freedom of speech would require strict scrutiny. However, both the Court of Appeals of New Mexico and the New Mexico Supreme Court rejected this claim. The Court of Appeals held that 'Elane Photography's commercial business ... is not so inherently expressive as to warrant First Amendment protections. The conduct of taking wedding photographs, unaccompanied by outward expression of approval for same-sex ceremonies, would not express any message.'[36] It also stated that they could have placed a message on their website that they disapproved of same-sex marriage.

The New Mexico Supreme Court's argument was broader. It too considered that the Huguenins were unlikely to be seen as endorsing same-sex marriage, but also held that whenever a business is a public accommodation, being required not to discriminate in providing services to the public would not affect its free speech rights. This is because the state is not thereby forcing the business to express a particular message. The Court held that 'this determination has no relation to the artistic merit of photographs produced by Elane Photography.'[37] Whichever route is taken to this conclusion, the Huguenins were not successful. While the Supreme Court's argument is perhaps too broad, the conclusion is unsurprising. The Huguenins' claim was a claim of conscience, not expression. Their real fear was not that people would misinterpret their beliefs, but that they believed aiding certain activities was wrong. Although the failure of the speech argument is recognised, it is a failure to appreciate the value of conscience which leads to the casting around for alternative arguments. The US approach is therefore far from satisfactory.

Proportionality

It will therefore be difficult to find an interference under US law due to the limited coverage of freedom of religion rights. Nevertheless, even under a proportionality approach, which takes a wide interpretation of rights, it could be objected that the disapproved-of act is too remote from the action a person is being asked to do to count as an interference. Thus for example, by providing a wedding cake, a service provider is not directly facilitating a same-sex marriage, still less being asked to enter into one herself. It could be argued that she cannot claim that her conscience is affected where she is not directly responsible for an 'immoral' act.

35 A. Lin, 'Sexual Orientation Antidiscrimination Laws and the Religious Liberty Protection Act: The Pitfalls of the Compelling State Interest Inquiry' (2001) 89 *Geo LJ* 719, 732.

36 NM Court of Appeals decision supra n.27, 439.

37 NM Supreme Court decision supra n.27, 66.

However, whilst in some cases involving the provision of services the link will be too remote, this is not always the case. Generally, aiding an 'immoral' act can be sufficient for both moral and even legal culpability.[38] If I sold a knife to someone knowing that he was going to use it to stab his partner it would not be an answer to my moral culpability that I sold knives in the ordinary course of my business. There would still be moral culpability even if there were no causal link, for example if I knew that another provider would sell the knife. This is of course an extreme example but my point is only that facilitation or approval of particular acts is generally seen as morally relevant.

There should also be no automatic bar to finding an interference in the commercial sphere. As discussed in Chapter 3, the fact that an act takes place in the public sphere may be very relevant to the question of justification because it may affect the rights of others, but that does not mean that there should be an automatic bar on such claims or that interference should be assessed so narrowly as to exclude them. There is still a relevant conflict between a person's perceived conscientious obligation and a state-enforced legal obligation. It may be true that there is no infringement of 'core' beliefs, in the sense of interference with religious worship, but, as has been demonstrated,[39] this is not a sufficient understanding of what freedom of religion requires. Although there is a need to protect the interests of others, this can be resolved by the use of a proportionality test, rather than by categorical exclusion.

Nevertheless, there still must be a close connection between the act and the belief and not every act motivated by a religious belief will be an interference.[40] Since whether or not there is an interference will depend on context and a fact-specific analysis, the exact point at which it becomes too remote is difficult to establish in the abstract. An example of where the act was too remote is the US case of *Blanding v Sports & Health Club.*[41] A gay man had his membership of a gym revoked because he performed 'a quick, impulsive dance step' during a conversation with other members about a piece of music.[42] This action was taken against a background of conflict. After gay members of the club had 'engaged in open sexual activity and sexual harassment', the gym, which was run by Evangelical Christians, enforced a policy of 'foreclos[ing] opportunities for what it considered to be inappropriate behavior', against its gay members and only them, limiting opportunities to socialise and putting posters up entitled 'What God thinks of Homosexuality'.[43] The owners claimed an exemption from the discrimination law on the basis of the Free Exercise Clause.[44] They claimed they had religious objections to same-sex sexual activity but stated that they had a 'heartfelt love for anybody … we can hate the sin but we love the sinner'.[45] However, as the Court held, since Blanding was discriminated against purely because of his sexual orientation, and this according to the owners' own testimony was not contrary to their religious beliefs, there was no interference with their religious rights. The act complained of was so remote from anything they had religious objections to that there could not be an interference.

38 For an analysis of Catholic teaching on cooperation with immoral acts see J. Garvey and A. Coney, 'Catholic Judges in Capital Cases' (1997) 81 *Marq L Rev* 303.
39 See Ch. 3.
40 See Ch. 4.
41 373 N.W. 2d 784 (Minn.App., 1985).
42 Ibid., 788.
43 Ibid., 787.
44 The case predates *Employment Division v Smith.*
45 Supra n.41, 791.

Rights of businesses?

A separate issue is whether businesses themselves can have religious freedom rights. In *Blanding,* the Court held that the company could not raise a free exercise claim because the club's purpose was to make a profit. It had no 'institutional free-exercise rights or derivative free-exercise rights.'[46] Responses to this issue across the three jurisdictions have not been uniform however. The issue has had some limited consideration in England. In *Exmoor Coast Boat Cruises Ltd v Revenue & Customs*[47] the owner of a company refused to file its VAT returns online because, he claimed,[48] of his religious beliefs. The tribunal rejected the claim, but held that it was possible in some limited circumstances for a company to have rights under Art. 9 where the company was the alter ego of a human person. The question of whether commercial organisations have their own rights under Art. 9 has also not yet been fully considered by the ECtHR. Early cases decided by the European Commission of Human Rights held that Art. 9 was only an individual right and even organised religions had no rights of their own.[49] This failed to perceive the communal nature of much religious belief, and the importance of institutional support in maintaining religious practices. More recently though a range of types of religious organisations have been able to bring claims. For example, in *Cha'are Shalom Ve Tsedek v France,*[50] a complaint by a Jewish liturgical association which wished to have access to slaughterhouses in order to perform ritual slaughter in accordance with its members' beliefs, was held to be admissible. Similarly, in *Verein Gemeinsam Lernen v Austria*[51] a private non-religious school could complain that it had been discriminated against compared to church schools. However, the Court has not yet accepted that purely commercial organisations can bring cases under Art. 9,[52] although cases may be considered under other Convention provisions such as Art. 10.[53]

It is in the US, though, that this question has been most hotly contested, particularly around the issue of the 'contraceptive mandate'. This requires certain employers to include contraception coverage in their employees' health plans. Some organisations and corporations owned or controlled by people with religious objections to this have claimed that this violates both their individual free exercise right and the free exercise right of the corporation. This issue reached the Supreme Court in *Burwell v Hobby Lobby.*[54] The case was brought by three companies: Hobby Lobby, Mardel, and Conestoga Wood Specialties. They all argued that providing emergency contraception (the 'morning after pill') and intrauterine devices (IUDs) contravened their religious beliefs that life begins at conception and was therefore a violation of RFRA.

In *Burwell,* the Supreme Court held that RFRA gave rights to 'closely held corporations'. It did not consider the position under the First Amendment. The companies who brought the cases were therefore entitled to an exemption. Despite the fact that Hobby Lobby owned 500 stores and had over 13,000 employees, it was, crucially, owned and controlled by a family group: the Greens and their three children. One son also founded Mardel, a

46 Ibid., 790.
47 [2014] UKFTT 1103 (TC).
48 The Tribunal rejected the sincerity of his religious beliefs.
49 *Church of X v UK* App No 3798/68, 29 CD 70 (17 December 1968).
50 9 BHRC 27 (2000).
51 (1995) 20 EHRR CD 78.
52 *Kustannus OY Vapaa Ajattelija AB et al. v Finland* (1996) 22 EHRR CD 69.
53 E.g. *Glas Nadejda EOOD v Bulgaria* App No. 14134/02 (11 Oct 2007).
54 573 US ___ (2014).

Christian book store, another claimant in the case. Similarly, Conestoga Wood Specialties had 950 employees but was owned and controlled by a family group. Is it therefore possible for the owners of a company to infuse an otherwise secular large company with religion, such that the company can claim its own religious freedom rights?

In the Supreme Court, Alito J rejected the argument that the fact the corporations were designed to make a profit was decisive, arguing that there was no requirement for corporations to make the pursuit of profit their only objective. He argued that 'A corporation is simply a form of organization used by human beings to achieve desired ends' and giving rights to corporations had the purpose of protecting those people's rights. He pointed out that under the Dictionary Act[55] a 'person' includes a corporation and there was nothing to the contrary in the text of RFRA. However, the ruling was limited to 'closely held corporations' such as the family-owned ones in issue.[56]

There was a strong dissent by Ginsburg J. She argued that the free exercise of religion was a 'characteristic of natural persons, not artificial legal entities'. While she accepted that non-profit religious organisations could exercise religion, she argued that there was a crucial difference between for-profit and non-profit organisations. Religious organisations existed, she argued, to 'foster the interests of persons subscribing to the same religious faith', which for-profit corporations do not. Unlike for-profit corporations, they may discriminate in order to ensure all employees share the same religious faith. Furthermore, she held that the act of incorporation itself made a difference. Since this permitted the individual to escape individual liability, this distanced the individual from the corporation's actions. The basis of incorporation is that the company and the individual are distinct legal entities. She queried why an individual should have the benefit of incorporation and none of the disadvantages.

Hobby Lobby was highly controversial and has given rise to a vast amount of discussion.[57] I will not address every aspect of the decision here or the question of whether, if corporations do have rights under RFRA, there was a less restrictive alternative means of ensuring women had access to all forms of contraception. I only wish to consider in what circumstances corporations may have rights of their own.

First, the case raises two unpersuasive arguments. The District Court's decision was that Hobby Lobby did not have its own religious freedom rights because 'general business corporations do not, separate and apart from the actions or belief systems of their individual owners or employees, exercise religion. They do not pray, worship, observe sacraments or take other religiously-motivated actions separate and apart from the intention and direction of their individual actors.'[58] This reasoning though is not entirely persuasive. It could be said about a religious institution, such as a church, that it does 'not pray, worship, observe sacraments or take other religiously-motivated actions separate and apart from the intention

55 1 U.S.C. § 1.

56 Although as Gedicks points out, this constitutes about 90 per cent of all employers in the US and they employ between one-half and four-fifths of all employees: F.M. Gedicks, 'One Cheer for *Hobby Lobby:* Improbable Alternatives, Truly Strict Scrutiny, and Third-Party Employee Burdens' (2015) 38 *Harv JL & Gender* 154.

57 See e.g. R. Ahdar, 'Companies as Religious Liberty Claimants' (2016) 5 *OJLR* 1; R. Colombo, *The First Amendment and the Business Corporation* (Oxford: Oxford UP, 2014); P. Horwitz, 'The Hobby Lobby Moment' (2014) 128 *Harv L Rev* 154; A. Koppelman and F.M. Gedicks, 'Is Hobby Lobby Worse for Religious Liberty Than Smith?' (2015) *St. Thomas Journal of Law & Public Policy* 223; I. Lupu, 'Hobby Lobby and the Dubious Enterprise of Religious Exemptions' (2015) 38 *Harv J L & Gender* 35.

58 870 F.Supp.2d 1278, 1291.

and direction of their individual actors'. After all, apart from metaphorically, an institution is incapable of acting except through its members.[59]

Second, while the act of incorporation is relevant, it is questionable whether this in itself should be sufficient to deny the claim. Incorporated organisations such as religious hospitals can more clearly be seen as religious organisations capable of advancing religious purposes. The profit motive is more difficult. Clearly there is a difference between a not-for-profit and a profit-making organisation in terms of their purpose, but, although this may be unlikely, a for-profit organisation may have a religious purpose. A church could conceivably operate as a for-profit organisation, and certainly many para-church organisations do, with the profits being used to fund religious activities.

If neither of these arguments is satisfactory, this still leaves the question open of whether businesses should have free exercise rights. Vischer contends that they should.[60] He argues that corporations can and should express moral views and that conscience is developed in association with others. Therefore, he claims that it is important to have a 'moral marketplace' which permits diversity of views through different providers, allowing customers to select those which have greatest affinity with their own beliefs. He states that 'when it comes to facilitating the living out of conscience, the relevance of the local church and Wal-Mart are different in degree, not in kind.'[61] Evidently, institutions are important in the development of conscience and belief and potentially this can include for-profit organisations. However, even if there is a difference only in degree this does not mean that all businesses should be able to claim religious freedom rights.

It seems clear that, even though they are not merely an aggregation of individuals' rights,[62] collective religious rights must ultimately derive from individual rights, otherwise an organisation could have rights even if it had no members.[63] If rights are derived from individuals, then it follows that two things must be demonstrated. First, there must be an identifiable group of people from whom rights can be derived, and second, there must be some purpose which the individuals intend the organisation to perform. While in religious organisations members, however defined, are the relevant original rights holders, in companies the rights could potentially derive from far more diverse groups with many more diverse interests, including directors, shareholders, employees and customers, as Ginsburg J contended in *Hobby Lobby*.[64] To consider just one of these, as Corbin points out, it is impossible to assume that employees share the religious views of their employer or have sufficient autonomy to move to employment run on religious lines of which they approve. As she argues, to ignore this affects the conscience rights of these employees.[65]

59 Colombo also makes this point in 'The Naked Private Sphere' (2013) 51 *Hous L R* 1.

60 R. Vischer, *Conscience and the Common Good: Reclaiming the Space Between Person and State* (Cambridge: Cambridge UP, 2009) and 'Do For-Profit Businesses Have Free Exercise Rights?' (2013) 21 *J Contemp Legal Issues* 369.

61 Ibid., 205.

62 J. Rivers, 'Religious Liberty as a Collective Right' in R. O'Dair and A. Lewis (eds), *Law and Religion* (Oxford: Oxford UP, 2001).

63 L. Vickers, 'Twin Approaches to Secularism: Organized Religion and Society' (2012) 32 *OJLS* 197.

64 This is a similar argument to J. Nelson, 'Conscience, Incorporated' (2013) 5 *Mich St L Rev* 1565.

65 C.M. Corbin, 'Corporate Religious Liberty' (2015) 30 *Const Commentary* 277. She therefore argues that granting free exercise rights to corporations would protect the rights of the elite at the cost of others.

The question of function is also more complex. The purpose of religious organisations is normally to spread particular viewpoints, develop doctrines and maintain exclusionary communities. This is not the purpose of ordinary businesses: they do not normally do anything that is recognisably religious. Therefore, it is difficult to show that businesses have religious freedom rights of their own. However, this should not be an absolute rule. *Some* for-profit organisations are designed around, and to spread, certain viewpoints. Since the right derives from its purposes, if an organisation has as one of its main aims the spreading or affirming of a religious viewpoint then it is possible that it can have free exercise rights.[66] For Hobby Lobby, although it does perform some religious activities, such as religious advertising, this is incidental compared to its major business of selling craft materials. There may though be an argument that Mardel falls within this category given that its business is selling Christian books and other materials. It describes itself as 'a faith-based company dedicated to renewing minds and transforming lives through the products we sell and the ministries we support'[67] and gives 10 per cent of its net profits to Wycliffe Ministries, an organisation which translates and distributes Bibles in numerous countries worldwide.

It should be stressed that this discussion is about how rights come to exist, rather than what the right entails. Even if an organisation's rights are derived from its members rather than freestanding, an organisation may still act to protect its own conception of conscience and autonomy. As long as the organisation has a recognisable religious purpose, an organisation's doctrines are not necessarily contingent on the opinions of the majority of its members and it does not have to be at all democratic in the selection of its leaders or in the development of doctrine. Furthermore, this discussion has left aside the fact that the claim might not be that the corporation's rights have been affected but that the owner's rights as an *individual* have been interfered with.[68] This is likely to be the case in very small businesses, where the owner must directly act in a way which is against her conscience. In larger companies, though, the link between the required act and the owner's beliefs are likely to be too remote.

Interference: conclusion

This section has considered whether an interference can potentially be found when a person or business is required not to discriminate in providing a service. It has been argued that in many circumstances it can be with regard to individual claims, but this will occur more rarely where a business itself claims rights. This approach is theoretically sound and practical. It excludes claims where the claimed right is very remote from the act that is objected to, as in *Blanding,* but at the same time it does not put formalistic barriers in the way of cases where there is a genuine conflict between a person's conscience and the law, such as in *Smith v*

66 *Tyndale House Publishers v Sebelius* 904 F.Supp.2d 106 (D.D.C., 2012) may also be an example. Colombo supra n.59 similarly argues that a business corporation can be 'a genuine community of individuals – investors, owners, officers, employees, and customers – coming together around a common vision or shared set of goals, values, or beliefs'. I would agree that a business could have free exercise rights in such a situation. However, Colombo appears to claim that businesses should have free exercise rights much more widely than this, arguing that a free exercise claim arises where a corporation adheres to a set of beliefs and undertakes conduct on account of these beliefs and government action substantially burdens such conduct, thus including cases such as *Hobby Lobby.*

67 http://www.mardel.com/our-story <last accessed 25 July 2016>.

68 As in *Exmoor Coast Boat Cruises* supra n.47.

Fair Employment and Housing Commission, since the rights of others can be considered at the justification stage.

In permitting a broad interpretation of interference[69] a proportionality approach is advantageous. Losing parties are explicitly held to have a constitutional interest that is worthy of protection, although outweighed in the current circumstances, rather than this interest simply being delegitimised in principle.[70] In doing so, proportionality requires justification: even if a party has to lose because of the rights of others, they still have a right to adequate justification as to why the right cannot be protected in a particular situation. This is missing in many of the cases, particularly from the US, which do not use a proportionality-type approach. Even if there is an interference, though, this certainly does not mean that the religious right should be found to be violated under a proportionality test. In order to decide that, each stage of the test must be considered in turn.

The provision of services and proportionality

Legitimate aim and rational connection

In a case where a person claims there has been an interference with a religious right the legitimate aim will normally be straightforward, since it will be to protect the rights of others by enforcing non-discrimination. In the converse situation, there will normally also be a legitimate aim in protecting the religious rights of others.

The next question is whether there is a rational connection between the legitimate aim and the action taken. Again, finding this is not generally a problem. However, in the Canadian case of *Eadie and Thomas v Riverbend Bed and Breakfast,*[71] the British Columbia Human Rights Tribunal held that a refusal to let a gay couple stay at a bed and breakfast had no rational connection to the function of the business in the context of deciding whether there was a bona fide and reasonable justification for the discrimination. There was therefore no defence to the claim of unlawful discrimination. The version of the rational connection test the Tribunal applied was whether a standard was adopted 'for a purpose or goal that is rationally connected to the function being performed'.[72] Since the services Riverbend provided were not religious in nature, the owners' religious beliefs were not relevant to the function of the business and therefore bore no rational connection to the refusal to let the couple stay.

As discussed previously, a business's function is relevant to whether it can claim a right of freedom of religion. It is therefore correct to say that in this situation there is no rational connection between the *business's* rights and the action taken. However, this is not a full answer because the *owners'* individual rights are also relevant. Here, unlike *Hobby Lobby,* there was a close connection between the act the owners would be required to do, providing accommodation for a same-sex couple in a business run from their own home, and their religious beliefs. They would personally be directly required to do something they considered to be contrary to their beliefs. Under a proportionality test, therefore, a rational connection would have been found.

69 See Ch. 5.
70 C. Taylor, 'Living with Difference' in A. Allen and M. Regan (eds), *Debating Democracy's Discontent: Essays on American Politics, Law, and Public Philosophy* (Oxford: Oxford UP, 1998) 218.
71 2012 BCHRT 247.
72 Ibid., para 117.

Instead the Tribunal used an undue hardship test. The test comes from *Meiorin*:[73] a case about whether it amounted to sex discrimination to require all fire-fighters to be able to run 2.5 kilometres in 11 minutes. This standard was easier for men to achieve than women. In this context, the test was effective. It meant that the employee had the right to be accommodated unless it could be demonstrated that to do so would impose undue hardship on the employer. The functions of the job were therefore relevant to the test: if a purpose is not rationally connected to the function of the job it cannot be undue hardship not to comply with it. However, given that *Riverbend* really involved individual rights of freedom of religion this test is unsuitable here. A person's individual right of conscience is not reducible, or even necessarily particularly related, to the functions she performs in her professional life. Problems of conscience can arise whatever functions a person performs and indeed can arise *because* of a conflict between these functions and her conscientious beliefs.

To apply the Canadian undue hardship test in this context would give those in employment unwarranted greater protection than those who are self-employed. In employment cases, the employer must justify their treatment of an employee by reference to the function of the job: thus giving the employee a potentially extensive right. In contrast, in claims brought by external parties, a focus on function could completely exclude the claim. This gives greater protection to employees, not because the interference with their rights is likely to be any greater, but because the test is unsuited to the situation of self-employed people.

In Canadian cases where a proportionality rather than undue hardship test was used, there is not the unsatisfactory conclusion there is in *Eadie* and the test is far simpler. For example, a rational connection was found in *Brockie*,[74] which involved the claimant's refusal to print materials for the Canadian Lesbian and Gay Archives.[75] In one sense, Brockie's purpose was to provide printing services, an entirely secular function, which could have no rational connection even to a refusal to print materials which directly denigrated his religious views, but no objection was made on this basis. In *Eadie* it should therefore have been found that there was a rational connection between the action the owners took and their right to religious freedom. This of course does not mean that the interference with the couple's rights was necessarily proportionate.

No less restrictive means

It could be argued that as a less restrictive alternative to forbidding such discrimination completely, the state should only intervene and prevent discrimination if a person is unable to obtain a service elsewhere. Vischer argues, continuing the line of reasoning explained above, that it is important for companies, like other associations, to be able to develop a 'distinct moral identity.'[76] Although he is in favour of non-discrimination rights in the context of employment and housing,[77] because there is unlikely to be a truly equal readily available alternative in these areas, he states that in most other commercial contexts, organisations should be able to raise a defence of 'market access' when providing services. This

73 *British Columbia (Public Service Employee Relations Commission) v British Columbia Government and Service Employees' Union* (1999) 3 SCR 3.

74 See Ch. 4.

75 The difference in tests is due to the fact that Riverbend claimed a statutory defence under the British Columbia Human Rights Code, but Brockie claimed that the British Columbia Human Rights Code infringed his rights under the Charter.

76 Vischer supra n.60, 202.

77 Ibid., 28.

would mean that there would be no breach of discrimination law where a service provider could demonstrate that a person could obtain the service from an alternative provider.

His starting point is that both the service provider and the customer have rights of conscience in the sense of 'an individual's capacity to develop and claim a moral worldview as her own ... and her ability to live consistently with that worldview'.[78] To take the example of *Elane Photography* mentioned above, he argues that both Willock's and the owners' consciences are relevant. The owners, the Huguenins, claim that they cannot provide photography for a same-sex commitment ceremony because they wish to live out their Christian convictions, which tell them that same-sex marriage is immoral and they should do nothing to approve it in every aspect of their lives. Willock also wishes to live out her convictions by marrying[79] her partner in a public ceremony with all the traditional trappings a wedding normally involves.[80]

Clearly, they have very different beliefs about the morality or otherwise of same-sex relationships and marriages. Vischer argues that the state should not take sides in the debate over these competing moral convictions and thus the state should not intervene if Willock can find an alternative photographer. He believes that if the Huguenins were forced to provide a service, when another provider could be found, then their conscience was unnecessarily trumped by an opposing claim of conscience, since Willock's conscientious belief in the morality of same-sex marriage could be protected by using another provider. He therefore criticises anti-discrimination laws because, he argues, they '[are] not premised on securing individuals' access to essential goods and services. Instead [they are] premised on the expressive value of non-discrimination as a universal norm in the marketplace'.[81]

Vischer's argument is not straightforward. Unlike McConnell,[82] he does not make the claim that the state should not intervene because it should not take sides in the dispute or even that it cannot deliberately declare that non-discrimination is a symbolically valuable norm. McConnell's argument is that the state should treat views on homosexuality in the same way as it treats religion under the First Amendment: it 'should not impose a penalty on practices associated with or compelled by any of the various views of homosexuality and should refrain from using its power to favor, promote or advance one position over the other', leaving 'private forces in the culture to determine the ultimate social response'.[83] That argument is unpersuasive because, as was discussed in the Introduction, the state has an obligation to demonstrate equal concern and respect to all as part of the non-discrimination right.[84] Not intervening does not demonstrate neutrality on this issue. Since there is no neutral place for the state to stand, it is more than justifiable that it symbolically states it is against this harm. A failure to act to prevent systemic discrimination demonstrates at least a lack of interest in those being discriminated against and perhaps tacit approval of the policy. As Dworkin stated with reference to the system of racial segregation as it existed in the Southern USA, a 'political and economic system that allows prejudice to destroy some people's lives does not treat all members of the community with equal concern.'[85] While

78 Ibid., 43.
79 This was not a legal marriage since same-sex marriage was not at the time recognised in New Mexico.
80 Vischer supra n.60, 2.
81 Ibid., 306.
82 M. McConnell, 'The Problem of Singling Out Religion' (2000) 50 *DePaul L Rev* 1.
83 Ibid., 44.
84 R. Dworkin, *Taking Rights Seriously* (Cambridge, Mass: Harvard UP, 1977).
85 R. Dworkin, 'What is Equality? Part 3: The Place of Liberty' (1987) 73 *Iowa L Rev* 1, 36–7.

permitting discrimination on the grounds of sexual orientation where there is a market access defence probably would not 'destroy some people's lives', at least under the social situations as currently exist in the three jurisdictions, it clearly causes real harm to those affected.

Indeed, Vischer recognises this, permitting the state not only to ensure practical access but also to embody an anti-discrimination norm by 'refusing to enter into contracts with discriminatory vendors, or by trumpeting the importance of non-discrimination through public awareness campaigns.'[86] The problem is then that Vischer's argument does not persuasively answer why the state may act coercively in these contexts but not others. Vischer's argument is also problematic because it is odd to say that a person has a right to a service which they need to live out their moral convictions. If Willock had been unable to find a photographer because none was available in the area, that would clearly be no concern of the state, even if she claimed this was necessary to live consistently with her worldview. Rather, in most situations,[87] she only has a right not to be discriminated against. Vischer's argument turns all the relevant interests into one of conscience, but not every choice is a conscientious one. It is thus better to see *Elane Photography* as a clash between conscience and non-discrimination, rather than between two ideas of conscience.

While it has been possible to consider a number of contexts at the first stages of the proportionality test, as the analysis is likely to be similar, there is likely to be wider variety in the relevant facts at the final balancing stage. Nevertheless, even if claims have not failed before this point, they have not been noticeably successful, regardless of jurisdiction and the legal test used. This is justifiable. These situations generally involve a minor interference with freedom of religion and a great interference with the right of non-discrimination. Although the right to freedom of religion includes more than mere religious worship, the right to manifest religious beliefs in the commercial sphere is normally on the periphery of the religious right. Whilst religionists may wish to run their business in accordance with their religious beliefs, running a secular business is not a direct outworking of religious beliefs in itself. Presumably a major, if not primary, reason for running the business will be to make a profit. In addition, while the fact that the person has chosen to provide the service should not exclude the claim entirely, this should be taken into account at the balancing stage. In contrast, the effects on those discriminated against can be pervasive and extensive. There are though still advantages to using a proportionality approach, most notably because it can recognise that there is a conflict of rights. I will now consider how the balancing test would apply in different contexts.

One-off commercial services

Conflicts can potentially result from a huge number of issues, and disputes have arisen over wedding cakes,[88] DJs,[89] rainbow-coloured cupcakes to celebrate National Coming Out

86 Supra n.60, 306.

87 C.f. *Griffin v County School Board of Prince Edward County* 377 US 218 (1964) (impermissible to avoid order to de-segregate schools by closing all public schools and providing vouchers to attend private segregated schools instead).

88 L. Moran, 'Baker Refuses to Make Wedding Cake for Lesbian Couple', *New York Daily News*, 4 Feb 2013, available at: http://www.nydailynews.com/news/national/baker-refuses-wedding-cake-lesbian-couple-article-1.1254776 <last accessed 25 July 2016>.

89 In *Posillico v Spitzer* No. 1300–06 (Sup. Ct. Nassau County) two Catholic DJs refused to accept a booking for a Gay Men's Health Crisis event. The case was withdrawn.

Day,[90] and photography.[91] This section will consider 'one-off commercial services': services with no intrinsic religious aspect, that are normally provided without restriction to the general public, and that do not involve an ongoing relationship. Often, but not necessarily, these are disputes related to same-sex marriage.

Proportionality

If these issues are to be addressed under a proportionality enquiry, as always, it is necessary to consider what interests are in question and how deeply they are affected. Some have seemed to suggest that the only interest opposing the religious one is that of practical access to a service. Laycock appears to see the opposing interest as one of 'inconvenience'[92] in finding an alternative. He states that 'in more traditional communities, same-sex couples planning a wedding might be forced to pick their merchants carefully, like black families driving across the South half a century ago.'[93] I am not sure why the analogy (although an imperfect one) does not lead Laycock to the opposite conclusion: that the symbolic harm caused by unequal treatment should at least be taken into account and may be decisive.[94] The harm caused to those families was not merely one of convenience. It was the constant reminder of a caste system which, by various mechanisms, highly circumscribed the lives of black people. Although the situation for those discriminated against on the grounds of their sexual orientation is not as extreme or pervasive as this, his analysis still ignores 'the dignitary and equality harm inherent in discrimination against a historically vulnerable minority'.[95]

Laycock has also suggested signage requirements alerting customers to the fact that they refuse to serve, for example gay couples, to minimise surprise.[96] However, it is arguable that this might in fact make the situation worse for gay people. In some areas it may mean more suppliers claim an exemption because of social pressure to conform to traditional mores[97] or because it may be easier to declare a discriminatory policy through a sign rather than face-to-face.[98] In addition a sign is an icon of second-class citizenship. Gay people may be forced to see it regularly, and this may act as a reminder of discriminatory attitudes even if they are not seeking that service. Finally, whether told by an employee or through a sign, the end result is still the same: a person is still denied a service because of her sexual orientation. While taken in isolation these issues may seem comparatively trivial, and only a minor interference

90 N. O'Callaghan, 'Death by a Thousand Cuts: Why Market Mechanisms Won't Solve the Culture Wars' (2010) 49 *Journal of Catholic Legal Studies* 335.

91 *Engel v Worthington* 23 Cal. Rptr.2d 329 (Cal. App., 1993).

92 D. Laycock, 'Afterword' in D. Laycock et al. (eds), *Same-Sex Marriage and Religious Liberty: Emerging Conflicts* (Lanham, Maryland: Rowman & Littlefield, 2008) 198.

93 Ibid., 199.

94 M. Curtis, 'A Unique Religious Exemption from Antidiscrimination Laws in the Case of Gays? Putting the Call for Exemptions for those who Discriminate Against Married or Marrying Gays in Context' (2012) 47 *Wake Forest L Rev* 173.

95 T. Flynn, 'Clarion Call or False Alarm: Why Proposed Exemptions to Equal Marriage Statutes Return Us to a Religious Understanding of the Public Marketplace' (2010) 5 *Nw J L & Soc Pol'y* 236.

96 Laycock supra n.92.

97 As Laycock admits.

98 Researchers posing as gay couples seeking accommodation for their honeymoon were more likely to be refused if they emailed rather than telephoned the owners. They concluded the personal nature of the contact made it more difficult to refuse. D. Howerton, 'Honeymoon Vacation: Sexual-Orientation Prejudice and Inconsistent Behavioral Responses' (2012) 34 *Basic and Applied Social Psychology* 146.

with the right of non-discrimination, focusing only on practical access does not take into account the broader context of discrimination and marginalisation or the emotional consequence of repeated refusals. As Hunter puts it, these cases involve a claim to 'cultural citizenship':[99] part of a claim to access the public, social sphere. These consequences of discrimination need to be taken into account.

Partly because a proportionality analysis can recognise this, religious claims have not been successful in this context when such a test is used. In the Canadian case of *Brockie,*[100] which involved a Christian printer's refusal to print stationery for a gay non-profit organisation, the Canadian Lesbian and Gay Archives, the Ontario Divisional Court used a proportionality approach which balanced the right of non-discrimination against Brockie's right to freedom of religion under the Charter.[101] It held that the interference with the religious right was justified and Brockie unjustifiably discriminated. The Court argued that discrimination on the grounds of sexual orientation demeaned 'the self-worth and personal dignity of homosexuals, with adverse psychological effects and social and economic disadvantages.'[102] It therefore held that avoiding this was a pressing and substantial objective. It pointed out that Brockie was acting in the commercial sphere and his actions were on the periphery of religious freedom. This reasoning, although entirely correct, does perhaps overlook the fact that Brockie did not refuse to serve gay people as such, but rather an organisation with particular aims relating to sexual orientation. Nevertheless, his refusal was still for discriminatory reasons and could still have a demeaning effect.

A proportionality approach therefore identifies the value in both sides' argument. Importantly and correctly, the Court in *Brockie* held that the balance of interests might be different in other cases and that 'there can be no appropriate balance if the protection of one right means the total disregard of another.'[103] This case demonstrates that proportionality can take both rights seriously, but still protect important non-discrimination rights where necessary. Here Brockie was only asked to print office stationery, but the Court indicated the outcome might be different if he were asked to print material 'that conveyed a message proselytizing and promoting the gay and lesbian lifestyle or ridiculed his religious beliefs'.[104] Although the reference to a 'gay and lesbian lifestyle' is somewhat perplexing, this does convey the idea that there is a balance to be made and both rights are important.

This case can be compared with a Northern Irish case, *Lee v Ashers Bakery Ltd.*[105] While Northern Irish discrimination law is different from the law in the rest of the UK, most notably in that it forbids discrimination on the grounds of political opinion, the law relating to sexual orientation discrimination is very similar. The case involved a Christian-run bakery which refused to ice a cake with a picture of the Sesame Street characters Bert and Ernie and the slogan 'Support Gay Marriage'. It was ordered for an event to mark the end of the Northern Ireland anti-homophobia week. The County Court held that this refusal

99 N. Hunter, 'Accommodating the Public Sphere: Beyond the Market Model' (2001) 85 *Minn L Rev* 1591.

100 Supra n.13.

101 The Charter did not apply directly to the dispute since it was between private parties. Brockie's argument was that the decision of the Board deciding he had been unlawfully discriminated was a violation of the Charter.

102 Supra n.13, para 47.

103 Ibid., para 56.

104 Ibid.

105 [2015] NICty 2.

amounted to direct discrimination 'on the grounds of'[106] sexual orientation and political opinion.[107] That this is discrimination on the grounds of political opinion is fairly straightforward: the service was refused because of Lee's opinion on a political matter. Whether it was also sexual orientation discrimination is more complex. The phrase 'on the grounds of' has been interpreted broadly and is not limited merely to the straightforward situation where a person is discriminated against because they are gay. Ashers' owners clearly refused to take the order because of their opinions about same-sex marriage, which is intrinsically related to sexual orientation. As a matter of interpretation of discrimination law the conclusion that there was direct discrimination appears to be correct.

The Court then went on to consider whether the law violated the owners' rights[108] under Art. 8 and 9 of the Convention. In doing so it applied a proportionality test, but in a highly deferential way. It was held an interference would be proportionate where the accommodation sought was discriminatory and not already part of a legislative exemption, otherwise it 'would be necessary for the civil courts to weigh the value of particular religious beliefs against the rights of other protected groups'.[109] A balancing of the extent and importance of the interference with the different rights (although not the *value* of religious beliefs themselves) is though exactly what is required by the proportionality test. Evidently this is a much more complex situation and interferes with the right of freedom of religion and expression to a greater extent than if the bakery had simply refused to supply a wedding cake for a same-sex couple, for example. It could be argued that not only are the owners being asked to act against their conscience, they are being required to actively express an opinion they do not agree with. However, merely because the bakery's owners fulfilled an order within the context of a usually available commercial service does not necessarily imply that they agreed with the statement iced. If a person had asked the bakery to ice an entirely innocuous message such as 'Happy Birthday' this would not normally be taken to mean that the bakery personally wished the recipient to have a happy birthday. It would be acting as a mere conduit. Nevertheless, these difficulties surrounding a 'right not to speak'[110] were not fully addressed in the case. While the result may well be justifiable, the court does not apply a principled process of analysis and therefore abdicates its responsibility.

USA

In contrast to cases decided in Canada and the UK, as described above, many US cases in this context fail at the first stage of demonstrating a prima facie case, even before justification is considered. In *Elane Photography*, although the link between the act objected to and the service required is limited, an interference should have been found and therefore the US's approach is unsatisfactory. However, even if the case were to be considered under a proportionality approach, the Huguenins' claim to discriminate must nevertheless fail. They were providing a commercial service which did not necessarily imply any sort of approval for

106 English law also used to refer to discrimination 'on the grounds of' a protected characteristic but the Equality Act replaced this with 'because of' as it was thought this was easier to understand. The difference in terminology was not meant to lead to substantive change.

107 This decision is at the time of writing being appealed.

108 Whilst this is a case brought against a business, it is the owners' individual rights which are in issue because of their personal involvement in performing an act they considered wrong. The initial order was taken by one of the owners.

109 Supra n.105, para 83.

110 H. Bosmajian 'The Freedom Not to Speak' (1994) 18 *Legal Stud F* 425.

same-sex marriage. Indeed, it would have been possible for the Huguenins to employ another photographer to cover same-sex weddings.[111] Although they may still argue that this would be contrary to their beliefs, and of course it might be, the interference with their rights would then be extremely limited.

It might be thought that this conclusion contradicts my argument in Chapter 6 that Ladele, the registrar who refused to perform civil partnerships, should have received an exemption from performing this part of her work. However, there are crucial differences between the cases. In *Elane Photography* the couple were directly confronted with a denial of service, whereas in *Ladele* all that was called for was a rearrangement of duties, albeit one that was required because of discriminatory beliefs. Furthermore, the distance from the act objected to, same-sex marriage, is much greater in *Elane Photography,* and therefore is less of a burden on the religionists' rights. Finally, since there is nothing distinctive about this case to distinguish it from any other supply of services case, granting an exemption would lead to an evisceration of the anti-discrimination principle.

The Huguenins are therefore left with a conflict between their legal obligations and their beliefs which cannot be lifted through the law. They must decide whether to give up their business or to comply with the anti-discrimination law. A proportionality analysis therefore leads to the same conclusion as that reached by the New Mexico Supreme Court. Nevertheless, deciding this case at the justification rather than at the interference stage, as a proportionality test allows, at least recognises the conflict between the rights, allowing an opportunity to express the loss caused to both rights, and focuses attention on the claims actually in issue.

It is even clearer that no exemption can be given in *Blanding,* the case involving a gay man who was banned from using a gym, even under a proportionality analysis. Even if there was an interference with the right of the company's owners, which is extremely doubtful, permitting Blanding to use the gym only posed a very limited burden on them. They were not required to facilitate or aid anything they were religiously opposed to: they were only required to let a gay man use a gym on the same terms as a heterosexual man. If an exemption was accepted here this would effectively prohibit all sexual orientation discrimination laws where a person had religious objections to homosexuality.

This section has considered the right to discriminate in the standard case of commercial services and concluded that such claims should not usually be successful because of the importance of the non-discrimination interest and the peripheral nature of the religious interest. It has also demonstrated that a proportionality analysis deals with these issues fully and provides a coherent method of balancing the interests. The rest of this chapter considers more complex situations that may involve a different balance of interests.

Housing

Housing raises issues separate from the general commercial provision of services, because it can simultaneously raise questions of forced association on one side and real need on the other. The question of exemptions to discrimination laws for landlords who, because of their religious beliefs, refuse to rent their properties to particular groups has especially arisen in the US in relation to discrimination against unmarried heterosexual couples. As in many other contexts, the law varies between states. While the federal Fair Housing Act prohibits

111 As suggested by Chai Felblum, now an EEOC (Equal Employment Opportunity Commission) Commissioner. Noted in Vischer supra n.60 at 303.

discrimination on many grounds, discrimination on the grounds of sexual orientation or marital status is only prohibited, if at all, at state level.[112] Different courts have reached different conclusions on these matters, some holding that there is no burden on the religious landlord's right at all and some holding that there has not only been an interference, but a violation. However, none of these cases are particularly satisfactory.

It was argued above that refusing to find an interference with the right of freedom of religion in these contexts, as occurred in *Smith v Fair Employment and Housing Commission,* does not take this right seriously,[113] since this ignores the fact that a person is being asked to act against her conscience. Some cases though make the opposite error. *Thomas v Anchorage Equal Rights Commission*[114] is a good example of this. Here the value of non-discrimination is entirely understated and is reduced to the level of minor inconvenience. Thomas refused to rent to unmarried couples because of his religious beliefs and claimed this was a violation of his free exercise rights on the basis that he had a hybrid right under *Smith.* Although the decision was withdrawn for technical reasons,[115] both the District Court and the Ninth Circuit Court of Appeals held that the law failed strict scrutiny. The majority of the Ninth Circuit held that 'the only palpable injury suffered by an unmarried tenant turned away by a Christian landlord for religious reasons is a marginal reduction in the number of apartment units available for rent'.[116] Preventing marital status discrimination did not therefore amount to a compelling interest for the purposes of the strict scrutiny test and therefore the state's defence of the law failed at the first hurdle.

The judgment thereby even minimises the practical interest in non-discrimination. As Failinger points out, housing is different from other sorts of goods because there is a restricted supply and it varies greatly in affordability, location, size and style.[117] To say that someone still has access to the housing market is not sufficient. More fundamentally, the majority in *Thomas* also completely failed to see the symbolic and accumulative effect of discrimination, including the fact that a prospective tenant 'has no way of knowing the next landlord will see things differently, or the next, and that ultimately he will find a decent place to live,'[118] which can have a substantial effect on the tenant's sense of inclusion and security.

A similar Canadian case looks at the question differently. In *Robertson and Anthony v Goertzen*[119] a landlord refused to rent to a gay couple, going so far as to retain their deposit and to threaten that if they moved in he would not renew the lease of Anthony's sister who lived in another apartment owned by him. The legislation at issue forbade discrimination on the grounds of sexual orientation but had an exemption where there was a bona fide and reasonable justification.[120] In order for this to be established it had to be proved that 'accommodation of the needs of an individual would impose undue hardship on a person

112 42 U.S.C. § 3601–19. It prohibits discrimination on the grounds of race, colour, religion, sex, familial status, or national origin but not sexual orientation.
113 12 Cal. 4th 1143 (Cal., 1996).
114 Supra n.17, 881.
115 Rehearing was granted and the opinion withdrawn on the basis that the dispute was not ripe for review: 192 F.3d 1208 (9th Cir., 1999).
116 Supra n.23, 718.
117 M. Failinger, 'Remembering Mrs. Murphy: A Remedies Approach to the Conflict Between Gay/ Lesbian Renters and Religious Landlords' (2001) 29 *Cap U L Rev* 383.
118 Ibid., 398.
119 2010 NTHRAP 1 (5 September 2010).
120 Northwest Territories Human Rights Act ss.5 and 12, SNWT 2002, c 18.

who would have to accommodate those needs.'[121] Although this is a slightly different enquiry to a proportionality test, it here involves the same kind of discussion in that it involves consideration of the effects on both sides and considers whether an appropriate balance has been struck between the rights. The decision deals with the two interests fully, clearly highlighting the effect on the couple of both the symbolic effect of discrimination and of being denied the apartment, as well as the importance of the claimant's religious beliefs to him, but rightly holds that there can be no exemption.

Quite clearly, even if the discrimination can be justified, the landlord's acts went beyond a 'mere' refusal and entirely failed to treat the couple with the respect owed to them. Therefore, if the case were to be considered under a proportionality test, it would fail the no less restrictive means test, since to permit such behaviour would interfere more deeply with the non-discrimination right whilst not giving any greater protection of the religious freedom right. Even if that were not the case, the negative effects on the prospective tenants, even given simply the practicality of finding alternative accommodation in a part of Canada with a limited rental market, outweigh the harm caused to Goertzen and therefore permitting discrimination would be disproportionate.

Of course consideration of the particular facts is essential, and a proportionality approach can always recognise this. To refer to a 'landlord' as if the situation and interests at stake did not vary is not appropriate. There can be a great difference between a landlord renting out a '100-unit apartment building and a widower who wants to rent out one bedroom in his home'.[122] In all three jurisdictions there are some legislative exemptions where living space is to be shared. The federal US Fair Housing Act exempts owner-occupied accommodation of less than five units.[123] Many US states also have legislative exemptions[124] as does Britain[125] and many Canadian provinces.[126] Although these exemptions include many cases where the objection is not based on conscience, privacy and associational interests nevertheless make this a proportionate solution.

Not to make a distinction between different types of landlords does not draw an appropriate balance between the rights, as the US case of *Wisconsin ex. rel. Sprague v City of Madison* illustrates.[127] Two women, Hacklander-Ready and Rowe, rented a four-bedroom house and wished to find housemates, with the permission of their landlord, to share the rent. Although they initially agreed to rent a room to a lesbian woman, Sprague, they changed their minds the next day. Sprague then sued and was successful. Unusually the ordinance in issue only permitted discrimination on the grounds of sex, even in shared accommodation.

The Court peremptorily dismissed the housemates' claim that the law unconstitutionally affected their right to privacy, stating that privacy rights were not relevant as 'appellants gave up their unqualified right to such constitutional protection when they rented housing for profit.'[128] This reasoning is unsatisfactory. Any profit seems very limited: the purpose was to

121 Northwest Territories Human Rights Act s.12.

122 S. Knutson, 'The Religious Landlord and the Conflict Between Free Exercise Rights and Housing Discrimination Laws – Which Interest Prevails?' (1996) 47 *Hastings LJ* 1669.

123 42 U.S.C. § 2000a(b)(1).

124 See C. Kolosov, 'Fair Housing Laws and the Constitutional Rights of Roommate Seekers' (2008) 4 *The Modern American* 1.

125 Equality Act Sch 5 para 3.

126 E.g. British Columbia Human Rights Code [RSBC 1996] s.10(2)(a).

127 1996 WL 544099 (Wis. Ct. App., 1996).

128 Ibid., 1.

share the rent rather than enter into commercial activity. There are legitimate concerns over privacy and 'intimate association'.[129] Indeed, the law was changed before the case was heard to add: 'Nothing in this ordinance shall affect any person's decision to share occupancy of a lodging room, apartment or dwelling unit with another person or persons.' The home is normally seen as a particularly protected space from outside intrusion, although of course this protection is not absolute. Selecting a housemate may be more akin to looking for friendship rather than the commercial provision of services, since in sharing living space there is inevitably some kind of personal relationship. Choosing a flatmate may therefore involve consideration of a huge range of concerns, some of which may be discriminatory. For this reason, there are many services which find flatmates for particular groups such as students, Christians or gay people. Of course, permitting such discrimination still limits available accommodation and may contribute to systemic discrimination, but given the importance of such potentially very personal relationships these issues are outweighed by the other interests. Indeed, in the later US case of *Fair Housing Council of San Fernando Valley v Roommate.com,*[130] it was held that it would be unconstitutional to apply the federal Fair Housing Act to housemates, even though the exemption in the legislation only covered owner-occupied accommodation.

As a proportionality analysis would demonstrate, there should therefore be a small landlord and housemate exemption where living space is to be shared. However, outside this context, in cases where there are not these privacy or associational interests, such as in the *Thomas* case described above, discrimination should not be permitted because of the importance of the need for living accommodation and the limited interference with religious rights, where there will only be limited contact with the tenant. In considering the balance of interests in different circumstances, proportionality thus provides workable solutions to this problem.

Bed and breakfast accommodation

If there is a justifiable claim not to share a house in some landlord and tenant situations, then is there a right to discriminate in allowing people to stay in bed and breakfast accommodation? Perhaps oddly, debates in England about the rights of bed and breakfast accommodation owners assumed a greater amount of attention than would be warranted by their number.[131] This is probably connected with 'the powerful rhetorical imagery of the home.'[132] The construction of the home as a private space though, although rhetorically useful for some,[133] is not a sufficient analysis of the issues. After all the owners have deliberately and for profit invited others into that space. In *Bull,*[134] the owners objected that when unmarried couples in their own family came to stay they made them sleep in different rooms. Evidently though, this is a very different situation. There is no commercial basis to it.

129 The seminal article on this concept is K. Karst, 'The Freedom of Intimate Association' (1980) 89 *Yale LJ* 624.

130 666 F.3d 1216 (9th Cir., 2012).

131 N. Cobb, '"Gay Couple's Break Like Fawlty Towers": Dangerous Representations of Lesbian and Gay Oppression in an Era of "Progressive" Law Reform' (2009) 18 *Social & Legal Studies* 333.

132 Ibid.

133 See for use of the 'home' argument: The Christian Institute, 'Christian B&B loses court case brought by gay couple', 18 Oct 2012, available at: http://www.christian.org.uk/news/christian-bb-loses-court-case-brought-by-gay-couple/ <last accessed 25 July 2016>.

134 Supra n.6.

Discrimination law tends not to intervene in personal situations such as this because of concerns over infringing privacy and individual autonomy. Bed and breakfast accommodation cases also involve different considerations from the flatmate example given above, because they do not usually involve the same degree of intimacy and will normally be for a very limited duration. There is little expectation of forming personal relationships.

No religious claim in any of the jurisdictions has been successful in this context. In the English case of *Bull*, referred to above, it was held that the owners of a bed and breakfast had unlawfully discriminated when they refused to allow a gay couple to share a double room as they would only allow a married couple to do so. The majority of the Supreme Court held that the Bulls had directly discriminated against Hall and Preddy by treating them differently from a married couple (since at the time same-sex couples could not marry). It may also be experienced as prurient and an invasion of privacy and therefore particularly demeaning. Direct discrimination cannot usually be justified unless a specific exemption applies, but Lady Hale considered whether the law was a violation of the Bulls' Convention rights.[135] She pointed out, using a proportionality analysis, that Article 9 included the right to manifest beliefs in 'worship, teaching, practice and observance' and held this right was of importance and that proportionality will require reasonable accommodation to be made for religious adherents in some cases.[136] However, she held that the claim had to fail because of the importance of the rights of others. In her judgment, she drew attention to the requirement for 'very weighty reasons' to justify sexual orientation discrimination and argued that discrimination involves an affront to gay couples' 'dignity as human beings'. This analysis is an excellent example of how proportionality can pay close attention to the rights of both parties, acknowledge the importance of each, and create a judgment which does not rest on a hierarchy of rights, but rather attempts to 'harmonise' the rights, based on the particular situation.[137]

Finally, as has been described, in the Canadian case of *Eadie and Thomas v Riverbend Bed and Breakfast*[138] the Tribunal held there was no rational connection between the bed and breakfast's purpose and the discrimination. This approach is flawed because it focuses only on the nature of the business and ignores the individual rights of the owners. However, the judgment also went on to consider whether the owners had reasonably accommodated the couple up to the point of undue hardship and here the reasoning is unassailable, although these issues could be considered more directly and simply under a proportionality rather than reasonable accommodation test. The Tribunal held that the owners were engaged in a commercial activity, that it was their 'personal and voluntary choice to start up a business in their personal residence' and that 'there are occasions when the exercise of personal religious beliefs in the public sphere may be limited or carry a cost.'[139]

135 Ibid., paras 41–55. The right not to be discriminated against on the grounds of sexual orientation was at the time contained in the Equality Act (Sexual Orientation) Regulations 2007. As these were delegated legislation, they had to comply with the Human Rights Act and could be struck down by the courts if they were not. However, now the right is contained in the Equality Act 2010 and as primary legislation the only option the courts would have is to issue a Declaration of Incompatibility.

136 See also, extrajudicially, B. Hale, 'Religion and Sexual Orientation: The Clash of Equality Rights' Yale Comparative and Administrative Law Conference, 7 March 2014. Available from: www.law.yale.edu/documents/pdf/conference/compadmin14_hale.pdf <last accessed 25 July 2016>.

137 L. Cariolou, 'The Search for an Equilibrium by the European Court of Human Rights' in E. Brems (ed.), *Conflicts Between Fundamental Rights* (Antwerp: Intersentia, 2008).

138 Supra n.71.

139 Ibid., paras 165 and 168.

There appears, quite rightly, to be a general conclusion that the right to non-discrimination outweighs the right to religious freedom in this situation. Importantly, the Canadian and English cases do not rest on an easy assertion that the owners should simply give up their businesses or that their religious beliefs are irrelevant in the public sphere, but rather on a careful analysis of the interests in question.

Conclusion

This chapter has addressed how religious claims should be treated in the secular marketplace. Again, it has been demonstrated that the proportionality test provides a valuable way of resolving these claims. It is far more coherent than the varying tests used in US law, which often do not permit such claims to be raised at all or do not address the clash of rights directly. This may either be because there is no cognisable religious claim, since the law forbidding discrimination is general and neutrally applicable under *Smith,* with the result that claims are brought on other unpersuasive bases such as freedom of speech, or because there is no claim for sexual orientation discrimination in the state jurisdiction. By contrast a proportionality test does not exclude claims at the interference stage unless the link between the religious belief and the discrimination is very attenuated, as occurred for example in *Blanding,* because interference is defined broadly and does not mean that the right has necessarily been breached. This distinction between justification and interference under a proportionality test is valuable. First, the question of whether a right has been interfered with is an analytically separate issue from whether it has been breached. In addition, the distinction emphasises that there is a loss to both rights and highlights the necessity of justification. As well as being advantageous compared to the US approach, proportionality is also simpler to apply than the undue hardship test used in some contexts in Canadian law as it addresses the conflict of rights more directly. This can be seen by contrasting the Canadian cases of *Brockie* and *Riverview.*

In attempting to fully understand and set out the interests in issue, including symbolic harm, a proportionality analysis leads to the conclusion that in most cases it will be necessary for religious individuals' interests to give way to non-discrimination interests. These situations are at the periphery of religious individuals' rights, but can greatly affect the right to be able to live in dignity, free from pervasive discrimination.

10 Conclusion

I began this book with two starting points. The first was that, at least in some contexts, aspects of the conflict between freedom of religion and gay rights are part of a 'culture war'. This does not mean that these issues are necessarily perceived by all as of fundamental importance, but rather that when disputes arise they are often characterised by rhetorical exaggeration, gain much media and other attention and are used to symbolically demonstrate fundamental cultural and political disagreements rather than being focused on the particular issue in question. The second starting point was that there was value in the broad rights being claimed: in the claims to protect religious conscience and autonomy and in the claims to non-discrimination. There was therefore a need for a legal mechanism of deciding cases which would encourage a situation whereby 'the irreconcilable can exist side by side, civilly, in the public sphere, and [find] ways of living together',[1] and which would protect both rights as far as possible.

I have argued that proportionality is an ideal method of resolving these issues and have suggested ways to resolve numerous specific conflicts between non-discrimination rights and freedom of religion in four broad contexts. These were: discriminatory acts or expression by employees in secular organisations; employment by religious organisations; the provision of services by religious organisations; and the provision of services by religious individuals. I will briefly outline my conclusions here, although it is important to note that summarising them in this way may appear to minimise the importance of the process of analysis by which they were reached.

First, in the context of secular employment I argued that the rejection of the specific situation rule in *Eweida v UK*,[2] meaning that the merits of Article 9 claims were fully assessed in employment cases, was a welcome development. Furthermore, in some cases it may be proportionate to accommodate employees' religious objections to certain acts such as performing same-sex marriages, where the discrimination will not be directly experienced, and that an exemption should not be ruled out automatically solely because it will lead to discrimination or because a person is a state employee. Clearly this is not to say that exemptions should always be given, and should not be granted where an obligation of non-discrimination is specifically related to the employment. This chapter also dealt with the question of discriminatory speech within employment, holding that where speech amounted to hate speech it is always permissible to prohibit it and that for some roles greater interferences with freedom of expression may be proportionate. Finally, while there may be some

1 C.F. Stychin, 'Faith in the Future: Sexuality, Religion and the Public Sphere' (2009) 29 *OJLS* 729, 753.
2 [2013] 57 EHRR 8.

cases where an employer may require employees to have particular non-discriminatory views, these cases would be very rare, and the employment must intrinsically require such beliefs.

With regard to religious employment, I argued that an absolute rule permitting any form of discrimination for clergy is not proportionate, but discrimination that is based on religious rules or on the religious beliefs of a religion's followers should be permissible. In the context of other religious employment, I argued that discrimination is permissible where there is a bona fide occupational requirement for a person to follow discriminatory religious rules. Whether this is the case will depend on a number of factors, including the religiosity of the organisation and the nature of the role.

In the context of the provision of services, I suggested that religious organisations should be able to discriminate in access to religious worship and similar activities. However, where the religious mission is far more attenuated, such as the hiring out of religious premises for profit, organisations should only have limited freedom to discriminate. Similarly, within the English context, there was no legal justification for discrimination where the activities of Catholic adoption agencies were publicly funded, and, in fact, most adoption agencies could find a way to both protect their religious conscience and provide services. The final chapter concluded that claims by religious individuals to discriminate in providing services will rarely be successful, particularly if there is no religious aspect to the service.

I have suggested that proportionality has numerous benefits for deciding these difficult issues. In particular, it provides a fact-specific and nuanced analysis, giving rise to a number of related benefits. Proportionality does not try to answer whether one right generally is more important than another, but rather only provides an answer for a specific fact situation. It was argued that this is particularly significant given that both freedom of religion and non-discrimination are valuable rights, which should both be protected as far as possible, but the weight to be given to each may not be equal in a particular case. For example, in considering whether and when it is permissible for religious schools to apply discriminatory religious rules to the selection and dismissal of teachers, I argued that a proportionality approach, which could take into account a number of factors, such as the religiosity of the school and the role of the employee, provides a far more subtle and appropriate way of deciding whether discrimination should be permissible than a categorical approach as employed, for example, in English law, where the only relevant issue is the type of school.

This fact and context-specific nature of proportionality is clearly evident from the range of different conclusions on particular cases I have drawn, some of which protect freedom of religion above non-discrimination rights, and some the opposite. Proportionality means that constitutional winners and losers are not created permanently because a decision is likely to depend on a number of factors. It thus means that there is no 'hierarchy of rights' with either right being seen as the exception to the other, but rather demands consideration based on the particular facts. In this way, the actual dispute in issue is highlighted, an important point when dealing with such potentially controversial matters.

I have also underlined the importance of protecting 'constitutional losers': those who raise a constitutional claim but who are unsuccessful, drawing on Calhoun's argument that these constitutional losers still possess 'constitutional stature' and should be treated as such.[3] I have argued that proportionality is a conciliatory form of reasoning because losing claims can be accepted as in principle worthy of protection, even if they are unsuccessful in a particular case. This point was particularly illustrated in the last chapter. Although most of the claims

3 E. Calhoun, *Losing Twice: Harms of Indifference in the Supreme Court* (Oxford: Oxford UP, 2012).

of religious individuals to discriminate when providing services to the public should be unsuccessful, a proportionality analysis makes it clear that these losing claims are in principle legitimate and that it is a loss that these claims cannot be protected, even though they are outweighed by other factors in particular contexts.

In addition to advantages related to proportionality's fact-specific and contextual nature, I have also argued that proportionality is intrinsically linked to justification. In particular proportionality always requires justification where a right is infringed and the justification must relate specifically to the injury at stake. Furthermore, rights can be defined broadly under a proportionality test, without overly restricting the autonomy of the state or other body, because the extent of the justification required will depend on the degree of interference. For example, it has been demonstrated that an interference with freedom of religion can be recognised under a proportionality analysis where a person is required to act contrary to their conscience in their employment. This is so even though the employee is only peripherally involved in an 'immoral' act and the dilemma could be avoided by resignation, because these factors can be taken into account at the justification stage.

This broad interpretation of rights is advantageous since it means that claims are not rejected at a preliminary point before the state or other body is required to justify its actions. It also helps to ensure that obligations to 'constitutional losers' are met since weaker claims can be accepted as interfering with a person's rights and therefore the loss to them acknowledged, even if the claim fails. My argument was that justification was not only important in a practical sense since it ensured that rights are not unnecessarily restricted, but also that it has symbolic significance. I argued that giving justification treats each party in a dispute as *worthy* of justification: as people who can be expected to accept the process of adjudication, even though they disagree with the result. Justification also adds to a process of dialogue, meaning that decisions are not simply imposed on losing claimants.

The advantages of a broad interpretation of rights have been particularly evident when comparing proportionality to the US approach to freedom of religion, which only requires justification to be given where a law is not neutral or generally applicable. In cases where a religious believer objects to providing a commercial service for discriminatory reasons, no justification is required, since religious rights are not considered to be infringed. This is so even though the rule or law may have a significant effect on her ability to live her life in accordance with her religious beliefs. In contrast, proportionality is compatible with a broad understanding of rights and therefore does require justification to be given in these circumstances. *Bull and Hall v Preddy*[4] is also a good example of this, involving owners of a private hotel who refused to allow a gay couple to stay in a double-bedded room. Even though the owners were unsuccessful, the Court clearly acknowledged their religious beliefs and that it was a loss to them to be required not to discriminate.

Throughout this discussion the differences between the usually proportionality-based reasoning of Canada and the UK, and the far more categorical approach used by the USA have become clear. In English law, indirect discrimination can be justified if it is a proportionate means of achieving a legitimate aim, thus incorporating a proportionality analysis into the decision. While there is no general justification available for direct discrimination, a proportionality requirement is relevant to the consideration of whether a genuine occupational requirement to be, for example, of a particular sexual orientation has been shown. In charity law, a proportionality test is used to decide whether it is permissible to restrict benefits to those who share a protected characteristic. Finally, a proportionality test,

4 [2013] UKSC 73.

although often not strictly applied, is used in assessing whether there has been a violation of Art. 9 under Convention law.

By contrast, analysis under the US Free Exercise Clause tends to focus on whether policies are neutral and generally applicable, rather than considering whether there is sufficient justification for interference with the right. While there are serious practical and theoretical reasons as to why the US has not embraced proportionality,[5] a return to the pre-*Employment Division v Smith* approach, which required strict scrutiny when considering freedom of religion claims, would go a long way in improving the law. There is though little sign that this is likely to occur, unless it occurs on a state by state basis through state RFRAs.[6] In addition, the complete lack of protection against sexual orientation discrimination in many US states is clearly highly problematic, although the situation is changing.

Proportionality provides a better method of analysis than other tests. To draw stark distinctions between action and belief or public and private in considering where the boundaries of religious freedom lie may lead to unfairness, since it does not consider the particular circumstances in which a right has been claimed and may both overly restrict and overly protect religious rights. For example, a strict public/private distinction is not suitable for resolving the question of when it is permissible to have discriminatory criteria for the selection of employees, or conversely for deciding when employees should be permitted religious exemptions from equality policies. It is disproportionate for employees, even those at the core of organised religions such as clergy, not to receive some protection from discrimination law, even though this is clearly not 'public' employment. The converse of this is also true: it is not sufficient to hold that because a person is a state official they can never be permitted a religious exemption, since this equates a person with the state in a way which is unwarranted, but rather in each case, a fact-specific analysis should be made which considers the nature of the role, the exemption claimed and the effect this would have on the non-discrimination right.

Concluding thoughts

Glendon argues that, 'in its simplest American form, the language of rights is the language of no compromise. The winner takes all and the loser has to get out of town. The conversation is over.'[7] This book has demonstrated though how a particular type of 'rights talk'[8] can be used to avoid such a stark analysis. As I have made clear, there is no reason why a discussion of contentious moral and political issues in terms of rights should necessarily 'lead one to think in absolute terms and to shun compromises'.[9]

5 J. Bomhoff, *Balancing Constitutional Rights: The Origins and Meanings of Postwar Legal Discourse* (Cambridge: Cambridge UP, 2013).

6 Unfortunately, many of these are weighted towards religious freedom claims against other concerns.

7 M. Glendon, *Rights Talk: The Impoverishment of Political Discourse* (New York: Free Press, 1991) 9.

8 Ibid.

9 A. Etzioni, 'Moral Dialogues: A Communitarian Core Element' in A. Allen and M. Regan (eds), *Debating Democracy's Discontent: Essays on American Politics, Law, and Public Philosophy* (Oxford: Oxford UP, 1998). Afridi and Warmington have argued the use of 'proportionality has the potential to elevate the level of debate beyond, "I invoke my claims as a right and this trumps consideration of all other issues". It can help to develop a better understanding of all of the rights and all of the people affected by a conflict.' A. Afridi and J. Warmington, *Managing Competing Equality Claims* (London: Equality and Diversity Forum, 2010).

In considering the conflict between freedom of religion and non-discrimination rights, Stychin hopes for a situation 'of accommodation and compromise which avoids intransigence and instead seeks out common ground'[10] in this context. Although legal methods like proportionality can only be part of the solution, and non-legal mechanisms should also be pursued,[11] since courts are inevitably called on to resolve some of these disputes, the law has an indispensable role to play in this process. While the culture war over homosexuality may perhaps be lessening as different sexual orientations become far more widely accepted, these kinds of disputes will continue to be fought internationally and over new frontiers such as transgender rights. I therefore end on a tentative but hopeful note: that these disputes need not be intransigent and that there is a way to resolve these complex and difficult conflicts, which are at times politically and socially sensitive, in a way which respects both rights as far as possible.

10 Stychin supra n.1, 755.

11 Many commentators have made this point including: A. Donald, *Religion or Belief, Equality and Human Rights in England and Wales* (Equality and Human Rights Commission, 2012); J.G. Brown, 'Peacemaking in the Culture War Between Gay Rights and Religious Liberty' (2012) 95 *Iowa L Rev* 747; J.D. Hunter, *Before the Shooting Begins: Searching for Democracy in America's Culture War* (New York: Free Press, 1994); J. Nedelsky and R. Hutchinson, 'Clashes of Principle and the Possibility of Dialogue: A Case Study of Same-Sex Marriage in the United Church of Canada' in R. Moon (ed.), *Law and Religious Pluralism in Canada* (Vancouver: UBC Press, 2008).

Bibliography

Abramowitz, A., and Saunders, K., 'Is Polarization a Myth?' (2008) 70 *Journal of Politics* 542

Adamczyk, A. et al., 'Religious Regulation and the Courts: Documenting the Effects of *Smith* and RFRA' (2004) 46 *J Church & St* 237

Aden, S., and Strang, L., 'When a "Rule" Doesn't Rule: The Failure of the *Oregon Employment Division v. Smith* "Hybrid Rights Exception"' (2003) 108 *Penn St L Rev* 573

Afridi, A., and Warmington, J., *Managing Competing Equality Claims* (London: Equality and Diversity Forum, 2010)

Ahdar, R., 'Companies as Religious Liberty Claimants' (2016) 5 *OJLR* 1

Ahdar, R., and Leigh, I., *Religious Freedom in the Liberal State*, 2nd ed. (Oxford: Oxford UP, 2013)

Alexy, R., *A Theory of Constitutional Rights*, tr. J. Rivers (Oxford: Oxford UP, 2002)

———'Constitutional Rights, Balancing and Rationality' (2003) 16 *Ratio Juris* 131

———'On Balancing and Subsumption' (2003) 16 *Ratio Juris* 433

———'Balancing, Constitutional Review, and Representation' (2005) 3 *ICON* 572

Araujo, R., '"The Harvest is Plentiful, but the Laborers are Few": Hiring Practices and Religiously Affiliated Universities' (1996) 30 *U Rich L Rev* 713

Audi, R., *Religious Commitment and Secular Reason* (Cambridge: Cambridge UP, 2000)

Baer, S., 'Privatizing Religion. Legal Groupism, No-Go-Areas, and the Public-Private-Ideology in Human Rights Politics' (2013) 20 *Constellations* 68

Bagni, B., 'Discrimination in the Name of the Lord: A Critical Evaluation of Discrimination by Religious Organizations' (1979) 79 *Colum L Rev* 1514

Baines, B., 'Contextualism, Feminism and a Canadian Woman Judge' (2009) 17 *Fem Leg Stud* 27

Baker, A., 'Proportionality and Employment Discrimination in the UK' (2008) 37 *ILJ* 305

Barak, A., 'Proportionality and Principled Balancing' (2010) 4 *Law & Ethics of Human Rights* 1

———*Proportionality: Constitutional Rights and their Limitations* (Cambridge: Cambridge UP, 2012)

Barendt, E., *Freedom of Speech*, 2nd ed. (Oxford: Oxford UP, 2005)

Barron, L.G. et al., 'The Force of Law: The Effects of Sexual Orientation Antidiscrimination Legislation on Interpersonal Discrimination in Employment' (2013) 19 *Psychology, Public Policy, and Law* 191

Bartlett, K., 'Feminist Legal Methods' (1989) 103 *Harv L Rev* 829

Battaglia, J., 'Religion, Sexual Orientation and Self-Realization: First Amendment Principles and Anti-Discrimination Laws' (1999) 76 *U Det Mercy L Rev* 190

Beaman, L., 'Defining Religion: The Promise and the Peril of Legal Interpretation' in R. Moon (ed.), *Law and Religious Pluralism in Canada* (Vancouver: UBC Press, 2008)

Beatty, D., *The Ultimate Rule of Law* (Oxford: Oxford UP, 2004)

Benjamin, M., *Splitting the Difference: Compromise and Integrity in Ethics and Politics* (Lawrence: University Press of Kansas, 1990)

Benson, I., 'The Freedom of Conscience and Religion in Canada: Challenges and Opportunities' (2007) 21 *Emory Int'l L Rev* 111

Berberick, K., 'Marrying into Heaven: The Constitutionality of Polygamy Bans Under the Free Exercise Clause' (2007) 44 *Willamette L Rev* 105

Berger, B., 'Law's Religion' in R. Moon (ed.), *Law and Religious Pluralism in Canada* (Vancouver: UBC Press, 2008)

Bernstein, D., *You Can't Say That: The Growing Threat to Civil Liberties from Antidiscrimination Laws* (Washington, D.C.: Cato Institute, 2003)

Bhagwat, A., 'Associations and Forums: Situating *CLS v. Martinez*' (2011) 38 *Hastings Const LQ* 543

Bielefeld, W., and Cleveland, W.S., 'Faith-Based Organizations as Service Providers and their Relationship to Government' (2013) 42 *Nonprofit and Voluntary Sector* 468

Bilchitz, D., 'Necessity and Proportionality: Towards a Balanced Approach' in *Reasoning Rights: Comparative Judicial Engagement* (Oxford: Hart Publishing, 2014)

Bingham, T., 'Discrimination in Education: Public Versus Private Universities' (2007) 36 *J L & Educ* 273

Blache, P., 'The Criteria of Justification under *Oakes*: Too Much Severity Generated Through Formalism' (1991) 20 *Man LJ* 437

Bold, F., 'Vows to Collide: The Burgeoning Conflict between Religious Institutions and Same-Sex Marriage Antidiscrimination Laws' (2009) 158 *U Pa L Rev* 179

Bomhoff, J., 'Lüth's 50th Anniversary: Some Comparative Observations on the German Foundations of Judicial Balancing' (2008) 9 *German LJ* 121

———'Genealogies of Balancing as Discourse' (2010) 4 *Law & Ethics of Human Rights* 107

———*Balancing Constitutional Rights: The Origins and Meanings of Postwar Legal Discourse* (Cambridge: Cambridge UP, 2013)

Borchers, D., and Vitikainene, A. (eds), *On Exit: Interdisciplinary Perspectives on the Right of Exit in Liberal Multicultural Societies* (Berlin: De Gruyter, 2012)

Bosmajian, H., 'The Freedom Not to Speak' (1994) 18 *Legal Stud F* 425

Bosset, P., 'Mainstreaming Religious Diversity in a Secular and Egalitarian State: The Road(s) Not Taken in *Leyla Sahin v. Turkey*' in E. Brems (ed.), *Diversity and European Human Rights: Rewriting Judgments of the ECHR* (Cambridge: Cambridge UP, 2013)

Bouchard, G., and Taylor, C., *Building the Future: A Time for Reconciliation* (Gouvernement du Quebec, 2008)

Boyle, C., 'A Human Right to Group Self-Identification? Reflections on *Nixon v. Vancouver Rape Relief*' (2011) 23 *Can J Women & L* 488

Brady, A., *Proportionality and Deference under the UK Human Rights Act: An Institutionally Sensitive Approach* (Cambridge: Cambridge UP, 2012)

Brandenburg, S., 'Alternatives to Employment Discrimination at Private Religious Schools' (1999) *Ann Surv Am L* 335

Brems, E., and. Lavrysen, L., 'Procedural Justice in Human Rights Adjudication: The European Court of Human Rights' (2013) 35 *Hum Rts Q* 176

Brest, P., 'The Supreme Court 1975 Term Foreword: In Defense of the Antidiscrimination Principle' (1976) 90 *Harv L Rev* 1

Brown, J.G., 'Peacemaking in the Culture War Between Gay Rights and Religious Liberty' (2012) 95 *Iowa L Rev* 747

Brown, R., 'Liberty: The New Equality' (2002) 77 *NYU L Rev* 1491

Brownstein, A., and Amar, V., 'Reviewing Associational Freedom Claims in a Limited Public Forum: An Extension of the Distinction Between Debate-Dampening and Debate-Distorting State Action' (2011) 38 *Hastings Const LQ* 505

Buchanan, G.S., 'The Power of Government to Regulate Class Discrimination by Religious Entities: A Study in Conflicting Values' (1994) 43 *Emory LJ* 1189

Buddel, N., 'Queering the Workplace' (2011) 23 *Journal of Gay & Lesbian Social Services* 131

Calhoun, E., *Losing Twice: Harms of Indifference in the Supreme Court* (Oxford: Oxford UP, 2012)

Cameron, E., 'Moral Citizenship and Constitutional Protection' in C. McCrudden (ed.), *Understanding Human Dignity* (Oxford: Oxford UP, 2013)

Campbell, A., 'Bountiful Voices' (2009) 47 *Osgoode Hall LJ* 183

Cariolou, L., 'The Search for an Equilibrium by the European Court of Human Rights' in E. Brems (ed.), *Conflicts Between Fundamental Rights* (Antwerp: Intersentia, 2008)

Carter, S., *The Culture of Disbelief: How American Law and Politics Trivialize Religious Devotion* (New York: Basic Books, 1993)

Casswell, D.G., *Lesbians, Gay Men and Canadian Law* (Toronto: Montgomery, 1996)

Chan, C., 'Proportionality and Invariable Baseline Intensity of Review' (2013) 33 *LS* 1

Chemerinsky, E., 'Substantive Due Process' (1998) 15 *Touro L Rev* 1501

Childress, J.F., 'Appeals to Conscience' (1979) 89 *Ethics* 315

Clark, B.R., 'When Free Exercise Exemptions Undermine Religious Liberty and the Liberty of Conscience: A Case Study of the Catholic Hospital Conflict' (2003) 82 *Or L Rev* 625

Cobb, N., '"Gay Couple's Break Like Fawlty Towers": Dangerous Representations of Lesbian and Gay Oppression in an Era of "Progressive" Law Reform' (2009) 18 *Social & Legal Studies* 333

Cochran, C., *Religion in Public and Private Life* (New York: Routledge, 1990)

Coffin, F., 'Judicial Balancing: The Protean Scales of Justice' (1988) 63 *NYU L Rev* 16

Cohen-Eliya, M., and Porat, I., 'The Hidden Foreign Law Debate in *Heller*: The Proportionality Approach in American Constitutional Law' (2009) 46 *San Diego L Rev* 267

———'American Balancing and German Proportionality: The Historical Origins' (2010) 8 *ICON* 263

———'Proportionality and the Culture of Justification' (2011) 59 *Am J Compl L* 463

———*Proportionality and Constitutional Culture* (Cambridge: Cambridge UP, 2013)

Colker, R., 'Section 1, Contextuality and the Anti-Disadvantage Principle' (1992) 42 *U Toronto LJ* 77

———'Religious Accommodations for County Clerks?' (2015) 76 *Ohio State LJ* 87

Collins, D., 'Culture, Religion and Curriculum: Lessons from the "Three Books" Controversy in Surrey, BC' (2006) 50 *Can Geogr-Geogr Can* 342

Colombo, R., 'The Naked Private Sphere' (2013) 51 *Hous L R* 1

———*The First Amendment and the Business Corporation* (Oxford: Oxford UP, 2014)

Corbin, C.M., 'Above the Law? The Constitutionality of the Ministerial Exemption from Antidiscrimination Law' (2007) 75 *Fordham L Rev* 2031

———'Corporate Religious Liberty' (2015) 30 *Const Commentary* 277

Cover, R., 'The Supreme Court 1982 Term Foreword: Nomos and Narrative' (1983) 97 *Harv L Rev* 4, 14

Craig, E., 'The Case for the Federation of Law Societies Rejecting Trinity Western University's Proposed Law Degree Program' (2013) 25 *CJWL* 148

Cram, I., 'The Danish Cartoons, Offensive Expression, and Democratic Legitimacy' in I. Hare and J. Weinstein, *Extreme Speech and Democracy* (Oxford: Oxford UP, 2010)

Cumper, P., and Lewis, T., '"Public Reason", Judicial Deference and the Right to Freedom of Religion and Belief under the Human Rights Act 1998' (2011) 22 *KLJ* 131

Curtis, M., 'A Unique Religious Exemption from Antidiscrimination Laws in the Case of Gays? Putting the Call for Exemptions for those who Discriminate Against Married or Marrying Gays in Context' (2012) 47 *Wake Forest L Rev* 173

Da Silva, V., 'Comparing the Incommensurable: Constitutional Principles, Balancing and Rational Decision' (2011) 31 *OJLS* 273

Darwall, S., 'Two Kinds of Respect' (1977) 88 *Ethics* 36

Davidov, G., 'Separating Minimal Impairment from Balancing: A Comment on *R v Sharpe (B.C.C.A)*' (2000) 5 *Rev Const Stud* 195

Davie, G., 'Religion in Europe in the 21st Century: The Factors to Take into Account' (2006) 47 *European Journal of Sociology* 271

———*Religion in Britain: A Persistent Paradox*, 2nd ed. (Oxford: Wiley-Blackwell, 2015)

Deakin, S., 'Equality, Non-discrimination and the Labour Market: A Commentary on Richard Epstein's Critique of Anti-discrimination Laws' in R. Epstein, *Equal Opportunity or More Opportunity? The Good Thing About Discrimination* (London: Civitas, 2002)

Demeyere, G., 'Discrimination in Employment by Religious Organizations: Exemptions, Defences, and the Lockean Concept of Toleration' (2010) 15 *Canadian Lab & Emp LJ* 435

Dershowitz, A., *Why Terrorism Works: Understanding the Threat, Responding to the Challenge* (Yale: Yale UP, 2002)

Dickey Young, P., 'Two by Two: Religion, Sexuality and Diversity in Canada' in L. Beaman and P. Beyer (eds), *Religion and Diversity in Canada* (Leiden: Martinus Nijhoff, 2008)

Dickey Young, P., Shipley, H., and Trothen, T. (eds), *Religion and Sexuality: Diversity and the Limits of Tolerance* (Vancouver: UBC Press, 2014)

Donald, A., *Religion or Belief, Equality and Human Rights in England and Wales* (Equality and Human Rights Commission, 2012)

Dworkin, R., *Taking Rights Seriously* (Cambridge, Mass: Harvard UP, 1977)

———'Liberalism' in *A Matter of Principle* (Cambridge: Cambridge UP, 1985)

———'What is Equality? Part 3: The Place of Liberty' (1987) 73 *Iowa L Rev* 1

———*Is Democracy Possible Here?* (Princeton: Princeton UP, 2006)

Dyzenhaus, D., 'Proportionality and Deference in a Culture of Justification' in G. Huscroft, B.W. Miller and G. Webber (eds), *Proportionality and the Rule of Law: Rights, Justification, Reasoning* (Cambridge: Cambridge UP, 2014)

Eberle, C., *Religious Conviction in Liberal Politics* (Cambridge: Cambridge UP, 2002)

Edge, P., 'Judicial Crafting of a Ministerial Exception: The UK Experience' (2015) 4 *OJLR* 244

Edge, P., and Vickers, L., *Review of Equality and Human Rights Law Relating to Religion or Belief* (EHRC Research Report 97, 2016)

Eisgruber, C.L., and Sager, L.G., 'The Vulnerability of Conscience: The Constitutional Basis for Protecting Religious Conduct' (1994) 61 *U Chi L Rev* 1245

———*Religious Freedom and the Constitution* (Cambridge, Mass: Harvard UP, 2010)

Ekklesia, *United We Stand: A Report on Current Conflicts between Christian Unions and Students' Unions* (London: Ekklesia, 2006)

Elias, P., 'Religious Discrimination: Conflicts and Compromises' (2012) 222 *EOR*

Ellison, G., and Gunstone, B., *Sexual Orientation Explored: A Study of Identity, Attraction, Behaviour and Attitudes in 2009* (Manchester: EHRC, 2009)

Epstein, R., *Forbidden Grounds: The Case Against Employment Discrimination Laws* (Cambridge, Mass: Harvard UP, 1992)

Equality and Human Rights Commission, *Beyond Tolerance: Making Sexual Orientation a Public Matter* (Manchester: EHRC, 2009)

———*Your Rights to Equality from Voluntary and Community Sector Organisations (Including Charities and Religion or Belief Organisations)* (Manchester: EHRC, 2011)

Esau, A., '"Islands of Exclusivity": Religious Organizations and Employment Discrimination' (1999) 33 *UBC Law Rev* 719

———'"Islands of Exclusivity" Revisited: Religious Organizations, Employment Discrimination and *Heintz v Christian Horizons*' (2009) 15 *Canadian Lab & Emp LJ* 389

Esbeck, C.H., 'Charitable Choice and the Critics' (2000) 57 *NYU Ann Surv Am L* 17

Eskridge, W., 'A Jurisprudence of "Coming Out": Religion, Homosexuality, and Collisions of Liberty and Equality in American Public Law' (1997) 106 *Yale LJ* 2411

———*Gaylaw: Challenging the Apartheid of the Closet* (Cambridge, Mass: Harvard UP, 1999)

———'Pluralism and Distrust: How Courts Can Support Democracy by Lowering the Stakes of Politics' (2004) 114 *Yale LJ* 1279

Eskridge, W.N., and Peller, G., 'The New Public Law Movement: Moderation as a Postmodern Cultural Form' (1990) 89 *Mich L Rev* 707

Etzioni, A., 'Moral Dialogues: A Communitarian Core Element' in A. Allen and M. Regan (eds), *Debating Democracy's Discontent: Essays on American Politics, Law, and Public Philosophy* (Oxford: Oxford UP, 1998)

Evans, C., and Gaze, B., 'Discrimination by Religious Schools: Views from the Coal Face' (2010) 34 *MULR* 392

Evans, C., and Hood, A., 'Religious Autonomy and Labour Law: A Comparison of the Jurisprudence of the United States and the European Court of Human Rights' (2012) 1 *OJLR* 81

Evans, S., and Stone Sweet, A., '*Balancing and Proportionality: A Distinctive Ethic?*', Paper given at VIIth World Congress of the International Association of Constitutional Law, Athens, 11–15 June 2007

Failinger, M., 'Remembering Mrs. Murphy: A Remedies Approach to the Conflict Between Gay/Lesbian Renters and Religious Landlords' (2001) 29 *Cap U L Rev* 383

Fallon, R., 'Strict Judicial Scrutiny' (2006) 54 *UCLA* 1267

Feinberg, J., *The Moral Limits of the Criminal Law – Volume 2: Offense to Others* (New York: Oxford UP, 1985)

Feldblum, C., 'Moral Conflict and Liberty: Gay Rights and Religion' (2006) 72 *Brook L Rev* 61

Figgis, J.N., *Churches in the Modern State* (London: Longmans, Green & Co, 1913)

Fink, J., De Jong, A., and Langan, M., 'New Challenges or Different Opportunities? Voluntary Adoption Agencies and the Shifting Terrain of Child Care Services' (2011) 15 *Voluntary Sector Review* 177

Finke, R., and Iannacone, L., 'Supply-Side Explanations for Religious Change' (1993) 527 *Annals Am Acad Pol & Soc Sci* 27

Fiorina, M., *Culture War? The Myth of a Polarized America*, 3rd ed. (Boston: Longman, 2010)

Fisher, L., 'A Miscarriage of Justice: Pregnancy Discrimination in Sectarian Schools' (2010) 16 *Wash & Lee JCR Soc Just* 529

Flynn, T., 'Clarion Call or False Alarm: Why Proposed Exemptions to Equal Marriage Statutes Return Us to a Religious Understanding of the Public Marketplace' (2010) 5 *Nw J L & Soc Pol'y* 236

Francart, K., 'No Dogs Allowed: Freedom of Association v Forced Inclusion. Anti-Discrimination Statutes and the Applicability to Private Organizations' (2000) 17 *TM Cooley L Rev* 273

Freeman, A., and Mensch, E., 'The Public-Private Distinction in American Law and Life' (1987) 36 *Buff L Rev* 237

Freeman, G., 'The Misguided Search for the Constitutional Definition of Religion' (1983) 71 *Geo LJ* 1519

Furedi, F., *On Tolerance: A Defence of Moral Independence* (London: Continuum, 2011)

Galeotti, A., *Toleration as Recognition* (Cambridge: Cambridge UP, 2002)

Gardbaum, S., 'The "Horizontal Effect" of Constitutional Rights' (2003) 102 *Mich L Rev* 387

Garvey, J., and Coney, A., 'Catholic Judges in Capital Cases' (1997) 81 *Marq L Rev* 303

Gavison, R., 'Feminism and the Public/Private Distinction' (1992) 45 *Stan L Rev* 1

Gedicks, F.M., 'Toward a Constitutional Jurisprudence of Religious Group Rights' (1989) 99 *Wisconsin LR* 100

———'Narrative Pluralism and Doctrinal Incoherence in *Hosanna-Tabor*' (2013) 64 *Mercer L Rev* 405

———'One Cheer for *Hobby Lobby*: Improbable Alternatives, Truly Strict Scrutiny, and Third-Party Employee Burdens' (2015) 38 *Harv JL & Gender* 154

Gerard, B., 'Imagining the Past and Remembering the Future: The Supreme Court's History of the Establishment Clause' (1986) 18 *Con L R* 827

Gilreath, S., 'Not a Moral Issue: Same-Sex Marriage and Religious Liberty' (2010) *U Ill L Rev* 205

Glendon, M., *Rights Talk: The Impoverishment of Political Discourse* (New York: Free Press, 1991)

Glenn, C., *The Ambiguous Embrace: Government and Faith Based Schools and Social Agencies* (Princeton: Princeton UP, 2000).

Gordon, S.B., *The Mormon Question: Polygamy and Constitutional Conflict in Nineteenth Century America* (Chapel Hill: North Carolina Press, 2012)

Gottlieb, S., 'The Paradox of Balancing Significant Interests' (1994) 45 *Hastings LJ* 825

Grace, A., and Wells, K., 'The Marc Hall Prom Predicament: Queer Individual Rights v. Institutional Church Rights in Canadian Public Education' (2005) 28 *Canadian Journal of Education* 237

Greenawalt, K., *Private Consciences and Public Reasons* (Oxford: Oxford UP, 1995)

———'Quo Vadis: The Status and Prospects of "Tests" under the Religion Clauses' (1995) *Sup Ct Rev* 323

———'Five Questions about Religion Judges are Afraid to Ask' in N. Rosenblum (ed.), *Obligations of Citizenship and Demands of Faith: Religious Accommodation in Pluralist Democracies* (Princeton: Princeton UP, 2000)

———*Religion and the Constitution Volume 1: Free Exercise and Fairness* (Princeton: Princeton UP, 2006)

Grimm, D., 'Proportionality in Canadian and German Constitutional Jurisprudence' (2007) 57 *U Toronto LJ* 383

Gunn, T.J., 'Adjudicating Rights of Conscience under the European Convention on Human Rights' in J. Van der Vyver and J. Witte (eds), *Religious Human Rights in Global Perspective: Legal Perspectives* (The Hague: Martinus Nijhoff, 1996)

———'The Complexity of Religion and the Definition of "Religion" in International Law' (2003) 16 *Harv Hum Rts J* 189

Gunther, G., 'In Search of Evolving Doctrine on a Changing Court: A Model for a Newer Equal Protection' (1972) 86 *Harv L Rev* 1

Habermas, J., *Between Facts and Norms: Contributions to a Discourse Theory of Law and Democracy*, tr. W. Rehg (Malden, MA: Polity Press, 1996)

Hafen, B., 'Institutional Autonomy in Public, Private, and Church-Related Schools' (1988) 3 *Notre Dame J L Ethics & Pub Pol'y* 405

Hale, B., 'Religion and Sexual Orientation: The Clash of Equality Rights' Yale Comparative and Administrative Law Conference, 7 March 2014, available from: www.law.yale.edu/documents/pdf/conference/compadmin14_hale.pdf <last accessed 25 July 2016>

Hambler, A., 'A No-Win Situation for Public Officials with Faith Convictions' (2010) 12 *Ecc LJ* 3

———'Recognising a Right to "Conscientiously Object" for Registrars whose Religious Beliefs are Incompatible with their Duty to Conduct Same-Sex Civil Partnerships' (2012) 7 *Religion and Human Rights* 157

———*Religious Expression in the Workplace and the Contested Role of Law* (Abingdon: Routledge, 2014)

Hamilton, M., 'The Belief/Conduct Paradigm in the Supreme Court's Free Exercise Jurisprudence' (1993) 54 *Ohio St LJ* 713

———*God vs. the Gavel: Religion and the Rule of Law* (Cambridge: Cambridge UP, 2005)

———'The Case for Evidence-Based Free Exercise Accommodation: Why the Religious Freedom Restoration Act is Bad Public Policy' (2015) 9 *Harv J L & Pub Pol* 129

Harmer-Dionne, E., 'Once a Peculiar People: Cognitive Dissonance and the Suppression of Mormon Polygamy as a Case Study Negating the Belief-Action Distinction' (1998) 50 *Stan L Rev* 1295

Harper, C., and Le Beau, B., 'The Social Adaptation of Marginal Religious Movements in America' (1993) 54 *Sociology of Religion* 171

Harvard Law Review Board, 'The Best of a Bad Lot: Compromise and Hybrid Religious Exemptions' (2010) 123 *Harv L Rev* 1494

Hatzenbuehler, M., 'How Does Sexual Minority Stigma "Get Under the Skin"? A Psychological Mediation Framework' (2009) *Psychol Bull* 135

Hellman, D., 'The Expressive Dimension of Equal Protection' (2000) 85 *Minn L Rev* 1

Henrard, K., 'The Effective Protection of the Freedom of Religion: The ECtHR's Variable Margin of Appreciation Regarding Religion-State Relations and the Rule of Law' in M. Foblets et al. (eds), *Belief, Law and Politics: What Future for a Secular Europe?* (Farnham: Ashgate, 2014)

Herek, G., 'Confronting Sexual Stigma and Prejudice: Theory and Practice' (2007) 4 *J Soc Issues* 905

Hoover, D., and Den Dulk, K., 'Christian Conservatives Go to Court: Religion and Legal Mobilization in the United States and Canada' (2004) 25 *Int Polit Sci Rev* 9

Horton, J., and Mendus, S. (eds), *John Locke: A Letter Concerning Toleration – In Focus* (Abingdon: Routledge, 1991)

Horwitz, P., 'Churches as First Amendment Institutions: Of Sovereignty and Spheres' (2009) 44 *Harv CR-CL L Rev* 79

———'The Hobby Lobby Moment' (2014) 128 *Harv L Rev* 154

Howard, E., 'Reasonable Accommodation of Religion and Other Discrimination Grounds in EU Law' (2013) *E L Rev* 360

Howerton, D., 'Honeymoon Vacation: Sexual-Orientation Prejudice and Inconsistent Behavioral Responses' (2012) 34 *Basic and Applied Social Psychology* 146

Hull, K., *Same-Sex Marriage: The Cultural Politics of Love and Law* (Cambridge: Cambridge UP, 2006)

Hunter, J.D., *Culture Wars: The Struggle to Define America* (New York: Basic Books, 1991)

———*Before the Shooting Begins: Searching for Democracy in America's Culture War* (New York: Free Press, 1994)

Hunter, J.D., and Wolfe, A. (eds), *Is there a Culture War? A Dialogue on Values and American Public Life* (Washington, D.C.: Brookings Institution Press, 2006)

Hunter, N., 'Accommodating the Public Sphere: Beyond the Market Model' (2001) 85 *Minn L Rev* 1591

Ingber, S., 'The Marketplace of Ideas: A Legitimizing Myth' (1984) *Duke LJ* 1

Jackson, V.C., 'Ambivalent Resistance and Comparative Constitutionalism: Opening Up the Conversation on "Proportionality," Rights and Federalism' (1999) 1 *U Pa J Const L* 583

Jacoby, W.G., 'Is There a Culture War? Conflicting Value Structures in American Public Opinion' (2014) 108 *American Political Science Review* 754

Johnson, P., and Vanderbeck, R.M., *Law, Religion and Homosexuality* (Abingdon: Routledge, 2014)

Kagan, E., 'Regulation of Hate Speech and Pornography After R.A.V.' (1993) 60 *U Chi L Rev* 873

Karst, K., 'Equal Citizenship Under the Fourteenth Amendment' (1977) 91 *Harv L Rev* 1

———'The Freedom of Intimate Association' (1980) 89 *Yale LJ* 624

———'Private Discrimination and Public Responsibility: *Patterson* in Context' (1989) *Sup Court Rev* 1

Katz-Wise, S., and Hyde, J., 'Victimization Experiences of Lesbian, Gay, and Bisexual Individuals: A Meta Analysis' (2012) 49 *J Sex Res* 142

Kenny, C., 'Law and the Art of Defining Religion' (2014) 16 *Ecc LJ* 18

Kip, A.K.T., 'Homophobia and Ethnic Minority Communities in the United Kingdom' in L. Trappolin, A. Gasparini and R. Wintemute, *Confronting Homophobia in Europe: Social and Legal Perspectives* (Oxford: Hart Publishing, 2011)

Klatt, M., and Meister, M., *The Constitutional Structure of Proportionality* (Oxford: Oxford UP, 2012)

———'Proportionality – A Benefit to Human Rights? Remarks on the ICON Controversy' (2012) 10 *ICON* 687

Knutson, S., 'The Religious Landlord and the Conflict Between Free Exercise Rights and Housing Discrimination Laws – Which Interest Prevails?' (1996) 47 *Hastings LJ* 1669

Kolosov, C., 'Fair Housing Laws and the Constitutional Rights of Roommate Seekers' (2008) 4 *The Modern American* 1

Koppelman, A., *Antidiscrimination Law and Social Equality* (New Haven: Yale UP, 1996)

———'Justice for Large Earlobes! A Comment on Richard Arneson's "*What is Wrongful Discrimination?*"' (2006) 43 *San Diego L Rev* 809

———'You Can't Hurry Love: Why Antidiscrimination Protections for Gay People Should Have Religious Exemptions' (2006) 72 *Brook L Rev* 125

———'Beyond Levels of Scrutiny: *Windsor* and "Bare Desire to Harm"' (2014) 64 *Case W Res L Rev* 1

Koppelman, A., and Gedicks, F.M., 'Is Hobby Lobby Worse for Religious Liberty Than Smith?' (2015) *St. Thomas Journal of Law & Public Policy* 223

Kumm, M., 'Who is Afraid of the Total Constitution? Constitutional Rights as Principles and the Constitutionalization of Private Law' (2006) 7 *German LJ* 341

———'What Do You Have in Virtue of Having a Constitutional Right? On the Place and Limits of the Proportionality Requirement' *New York University Public Law and Legal Theory Working Papers*, Paper 46 (2006), 1

———'Political Liberalism and the Structure of Rights' in G. Pavlakos (ed.), *Law, Rights and Discourse* (Oxford: Hart Publishing, 2007)

———'The Idea of Socratic Contestation and the Right to Justification: The Point of Rights-Based Proportionality Review' (2010) 4 *Law & Ethics of Human Rights* 141

Kuyper, A., 'Sphere Sovereignty' in J.D. Beatt (ed.), *Abraham Kuyper: A Centennial Reader* (Grand Rapids: Eerdmans Publishing, 1998)

Lacey, L., '*Gay Rights Coalition v Georgetown University*: Constitutional Values on a Collision Course' (1985) 64 *Or L Rev* 409

Laycock, D., 'Toward a General Theory of the Religion Clauses: The Case of Church Labor Relations and the Right to Church Autonomy' (1981) 81 *Colum L Rev* 1373

———'The Remnants of Free Exercise' (1990) *Sup Ct Rev* 1

———'The Religious Exemption Debate' (2009) 11 *Rutgers J L & Religion* 139

———'Afterword' in D. Laycock et al. (eds), *Same-Sex Marriage and Religious Liberty: Emerging Conflicts* (Lanham, Maryland: Rowman & Littlefield, 2008)

———'*Hosanna-Tabor* and the Ministerial Exception' (2012) 35 *Harv J L & Pub Pol'y* 840

Layman, G., *The Great Divide: Religious and Cultural Conflict in American Party Politics* (New York: Columbia UP, 2001)

Leigh, I., 'Balancing Religious Autonomy and Other Human Rights under the European Convention' (2012) 1 *OJLR* 109

Leigh, I., and Hambler, A., 'Religious Symbols, Conscience and the Rights of Others' (2014) 3 *OJLR* 2

Levinson, R.B., 'Gender Equality vs. Religious Autonomy: Suing Religious Employers for Sexual Harassment after *Hosanna-Tabor*' (2015) 11 *Stanford J C R & CL* 89

Lin, A., 'Sexual Orientation Antidiscrimination Laws and the Religious Liberty Protection Act: The Pitfalls of the Compelling State Interest Inquiry' (2001) 89 *Geo LJ* 719

Loeb, H., and Rosenberg, D., 'Fundamental Rights in Conflict: The Price of a Maturing Democracy' (2001) 77 *ND L Rev* 27

Long, R., and Bolton, P., *Faith Schools: FAQs* (House of Commons Library Briefing Paper Number 06972, 14 Oct 2015)

Lund, C., 'Religious Liberty After *Gonzales*: A Look at State RFRAs' (2010) 55 *SD L Rev* 466

Lupu, I., 'Free Exercise Exemption and Religious Institutions: The Case of Employment Discrimination' (1987) 67 *BU L Rev* 391

———'Where Rights Begin: The Problem of Burdens on the Free Exercise of Religion' (1989) 102 *Harv L Rev* 933

———'The Trouble with Accommodation' (1991) 60 *Geo Wash L Rev* 743

———'The Lingering Death of Separationism' (1994) 62 *Geo Wash L Rev* 230

———'Hobby Lobby and the Dubious Enterprise of Religious Exemptions' (2015) 38 *Harv J L & Gender* 35

———'Moving Targets: *Obergefell*, *Hobby Lobby*, and the Future of LGBT Rights' (2015) 7 *Ala CR & CL L Rev* 1

Lupu, I., and Tuttle, R., 'Same-Sex Equality and Religious Freedom' (2010) 5 *Nw J L & Soc Pol'y* 274

Luther, R., 'Marketplace of Ideas 2.0: Excluding Viewpoints to Include Individuals' (2011) 38 *Hastings Const LQ* 673

McClellan, M., 'Faith and Federalism: Do Charitable Choice Provisions Preempt State Nondiscrimination Employment Laws?' (2004) 61 *Wash & Lee L Rev* 1437

McConnell, M., 'Religious Freedom at a Crossroads' (1992) 59 *U Chi L Rev* 115

———'The Problem of Singling Out Religion' (2000) 50 *DePaul L Rev* 1

McCoy, T., 'A Coherent Methodology for First Amendment Speech and Religion Clause Cases' (1995) 48 *Vand L Rev* 1335

McCrea, R., *European Law, Religion and the Public Order of the European Union* (Oxford: Oxford UP, 2010)

———'Religion in the Workplace: *Eweida and others v United Kingdom*' (2014) 77 *MLR* 277

McCrudden, C., 'Human Dignity and Judicial Interpretation of Human Rights' (2008) 19 *EJIL* 655

———(ed.) *Understanding Human Dignity* (Oxford: Oxford UP, 2013)

MacDougall, B., 'Refusing to Officiate at Same-Sex Civil Marriages' (2006) 69 *Sask L Rev* 351

MacDougall, B., and Short, D., 'Religion-based Claims for Impinging on Queer Citizenship' (2010) *Dalhousie LJ* 133

Macedo, S., 'Transformative Constitutionalism and the Case of Religion: Defending the Moderate Hegemony of Liberalism' (1998) 26 *Pol Theory* 56

McGoldrick, D., 'The Limits of Freedom of Expression on *Facebook* and Social Networking Sites: A UK Perspective' (2013) 13 *HRLR* 125

McIlroy, D., 'Legislation in a Context of Moral Disagreement: The Case of the Sexual Orientation Regulations' (2007) 159 *Law & Just – Christian L Rev* 114

MacKinnon, C., *Toward a Feminist Theory of the State* (Cambridge, Mass: Harvard UP, 1989)

Maclure, J., and Taylor, C., *Secularism and Freedom of Conscience* (Cambridge, Mass: Harvard UP, 2011) 11–12

Mahlmann, M., 'Six Antidotes to Dignity Fatigue in Ethics and Law' in C. McCrudden (ed.), *Understanding Human Dignity* (Oxford: Oxford UP, 2013)

Malik, M., 'Religious Freedom, Free Speech and Equality: Conflict or Cohesion?' (2011) 17 *Res Publica* 21

Malloy, J., 'Bush/Harper? Canadian and American Evangelical Politics Compared' (2009) 39 *American Review of Canadian Studies* 352

Marshall, W.P., 'Solving the Free Exercise Dilemma: Free Exercise as Expression' (1983) 67 *Minn L Rev* 545

———'Discrimination and the Right of Association' (1986) 81 *Nw U L Rev* 68

Marshall, W.P., and Blomgren, D.C., 'Regulating Religious Organizations Under the Establishment Clause' (1986) 47 *Ohio State LJ* 293

Matsuda, M. et al., *Words that Wound: Critical Race Theory, Assaultive Speech and the First Amendment* (Boulder: Westview Press, 1993)

Messenger, T.W., *Holy Leisure: Recreation and Religion in God's Square Mile* (Philadelphia: Temple UP, 2000)

Miller, B., 'Proportionality's Blind Spot: "Neutrality" and Political Philosophy' in G. Huscroft, B.W. Miller and G. Webber (eds), *Proportionality and the Rule of Law: Rights, Justification, Reasoning* (Cambridge: Cambridge UP, 2014)

Minow, M., 'Should Religious Groups be Exempt from Civil Rights Laws?' (2007) 48 *BCL Rev* 781

———'Is Pluralism an Ideal or a Compromise?' (2008) 40 *Conn L Rev* 1287

Mnookin, R., 'The Public/Private Dichotomy: Political Disagreement and Academic Repudiation' (1982) 130 *U Pa L Rev* 1429

Möller, K., 'Proportionality: Challenging the Critics' (2012) 10 *ICON* 709

———*The Global Model of Constitutional Rights* (Oxford: Oxford UP, 2012)

———'Proportionality and Rights Inflation' in G. Huscroft, B.W. Miller and G. Webber (eds.), *Proportionality and the Rule of Law: Rights, Justification, Reasoning* (Cambridge: Cambridge UP, 2014)

Monsma, S., *When Sacred and Secular Mix: Religious Nonprofit Organizations and Public Money* (London: Rowman & Littlefield, 1996)

Moon, G., 'From Equal Treatment to Appropriate Treatment: What Lessons Can Canadian Equality Law on Dignity and on Reasonable Accommodation Teach the United Kingdom?' (2006) 6 *EHRLR* 695

———(ed.) *Law and Religious Pluralism in Canada* (Vancouver: UBC Press, 2008)

Moon, R., *Freedom of Conscience and Religion* (Toronto: Irwin Law, 2014)

Morris, D., Morris, A., and Sigafoos, J., 'Adopting (In)Equality in the UK: The Equality Act 2010 and its Impact on Charities' (2016) 38 *Journal of Social Welfare and Family Law* 14

Motilla, A., 'The Right to Discriminate: Exceptions to the General Prohibition' in M. Hill (ed.), *Religion and Discrimination Law in the European Union* (Trier: Institute for European Constitutional Law, 2012)

Murray, J.C., 'Law or Prepossessions' (1949) 14 *Law and Contemp Probs* 23

Mustanski, B., and Liu, R.T., 'A Longitudinal Study of Predictors of Suicide Attempts Among Lesbian, Gay, Bisexual, and Transgender Youth' (2013) 42 *Arch Sex Behav* 437

Muste, C., 'Reframing Polarization: Social Groups and "Culture Wars"' (2014) 47 *Political Science & Politics* 432

Myers, R.S., 'The Right to Conscience and the First Amendment' (2011) 9 *Ave Maria L Rev* 123

National Council for Voluntary Organisations, *Faith and Voluntary Action: An Overview of Current Evidence and Debates* (London: NCVO, 2007)

Nedelsky, J., and Hutchinson, R., 'Clashes of Principle and the Possibility of Dialogue: A Case Study of Same-Sex Marriage in the United Church of Canada' in R. Moon (ed.), *Law and Religious Pluralism in Canada* (Vancouver: UBC Press, 2008)

Nelson, J., 'Conscience, Incorporated' (2013) 5 *Mich St L Rev* 1565

Nelson, R., 'Sexual Orientation Discrimination Under Title VII after *Baldwin v Foxx*' (2015) 72 *Wash & Lee L Rev Online* 255

Newman, D., 'On the Trinity Western University Controversy: An Argument for a Christian Law School in Canada' (2013) 22 *Const Forum* 1

Nice, J., 'How Equality Constitutes Liberty: The Alignment of *CLS v. Martinez*' (2011) 38 *Hastings Const LQ* 631

Nolan, J. (ed.), *The American Culture Wars: Current Contests and Future Prospects* (Charlottesville: University Press of Virginia, 1996)

Nussbaum, M., 'A Plea for Difficulty' in S. Okin (ed.), *Is Multiculturalism Bad for Women?* (Princeton: Princeton UP, 1999) 106

———*Women and Human Development: The Capabilities Approach* (Cambridge: Cambridge UP, 2000)

———*Liberty of Conscience* (New York: Basic Books, 2008) 19

———*From Disgust to Humanity: Sexual Orientation and Constitutional Law* (New York: Oxford UP, 2010)

O'Brien, D., 'Chant Down Babylon: Freedom of Religion and the Rastafarian Challenge to Majoritarianism' (2002) 18 *J L & Religion* 219

O'Callaghan, N., 'Death by a Thousand Cuts: Why Market Mechanisms Won't Solve the Culture Wars' (2010) 49 *Journal of Catholic Legal Studies* 335

———(ed.), *Is Multiculturalism Bad for Women?* (Princeton: Princeton UP, 1999) 106

Okin, S.M., '"Mistresses of Their Own Destiny": Group Rights, Gender, and Realistic Rights of Exit' (2002) 112 *Ethics* 205

Oleske, J., 'Federalism, Free Exercise and Title VII: Reconsidering Reasonable Accommodation' (2004) 6 *U Pa J Const L* 525

Olsen, F., 'Constitutional Law: Feminist Critiques of the Public/Private Distinction' (1993) 10 *Const Comment* 319

O'Neil, R., 'Religious Freedom and Nondiscrimination: State RFRA Laws Versus Civil Rights' (1999) 32 *UC Davis L Rev* 785

O'Reilly, J., and Chalmers, M., *The Clergy Sex Abuse Crisis and the Legal Responses* (Oxford: Oxford UP, 2014)

Panaccio, C., 'In Defence of Two-Step Balancing and Proportionality in Rights Adjudication' (2011) 24 *Can J L & Jurisprudence* 109

Pasquinelli, C., 'Fundamentalisms' (1998) 5 *Constellations* 10

Paterson, H., 'The Justifiability of Biblically Based Discrimination: Can Private Christian Schools Legally Refuse to Employ Gay Teachers?' (2001) 59 *U Toronto Fac L Rev* 59

Pearson, M., 'Article 9 at a Crossroads: Interference Before and After *Eweida*' (2013) 13 *HRLR* 580

———'Religious Claims vs. Non-Discrimination Rights: Another Plea for Difficulty' (2013) 15 *Rutgers J of L & Relig* 47

———'Offensive Expression and the Workplace' (2014) *ILJ* 429

Perry, M., *The Political Morality of Liberal Democracy* (Cambridge: Cambridge UP, 2010)

Philpot, T., 'Keeping the Faith', *Community Care*, 22 January 2009

Pitt, G., 'Keeping the Faith: Trends and Tensions in Religion or Belief Discrimination' (2011) 40 *ILJ* 384

Plant, R., 'Religion, Identity and Freedom of Expression' (2011) 17 *Res Publica* 7

Poole, T., 'Tilting at Windmills? Truth and Illusion in "The Political Constitution"' (2007) 70 *Mod L Rev* 250

Porat, I., 'Mapping the American Debate over Balancing' in G. Huscroft, B.W. Miller and G. Webber (eds), *Proportionality and the Rule of Law: Rights, Justification, Reasoning* (Cambridge: Cambridge UP, 2014)

Quong, J., 'The Rights of Unreasonable Citizens' (2004) 12 *J Polit Philos* 314

Rayside, D., and Wilcox, C. (eds), *Faith, Politics and Sexual Diversity in Canada and the United States* (Vancouver: UBC Press, 2011)

Rees, J., 'Public Sector Commissioning and the Third Sector: Old Wine in New Bottles' (2014) 29 *Public Policy and Administration* 45

Rekart, J., *Public Funds, Private Provision: The Role of the Voluntary Sector* (Vancouver: UBC Press, 2011)

Richardson, D., 'Locating Sexualities: From Here to Normality' (2004) 7 *Sexualities* 391

Rivers, J., 'Religious Liberty as a Collective Right' in R. O'Dair and A. Lewis (eds), *Law and Religion* (Oxford: Oxford UP, 2001)

———'Proportionality and Variable Intensity of Review' (2006) 65 *CLJ* 174

———'Proportionality, Discretion and the Second Law of Balancing' in G. Pavlakos (ed.), *Law, Rights and Discourse* (Oxford: Hart Publishing, 2007)

———'Law, Religion and Gender Equality' (2007) 9 *Ecc LJ* 24

———*The Law of Organized Religions: Between Establishment and Secularism* (Oxford: Oxford UP, 2010)

———'Promoting Religious Equality' (2012) 1 *Ox J Law & Religion* 386

———'Justifying Freedom of Religion: Does Dignity Help?' in C. McCrudden (ed.), *Understanding Human Dignity* (Oxford: Oxford UP, 2013)

Robinson, J., 'Neither Ministerial Nor an Exception: The Ministerial Exception in Light of *Hosanna-Tabor*' (2014) 37 *Harv J L & Pub Pol'y* 1151

Rosenblum, L., 'Equal Access or Free Speech: The Constitutionality of Public Accommodations Law' (1997) 72 *NYU L Rev* 1243

Rosenblum, N., '*Amos*: Religious Autonomy and the Moral Uses of Pluralism' in N. Rosenblum (ed.), *Obligations of Citizenship and Demands of Faith: Religious Accommodation in Pluralist Democracies* (Princeton: Princeton UP, 2000)

Rosenfeld, M., 'Hate Speech in Constitutional Jurisprudence: A Comparative Analysis' (2003) 24 *Cardozo L Rev* 1523

Russ, J.A., 'Shall We Dance? Gay Equality and Religious Exemptions at Private Californian High School Proms' (1988) 42 *NYL Sch L Rev* 71

Rutherford, J., 'Equality as the Primary Constitutional Value: The Case for Applying Employment Discrimination Laws to Religion' (1996) 81 *Cornell L Rev* 1049

Rutledge, C.T., 'Caught in the Crossfire: How Catholic Charities of Boston was Victim to the Clash Between Gay Rights and Religious Freedom' (2008) 15 *Duke J Gender L & Pol'y* 297

Ryan, J., '*Smith* and the Religious Freedom Restoration Act: An Iconoclastic Assessment' (1992) 78 *Va L Rev* 1407

Ryder, B., 'The Canadian Conception of Equal Religious Citizenship' in R. Moon (ed.), *Law and Religious Pluralism in Canada* (Vancouver: UBC Press, 2008)

Sadurski, W., 'On Legal Definitions of "Religion"' (1989) 63 *Aust LJ* 834

———'"Reasonableness" and Value Pluralism in Law and Politics' in G. Bongiovanni et al. (eds), *Reasonableness and Law* (Dordrecht: Springer, 2009)

Sala, R., 'The Place of Unreasonable People Beyond Rawls' (2013) 12 *European J of Political Theory* 253

Salmons, D., 'Toward a Fuller Understanding of Religious Exercise: Recognizing the Identity-Generative and Expressive Nature of Religious Devotion' (1995) 62 *U Chi L Rev* 1243

Samuels, H., 'Feminizing Human Rights Adjudication: Feminist Method and the Proportionality Principle' (2013) 21 *Fem Leg Stud* 39

Sandberg, R., 'The Right to Discriminate' (2011) 13 *Ecc LJ* 157

———*Religion, Law and Society* (Cambridge: Cambridge UP, 2014)

Schacter, J., '*Romer v. Evans*: Democracy's Domain' (1997) 50 *Vanderbilt Law Rev* 411

Schauer, F., *Free Speech: A Philosophical Enquiry* (Cambridge: Cambridge UP, 1982)

———'Proportionality and the Question of Weight' in G. Huscroft, B.W. Miller and G. Webber (eds), *Proportionality and the Rule of Law: Rights, Justification, Reasoning* (Cambridge: Cambridge UP, 2014)

Schneiderman, D., 'Associational Rights, Religion and the Charter' in R. Moon (ed.), *Law and Religious Pluralism in Canada* (Vancouver: UBC Press, 2008)

Schragger, R., and Schwartzman, M., 'Against Religious Institutionalism' (2013) 99 *Va L Rev* 917

Secretary of State for the Home Department, *Prevent Strategy* (HM Stationery Office, 2011)

Selwyn, J., *Adoption and the Inter-agency Fee* (Department for Children, Schools and Families, 2009)

Sheppard, C., 'Equality Rights and Institutional Change: Insights from Canada and the United States' (1998) 15 *Ariz J Int'l & Comp L* 143

Sherry, S., 'Civic Virtue and the Feminine Voice in Constitutional Adjudication' (1986) 72 *Va L Rev* 543

Skjeie, H., 'Religious Exemptions to Equality' (2007) 10 *Critical Review of International Social and Political Philosophy* 471

Smith, S., 'Religious Freedom and its Enemies, or Why the *Smith* Decision May Be a Greater Loss Now Than it was Then' (2011) 32 *Cardozo L Rev* 2033

———'The Jurisprudence of Denigration' (2014) 48 *UC Davis LR* 675

Smyth, M., and Jenness, V., 'Violence Against Sexual and Gender Minorities' in R. Gartner and B. McCarthy (eds), *The Oxford Handbook of Gender, Sex and Crime* (Oxford: Oxford UP, 2014)

Stahl, R., 'Carving Up Free Exercise: Dissociation and "Religion" in Supreme Court Jurisprudence' (2002) 5 *Rhetoric & Public Affairs* 439

Stone Sweet, A., and Mathews, J., 'Proportionality Balancing and Global Constitutionalism' (2008) 47 *Colum J Transnat'l L* 73

———'All Things in Proportion? American Rights Doctrine and the Problem of Balancing' (2011) 60 *Emory LJ* 797

Stonewall, *Living Together: British Attitudes to Lesbian, Gay and Bisexual People in 2012* (London: Stonewall, 2012)

———*Gay in Britain: Lesbian, Gay and Bisexual People's Experiences and Expectations of Discrimination* (London: Stonewall, 2013)

Stychin, C.F., 'Faith in Rights: The Struggle Over Same-Sex Adoption in the United Kingdom' (2008) 17 *Const F* 7

———'Faith in the Future: Sexuality, Religion and the Public Sphere' (2009) 29 *OJLS* 729

———'Pluralism, Equality and the Challenge of Faith Based Services' (2014) 1 *JICL* 141

Sullivan, E.T., and Frase, R., *Proportionality Principles in American Law* (Oxford: Oxford UP, 2008)

Sullivan, W.F., *The Impossibility of Religious Freedom* (Princeton: Princeton UP, 2005)

Sunstein, C., 'Incompletely Theorized Agreements' (1994) 108 *Harv L Rev* 1733

———*One Case at a Time: Judicial Minimalism on the Supreme Court* (Cambridge, Mass: Harvard UP, 1999)

———*Designing Democracy: What Constitutions Do* (Oxford: Oxford UP, 2001)

Svensson, E., 'Religious Ethos, Bond of Loyalty, and Proportionality – Translating the "Ministerial Exception" into "European"' (2015) 4 *OJLR* 224

Swaine, L., *The Liberal Conscience* (New York: Columbia UP, 2006)

Taylor, C., 'Living with Difference' in A. Allen and M. Regan (eds), *Debating Democracy's Discontent: Essays on American Politics, Law, and Public Philosophy* (Oxford: Oxford UP, 1998)

Taylor, P., 'The Costs of Denying Religious Organizations the Right to Staff on a Religious Basis When They Join Federal Social Service Efforts' (2002) 12 *Geo Mason U CR LJ* 159

Tebbe, N., 'Religion and Marriage Equality Statutes' (2015) 9 *Harv Law & Pol Rev* 25

Trakman, L. et al., '*R. v Oakes* 1986–1997: Back to the Drawing Board' (1998) 36 *Osgoode Hall LJ* 83

Trappolin, L., Gasparini, A., and Wintemute, R., *Confronting Homophobia in Europe: Social and Legal Perspectives* (Oxford: Hart Publishing, 2011)

Trigg, R., *Religion in Public Life: Must Faith be Privatized?* (Oxford: Oxford UP, 2007)

Trotten, T.J., 'Shattering the Illusion: Child Sexual Abuse and Canadian Religious Institutions' (Waterloo, Ont: Wilfrid Laurier UP, 2002)

Trotter, G., 'The Right to Decline Performance of Same-Sex Civil Marriages: The Duty to Accommodate Public Servants' (2007) 70 *Sask L Rev* 365

Tsakyrakis, S., 'Proportionality: An Assault on Human Rights?' (2009) 7 *ICON* 468

Tyler, T., 'Procedural Justice and the Courts' (2007) 44 *Ct Rev* 26
Uecker, J., and Lucke, G., 'Protestant Clergy and the Culture Wars: An Empirical Test of Hunter's Thesis' (2011) 50 *J Sci Study Relig* 692
Underkuffler-Freund, L., 'The Separation of the Religious and the Secular: A Foundational Challenge to First Amendment Theory' (1995) 36 *Wm & Mary L Rev* 837
Urbina, F., '"Balancing as Reasoning" and the Problems of Legally Unaided Adjudication: A reply to Kai Möller' (2014) 12 *ICON* 214
Van der Vyver, J., 'Sphere Sovereignty of Religious Institutions: A Contemporary Calvinistic Theory of Church-State Relations' in G. Robbers (ed.), *Church Autonomy* (Bern: Peter Lang, 2001)
Vartanian, J., 'Confessions of the Church: Discriminatory Practices by Religious Employers and Justifications for a More Narrow Ministerial Exception' (2009) *U Tol L Rev* 40
Vazquez, R., 'The Practice of Polygamy: Legitimate Free Exercise of Religion or Legitimate Public Menace?' (2001) 5 *NYU J Legis & Pub Pol'y* 225
Vickers, L., 'Religious Discrimination and Schools: The Employment of Teachers and the Public Sector Duty in Law' in M. Hunter-Henin (ed.), *Law, Religious Freedoms and Education in Europe* (Farnham: Ashgate, 2012)
———'Twin Approaches to Secularism: Organized Religion and Society' (2012) 32 *OJLS* 197
———'Religion and Belief Discrimination in Employment Under the Employment Equality Directive: A Comparative Analysis' (2015) *European Equality Law Review* 25
Vischer, R., *Conscience and the Common Good: Reclaiming the Space Between Person and State* (Cambridge: Cambridge UP, 2009)
———'Do For-Profit Businesses Have Free Exercise Rights?' (2013) 21 *J Contemp Legal Issues* 369
Waldron, J., 'A Right to do Wrong' (1981) 92 *Ethics* 21
———*The Harm in Hate Speech* (Cambridge, Mass: Harvard UP, 2012)
Waldron, M., *Free to Believe: Rethinking Freedom of Conscience and Belief in Canada* (Toronto: University of Toronto Press, 2013)
Walton, A. et al., *Is there a 'Religious Right' Emerging in Britain?* (London: Theos, 2013)
Webber, G., *The Negotiable Constitution: On the Limitation of Rights* (Cambridge: Cambridge UP, 2009)
———'Proportionality, Balancing, and the Cult of Constitutional Rights Scholarship' (2010) 23 *Can J L Jurisprudence* 179
———'On The Loss of Rights' in G. Huscroft, B.W. Miller and G. Webber (eds), *Proportionality and the Rule of Law: Rights, Justification, Reasoning* (Cambridge: Cambridge UP, 2014)
Weinrib, L., 'Postwar Paradigm and American Exceptionalism' in S. Choudhry (ed.), *The Migration of Constitutional Ideas* (Cambridge: Cambridge UP, 2006)
Westen, P., 'The Empty Idea of Equality' (1982) 95 *Harv L Rev* 537
White, S., 'Freedom of Association and the Right to Exclude' (1997) 4 *J Pol Phil* 373
Wilson, R.F., 'A Matter of Conviction: Moral Clashes over Same-Sex Adoption' (2008) 22 *BYU J Pub L* 475
Winkler, A., 'Fatal in Theory and Strict in Fact: An Empirical Analysis of Strict Scrutiny in the Federal Courts' (2006) 59 *Vand L Rev* 793
Wintemute, R., 'Religion vs. Sexual Orientation: A Clash of Human Rights?' (2002) *Journal of Law & Equality* 125
———'Accommodating Religious Beliefs: Harm, Clothing or Symbols, and Refusals to Serve Others' (2014) 77 *MLR* 223
Woodhead, L., 'Liberal Religion and Illiberal Secularism' in G. D'Costa et al. (eds), *Religion in a Liberal State* (Cambridge: Cambridge UP, 2013)
Woodhead, L., and Catto, R. (eds), *Religion and Change in Modern Britain* (Abingdon: Routledge, 2012)
Wragg, P., 'Mill's Dead Dogma: The Value of Truth to Free Speech Jurisprudence' (2013) *PL* 363
Yarel, C., 'Where are the Civil Rights for Gay and Lesbian Teachers?' (1997) 24 *Human Rights* 22
Yowell, P., 'Proportionality in United States Constitutional Law' in *Reasoning Rights: Comparative Judicial Engagement* (Oxford: Hart Publishing, 2014)

Index

absolute rights 48
action/belief test 25–31
adoption agencies 161–7
Alberta v Hutterian Brethren of Wilson Colony 18, 51
Alexy, Robert 58, 67, 68
American Postal Worker's Union v Postmaster General 95
animus 63
Apelogun-Gabriels v London Borough of Lambeth 104
appraisal respect 12
Arrowsmith v UK 53
atmospheric burdens 54, 64
autonomy: argument 114; and freedom of religion 5–6; religious 122; right to 45–7

Bagni, Bruce 113, 123
balancing 67–8, 72, 76–7, 81, 94–7, 114–18, 130, 146, 153, 156
Baldwin v Fox 23
Beatty, David 70, 74, 94
bed and breakfast accommodation 189–91
belief: conduct/belief test 25–31; and employment 29–30; proportionality and 107–8
Benner v Canada (Secretary of State) 65
Bernstein and Paster v Ocean Grove Camp Meeting Association (OGCMA) 155–7
biblical chain of command 122
Blanding v Sports & Health Club 174–5, 186
bona fide occupational requirement (BFOR) 129, 130, 132, 135, 139
Bowen v Roy 51
Bowers v Hardwick 22
Brady v Dean 85, 86, 87, 91, 94, 97
British Columbia College of Teachers v Trinity Western University 149–50
Bull v Hall and Preddy 169–70, 189–90
Buonanno v AT&T Broadband 108
Burwell v Hobby Lobby 175–8
businesses: functions of 178, 179–80; religious freedom rights of 175–8. *See also* commercial services
Caldwell v St Thomas Aquinas High School 129
Campbell and Cosans v UK 49
Canada: bona fide occupational requirement (BFOR) 129; Charter of Fundamental Rights and Freedoms 17, 18, 19, 44, 79–80; commercial services 170, 180, 184; educational services provided by religious organisations 148–54; freedom of religion legislation 18; housing 187–8; Human Rights Act 17, 18; legal frameworks 17–19; legitimate aims in infringement of rights 59; *Meiorin* test 79–80; proportionality 13, 58, 79–80; religious ministers, employment of 116; same-sex marriage cases 84; secular employment, religious claims in 84; services provided by religious organisations 155; sexual orientation discrimination legislation 18–19; social service organisations 135–7; teachers in religious organisations 129–32; and UK and US comparison 194–5; university religious societies 144
Cannata v Catholic Diocese of Austin 117
case-specific nature of proportionality 69–73, 146–7, 193–4
case studies: jurisdictions 12–13; proportionality in 13
categorisation 76
Catholic Care (Diocese of Leeds) 161, 162, 163, 164–5
Catholic Charities of the Diocese of Springfield v State of Illinois 163–4
Cha'are Shalom Ve Tsedek v France 51, 52, 175
Chamberlain v Surrey School District No. 36 11, 32–3, 150
Charter of Fundamental Rights and Freedoms (Canada) 44
children: adoption agencies 161–7; child neglect laws 36; foster parenting 107–8; safeguarding 35–6
Christian Legal Society v Martinez 144–7
Church of Latter Day Saints (Mormons) 26–7
Church of the Lukumi Babalu Aye v City of Hialeah 41

City of Boerne v Flores 21, 171
City of Cleveland v Nation of Islam 142–3
Civil Partnership Act 2004 16, 84
Civil Rights Act 1964: Title IX 148; Title VII 21, 116, 128
cognitive dissonance 28
collective religious freedom 111–12, 127
commercial services: bed and breakfast accommodation 189–91; Canada 180, 184–5; England 169–70, 172; housing 186–9; interference 169–79; one-off services 182–6; proportionality 183–6; state, intervention by 181–2; United States 170–8, 185–6
communication: of discrimination 183; of religious rules to teachers in religious organisations 131
compulsion/motivation distinction 53
conduct based on religious beliefs, protection of 6
conduct/belief test 25–31
conscientious objection argument 114
constitutional losers 73–4, 193–4
context-specific nature of proportionality 69–73, 146–7, 193–4
contraceptive mandate 175–8
core/periphery distinction 37–9
Corporation of Presiding Bishop v Amos 137
counselling 99–104
Criminal Justice and Immigration Act 2008 16
criteria for decisions on religious claims: conduct/belief test 25–31; core/periphery 37–9; hybrid rights 42–3; neutral laws of general applicability 38–42; public/private 31–7
culture of justification, proportionality as part of 73–5
culture wars 2–3, 70, 72, 192

Davis, Kim 85, 87, 97
decriminalisation of homosexual acts 16, 19, 22
Defense of Marriage Act (DOMA) 23, 63
deliberation, norm of 73, 74–5, 90–3
dialogue, norm of 90–3
Dias v Archdiocese of Cincinnati 126
dignity 50, 61–2, 183
Dignity Twin Cities v Newman Center & Chapel 157–8
direct/indirect discrimination 15
discrimination: communication of 183; defining 110; direct/indirect 15; impact of 112; justification 55. *See also* commercial services; employment; freedom of religion; non-discrimination; religious employment; religious organisations, services provided by; secular employment, religious claims in; sexual orientation discrimination
Dixon v University of Toledo 99n,93
Donaldson v Farrakhan 143
Dudgeon v UK 17, 62
Dworkin, Ronald 9, 181

Eadie and Thomas v Riverbend Bed and Breakfast 179–80, 190
Edmunds Act 1887 27
educational services provided by religious organisations 147–54. *See also* teachers in religious organisations
EEOC v Fremont Christian Schools 128
EEOC v Hosanna-Tabor 35, 42, 117, 119, 120, 121, 122, 126, 128
Egan v Canada 19
Elane Photography LLC v Willock 171–2, 173, 181–2, 185–6
Eldridge v British Columbia 66
employment: and belief 107–8; belief and 29–30; freedom of religion 20–1; interference with rights 51–2, 54; United States 22–3; voluntary situations 54. *See also* religious employment; secular employment, religious claims in
Employment Division v Smith 20–1, 39–40, 41–2, 43, 74, 170–1
Employment Equality (Sexual Orientation) Regulations 2003 16, 121
Employment Non-Discrimination Act (ENDA) 22
Employment Opportunity Commission (EEOC) 23
England: adoption agencies 161–2, 161–7, 163, 164–6; businesses, religious freedom rights of 175; commercial services 169–70, 172; decriminalisation of homosexual acts 16; educational services provided by religious organisations 147–8; European Convention on Human Rights (ECHR) 14–15; freedom of religion legislation 14–16; Human Rights Act 1998 15–16; legal frameworks 14–17; proportionality (overview) 13, 58, 79; race discrimination law 14; same-sex marriage cases 84; secular employment, religious claims in 84; services provided by religious organisations 154–5, 159–60; sexual orientation discrimination legislation 16–17; teachers in religious organisation 124–6
Equality Act 2006 15, 121
Equality Act 2010 15, 125, 159, 162
Equality Act (Sexual Orientation) Regulations (Northern Ireland) 2006 62
Equality Act (Sexual Orientation) Regulations 2007 16, 93
Equality and Human Rights Commission (EHRC) 160
Esau, Alvin 136, 139
European Convention on Human Rights (ECHR) 14–15, 172; Art. 8 17; Art. 9 26, 37, 44, 64; Art. 14 17

Eweida and others v UK 91, 163
Eweida v British Airways 52, 53
Exmoor Coast Boat Cruises Ltd v Revenue & Customs 175

fact-specific nature of proportionality 69–73, 146–7, 193–4
Fair Housing Council of San Fernando Valley v Roommate.com 189
Fernandez Martinez v Spain 120
First Amendment 20–1, 127–8, 148, 155
flexibility of proportionality 75
foster parenting 107–8
Free Exercise Clause 20–1, 26, 27, 170–1, 172, 173
freedom of expression 60–1
freedom of religion: arguments for 4–6; autonomy 5–6; businesses, rights of 175–8; Canadian legislation 18; collective religious freedom 111–12, 127; conduct based on 6; and employment 20–1; English legislation 14–16; historical background 4; human dignity, belief's compatibility with 50; identity-generative nature of 4; legal frameworks 14–16, 18, 20–1; and offence 60–1; protection of 6–7; reasonable co-existence, acceptance of 50; respectability of beliefs 49–50; right of 4–7; seriousness of conflict with non-discrimination 11–12; substantive limits to protection 48–50; United States legislation 21–4. *See also* criteria for decisions on religious claims; religious employment; religious organisations, services provided by; secular employment, religious claims in
functions of individuals/businesses 137–8, 178, 179–80

Gay Rights Coalition v Georgetown University 71
Gedicks, F.M. 119, 138
Germany: Basic Law 46; necessary measures 66; proportionality 58; proportionality-type tests 82
Gibson v Brewer 35
ground projects 5, 6

Hall v Baptist Memorial Health Care Corp 134–5
Hall v Bull 72
Hall v Powers 152–4
Halpern v Canada 19
Hämäläinen v Finland 17, 17n26
Hamilton, Marci 26, 30, 119
harm to others: broad interpretation of interference 73; symbolic harms 160–1, 183
Hasan v Bulgaria 120–1
hate speech: prohibition of 61–2; United States 23–4
Heintz v Christian Horizons 135–7
Hender v Prospects 133
Hendricks and Leboeuf v Quebec 19
heterosexual norm 10–11
hiring of premises 155–60
Hollingsworth v Perry 23
Hollon v Pierce 29
homosexuality: decriminalisation of homosexual acts 16, 19, 22. *See also* same-sex marriage; sexual orientation discrimination
Horev v Minister of Transportation 70–1, 72
housing services 186–9
human dignity, belief's compatibility with 50
Human Rights Act 1998 15–16
Human Rights Act (Canada) 17, 18
hybrid rights 42–3, 171

impartiality as essence of employment role 97–9
indirect/direct discrimination 15
interference with rights: atmospheric burdens 54; balance with justification 67–8; broad interpretation of 73; broadness of right 51–4; commercial services 169–79; compulsion/motivation distinction 53; employment 51–2, 54; legally forbidden acts 51–4; proportionality 85–7; same-sex marriage 85–7; secular employment, religious claims in 85–7; substantive limits to protection 48–50; voluntary situations 54
islands of exclusivity 138–40

Jefferson, Thomas 26
judges, impartiality of 97–9
jurisdictions of case studies 12–13. *See also* Canada; England; United Kingdom; United States
justification: balance with interference with rights 67–8; broad definition of rights 44–5; culture of, proportionality as part of 73–5; discrimination 55; of interference under proportionality 73; proportionality 194; religious ministers, employment of 122; requirement for in proportionality 73–5; same-sex marriage 90–4; secular employment, religious claims in 90–4

Kant v Lexington Theological Seminary 127
Keeton v Anderson-Wiley 100–1, 101
Kirby v Lexington Theological Seminary 127
Kruse v Johnson 41
Kuyper, Abraham 34

Ladele v Islington LBC 38, 65, 79, 84, 87, 88, 90, 91–2, 92–3, 94–6, 163, 169, 186
law. *See* legal frameworks

Laycock, D. 8, 53, 114, 119, 183
least restrictive means test 66–7, 81, 88–9, 99, 114, 143, 145, 153, 156, 158–9, 180–2
Lee v Ashers Bakery Ltd 184–5
legal frameworks: Canada 17–19, 19–24; England 14–17; freedom of religion 14–16, 18, 20–1; law as solution to conflicts 13; sexual orientation discrimination 16–17, 18–19, 21–4; United States 19–24
legitimate aim 59–65, 73, 81, 87–8, 98–9, 114, 143, 145, 149, 153, 156, 179–80
Lemon v Kurtzman 32
Little v Wuerl 128
lived religion 30
losers, constitutional 73–4, 193–4
Lown v Salvation Army 133
Lumpkin v Brown 99
Lustig-Prean v UK 17
Lyng v Northwest Indian Cemetery Protective Association 51

Madsen v Erwin 137–8
Mandla v Dowell Lee 14
Marriage Commissioners Case (Canada) 84, 86, 89, 94, 97
Marriage (Same Sex Couples) Act 2013 16–17
McClintock v. Department of Constitutional Affairs 6n37, 97–8
McClure v Salvation Army 116–17
McFarlane v Relate (Avon) Ltd 65, 86, 100–2
Meiorin test 79–80, 180
Miller v Davis 85, 87, 97
Minersville School District v Gobitis 27–8, 29
minister, religious, employment of 113–23
ministerial exception 116–17, 126, 127, 140
Mississippi Commission on Judicial Performance v Wilkerson 98
moral recognition respect 12, 90
morality: and legitimate restriction of rights 64; proportionality 78
Mormonism 26–7
motivation/compulsion distinction 53
Multani v Commission Scolaire Marguerite-Bourgeoys 18
Murphy v Ramsey 27

necessity test 66–7, 81, 88–9, 99, 114, 143, 145, 153, 156, 158–9, 180–2
neutral laws of general applicability 38–42
new religions 40
Nichols v M.J. 84, 86, 90, 93–4, 94
no less restrictive means 66–7, 81, 88–9, 99, 114, 143, 145, 153, 156, 158–9, 180–2
nomos, religion as 5
non-discrimination: importance of 7–8; jobs based on 99; right of 7–11; right to 54–5; seriousness of conflict with freedom of religion 11–12. *See also* commercial services; employment; religious employment; religious organisations, services provided by; secular employment, religious claims in
Northern Ireland 184
Nussbaum, Martha 4, 5, 70

Obergefell v Hodges 23
offence 60–1
O'Neill v Governors of St Thomas More RCVA Upper School 125
Ontario (Human Rights Commission) v Brockie 170, 180, 184
Ontario Human Rights Division v Simpson-Sears 18
Otto Preminger Institut v Austria 60–1
over-inclusivity 67, 150

Parry v Vine Christian Centre 142
Pedeira v Kentucky Baptist Homes for Children 134
Pemberton v Inwood, Acting Bishop of Southwell and Nottingham 118
Percy v Church of Scotland 117–18, 120
performative religions 30, 39–40, 43
periphery/core distinction 37–9
pervasive religiousness 130, 138–40
Peterson v Hewlett-Packard Co. 104–5
peyote religions 30, 39–40, 43
Pichon and Sajous v France 32, 51–2, 54, 169
pluralism, religious 28
polygamy 26–7
premises, hiring of 155–60
private/public distinction 31–7
proportionality: advantages of 68–76, 193–5; balancing 67–8, 72, 76–7, 81, 90–7, 114–18, 130, 143, 146, 153, 156; and belief 107–8; Canada 58; Canada (overview) 79–80; case-specific nature 69–73; case studies, variations in 13; categorisation 76; commercial services 183–6; as complex/uncertain 77–8; criticisms of 76–9; England (overview) 58, 79; fact-specific nature 69–73, 146–7, 193–4; factually contingent nature 72; flexibility and structure of 75; German law 58; Germany 82; incommensurables, measuring 78–9; increased use of 57; interference 85–7; justification requirement 73–5, 194; legitimate aim 59–65, 73, 81, 87–8, 98–9, 114, 143, 145, 149, 153, 156, 179–80; morality 78; necessity test 66–7, 81, 88–9; no less restrictive means 66–7, 81, 88–9, 99, 114, 143, 145, 153, 156, 158–9, 180–2; as part of culture of justification 73–5; public reason, requirement of 75; rational connection 65, 88, 114, 130, 143, 149, 153, 179–80; rights under 2; as subjective 77; teachers in religious organisations 129–32; thoughtlessness, guarding against 75;

transparency 75–6; United States (overview) 80–2; as unprincipled/pragmatic 77; use of to resolve conflicts 1–2; variations between jurisdictions 58–9
public policy and rights, distinction between 55, 59
public/private distinction 31–7
public reason, requirement of 75

qualified rights 48

R (Amicus) v Secretary of State for Trade and Industry 121–2, 125
R (Begum) v Denbigh High School 15, 45, 52
R (Johns) v Derby City Council 107–8
R (Raabe) v Secretary of State for the Home Department 105–6
R v Big M Drug Mart 18
R v Oakes 58, 59
R (Williamson) v Secretary of State for Education and Employment 37, 48–9
race discrimination law in England 14
rational connection 65, 88, 114, 130, 143, 149, 153, 179–80
Reaney v Hereford Diocesan Board of Finance 118
reasonable co-existence, acceptance of 50
religion: new/small religions 40; as nomos 5; as not intrinsically discriminatory 3; public/private distinction 31–7. *See also* criteria for decisions on religious claims; freedom of religion; religious employment; secular employment, religious claims in
religious employment: collective religious freedom 111–12; discrimination, defining 110; impact of discrimination 112; islands of exclusivity 138–40; ministers 113–23; pervasiveness of religion 138–40; secular function employees 137–8; social service organisations 132–7; spiritual/secular activities 113; teachers 123–32
religious expression, discriminatory, in secular employment 104–7
Religious Freedom Restoration Act (RFRA) 21, 171–2
religious ministers, employment of 113–23
religious organisations, services provided by: adoption agencies 161–7; educational services 147–54; general public 160–7; hiring of premises 155–60; non-members 154–67; and proportionality 179–82; religious activities 141–4; university religious societies 144–7; variety of reactions to legislation 166–7; welfare services 160–7
respect 12, 90, 152–3
respectability of beliefs 49–50
Reynolds v US 26–7, 28
rights: absolute 48; to autonomy 45–7; balancing 76–7, 94–7; broad definition of 44–8, 194; broadness of right 51–4; of businesses 175–8; hybrid rights 42–3, 171; importance of 3; justification of interference with 55; legitimate aims in infringement 59–65; motivation/compulsion distinction 53; non-discrimination 7–11, 54–5; under proportionality 2; and public policy, distinction between 55, 59; qualified 48; to refuse to associate 141–4; seriousness of conflicts between 11–12; two stages process in analysis of 44–8. *See also* freedom of religion
Robertson and Anthony v Goertzen 187–8
Romer v Evans 62–3
Rushton v Nebraska Public Power District 53

same-sex marriage: balancing 90–7; English cases 84; exemption claims by employees 83–5; interference 85–7; justification 90–4; legitimate aim 87–8; no less restrictive means 88–9; rational connection 88; rights, balancing 94–7; specific situation rule 85–6; state employees 94–7; United States cases 23, 84–5. *See also* sexual orientation discrimination
Schalk and Kopf v Austria 17
School Standards and Framework Act 1998 125
Schroen v Steinbach Bible College 138–40
Scotland, adoption agencies in 163
Section 28 11
secular employment, religious claims in: balancing 90–7; counsellors 99–104; discriminatory religious expression 104–7; employers' aims 88; England 84; impartiality as essence of employment role 97–9; interference 85–7; justification 90–4; legitimate aim 87–8; no less restrictive means 88–9; non-discrimination, jobs based on 99; rational connection 88; rights, balancing 94–7; same-sex marriage cases 83–5; specific situation rule 85–6; state employees 94–7; subjective approach 95; United States cases 84–5
secular function employees 137–8
secular marketplace: bed and breakfast accommodation 189–91; Canada 170, 180, 184–5; England 169–70, 172; housing 186–9; interference 169–79; one-off services 182–6; proportionality 183–6; state, intervention by 181–2; United States 170–8, 185–6
Seide v Gillette Industries Ltd 14
services provided by religious organisations: adoption agencies 161–7; educational services 147–54; general public 160–7; hiring of

premises 155–60; non-members 154–67; and proportionality 179–82; religious activities 141–4; university religious societies 144–7; variety of reactions to legislation 166–7; welfare services 160–7. *See also* commercial services
sexual orientation discrimination: Canadian legislation 18–19; characterising 110–11; cumulative nature 8; employment 16; English legislation 16–17; extent of 10; heterosexual norm, challenging 10–11; impact of 8; legal frameworks 16–17, 18–19, 21–4; state obligation 8–9; stigmatic effect 8. *See also* same-sex marriage
Sherbert v Verner 20, 172
signage 183
Slater v Douglas County 85, 86, 92, 96–7
small religions 40
Smith and Grady v UK 17
Smith v Fair Employment and Housing Commission 172, 187
Smith v Knights of Columbus 158–9
Smith v Trafford Housing Trust 106–7
social service organisations: Canada 135–7; religiousness of 132; United Kingdom 132–3; United States 133–5
specific situation rule 85–6
sphere sovereignty 34–5
St Margaret's Children and Family Care Society 163
states: attitude of 7; employees of 94–7; intervention by 181–2; resistance to intervention by 35
strict scrutiny 20–1, 78, 80–2
structure of proportionality 75
student religious societies 144–7
Stychin, C.F. 12, 86, 96, 161
substantive limits to protection 48–50
symbolic harms 160–1, 183

teachers in religious organisations: Canada 129–32; communication of religious rules to 131; consistency of approach towards 131; England 124–6; impact of discriminatory policies on 124; ministerial/non-ministerial employees distinction 126–8; as ministers 126–8; pervasive religiousness of school 130; proportionality approach 129–32; religiousness of post 131; as role models 123; role of 123–4
Thlimmenos v Greece 39–40
Thomas v Anchorage Equal Rights Commission 171, 187
Thorson v Billy Graham Evangelistic Association 133
thoughtlessness, guarding against 75
tolerance 59–60
Torcaso v Watkins 29
transparency of proportionality 75–6
Trinity Western University (TWU) 148–51
TWU v Nova Scotia Barristers' Society 149, 150–1

under-inclusivity 150
United Kingdom: and Canada and US comparison 194–5; commercial services 184–5; Northern Ireland 184–5; religious ministers, employment of 116, 117–18, 121–2; Scotland, adoption agencies in 163; social service organisations 132–3; university religious societies 144. *See also* England
United States: and Canada and UK comparison 194–5; commercial services 170–8, 185–6; educational services provided by religious organisations 148–51; employment 22–3; First Amendment 20–1, 127–8, 148, 155; Free Exercise Clause 20–1, 26, 27, 170–1, 172, 173; freedom of religion legislation 20–1; hate speech 23–4; housing 186–7, 188–9; legal frameworks 19–24; proportionality in 13, 80–2; religious ministers, employment of 116–17, 118–21; same-sex marriage 23, 84–5; secular employment, religious claims in 84–5; secular function employees 137–8; services provided by religious organisations 142–3, 155; sexual orientation discrimination legislation 21–4; social service organisations 133–5; strict scrutiny 20–1, 78, 80–2; university religious societies 144–7
United States v Windsor 23, 63
universities, religious 147–51
university religious societies 144–7

Vejdeland v Sweden 61–2
Verein Gemeinsam Lernen v Austria 175
voluntary situations 54
Vriend v Alberta 19

Ward v Polite 100, 102–4
Webber, Grégoire 46, 47, 76
Weishuhn v Catholic Diocese of Lansing 126
Weiter v Kurtz 36
welfare services 160–7
West Virginia v Barnette 28–9
Williams, Bernard 5
Wisconsin ex. rel. Sprague v City of Madison 188–9
Wisconsin v Yoder 80–1

Yoder v Wisconsin 36, 42

For Product Safety Concerns and Information please contact our EU
representative GPSR@taylorandfrancis.com
Taylor & Francis Verlag GmbH, Kaufingerstraße 24, 80331 München, Germany

www.ingramcontent.com/pod-product-compliance
Ingram Content Group UK Ltd.
Pitfield, Milton Keynes, MK11 3LW, UK
UKHW050054200926
475702UK00019B/2832
* 9 7 8 0 3 6 7 1 8 9 9 1 4 *